The Jewish Women of Ravensbrück Concentration Camp

The Jewish Women
of Ravensbrück
Concentration Camp

Rochelle G. Saidel

Terrace Books
A trade imprint of the University of Wisconsin Press

This book was made possible in part by the support of
the Five Millers Family Foundation, the Lucius N. Littauer Foundation,
Richard J. and Joan G. Scheuer Family Foundation, and
the Remember the Women Institute.

The University of Wisconsin Press
1930 Monroe Street, 3rd Floor
Madison, Wisconsin 53711-2059
uwpress.wisc.edu

3 Henrietta Street, Covent Garden
London WC2E 8LU, United Kingdom
eurospanbookstore.com

Printed in the United States of America

Library of Congress Cataloging-in-Publication Data
Saidel, Rochelle G.
The Jewish women of Ravensbrück Concentration Camp / Rochelle G. Saidel
p.   cm.
ISBN 0-299-19860-X
ISBN 0-299-19864-2 (pbk.:   )
1. Jewish women in the Holocaust—Germany (East).
2. Ravensbrück (Concentration Camp).
3. Women concentration camp inmates—Germany (East).
4. World War, 1939–1945—Prisoners and prisons, German.
5. World War, 1939–1945—Conscript labor—Germany (East).   I. Title.
D804.47.S35   2004
940.53'1853154—dc22
2003020576

ISBN 978-0-299-19864-0 (pbk.:   )
ISBN 978-0-299-19863-3 (e-book)

In loving memory of my cousins, the Miller family, and my grandmother Esther Ovchinskas Saidel, whom they brought from Kopcheva, Lithuania, to the United States in 1908.

A Dance on the Poems of Rilke

Charles Fishman

I remember a Czech dancer who danced on the poems of Rilke.
Stennie Pratomo-Gret

In the particular hell of Ravensbrück
where Gypsy girls were sterilized and babies
were drowned at birth   where dysentery
lung cancer and typhus   took life after life
and grotesque experiments in the inducement
of infection and pain were cultivated as a fine art

where women of every European nation slaved
for *Siemens*   through endless moonless nights
and cut trees   dug pits   loaded and unloaded
railway cars and barges   where abortion was
inevitable   and sexual cruelty the rule   and where

a woman could be duly tortured for using rags
as tampons   or merely for adjusting her dress
a certain Czech woman who knew every word
danced to the poems of Rilke   moving sinuously
to each of his Orphean sonnets bowing gracefully
with the first notes of each *Elegie*: she felt the dark music

of Rilke's heart   each soaring leap of the spirit   each lunge
toward grief   Though she is long gone   and we
no longer know her name   she is the one who showed
even a halting step could be a triumph   and a dance
on the poems of a dead poet   might redeem.

Contents

Illustrations

xi

Illustrations

Illustrations

Preface to the 2006 Edition

After more than a quarter of a century of involvement with Ravensbrück women's concentration camp and specifically with its Jewish victims and survivors, I am convinced that it is of utmost importance to appropriately memorialize these women and tell their stories. Because we are rapidly approaching a time when there will be nothing left but memory, it is urgent that we capture and give voice to these individual memories now.

In April 2005 I participated in the sixtieth anniversary of the liberation of Ravensbrück, held at the official memorial site, *Mahn- und Gedenkstätte Ravensbrück*. It was obvious at this gathering of survivors, family members, government officials, and scholars that the number of survivors in attendance had shrunk considerably since the previous major event in 1995. If there is another public commemoration in 2015, there will surely be very few survivors young and healthy enough to travel to Germany for the event. Survivors who were only twenty at liberation will by then be ninety years old, and those who were teenagers will be over eighty. The youngest Jewish survivor I know, a baby who was less than three years of age at liberation, will be seventy-two in 2015. Her case is unusual as few Jewish or other young children survived.

At the concentration camp memorial site there is some good news regarding the politics of memory and the Jewish women of Ravensbrück. The situation has improved tremendously from zero representation of the camp's Jewish victims before 1988. Now visitors can find a Jewish memorial room, a monument (albeit with outdated German Democratic Republic language), and references to individual Jewish victims among the various exhibitions.

Despite these changes, even after more than sixty years, the Jewish victims have not been sufficiently recognized. This is true both at the camp memorial and for Holocaust memorialization in the United States and elsewhere. At the sixtieth anniversary commemoration at the camp memorial, as at the fiftieth anniversary, there was a delegation of survivors from Israel, as well as individual Jewish survivors from the United States, Europe, and Canada. However, the Jewish survivors received more recognition and attention at the 1995 anniversary commemoration than at the 2005 event.

For example, the commemorative brochure that participants received in 2005 mentioned the Jewish victims only once, after the Gypsy victims. One of the events featured during the ceremonies was a new German documentary that by no means did justice to the camp's Jewish victims. One Jewish survivor speaking in the film chose to emphasize her Jewish background, but the presence of Jewish prisoners in the camp was generally played down. The film highlights the story of Stella Kugelman Nikiforova, a Jewish survivor born in Belgium, but there is no mention of the fact that she is Jewish. She was a small Jewish child in Ravensbrück, and was taken to the Soviet Union by a prisoner-of-war after the camp's liberation. Her story is told in this book, which makes her Jewish identity clear. Thus the sixtieth anniversary commemoration should have included more references to Jewish victims. The end result seemed somewhat retrogressive to me, and to some of the Jewish survivors.

On the positive side, there was a session about this book, as well as an interfaith service that included a rabbi and hazzan. The general memorial commemoration even included the chanting of *El Moley Rachamim*, the Jewish memorial prayer. But overall and perhaps subjectively, something was missing. The recognition seemed perfunctory, and some of the Jewish survivors attending the ceremonies felt they had been forgotten, or at least not sufficiently remembered.

And in the United States and elsewhere, it is still difficult to find the Jewish women of Ravensbrück included in most Holocaust exhibits and general books on the Holocaust. With all of the newspaper and television coverage about sixtieth anniversaries of camp liberations, we read a lot about Auschwitz and Bergen Belsen, but rarely or not at all about Ravensbrück. This is the first book in English to deal with the subject of the camp's Jewish victims; others are only now beginning to follow.

One of the most rewarding parts of writing this book has been the warm friendships I have forged with some of the Jewish survivors. I was pleased to again see at the sixtieth anniversary event some of the women whose stories are recounted here, including Chaya Moskovits Dana, Sali Solomon Daugherty, Nomi Moskovits Friedmann, Judith Rosner Gertler, Stella Kugelman Nikiforova, and Lidia Rosenfeld Vago. I also met other Jewish survivors for the first time.

Aside from the sixtieth anniversary event, the publication of the first edition of this book has led to my meeting or hearing about other Jewish survivors. After reading the book, some survivors or their relatives contacted me and told me stories of Jewish women in Ravensbrück. For example, Antoine Bernheim found me and related the remarkable saga of his mother, Ginette Kahn-Bernheim, a heroic member of the French Resistance who was captured posing as a non-Jew, brought to Ravensbrück, and survived the camp.

I was especially pleased to make the acquaintance of the granddaughters of two women whose stories are told here: Gladys Gemma McMillion, named for her grandmother Gemma La Guardia Gluck, and Kathy Leichter, named for her grandmother, Dr. Käthe Pick Leichter. The interest of the third generation in their grandmothers' experiences in Ravensbrück offers hope that the Jewish victims of the camp will not be forgotten in the future.

I have visited the Ravensbrück concentration camp memorial six times between 1980 and 2005, and each time it has seemed as though I was in a different place. The memorial was different because the world was different. History and politics and time had impacted on the memorial and how Jewish women are memorialized there. A new director, Dr. Insa Eschebach, took over in June 2005 and I look forward to further positive changes that will be more inclusive of the Jewish victims. Let's hope this happens while some of the camp's Jewish survivors can still appreciate this recognition and contribute to shaping the memory.

Ravensbrück women's concentration camp and the experiences of the forgotten Jewish female victims who suffered there have been on my mind for more than twenty-five years. Whether we like it or not, all historical events are obscured by the passing of time and the development of new world situations, and it takes a tremendous effort to keep any collective memory publicly alive. It is not enough to simply say that we must remember the Holocaust. We must remember all of the victims, including the Jewish women of Ravensbrück. This book is intended to contribute to that effort.

Acknowledgments

The idea for this book goes back to my visit to the German Democratic Republic (GDR) in 1980, and its gestation period has been so long that I am grateful to many people and institutions. Journalist Charles R. Allen, Jr. and Murray Zuckoff, then editor of the Jewish Telegraphic Agency, arranged my 1980 trip, and feminist journalist Aviva Cantor suggested that I visit Ravensbrück. Werner Händler of Berlin was the official GDR host on that first trip, and he and his wife Hella have remained supportive of my work.

At *Mahn- und Gedenkstätte Ravensbrück,* the Ravensbrück memorial, the professional staff, headed by Sigrid Jacobeit and including Christa Schulz, Monika Herzog, Britta Pawelke, and Cordula Hoffmann, has always been gracious and helpful, as have Horst Seferens of the *Stiftung Brandenburgische Gedenkstätten,* the Brandenburg Memorials Foundation, and Insa Eschebach, a German independent scholar.

Research was carried out under the auspices of The Remember the Women Institute and in cooperation with NEMGE—The Center for the Study of Women and Gender, University of São Paulo, where I am especially grateful to Eva Alterman Blay and Rosa Ester Rossini. I also thank the Center for the Study of Women and Society at The Graduate School and University Center of City University of New York, then directed by Joyce Gelb, and The Philadelphia Center on the Holocaust, Genocide, and Human Rights, directed by Marcia Sachs Littell, for inviting me to serve as a visiting scholar during phases of the research.

I worked in libraries and archives, including *Mahn- und Gedenkstätte Ravensbrück,* Yad Vashem, the United States Holocaust Memorial Museum, the Public Record Office in London, the Shneiderman Family

Archive at Tel Aviv University, Lund University Library (with thanks to Manuscript Division Director Birgitta Lindholm and Paul Levine, who suggested my visit), the Leo Baeck Institute and the YIVO Research Institute in New York, the Committee for the International Red Cross in Geneva, and the Division of Oral History of the *Arquivo Histórico Judaico Brasileiro* in São Paulo. Other archives and institutions that provided photographs and materials include: The LaGuardia and Wagner Archives, LaGuardia Community College/The City University of New York, *Dokumentationsarchiv des Österreichischen Widerstandes* in Vienna, *Staatsarchiv Nürnberg, Museen der Landeshauptstadt Schwerin— Stadtgeschichtsmuseum*, the Florida Holocaust Museum in St. Petersburg, Sovfoto/Eastfoto, and The Watch Tower Bible and Tract Society. The United States Holocaust Memorial Museum's Survivor Registry sent my mailing to Ravensbrück survivors, and Roberta S. Kremer, Executive Director of the Vancouver Holocaust Education Centre, brought Rebecca Teitelbaum's story to my attention.

Others who shared valuable materials and information include: Stennie and Djajeng Pratomo-Gret and Rabbi David Lilienthal of Holland, Eileen Shneiderman of Tel Aviv, Ben Shneiderman of Maryland, Senator Franz Leichter and Henry O. Leichter of New York, Charles Fishman of Patchogue, New York, Alex Buckman of Vancouver, Canada, Marie-Jo Chombart de Lauwe of Paris, Amichai Lau-Lavie of New York, Larry Gropman of Canton, Michigan, Magdelena Kusserow Reuter of Spain, and Karl Heinz Schütt of Neustadt-Glewe, Germany.

The circle of scholars working on women and the Holocaust is still small, and I would like to acknowledge the encouragement of colleagues including Elizabeth Baer, Susan Benedict, Myrna Goldenberg, S. Lillian Kremer, Dalia Ofer, Nechama Tec, and especially Sonja Hedgepeth. Dr. Hedgepeth has been a true comrade, bringing me books from Germany, sharing educational presentations, helping with German translation and proofreading, and accompanying me to Ravensbrück in 2001. I met her at Brandeis University at a National Endowment for the Humanities summer seminar in 1996. Led by Alan Mintz, the seminar enabled me to discuss ideas for this book with colleagues. In addition to Dr. Hedgepeth and Dr. Kremer, Ilya Altman of Moscow and Monika Adamczyk-Garbowska of Lublin continued to follow my project afterward. Later, the Ma'yan Jewish Feminist Research group in New York gave me the opportunity to present a book chapter and receive feedback.

I am grateful to the Florida Holocaust Museum, especially Museum Director Stephen Goldman and Education Director Noreen Brand, for inviting me to serve as guest curator for their exhibit, *Women of Ravensbrück—Portraits of Courage: Art by Julia Terwilliger*. The museum later made some of the exhibit visuals available for this book. Herbert

Acknowledgments

Obererlacher, my intern in Florida, and my son, Daniel Wolk, were helpful in providing digital images. The exhibit had as its core panels by Florida artist Julia Terwilliger, a dear friend of blessed memory whose devotion to the women of Ravensbrück was inspirational.

To complete the research for this book, I counted on the assistance of able interviewers Evie Joselow, Susan Sapiro, and Robin Ostow. Julia Klimek was my capable official German-English translator, with the help of friends including Ester Golan and Miriam Oelsner. For Polish translation I am indebted to another friend, Moshe Borger. Alla Millstein Gonçalves served as my Russian translator for one interview. Deborah Lattimore's transcription service was outstanding and publishing consultant Katharine Turok offered sound advice. I thank the University of Wisconsin Press and especially Director, Robert Mandel, and editorial committee member Ruth Schwertfeger for making this book a reality.

The Jewish survivors of Ravensbrück listed at the end of the book generously granted interviews, provided photographs, and offered other materials, as well as encouragement. Survivors Lore Shelley and Lidia Vago, authors in their own right, made suggestions and provided me with information about other Jewish survivors. Without the shared memories of the survivors, this book would not be possible, and I deeply appreciate their contributions.

Funding for research was primarily the generous gift of The Five Millers Family Foundation, especially Dora Miller. A grant from the National Endowment for the Humanities allowed me to participate in the Brandeis University seminar, and grants from the Lucius N. Littauer Foundation enabled me to attend the fiftieth anniversary of Ravensbrück and to include visuals in this book. Further publishing grants were provided by the Littauer Foundation and the Richard J. and Joan G. Scheuer Family Foundation. I am grateful to them and others who made donations to The Remember the Women Institute, through which this project was carried out.

Elizabeth Howitt of New York, Nancy Ordway of Jerusalem, and Suzanna Sassoun of São Paulo, three special friends not in this field of studies, offered intelligent ideas and patient ears in many conversations over the years. Other family members, friends, and colleagues not named here also lived through all or part of my twenty-three-year passion to tell the story of the Jewish victims of Ravensbrück. I thank all of them. I especially thank my husband, Guilherme Ary Plonski, who for seventeen years has encouraged my work, provided feedback and ideas, and can always be counted on for translation help in various languages.

The Jewish Women of Ravensbrück Concentration Camp

Introduction

Ravensbrück on My Mind

THE JEWISH victims of Ravensbrück concentration camp have been doubly ignored and forgotten. For most of the time that the camp memorial was under the jurisdiction of the Soviet Union and then the German Democratic Republic (GDR), the victims' identity as Jews was minimized or submerged in memorial exhibits and monuments. They share this fate with other Jewish women and men who were interned in camps that later became part of or were under the domination of the Soviet Union. However, in the case of the Jewish women of Ravensbrück, they were also ignored in memorial exhibits, monuments, and publications in the United States.

Located approximately fifty-five miles from Berlin, Ravensbrück is now an official memorial site of the state of Brandenburg. Of the about 132,000 women and children who were in the camp at some time between 1939 and 1945, an estimated 100,000 to 117,000 of the total population of prisoners did not survive. About 20 percent of the prisoners were Jewish, and this book seeks to tell their stories and interweave their presence in the history of the camp. The camp was originally intended as a work camp for dissident women, some of them Jewish, but by its final days was responsible for the murder of tens of thousands of women—it even had its own operating gas chamber.

From the end of World War II until the dismantling of the Soviet bloc, concentration camp memorial sites in the East, such as Ravensbrück, were conceptualized as Communist shrines. The Ravensbrück site was first under the jurisdiction of the Soviet Union and in 1959 became a national *Mahn- und Gedenkstätte*, or memorial site, of the GDR. The exhibits, books, and audiovisual materials produced by the GDR-administered memorial site highlighted the histories of the Communist heroines, especially German Communists, who had been imprisoned in the camp, and did not mention that Jewish women were among the victims. Additionally, as in all of the countries in the Communist bloc, there was a tendency to downplay or eliminate mentioning Jewish victims.

Furthermore, many Communist women had been incarcerated in the camp, and they dominated the active survivor committees not only in the GDR but also throughout Europe. There was little or no attempt to acknowledge that Jews, even Jewish Communists, had been imprisoned and murdered there. Much has been written about political prisoners at the camp, especially in German, French, Polish, Russian, and Dutch, and a few of these works have been translated into English.[1] However, with the exception of a small number of memoirs that only marginally address Ravensbrück, nothing has been published specifically about the camp's Jewish victims. The women arrested as Jews were in the camp along with political prisoners (some of whom were also Jewish), prisoners-of-war, Jehovah's Witnesses, criminals, and "asocials" (a category that included Gypsies, lesbians, and prostitutes) from more than forty nations.

I first saw the Ravensbrück memorial site in 1980, a rare opportunity for a visitor from the United States. That year I was invited to represent the Jewish Telegraphic Agency (JTA), the international wire service that serves Jewish communal and other newspapers, on a visit to East Germany, along with colleagues from two other Jewish publications, *Reform Judaism* and *Martyrdom and Resistance*, a survivor newspaper.

The memorial site that I saw in 1980 was designed to be a Communist shrine.[2] In addition to an "off-limits" and walled-off area that housed Soviet troops, there was a public memorial complex that included the former SS headquarters, the prison and torture cell building, the crematorium, and surrounding space. All of the exhibits and monuments were designed to glorify communism and the Communist heroines of the resistance who had been imprisoned in Ravensbrück. There was no evidence that any Jewish woman had ever even passed through the camp.

Arriving at the Ravensbrück memorial on that day in 1980, I had virtually no information about the existence of Jewish women in the camp. It merely seemed logical that Hitler would use all methods, including this particular women's camp, in his genocidal Final Solution. I decided to ask the Communist survivor who served as my guide whether there had been Jewish women at the camp, and, if so, what she could tell me about them. She tried to evade the question but, when pointedly pressed, said that one barrack had been known as the Jewish barrack. She added that one of the Communist heroines, Olga Benário Prestes, was a Jew. This was the

She Who Carries, a sculpture by Will Lammert, considered to be the symbol of the Ravensbrück memorial site, shown with the church steeple of the town of Fürstenberg in the background. Photo by Heinz Heuschkel, Berlin. Collection of Mahn- und Gedenkstätte Ravensbrück/Stiftung Brandenburgische Gedenkstätten (Ravensbrück Memorial/Brandenburg Memorials Foundation MGR/SBG).

extent of official available information about Jewish victims, and I felt that it was probably a gross distortion of the facts. Sadly, I later discovered that my hunch was accurate, and Ravensbrück was indeed a site of Jewish suffering and genocide.

There was no memorial room for Jewish victims because memorialization was portrayed by nationality and not religion, according to the guide. Each nation was given a small room (former prison block cell), and the survivor committee from that nation was responsible for creating its memorial. The Polish exhibit, for example, had a Roman Catholic religious orientation that obliterated the memory of the thousands of Jewish Polish women that had been Ravensbrück prisoners. (In a strange exception, the Dutch room included a display on Anne Frank, but she was never in the camp.)

A film I viewed at the camp memorial in 1980 presented various forms of resistance, emphasizing the role of the Communist inmates. The Communist women were portrayed as the first prisoners in the camp, at the heart of the resistance movement. (Other early inmates, such as Jehovah's

Witnesses, were not mentioned.) The Communist resistance described in the film included sabotage in the Siemens armaments plant and daily demonstrations of human kindness, such as creating toys for the children and teaching secret classes. The women in the camp also commemorated the Communist holidays, such as the anniversary of the death of Lenin, and everyone sang the *International* in her own language, according to the film.

In short, the purpose of the film I saw in 1980 was the exaltation of communism. It even pointed out that socialism was a reality in two-thirds of Europe. The president of the International Ravensbrück Committee said in the film that the real work was to warn young people about fascism, especially in West Germany. Jewish victims were not mentioned, nor was it even explained that some of the Communists were Jewish (and always singled out as Jews as well as political prisoners).

While the situation of access to the camp began to change after reunification, the Soviet troops did not completely pull out of Ravensbrück until August 1993. The site was in a state of transitional chaos when I returned in March 1994, accompanied by a Jewish survivor, and could finally see how huge the camp had been. I was told that a new Jewish memorial space had been created in one of the prison cells, where in 1980 memorial displays organized according to nation had no mention of Jewish victims. Camp officials said that I could not see the Jewish exhibit, because it was being revised for the forthcoming 1995 ceremonies marking the fiftieth anniversary of the camp's liberation. The national displays (some of which were also being revised and "westernized") had been created by the individual national memorial committees, but camp staff members had designed the Jewish display, I was told.

Even in 1994, it was still difficult to begin to grasp the role of Ravensbrück as a camp that affected the lives of thousands of Jewish women. Perhaps the memorial's highlighting of communism and Communists was one reason that the camp was virtually unknown for decades in the United States. This remained the case even after Holocaust memorialization became a powerful force in the Jewish community and was institutionalized in the greater population with the NBC-network television series *Holocaust* in 1978, and then culminated in the opening of the United States Holocaust Memorial Museum in Washington, D.C., in 1993. If it was mentioned at all by western Holocaust scholars, it was considered a camp for political prisoners or a site of slave labor, but not a significant or even a peripheral part of the story of the attempted genocide of the Jewish people. The monolithic thrust of the site's approach to memorialization certainly reinforced this assumption.

"The intentions behind the memorial site, and the monument at the time it was erected, may be discerned in a book which was published in four languages and ten thousand copies shortly after the memorial site opened," German researcher and author Insa Eschebach correctly observed. According to the book, distributed during the GDR era, the site "is a memorial to the women of strong will, to the women with knowledge, who held firmly together and who supported and sustained their weaker comrades, the defenseless victims; it is a monument, built here to the everlasting glory of the heroines, who fought here to the very last breath."[3] Like the film I saw in 1980, this book demonstrates that the memorial site was dedicated to the Communist heroines. "Acts of solidarity and compassion are presented as a particular characteristic of German antifascists," Eschebach said. "The genocide of the Jewish people is not mentioned once—indeed, Jewish inmates occur only twice in this book," as being forced to unload bricks and as recipients of smuggled food from other comrades.[4]

In an odd twist, when the site was dedicated as a GDR memorial in 1959, an Israeli was among the international representatives but did not mention the Jewish victims.[5] No other Israeli was permitted to appear at any memorial ceremony at the camp during the years of the GDR. "By 1985 Ravensbrück's Jewish inmates had become forgotten to such an extent that, for example, when the GDR government representative Kurt Hager made a speech for the ceremonies marking the fortieth anniversary of the liberation, he failed to mention them once," Eschebach pointed out.[6]

The non-Jewish political prisoners, especially Communists, ran the national and international survivor organizations of memorial committees after World War II. As the former leaders of the French and Dutch survivor committees explained to me, the ideology of these groups did not allow for the separate memorialization of Jewish women. Since there was never an organized group of Jewish Ravensbrück survivors, and for the most part they did not participate in the national politically oriented groups, they "got lost in the shuffle" of memorialization. Furthermore, most of the Jewish women who survived settled in Israel or the United States, where the emphasis was on general survivor organizations, rather than specific camp organizations.

The heavy Communist orientation was, of course, compounded by inaccessibility. Even if American or other western scholars were able to reach East Berlin before the unification, it was still difficult to travel the local bad roads or worse railroad connections to the camp. Since there were Soviet troops stationed there, visits by scholars from the United States and its allies were certainly not encouraged. Even those who wanted to learn about the camp through writings in English had a difficult time.

It could also be speculated, although not proven, that the camp's definition as a women's camp added to the lack of interest among the predominantly male circles of Holocaust scholars and survivor leaders. After scholars in the United States finally began to seriously study the many aspects of the Holocaust, beginning in the late 1960s, and even as documentation, literature, courses, and memorials have proliferated until the present, Ravensbrück and its female Jewish victims seem to have remained nearly invisible.

The Jewish victims' silence about the camp has compounded the lack of interest and information. Many of them were no longer alive to tell their stories, because they had either been murdered or worked to death at Ravensbrück, or sent on to be eliminated at Auschwitz-Birkenau or another camp. In the fall of 1942, the camp was mostly "cleansed" of its Jewish prisoners, and then, shortly afterward, other groups of Jewish women arrived until the very end of the war.[7] Most Jewish women who survived arrived between the spring of 1944 and the camp's liberation in April 1945—this was a pivotal year for massive transports of Jewish women to the camp. Most of these survivors had longer and more intense memories of other camps. They arrived at Ravensbrück after many other hellish experiences or stayed there a relatively short time and then were sent on to other camps, so they considered their time there short and unimportant in relation to the totality of what they endured. There are almost no published memoirs by Jewish Ravensbrück survivors.[8]

This book seeks to address the failure to acknowledge the victimization of Jewish women. Based on discussions with the camp's Jewish victims and other research, it offers testimonies of Jewish survivors. More than a collection of narratives, the individuals' stories are in documented context that includes previously unpublished archival material, information on murdered Jewish victims, and background facts. The book is intended to enrich and augment the reader's understanding of the Holocaust, especially regarding women's experiences. It specifically seeks to contribute to a deeper understanding of this notorious women's camp where the number of Jewish women was most likely more than twenty thousand, a considerably higher number than earlier estimates.[9]

Beginning in the spring of 1995, it was finally possible to study the Jewish women of Ravensbrück in a methodological way. At the ceremonies marking the fiftieth anniversary of the liberation of Ravensbrück, and fifteen years after my first visit—after too many years of delay—I learned there were hundreds of Jewish survivors, many of whom were willing to talk about their experiences. Soon afterward, I augmented my Jewish survivor list by contacting the United States Holocaust Memorial Museum's Registry of Jewish Holocaust Survivors. The Registry sent a mailing on my behalf to some three hundred Jewish Ravensbrück survivors, most living in the United States. More than sixty answered me, and most of these then sent back my preliminary questionnaires. Even this introductory contact produced rich materials: along with the questionnaires, some shared a poem, a diary excerpt, or a memoir. Some provided other names or brief anecdotal comments, and the list that had been accumulated at the fiftieth anniversary of the camp's liberation grew considerably. Since then I have interviewed many of the women, and their stories and memories, some sparse and some taking many pages, collectively help us to begin to understand the horrors that Ravensbrück inflicted on the Jewish women who were there at different times from 1939 until 1945.[10]

Much of the information in this book is from first-hand interviews with Jewish survivors, as well as the unpublished memoirs they shared with me. Books and articles published in languages other than English, archival documents and testimonies, and out-of-print books provided background. The methodology for the interviews was free-flowing discussion, using minimal guidance to allow the survivors to tell their stories. I then put the information into readable narratives, checking facts, geography, and dates of historically verifiable events. "The political is personal" in a deeply visceral way for these survivors who suffered both as Jews and as women, and I have tried to use humility and caution in both the interviews and my presentation of them. However, because of the emotional and personal nature of this subject matter and my own involvement with the camp and its victims, I could not and did not approach this book as a completely neutral observer.

As political scientist Karl Deutsch, sociologists Peter Berger and Thomas Luckmann, and others have concluded, knowledge is an activity in which subjective and objective perspectives meet.[11] "Once the project begins, a circular process ensues: the woman doing the study learns about herself as well as about the woman she is studying," sociologist Shulamit Reinharz observed regarding feminist biographical methods.[12] I certainly agree with this statement, and would add that once interviewing women about their experiences during the Holocaust begins, the depth and breadth of their stories can keep this circle revolving.

Before reading the poignant stories of some of the Jewish women who survived Ravensbrück or perished there, readers will learn in chapter 1, "A Special Hell for Women," about the camp's history and how it constantly deteriorated during its six years of existence. Then, in chapter 2, "Triangles of Many Colors," we meet some of the non-Jewish prisoners and learn how they interacted with the Jewish women. While Jewish women who were in Ravensbrück are the focus of this book, their stories can be better understood in the context of the other prisoners' experiences.

Within this framework, chapter 3, "Olga Benário Prestes and Käthe Pick Leichter," recounts how Jewish women were in the camp from the earliest days and highlights the stories of these two Jewish political prisoners, both murdered in the winter of 1942. They and many other women, some Jewish, were remarkable for the resistance they were able to sustain under almost impossible conditions and with severest penalties if caught.

With few exceptions, we can learn about Jewish women's life in the camp before 1944 only by reading what non-Jewish prisoners have written about their Jewish camp sisters. The relatively in-depth information about these two early Jewish political prisoners can also shed some light.

In addition to their activities, chapter 4, "Resistance that Lifted the Spirit," documents other acts of resistance that kept the women going and helped them survive, including teaching, preparing clandestine cookbooks, fashioning various gifts for friends to mark birthdays and special occasions, and writing poetry for themselves and each other.

Children were sometimes brought to the camp with their mothers, and some managed to survive, although most either perished at the camp or were sent on to death camps. The stories of some of the Jewish children are discussed in chapter 5, "Joyless Childhoods." For example, Stella Kugelman Nikiforova, only four years old when she entered the camp with her mother, shared with me her sad memories of life in and after Ravensbrück. Other child survivors from Israel and the United States also told me their stories, which are rounded out by adult survivors' recollections about the children.

Although there may have been some exceptions, Jewish women who were in Ravensbrück before 1942 were murdered at the camp or sent to Auschwitz-Birkenau or another camp by the fall of that year. One Jewish survivor included in this book came as a child from Holland at the end of 1942 (soon after the camp was made *Judenrein,* or free of Jews), and I know of only one Jewish prisoner who came earlier and survived. Most Jewish survivors of the camp came in late 1944, or after the evacuation of Auschwitz in 1945. The 1944 arrivals' stories are told in chapter 6, "A Year of Comings and Goings."

Since slave labor was so varied, so physically and mentally brutal, and played such a major role in the daily existence of the women in Ravensbrück, chapter 7, "Women at Work," is devoted to the various ways in which the women were forced to toil. Among the many work details at the camp, perhaps the most infamous "employer" was the Siemens electric company.

It is an extraordinary and almost unknown fact that at least one Jewish woman from the United States was a prisoner in Ravensbrück. Gemma LaGuardia Gluck, the sister of New York City Mayor Fiorello LaGuardia, was kept in the camp as a political hostage, and her story is told in chapter 8, "Gemma LaGuardia Gluck—A Jewish American." She was arrested in Budapest in the spring of 1944 and kept at the camp until almost the time of liberation in April 1945. She left a published memoir, and I was able to locate unpublished documents that augment her unique story.[13]

Of all of the survivors I have had the opportunity to meet, most came to Ravensbrück on death marches after Auschwitz-Birkenau was evacuated in January 1945. They had relatively short-term experiences at Ravensbrück but remember the appalling conditions and some specific details that provide vivid images of the camp's last weeks. Chapter 9, "Jewish Evacuees Arrive from Auschwitz," is devoted to the recollections of this group of women, and the odyssey of several other women who came from elsewhere at that time is told in chapter 10, "Late Arrivals from Other Camps."

Ravensbrück had a number of satellite work camps, and survivors spoke most often of being sent to either Malchow or Neustadt-Glewe. Survivor accounts and background about Neustadt-Glewe and other generally unknown subcamps are included in chapter 11, "The Satellite Work Camps," while chapter 12 discusses "Malchow and the Death Marches." Some survivors were fortunate that the Red Cross rescued them before the initiation of the death marches out of Ravensbrück at the end of April 1945. They were brought to Sweden to recuperate, and chapter 13, "Rescue to Sweden," provides first-hand accounts by some of those who were saved.

Chapter 14, "Reconstructing Lives in the Aftermath," discusses how some of the Jewish women were able to begin their lives anew after liberation, especially in the United States and Israel. Chapter 15, "Gender and Women's Bodies," returns to the issue of women and the Holocaust, using examples from the testimonies and histories of survivors and victims to better understand the Holocaust in the context of social relations and physiological differences between men and women. Finally, the epilogue, "Ravensbrück Still on My Mind," addresses my own involvement with the camp memorial site and its Jewish victims.

This book is intended to rightfully include within Holocaust history the voices and stories of the female Jewish victims of Ravensbrück. In addition to recounting their experiences, it offers the reader the opportunity to use these particular stories to better understand the unfathomable entirety of the Holocaust, and to explore whether and how women and men experienced the Holocaust differently.

1

A Special Hell for Women

B EFORE meeting some of the remarkable Jewish women who survived Ravensbrück, and others who did not, we need to understand
the history of the camp and how conditions deteriorated over time.
Construction began in November 1938, when the Nazis determined that
war was imminent and a large women's camp for political prisoners and
resisters was necessary. Ravensbrück was built using the slave labor of
about five hundred male inmates from nearby Sachsenhausen concentration camp. According to SS records, it was originally planned to hold
three thousand female inmates.

THE CAMP'S EARLY HISTORY

The first negotiations by representatives of the German Reich, the Nazi
Party, and the *Waffen-SS* to purchase land in the small community of
Ravensbrück, north of Fürstenberg on the Havel River in Mecklenburg,
can be dated to 1934. As the camp was enlarged several times until 1944,
additional land was later purchased. The location offered transportation,
via the Fürstenberg train station (on the Berlin-Neustrelitz railroad line)
and Highway 96, as well as well-camouflaged seclusion. Schwedtsee, a
lake, separated the camp from the residential areas in Fürstenberg, with
large forested areas to the northeast of the camp and the Havel River to
the south.[1]
    The first transport consisted of 867 women who arrived in May 1939,
mostly German anti-fascists, either Social Democrats or Communists,
some coincidentally Jewish. They arrived from Lichtenburg in Saxony, a
fortress that had been used as a women's camp from March 1938 until

May 1939.[2] Before that (from October 1933 until March 1938) the first women's camp was located in a workhouse in Moringen, near Hanover, but women were generally incarcerated in prisons during the early years. The Ravensbrück camp ledger for 21 May 1939 lists 974 female prisoners, 137 of them Jewish. While there were Jewish prisoners from the camp's first days, I know of only one who was there during its first three years and survived.[3] It is rare to find a Jewish survivor who arrived before 1943 or during that year.

The original purpose of the camp was to incarcerate and punish female political prisoners as Germany prepared for war, and to use the women as slave laborers. After the invasion of Poland initiated World War II in September 1939, transports came every day from the countries that the Nazis occupied. The imprisoned women wore color-coded triangles that identified them as political prisoners, Jews, "asocials," criminals, or Jehovah's Witnesses. They were forced to work at different kinds of jobs, from heavy outdoor physical labor to building rocket parts for the Siemens electric company.

SLAVE LABOR AND CRUEL PUNISHMENT

Harsh slave labor was always an integral part of life at Ravensbrück, with the workload and brutality increasing as the demands of the war escalated. The early prisoners were required to build the roads within the camp and the adjacent housing for the SS guards. Stones were brought from near the lake, the women forming a human chain to move them to the road. The women were used like animals, with a team of twelve to fourteen pulling a huge roller to pave the streets. After the war began, the camp's growing slave labor force was exploited to the utmost. There were factory workers and farm and forest workers, and the prisoners were also required to extend the camp. Some of the women worked outside the camp, for example, in Fürstenberg. Even those who were too old or disabled to perform other duties had to stay in the barracks and knit clothing for the army (with angora from the camp's rabbit farm), or clean the barracks and latrines. There was also a sizable and widespread network of satellite camps, many of which held contracts with private companies that contributed to the war effort.

The "Bunker," a building of cellblocks completed in 1939, served as the camp prison, where solitary confinement and torture became routine. During the entire time of its existence, Ravensbrück also served as a centralized training camp for newly hired female SS auxiliary guards who were then transferred to other camps, such as Auschwitz or Majdanek.

One survivor, Gemma LaGuardia Gluck, recalled a particularly bizarre and sadistic torture: "There was the 'ice room' in Ravensbrück,

Beating sentence. Drawing by an unknown prisoner artist, from the exhibit in the former cellblock building. Collection of MGR/SBG.

where for some minor offense one had to stand barefooted for hours on the ice. For a severe punishment many prisoners were stripped of their clothes and thrown into the ice room. Is it any wonder that so many have come out permanently ill from these camps?"[4]

More conventional and routine torture methods included beatings and attacks by SS dogs. Solitary confinement in the dark and airless prison cells of the Bunker—often punishment for acts considered sabotage or resistance—was frequently accompanied by severe beatings. Punishment by up to twenty-five lashes with a whip was officially instituted in 1940. Beginning in April 1942, according to a memo from SS Reich Leader and Head of the German Police Heinrich Himmler, whippings were to be given on the naked buttocks. A prisoner categorized as a criminal carried out the whippings in the basement of the prison building, receiving extra rations for her work. The camp doctor was required to be present at each punishment, to confirm it had been carried out, and Himmler was supposed to approve each instance of corporal punishment. On 2 December 1943, Himmler ordered whipping to be used only as a last resort, as it did not constitute an "educational punishment."[5]

Until 1940, the area of the camp was about 25,000 square yards, surrounded by a wall more than thirteen feet high, topped with electrified barbed wire. Inside the walls stood a wooden building for washing and cooking, and sixteen barracks. Of these, two were used as inmate infirmaries, or *Reviers,* and the other fourteen were living quarters for the inmates, arranged on both sides of the *Lagerstrasse,* the main camp road. These first barracks were equipped with 135 sleeping places and subdivided into two dormitories, two dining halls, one washroom, and one office for the SS Block Overseer.[6]

By the beginning of 1945, the women's camp included a clothing warehouse, a tool and machinery depot, a barrack office for administration of work details, a laundry, the office for an *Oberaufseherin* (female executive commander), kitchen, bath, morgue, and SS kitchen-cafeteria, as well as thirty-two living barracks, among them seven infirmary blocks, and three barracks that held the *Reviers.*[7]

EARLY PRISONERS' DESCRIPTIONS OF THE CAMP

Most early Jewish prisoners from 1939 to 1942 did not live to tell their stories. However, a non-Jewish political prisoner with family ties to Judaism survived Ravensbrück and wrote a valuable memoir describing the camp in its early years. Margarete Buber-Neumann had been married to the son of Rabbi Martin Buber, and then divorced. When I met her daughter, Dr. Judith Buber Agassi, at the ceremonies for the fiftieth anniversary of the camp's liberation in April 1995, she told me that she was sure her mother would not have survived had she been Jewish.

After Margarete Buber divorced her first husband, she married Heinz Neumann, a leader of the German Communist party between 1928 and 1932. He was then removed from the leadership because of "political deviations." The couple was brought to Moscow in 1934 and watched by the Secret Police until they were arrested in the spring of 1937. She was sent to Siberia and, as a result of the Molotov-Ribbentrop Pact of cooperation between the Nazis and the Soviet Union (signed 23 August 1939), was sent back to Germany. In July 1940 she was placed under "preventive arrest" in Berlin, the Nazis claiming that, if free, she would work for the Communist party. On 3 August 1940, she was part of a fifty-woman transport that left Berlin for Ravensbrück. She recalled her first impression of the camp on the day of her arrival, a year and a few months after it was established:

> We lined up in fives in front of a newly painted wooden hut before which was a neat garden plot. . . . I was astonished at what I saw: neat plots of grass with beds in which flowers were blooming. A road leading away from the entrance square was lined with young trees, and before the wooden huts which extended away on either side were more flowerbeds. The square and the street were obviously most carefully kept and even the gravel paths had been freshly raked over. To the left of us, towards the watch-tower, there was a large timber barracks painted white, and next to it was a great aviary as though in a zoological garden.[8]

When I first saw the camp's location in 1980, I also was struck by the beauty of the landscape, and especially the picture postcard view of the medieval town of Fürstenberg on the other side of the lake. However, like Margarete Buber-Neumann's, my first impression rapidly vanished. Next to the picturesque lake is the high wall that enclosed the women in Ravensbrück, and this very lake received the women's ashes from the camp's crematorium.

In 1940, Margarete soon discovered that the camp's outside appearance was misleading. Even the manicured paths and vegetation were the result of the prisoners' backbreaking slave labor. She continued her narrative:

> From the outside everything looked beautiful—more like a neat holiday camp than a concentration camp. But behind the aviary we could see part of the barbed wire fencing which surrounded the camp and served to remind us where we were. . . . A column of prisoners came by and I saw German camp inmates for the first time. They marched in orderly ranks. Each woman wore a clean white kerchief bound round her head and fastened at the back, a broad-striped dress and a dark-blue apron. They were all barefooted. . . . Their faces were impassive as they passed. One looked just like the other. My heart fell as I realized that this was how I was going to live: regimented, drilled and shouted at day in, day out, for year after year. . . . And all the while the dogs bayed and growled and the guards bawled out orders.[9]

Margarete's description of the camp in 1940 demonstrates that during its first one to two years, it was organized and orderly, even though slave labor, brutality, and torture were routine. The women wore no shoes, but were dressed in clean, matching uniforms. During 1940, only forty-seven prisoners died in Ravensbrück, according to her testimony.[10]

By May 1940, a year after the camp opened and three months before Margarete's arrival, the number of inmates already exceeded the original capacity of three thousand. By the summer of 1941 there were over five thousand women.[11] One report states that "after 1941, the nutrition became worse by the week. The ration was five hundred grams of bread, one-half to three-quarters of a liter of vegetables, a few potatoes, and morning or evening soup. And on Saturdays or Sundays, sausage or a little cheese, and weekly a spoon of malt and some marmalade. Meat dishes were only given on Sunday."[12]

Nanda Herbermann, a Catholic German political prisoner who entered the camp at the beginning of August 1941, wrote in her memoir about the arrival routine at that time:

> For hours we stood there in our nakedness. . . . Then we were led into yet another room, where the new arrivals were deloused, one after the other, by two Jehovah's Witnesses who were also inmates. Wherever a single louse or a bug was found, the poor creatures' heads were fully shaved. . . . Then we went under the hot downpour, which did us good. . . . After this shower bath everyone received a blue towel and was then "clothed" as a proper prisoner. Underwear and clothing were for the most part uniform. Everyone received a shirt, which was more gray than white, a skirt, and, as long as the supply lasted, knickers. These gray knickers were so long that they stuck out ten, and sometimes even twenty, centimeters [four to eight inches] below the skirts.[13]

According to Nanda's description, in August 1941 the women were still receiving decent uniforms and towels. Like Margarete Buber-Neumann, she documented that the women were required to go barefoot in summer, even while performing heavy outdoor labor. Throughout her memoir she recounted the suffering that this caused her and others. Women who arrived in later years received clothes that formerly belonged to other prisoners, often inappropriate and of the wrong size.

DETERIORATING CONDITIONS

Because of the evolving situation at the camp during its six years of existence and the destruction of many records by the Nazis as the Soviet Army approached, it is difficult to present a complete and accurate picture. This is particularly true regarding the fate of the Jewish victims, because early Jewish prisoners were either murdered or transferred to death camps by October 1942. However, within two months of that date, Jewish women began to arrive at Ravensbrück again, and they continued to do so until its last days. 1942 was a pivotal year for the Jewish prisoners, because the Nazis decided that year to cleanse camps within Germany of their Jewish prisoners. Between February and April 1942, about 1,500 Ravensbrück prisoners, including at least 700 to 800 Jewish women, were gassed at the Bernburg euthanasia center under the "14f13" project.[14] There were also two large transports of Jewish women to Auschwitz that year, 1,000 on 26 March and 522 on 6 October. Meanwhile, in mid-1942 the *Neue Lager* (New Camp) was added, and the camp was later enlarged several times, with women doing much of the hard physical labor. In April 1942 about 6,400 to 7,500 female inmates were listed in ledger counts.[15]

The deportation to Ravensbrück of Jewish and non-Jewish women from prisons and camps in Poland, Austria, France, Belgium, Holland, Norway, Yugoslavia, and other occupied countries caused the number of inmates to rise dramatically from 1943 onward. Camp records account for about 10,000 new arrivals in 1943.[16] In January 1944, about 17,300 prisoners were held in Ravensbrück. One reason for the increased population of the camp in 1944 was the deportation of 12,000 non-Jewish women and children from Warsaw after the August uprising. By December of that year the number had risen to between 32,000 and 43,700.[17] Whatever the exact number, the conditions, with so many women living together, were unimaginable. As the camp's population grew to more than ten times the originally planned number of women, the living conditions and treatment rapidly deteriorated. Some of the barracks built for a maximum of 250 women eventually housed as many as 2,000, with three or four to a bunk. Thousands of women did not even have part of a bunk and slept on the floor, without even a blanket. Already insufficient rations became more and more meager as time went on.

By September 1944 there were 1,100 women in each barrack building, originally designed for about 250. Every straw sack in the three-tiered bunk beds held at least two to three women. There was a plague of lice and danger of disease from the water. The women were awakened for roll call at four o'clock in the morning; five hundred women stood in the bathroom around three toilets, with no doors. Everything in the rooms was fair game for thieves, especially clothing and shoes.[18]

Nearly all of the Jewish women who survived came when Ravensbrück was in this deteriorated state or worse. Mass transports of Jewish prisoners, mostly from Hungary, began to arrive by the fall of 1944. Other women were shipped to Ravensbrück when evacuations began from Majdanek, Auschwitz, and other camps. When five hundred or more Jewish women arrived from Hungary in the fall of 1944, a big tent with a straw floor was erected. The women lay in their own dirt in the freezing cold and died in masses. Some two thousand Hungarian Jewish women arrived at the camp between 19 and 28 November. The tent, erected between Blocks Twenty-Four and Twenty-six in the middle of the camp, "housed" Hungarian Jews as well as women evacuated from Auschwitz, and up to three thousand women were left to perish with virtually no water, food, or blankets.[19]

Charlotte Müller, a German political prisoner who worked as a plumber at the camp, described the tragic reason for a major drainage blockage that she was sent to correct. After days of pumping, the body of a newborn dead baby was pulled out of the sewage drain adjacent to the tent of the Hungarian Jewish women. "Was the baby born dead?" she asked. "Did he die shortly after birth, or did the mother kill him herself, to spare him an agonizing death from hunger?"[20]

The Jewish population continued to grow when women arrived on the death marches from Auschwitz in January and February 1945. By then the camp was in chaos, and not all of the thousands of Jewish women who arrived were even counted. Many of them were sent on to satellite camps, while the conditions in Ravensbrück kept getting worse.

I. Judith Becker, a Jewish woman who arrived from Auschwitz in early February 1945, has a vivid and dramatic recollection of the horrendous conditions of the camp at that time. She told me that the women in her barrack were packed so tightly that they had to stand. There were so many women in the small space that some of them were actually kept vertical among the other women, without their feet touching the floor. "It must have been a thousand women," she said:

> And the barrack, if the barrack had been functioning, in other words with bunks and so on, the space would have been for a hundred to a hundred and fifty. . . . We had a regular Chagall situation, where people were up in the air. And the people who were up in the air were being pushed, because I didn't want somebody standing on my shoulders, and neither did the next person, so the people in the air became the first victims, because we were not strong enough to be able to have somebody. . . . And then, of course, we found out when this persisted a little longer, that this was the method of killing us. That the lack of oxygen and the lack of space and the violence that erupted from the people in the air wanting to get down, that that was supposed to kill us all. And, of course, many died.[21]

MURDER BY GASSING AND OTHER MEANS

There were many methods of murdering the women at Ravensbrück, in addition to unviable overcrowding and starvation rations. These included hard slave labor, torture, shooting (in a specially designed alley), lethal injection, "medical" experiments, starvation, or gassing, both inside and outside the camp. Jewish political prisoners and others were gassed in the winter–spring of 1942 in the Bernburg psychiatric facility, and by the end of 1944 Ravensbrück became an extermination camp with its own gas chamber. In the summer of that year, inmates from the men's camp attached to Ravensbrück had started constructing the gas chamber in a wooden barrack just outside the camp walls, near the crematorium. The first female inmates were probably killed there in January 1945. According to witnesses, the gas chamber was preceded by the use of carbon monoxide from car engine exhaust.

The SS tried to keep the gassings secret by pretending the transports were headed towards a nonexistent camp named *Schonungslager Mittwerda* (special care/indulgence camp Mittwerda). However, the inmates quickly guessed that the destination of these transports was a gas chamber located nearby, because the empty trucks returned after only a few minutes. The inmates were absolutely sure about the gas chamber when Czech women working in the clothing storage area found it by accident. The work connected with the gassing and the burning of the corpses was relegated to a detail of eleven men from the Ravensbrück men's camp, and continued until April 1945.

SS-Obersturmbannführer (Major) Johannes Schwarzhuber admitted at the Ravensbrück war crimes procedures in Hamburg after World War II that he had been present at one gassing: "One hundred and fifty women were driven into the gas chamber at a time," he testified. "*Hauptscharführer* Moll commanded the women to take off their clothes so the lice could be killed. After that, they were led to the chamber and the door was locked. Some man, an inmate, climbed on the roof and dropped a container with gas into the room and immediately closed the hatch. You could hear moans and screams from the inside. [There was] silence after two or three minutes. I can't say if the women were passed out or dead, because I wasn't present when the gas chamber was cleaned out."[22]

By comparing lists of names of women sent to the nonexistent camp "Mittwerda" (i.e., the gas chamber) with arrival lists, Bernhard Strebel, a historian of the camp, concludes that the majority of those killed by gas were Hungarian, mostly Jewish, then Polish (after the Warsaw uprising), then Russian. Women prisoners who worked as scribes counted a total number of 3,660 names on lists for "Mittwerda." However, since some of the transports went directly from the satellite camps to the gas chamber without reference being made to "Mittwerda," the number of women killed torturously in the gas chamber at Ravensbrück is estimated to be around 5,000 to 6,000.[23]

"It was Himmler who ordered a gas chamber to be built at Ravensbrück in November, 1944—for greater efficiency of extermination," according to survivor Gemma LaGuardia Gluck. "The gas room resembled a bathroom and its door was labeled 'Bathroom.' The poor victims were told to undress, were given a piece of soap and a towel, and were led to the 'showers.' Instead of water, the gas was turned on. . . . During Easter week in 1945 the crematory burned day and night: the frenzied Nazis wanted to get rid of as much 'evidence' as they could. Just before the Russians arrived at Ravensbrück in April, the gas chamber itself was totally destroyed."[24]

The so-called youth concentration camp Uckermark, established about a mile from Ravensbrück in 1941–1942, was under command of the main camp and was sometimes the conduit to the gas chamber. After the first barracks were completed, young girls who didn't fit the Nazi image of proper German girls were admitted, after being declared criminals or persecuted as runaways and "asocials." Between its inauguration and 1945, about one thousand girls were held in custody under inhuman conditions.[25] In addition, in December 1944 or January 1945, Uckermark was partially cleared of youngsters and used as a selection and extermination camp for Ravensbrück. The SS sent to this nearby Ravensbrück auxiliary camp the old, sick, and weakened women who had been selected as "unable to work."

By the end of January 1945, the first selected women were sent to Uckermark from the main camp, stripped of most of their clothing and the gold from their teeth. Czech survivor Dagmar Hajkova described the abysmal conditions: "Five barracks had been separated into large rooms in the new camp. Instead of beds, boards along the walls. There were no blankets, and the women only had rags. They had no underwear, jackets, kerchiefs, not even wooden clogs. There was no water; there were no toilets—only a latrine behind the fifth barrack, and buckets. During the first three days, no food arrived at all. Instead, you stood the whole day at roll call—twice a day, six to eight hours each time. At night, the women were lying on the floor, without blankets. They died quickly, thirty-five, thirty a day."[26]

Lotte Brainin, an Austrian Jewish woman who arrived in Ravensbrück after the death march from Auschwitz in January 1945, told me of her transfer to Uckermark:

A large group of Jewish women prisoners came together with me from Auschwitz to Ravensbrück and were taken to the infamous tent in the camp under extremely dreadful conditions in the very harsh winter of 1945. I came out of the tent very soon through the help of a non-Jewish prisoner, whom I had known in Vienna before the war. From Ravensbrück I was sent to the so-called Youth Camp in Uckermark, which was in fact a *Nebenlager* [auxiliary camp] of Ravensbrück and turned out to be again an annihilation camp. Many women, Jewish and non-Jewish, were murdered there by the Nazis.[27]

21

Polish historian Wanda Kiedrzynska corroborates Dagmar Hajkova and Lotte Brainin's descriptions of catastrophic conditions at Uckermark. She wrote in Polish that most of the women died of hunger, exhaustion, or disease, and some were murdered with poison powder and injections or selected to die in the Ravensbrück gas chamber. One way the women knew of the gas chamber was that the large volume of clothes returned from Uckermark had a heavy sweet smell that caused headaches and nausea. A total number of 8,000 women were brought to Uckermark before it was evacuated in mid-April, when 1,557 women were transported back to the main camp.[28]

THE SUFFERING OF WOMEN

The Jewish women in Ravensbrück had to confront certain questions both as Jews and as women. Every survivor's story is distinct, but women's experiences were in some ways different from those of men in the context of the universal suffering of all victims of the Holocaust. Learning about the experiences of Jewish women in a women's camp can help us to better understand these distinctions. On one hand, there were positive aspects related to gender that enabled women to better struggle against the subhuman conditions of degradation, deprivation, terror, and death at Ravensbrück. For example, homemaking and nurturing skills were "women's work," and women's familiarity with these roles equipped them to form surrogate families, care for each other, and perform the hygienic and housekeeping routines that helped to sustain life.

On the other hand, gender-associated qualities caused some of the women to suffer. For example, because of the social relations between women and men at that time, girls were brought up to be modest, and many women were traumatized when forced to parade naked before men, and even other women. Women were also taught to be submissive, "the weaker sex," and they had to overcome this ingrained self-image in order to stay alive.

As for physiological differences between men and women, both common sense and survivor testimonies point to women's vulnerabilities. Pregnancy could be punishable by death, or at least by forced abortion. There are many testimonies about women prisoners in various camps helping other women to miscarry or abort, in order to save the life of the mother. Likewise, there are stories of women who killed their own newborn infants, because there was no hope for the babies, and their presence could cause suffering or death to others. Menstruation or its cessation was also a problem specific to women in Ravensbrück and other concentration camps.

Fear of rape and sexual abuse was another issue that affected the women in the camp. The racial laws enacted in Germany in 1935, which made it illegal for "Aryans" to have sexual relations with Jews, should have protected Jewish women against rape and forced prostitution. However, there is evidence in historical accounts and testimonies that these laws were often broken. Most women survivors do not talk about their own sexual exploitation, but some of them tell stories of their comrades' suffering. The question of gender during the Holocaust began to be explored only twenty years ago, and its significance has not yet been resolved.[29]

A particular form of torture and abuse aimed at Ravensbrück women was forcing them to serve as prostitutes. Beginning in mid-1941, the SS set up bordellos for themselves or privileged prisoners in some of the men's camps. Some women were forced to participate, while others agreed in exchange for false promises of release. When they were later sent back to Ravensbrück, they were often either pregnant or infected with disease.[30]

TRYING TO UNDERSTAND THE NUMBERS

Regarding the total number of prisoners at Ravensbrück, and the breakdown of this total into the Nazi categories of prisoners, there is no firm consensus. Although only an estimate, the camp memorial continues to use the figure of 132,000 for the total number of women who were at some time prisoners in Ravensbrück. Documents of the International Search Service in Arolsen substantiate that between the founding of the camp and February 1945, a total of 107,753 women were brought to Ravensbrück. Hermine Salvini, a former inmate who was employed until the end of April 1945 in the office of the camp commander, said that the continuous numbering of inmates had reached approximately 123,000. Since an unknown number of transports arrived in Ravensbrück toward the end of the camp's existence, and some of these women were not registered (or numbers were sometimes repeated), the assumed figure of 132,000 inmates has been generally accepted.[31]

Kiedrzynska estimates the number of deaths at 92,000, but much of the documentation within the camp, which could give more precise numbers, was apparently destroyed immediately before the SS left the camp. Her study uses the following numbers, referring to the British charges brought up in the first Ravensbrück war crimes trial in Hamburg: 123,000 total number of female inmates; 12,000 survivors at the end of April 1945; 20,000 prisoners sent from Ravensbrück to be murdered in other camps; 91,000 women who did not survive Ravensbrück. These figures are not entirely accurate because they include the women who died in Ravensbrück's satellite camps, and there is confusion about counting as dead the women who were liberated from the satellite camps and the estimated 7,500 female inmates freed in April 1945 by the Red Cross.[32]

The incomplete documentation found in the camp ledgers accounts for only 55,549 new arrivals, and the camp memorial extrapolates estimates of numbers and percentages to arrive at a total of 132,000. For example, the total number of Jewish women listed in the ledgers is 7,586, which the camp memorial estimates as 17,780 women or 13.47 percent of the camp's population. The problem with this low estimate of the percentage of Jewish women is that thousands of them arrived during the severely overcrowded and disorganized last days when they were not always counted. Others, like some whose stories are told in this book, entered the camp as non-Jews, using false identity papers. Furthermore, many hundreds of Jewish women passed through the camp and stayed a short time before being deported to extermination camps or satellite camps, and these women may also not have been counted. Since there are only 55,549 names accounted for out of an estimated total of 132,000 women, and a high percentage of those unaccounted for could well have been Jewish, the estimated percentage of 10–13.47 percent that has been used officially at the camp memorial is probably much too low. Researchers at the memorial have recently begun to use a figure that is closer to twenty percent.[33]

On 30 April 1945, the Soviet Army reached Ravensbrück. Between the camp's initiation on 18 May 1939 and the day of liberation, an estimated 117,000 of the 132,000 women who passed through the camp had been murdered. When the Soviet Army arrived, they found in the concentration camp only 3,000 desperately weak, sick, and dying prisoners. At least 7,500 to 8,000 women had been evacuated by the Red Cross to Switzerland and Sweden during the last month of the camp's existence. The remaining 15,000 women prisoners had been driven out on 28 April and, under Nazi guard, had embarked on a death march toward the northwest. The SS had intended to dynamite the camp and murder the remaining women, but some prisoners from the nearby men's camp destroyed the explosives.

THE MEMORIES OF INDIVIDUALS

Every survivor of Ravensbrück has her own individual memories about the camp, and sometimes the recollections are different or contradictory. For example, among the Jewish women who arrived on the death marches from Auschwitz and some of its subcamps in January–February 1945, there were divergent comments about the food. One survivor, Lea Ferstenberg, remembered there was virtually nothing to eat at Ravensbrück.

"In Auschwitz you knew that you'd get soup, that you'd get a portion of bread. You knew that you'd get some coffee, something in the morning," she said.[34] Another survivor, Fela Kolat, who came at the same time from the Auschwitz subcamp of Gleiwitz, summed up her time in Ravensbrück with the memory that the soup was thicker there than in Gleiwitz.[35] "The only thing [that] I know from Ravensbrück, the soup was a little thick, it was not so watery, and they didn't catch us to go to work, we could just sit around," she said.

In addition to selective memory and forgetfulness over more than fifty years, individuals can obviously remember only what happened specifically to them. It was not possible for Ravensbrück prisoners to have a conception of the camp as a whole or the experiences of other women. Thus, Fela remembers her good luck of getting a bowl of soup from the bottom of the pot, while Lea remembers nearly starving.

This is just one example of survivors who arrived at the same time but had different individual experiences that influence their recollections of conditions at the camp. Besides individuals' ability to report only on their own specific and limited familiarity with the totality of the camp, those who arrived at different times during the camp's six years of existence actually found extremely dissimilar situations. Ravensbrück cannot be described in a monolithic way, because, like all concentration camps, it changed for the worse over time. It was drastically different at the end of World War II than it was intended to be when it was inaugurated in 1939.

2

Triangles of Many Colors

THE STORIES of Jewish prisoners, a minority in Ravensbrück, can best be told in the context of the camp's population at large. Women from twenty-three nations, including a Jewish woman from the United States, suffered the horrors of Ravensbrück concentration camp. The Nazis divided the prisoners into specific categories, and identified them by way of distinctive color-coded triangles on their uniforms: yellow for Jews, red for political prisoners, purple for Jehovah's Witnesses, black for asocials, and green for criminals. Some Jewish prisoners were also classified as political and wore both a red and a yellow triangle, arranged as a Star of David. Jewish women were always set apart by their "race" on camp lists, even when they were also in another category.

Female prisoners of war (POWs) from the Soviet Army and Great Britain, as well as "special treatment" hostages wore the red badge of political prisoners. The categories of "political" and "asocial" were extremely broad, encompassing a variety of Nazi-defined crimes. Triangles sometimes also had a capital letter to identify the women's countries of origin, (such as a P for Polish prisoners and an F for the French.) When the women arrived, after their hair was cut short or shaved and they were given clothing (uniforms in the early years and then discarded clothing from dead inmates), they had to sew on their designated numbers and triangles.

THE RED TRIANGLE — POLITICAL PRISONERS

Political prisoners included those arrested for such activities as spying for the Allies, helping Jews, publishing illegal materials, participating in

Sculptures of women in front of a memorial wall of nations at the Ravensbrück memorial site, by Will Lammert. Photo by Heinz Heuschkel, Berlin. Collection of MGR/SBG.

outlawed political parties (usually Communists or Social Democrats), or carrying out other forms of organized or individual resistance. The Jewish political prisoners were part of a much larger mix of red-triangle prisoners. Those women arrested as political prisoners ranged from Jewish and non-Jewish confirmed atheists to Roman Catholic nuns and Orthodox Jews, and came from many countries in Europe. The largest groups were from Poland, France, Germany, and Russia; and some individuals from these and other countries have published descriptions of their ordeals in their own languages.[1] Some non-Jewish political prisoners worked with Jewish prisoners in resistance activities, helped to rescue Jews, or served as witnesses to the suffering of Jewish women in the camp.

German Political Prisoners

The fate of Elisabeth Saborowski Ewert[2] (known as Sabo) is integrally intertwined with that of Olga Benário Prestes, a Jewish Communist whose story is told in the next chapter. Sabo, a German national and member of the Communist Party, came from a working class family in East Prussia. She and her German Communist husband, Arthur Ernst Ewert, were sent to Brazil by the Comintern (Communist International) in 1934 to help Brazilian Communist leader Luís Carlos Prestes organize a revolution. They were arrested in Rio de Janeiro on 26 December 1935 after the revolution failed, and tortured by Brazilian and German police. Torture methods in Brazil included nightly beatings and the rape of Sabo in front of her husband. She was taken from the Rio prison in 1936, placed on a Nazi ship, brought to the Barnimstrasse Prison in Berlin, and then sent to Lichtenburg early in 1938. She arrived at Ravensbrück in the late spring of 1939.[3] Even though she had tuberculosis and weighed only about ninety pounds, she was made *Blockälteste* (a prisoner in charge of a barrack) for a group of "asocial" prisoners, including prostitutes.[4] She was responsible for the barrack, and demonstrated both firmness and compassion for the women. Sabo continued to organize her comrades, and when she refused to give the names of "offenders" to the camp commander, he beat and kicked her and sent her to the punishment block.

Sabo was also on an outdoor forced labor detail, required to carry heavy rocks. When she broke down physically, *Aufseherin* (Nazi work overseer) Rabenstein brought her back to consciousness by kicking her and sending dogs to bite her, forcing her back to work. Her comrades often carried her back to the barrack at the end of the day. When it rained, her body was bathed in perspiration, she shivered and lost consciousness, and remained lying in the open field until evening. At some point during the winter of 1939–1940, when Sabo was extremely ill and could no longer

28

lift heavy stones, her political comrades took her to the *Revier* (camp in-firmary). By then, she had pneumonia and a fever of 40° C (104° F). Two comrades who worked as a doctor and nurse in the *Revier* did their best but were unable to save her.

There were many other members of the German Communist resis-tance at the camp. I met one such survivor, Charlotte Uhrig, when I visited the camp memorial in 1980 (nine years before the Berlin wall fell).[5] There is considerable literature in German on the Communist German heroines who were imprisoned in Ravensbrück, but very little has been translated into English.[6] In addition to the Communists, other German women arrested as political or religious resisters were imprisoned in the camp.

For example, Nanda Herbermann was drawn to resistance activities because of her religious beliefs rather than her political ideology. A devout Roman Catholic born to a middle-class family in Münster in 1903, she was arrested there in 1941 and spent two years in Ravens-brück.[7] She had been the editorial assistant for a Catholic journal, *Der Gral* (The Grail), edited and published by an outspoken anti-Fascist priest, Father Friedrich Muckermann. After Father Muckermann was forced to flee to Holland to escape arrest in the summer of 1934, Nanda took over as editor. The Nazis invaded and destroyed the offices of *Der Gral* in 1938, and Nanda was arrested in February 1941, charged with sending clothing and papers to Father Muckermann in exile. In Ravens-brück she was placed in charge of Block Two, which housed the "aso-cials" (many of whom had been arrested for prostitution), and was later given an office job. She was released from the camp after two years and returned to Münster, after one of her brothers, a soldier in the German army, interceded. She resumed her literary activities, including the publi-cation of a memoir about her time in Ravensbrück, and served as the chair of the Münster Committee for the Recognition of People Persecuted for Political, Racial, or Religious Reasons. Nanda died in Münster in 1979.[8]

Sister Theodolinde, another Catholic member of the resistance, was born Katharina Katzenmaier in Heppenheim on 24 April 1918. She was imprisoned on 21 July 1943, after speaking out during a religion class against the mistreatment of people with deficiencies. She was taken to Ravensbrück on 21 October 1943 in a transport of eight hundred women and received inmate number 24295. She was assigned to work at the Siemens factory, and her innate good humor helped people overcome difficult situations. A committed Catholic who remained strong because of her religious beliefs, she tried to prevent confrontations between differ-ent groups of prisoners, such as Communists and religious women. After liberation she returned to her hometown and became a primary school teacher. In November 1949, after studying theology in the Gutenberg University in Mainz, she joined the Benedictine order in Freiburg-Günterstal and received the name Sister Theodolinde. Like Nanda Herbermann, she wrote a memoir of her time in the camp.[9] I met Sister Theodolinde at the 1995 ceremonies commemorating the fiftieth anniversary of Ravensbrück's liberation, and observed her warm reunion with a Jewish survivor who had worked with her at the Siemens factory. Sister Theodolinde died on 5 August 2000.

Polish Political Prisoners

Many women arrived from Poland, and by 1940 there were some one thousand Polish prisoners. They became the largest group of political prisoners, about 75 to 80 percent of the category, and 25 percent of the total population. Their number rose dramatically in August 1944, after the general Warsaw uprising.[10]

Between 1 August 1942, and 16 August 1943, experimental surgical tests on seventy-four Polish women and twelve women of other nationalities were conducted under simulated battlefront conditions, to explore the effectiveness of medications necessary for the war effort. The operations were designed to lead to infections (*Gasbrand*) so that the effects of a treatment with sulfonamides could be studied. Other experimental operations inflicted simulated war wounds on the women's bones, muscles, and nerves. The camp jargon referred to the women who were being operated on as "rabbits" (the equivalent of guinea pigs in English). Many of the women were later exterminated, and those who lived suffered lifelong disfigurement and pain.

One of the "rabbits," Wanda Półtawska, wrote a book about her time in Ravensbrück, full of details about daily life in the camp.[11] A courier for the resistance in Lublin, she was arrested at the age of nineteen in 1941 and arrived in Ravensbrück on 23 September. She recounted how thirteen Polish friends were murdered by firing squad on 18 April 1942. Then, on 27 July of that year, she was among a group of Polish women who were ordered to the main square of the camp to show their legs to a group of civilian and military visitors. Półtawska was one of the first six women whose legs were operated on, and she described in grim detail the inhuman ordeal that she and her friends were forced to undergo in the infamous "rabbit" experiments.[12]

She also told how she and her comrades tried unsuccessfully to resist against further operations on other women, and how her friend Krysia managed to write secret letters on scraps of paper, which were smuggled back to Poland. She was selected to be executed at the time the Polish Jewish transports arrived from Auschwitz in January–February 1945 and managed to hide among them, even writing a false tattooed number on her arm. She was with this group when they were transferred to Neustadt-Glewe, and then liberated from there by the Russian army.

French Political Prisoners

Women from the French resistance in Ravensbrück were highly united and organized and did whatever they could to resist and sabotage the slave labor. Most of the books written by these former prisoners are in French, but a few have been translated into English.[13] A leader of the Amicale of French survivors, Marie-Jo Chombart de Lauwe, spoke with me about her experiences in her home outside of Paris in January 1995. She told me that she had been arrested at age eighteen because she had joined the French resistance in Brittany. She was part of a resistance network on the coast that had been spying for the British. Her father was murdered at Buchenwald, and her mother died soon after liberation. She wrote everything down as soon as she returned to France at the end of World War II, she said.[14]

Marie-Jo arrived in Ravensbrück on 31 July 1943 from a prison in France. She worked for the Siemens company, as well as performing hard manual labor. She also worked in the hospital, where she had personal knowledge of the sterilization of Gypsy women and children, and the experiments on Polish women. She recounted that she was present when a newborn baby was killed. She was sent to Mauthausen toward the end of the war and liberated from there on 2 March 1945 by the Canadian and Swiss Red Cross. She believes that ten thousand French women were imprisoned in Ravensbrück, and two thousand of them survived.

Germaine Tillion is the French survivor best known to readers in the United States; her book was translated into English and published as a popular paperback in 1975.[15] She was arrested on 13 August 1942 in Paris, after a traitor had penetrated the *Musée de l'Homme* (Museum of Man) resistance network to which she belonged. She was accused of five acts that resulted in a death sentence, including harboring English agents. Deported to Ravensbrück from France on 21 October 1943 on a transport of *Nacht und Nebel* (Night and Fog) prisoners, she was destined to be exterminated. Her mother arrived on 3 February 1944, on the transport of 958 French women known as the "twenty-seven thousands" because of the numbers designated to them. Tillion managed to secretly record information and hide her notes during her time at the camp, coding and disguising as recipes the identities of the principal SS personnel. When she was rescued on 23 April 1945 by the Swedish Red Cross, she smuggled out a roll of film with photographs of the maimed legs of the Polish victims of medical experiments. Her record of daily life at the camp, including information on Jewish inmates, was published in its first version in French in 1946 and serves as one of the earliest and most detailed eyewitness accounts.

Two nuns who had been arrested for resistance activities in France made the ultimate sacrifice in Ravensbrück. Mother Maria, whose civil name was Elisabeth Skobzoff, was born in 1891 and emigrated from Russia to France after the Russian Revolution. She settled in Paris and helped the needy, especially other refugees. Her four-year-old daughter died in 1926, and six years later she became a nun in the Russian Orthodox Church. After the Nazi occupation of France, she sheltered Jews and helped them flee to relative safety in southern France. She worked with Father Dimitri Klepinin, the chaplain at her house, who from 1940 to 1943 issued false baptismal certificates to Jews in order to protect them. Mother Maria was arrested and sent to Ravensbrück in 1943. Her final act of kindness and generosity occurred on Good Friday, 30 March 1945. Although she was not selected for the gas chamber that day, she could not bear the panic among those women who had been selected. She therefore took the place of one of the condemned, in order to help her companions face their deaths.[16]

Mother Superior Élise Rivet did likewise. She was born on 19 January 1890 in Draria, Algeria, the daughter of a French navy officer. Élise joined the convent of the medical sisters, *Notre Dame de Compassion* in Lyon, took her vows, and became Mother Superior in 1933. She was denounced for suspicion of hiding weapons, arrested by the Gestapo, and taken to the prison at Fort Montluc in Lyon. From there she was taken to Ravensbrück on 28 July 1944. In March 1945 she and 1,500 other women were transferred to Uckermark, a location for those marked for death. She also chose Good Friday to volunteer to go to the gas chamber in Ravensbrück, in the place of a mother.[17]

Dutch Political Prisoners

Cornelia Ten Boom, who was born in Amsterdam in 1892 and moved to Haarlem at a young age, is perhaps one of the best-known members of the Dutch resistance outside of the Netherlands. She recounted her experiences in a book that has been translated into English and many other languages, and made into a film. Motivated by their Christian faith, Corrie and her family spearheaded a rescue operation that helped many Jews in Holland, including hiding them in their home. The whole family was arrested after a traitor betrayed them, and Corrie and her sister Betsie were sent to Ravensbrück. Betsie died there of disease and malnutrition, but Corrie managed to survive. At the camp she became a source of comfort for the other women, especially by telling them Bible stories.[18]

There were more than 860 Dutch women at Ravensbrück, according to Stennie Pratomo-Gret, a leader of the Dutch Committee of survivors of the camp.[19] Most of the Dutch women were in the camp because of their resistance activities, according to Stennie. They not only hid Jews but also transported weapons for the underground, participated in armed raids on Nazis, printed underground leaflets, and helped allied pilots who landed by parachute after their planes were shot down over the Netherlands.

Women who were arrested early were sent to a provisional Nazi concentration camp in Schoorl, in the dunes of the province of North Holland, and most of them were transported directly from there to Ravensbrück. In June 1943 the first women members of the Dutch resistance movement arrived in Vught, a Nazi concentration camp in the south of Holland. On 6 September 1944, with the Allies approaching the camp, the Nazis evacuated Vught and sent 516 Dutch women, including Stennie Pratomo-Gret, to Ravensbrück. She recounted the overcrowding, her work in the Siemens factory office, the existence of an illegal prisoners' committee that encouraged sabotage, and the birth of a baby that survived. She and most of the surviving Dutch women were liberated by the Swedish Red Cross on 25 April 1945, but at least 135 Dutch women died or were murdered at the camp.

Hetty Dutihl Voûte, Gisela Wieberdink, and Anje Roos were among other Dutch women who were sent to Ravensbrück for helping to hide Jews. As part of the Utrecht Children's Rescue Operation, university students Hetty and Gisela worked together with other friends to hide Jewish children in Utrecht, finding foster homes, providing false identity papers and ration cards. They were arrested by the Gestapo in June 1943, Hetty's twenty-fifth birthday. They were first sent to Vught, then to Ravensbrück. Anje Roos, a nurse, helped hide Jews and deliver food, money, and documents in Amsterdam. She joined the Arondius Group, an underground sabotage organization, and was caught after the group set fire to the Nazi registration office. She was sentenced to serve one year of hard labor at Ravensbrück.[20]

Red Army Women—Soviet Political Prisoners

A large group of women came from the Red Army, and a document from the *Wehrmacht* (German Armed Forces) from 1944 stated that the Soviet female POWs should be placed in Ravensbrück. However, the first female members of the Red Army were sent to the camp on 27 February 1943, even before this *Wehrmacht* order. Most reports indicate that the Red Army women who arrived at the camp had high-level educations, including a large proportion of doctors and health professionals.

The Red Army women were very active in efforts at resistance, working in the secret Communist underground activities in the camp. They tried to slow down or sabotage work efforts. Groups of four or five women comprised surrogate families, and at night they sang songs and recited poems for each other. They also recounted film and theater plots and had political discussions. Some of the women taught French or German to their comrades. Despite their intelligence, the Red Army prisoners did not receive office jobs working for the Nazis, because the SS did not trust them.

One important eyewitness account was written in Russian by Antonina Alexandrowna Nikiforova, a Red Army doctor considered a great heroine of the camp. Born in Leningrad, she attended medical school there and worked in a major hospital. She joined the army when World War II broke out and served in an army hospital. Nikiforova was put into POW and concentration camps beginning in 1941 and then sent to Majdanek because she refused to do forced labor. She entered Ravensbrück on 20 April 1944 and stayed there until the end of the war. Following her quarantine period, she was placed in charge of pathology. After the camp's liberation she stayed for a while and ran an army-style hospital to care for the sick survivors, before returning to the Soviet Union.[21]

The British Spies

In addition to the Soviet POWs, British military women including Lillian Rolfe, Denise Bloch (whose code name was Denielle Williams), and Violette Szabo were incarcerated in Ravensbrück. These three women had joined the British Paratrooper unit (FANY) and were working with the underground, serving as spies in France when they were arrested by the SS. They were brought to Ravensbrück in the summer of 1944 and then transferred to the Konigsberg subcamp. They were later returned to the main camp and placed in the punishment block. In January 1945 they were executed by a firing squad at Ravensbrück. Violette had volunteered for the underground even though she had an infant daughter, Tania, born in June 1942.

At the Hamburg trials of the Ravensbrück Nazi perpetrators, *SS-Obersturmbannführer* (Major) Johannes Schwarzhuber, whose statement regarding the camp's gas chamber was recounted in chapter 1, testified on 12 March 1946 that he had been an eyewitness to this execution:

> One evening towards 1900 hours, they [the three British women] were called out and taken to the cemetery yard by the crematorium. Camp Commandant Suhren made these arrangements. He read out the order for their shooting in the presence of the Chief Camp Doctor, Dr. Trommer, SS Sergeant Z [illegible], SS Lance Corporal Schult (a block leader

from the men's camp), SS Corporal Schenk (in charge of the crematorium), Dentist Dr. Hellinger. I was myself present.

The shooting was done only by Schult with a small caliber gun
through the back of the neck. They were brought forward singly by
Corporal Schenk. Death was certified by Dr. Trommer. The corpses
were removed singly by internees who were employed in the crematorium and burnt. The clothes were burnt with the bodies.

I accompanied the three women to the crematorium yard. A female
camp overseer was also present and was sent back when we reached the
crematorium. Z [illegible] stood guard over them while they were waiting to be shot.

All three were very brave and I was deeply moved. Suhren was also
impressed by the bearing of these women. He was annoyed that the
Gestapo did themselves not carry out these shootings.[22]

THE PURPLE TRIANGLE — JEHOVAH'S WITNESSES

The Jehovah's Witnesses in Germany numbered only about twenty thousand in a general population of sixty-five million Germans. Because of
their strong religious convictions, they refused to say "*Heil Hitler,*" enlist
in the army, or desist from their banned publishing activities. They were
persecuted and isolated by the Nazis beginning in 1933, placed in "preventive detention" beginning in 1936 and ultimately sent to concentration camps. A total of some ten thousand male and female Jehovah's
Witnesses, most of them German, ended up in camps, and the others lost
their jobs, pensions, civil rights, and sometimes their children. Those who
were incarcerated were often brutally tortured, and some were murdered
by firing squad, decapitation, and other methods. It is estimated that
between twenty-five hundred and five thousand Jehovah's Witnesses did
not survive the concentration camps or prisons. Almost none of them
renounced their faith, even though they could have done so and been
freed by simply signing a piece of paper.[23]

The women who were arrested were sent first to prisons, then to
Lichtenburg; there were Jehovah's Witnesses in the first transport to
Ravensbrück. They refused to participate in any slave labor that resulted
in helping the war effort, such as the Siemens factory at the camp. Because
they were completely honest and trustworthy, they were often assigned
jobs cleaning the homes of the SS officers and caring for their children.

Jewish special prisoner Gemma LaGuardia Gluck admired the Jehovah's Witnesses for their strength of character. "They had been in prison
for eight, ten, or twelve years, right from the beginning of Hitler's regime
in 1933, when members of their sect refused to answer or acknowledge
the official Nazi greeting, 'Heil Hitler,'" she wrote. "At one point the
Gestapo had announced that any [Jehovah's Witness] who renounced his

beliefs and signed a statement to that effect would be given his freedom and be persecuted no longer. . . . They preferred to go on suffering and patiently waiting for the day of liberation."[24]

Magdalena Kusserow Reuter was a teenager when she was sent to the camp for the "crime" of being a Jehovah's Witness and refusing to say "*Heil Hitler.*"[25] Her ready smile and tranquil manner belie the suffering that she and her family endured at the hands of the Nazis. Magdalena was the seventh of eleven children, and all thirteen members of her family were in prison or "protective custody" at some time during the Nazi regime. At the age of seventeen, she was sentenced to a solitary confinement cell in the Vechta youth prison, and ten months later, along with her mother, Hilda, and her sister Hildegard, she was transferred to Ravensbrück. She remained there for three and a half years, until the camp's last days, and was permitted to write one letter a month, with a maximum of six lines. She remembered the day when some of the Jehovah's Witness women in the camp informed her of the murder of her brother Wolfgang, who was decapitated in the Brandenburg prison. Another brother, Wilhelm, was killed by a firing squad in Münster. Magdelena settled in Spain after the war, and her family's tragic story is often used by the Jehovah's Witnesses as an example of the brutal persecution that this religious group underwent during the Nazi regime.

Ilse Unterdorfer, another Jehovah's Witness who survived Ravensbrück, recalled:

> We would build one another up spiritually by sharing the Bible knowledge that we had acquired before we were imprisoned. Also, newcomers to the camp would share what they had learned more recently in their Bible studies. How glad we were when several Bibles were smuggled into the camp! . . . Nothing could stop us from demonstrating our faithfulness to Jehovah. Our decision was: "rather die than give up." . . . The Gestapo quite unexpectedly appeared in Ravensbrück on 4 May 1944. They made a sudden search for Bibles and Bible literature, particularly the *Watchtower.* . . . Finally it was determined that fifteen sisters regarded as the ones responsible, would suffer for all. . . .
>
> First, we were locked in the notorious cell block. There we were crammed into small dark cells, and for seven weeks we were not allowed into the open air. Then we were taken to the "punishment building." . . . What we lived through there during our last year in Ravensbrück can hardly be expressed in words.[26]

Margarete Buber-Neumann was the Block Elder in charge of 275 Jehovah's Witnesses at Ravensbrück. She wrote in her memoir of the calm and order that prevailed in these barracks. After she realized that the women were secretly bringing in Bibles and other forbidden literature in their pails and floor cloths, she encouraged them to hide their literature in the block. "After that, Bible study went on quite openly in the block in the evenings and on Sundays," she wrote. "And in bed at night, before the SS women came around with their dogs, they would sing their songs softly." She was impressed with the Jehovah's Witnesses' strength of conviction, honesty, and selflessness.[27]

THE BLACK TRIANGLE — ASOCIAL WOMEN

Like the category of "political prisoners" who wore the red triangle, the category of "asocial" was extremely broad. It included prostitutes, lesbians, and Gypsies (Sinti and Roma), as well as women who were considered sexually promiscuous or had elected to have abortions. In general, the majority of the men and women who were considered "asocial" by the Nazis were poor and dependent on state support. Many did not have fixed residences, or were beggars, charity cases, homeless people, alcoholics, homosexuals, prostitutes, or "immoral priests." The nomadic way of Gypsy life placed the Sinti and Roma in this category, although they were also considered racially inferior. Criminals and male homosexuals living under the Nazis, at first included in the asocial category, later had their own categories and corresponding triangles—green for criminals and pink for male homosexuals.[28]

Lesbians

At the historic and groundbreaking "Conference of Women Surviving the Holocaust" organized by Esther Katz and Joan Ringelheim at Stern College in New York in March 1983, I witnessed the bitter conflict between lesbians and female Holocaust survivors that almost halted the proceedings.[29] When one of the politically militant lesbians in attendance raised the question of lesbian affection in the camps, a number of the survivors in attendance became enraged. To paraphrase and summarize their responses, they were deeply insulted that anyone could even think of such a possibility in the midst of their terrible suffering. However, despite their blanket denials, lesbians were indeed imprisoned in Ravensbrück as lesbians, considered as "asocial."

There is even evidence that at least two women, Jenny (Henny) Sara Schermann and Mary Pünjer, were condemned to death at Ravensbrück because the Nazis classified them as both Jews and lesbians. Jenny was "described as a 'practicing lesbian' who 'shuns the [Nazi-imposed] name *Sara*,' the 'Jewess without a nationality' was diagnosed by [Nazi euthanasia expert] Dr. [Friedrich] Mennecke as 'suffering from mental disorders.'" She was accused of "unnatural fornication" and selected for extermination by gas at the Bernburg killing facility in 1942. Jenny was born to Jewish parents on 19 February 1912 in Frankfurt and had two younger sisters. Her father was an immigrant from Russia. In 1936 she was working as a shop assistant and still living with her family, and in early 1940 she was arrested in Frankfurt and deported to Ravensbrück. The back of her prison photo identifies her and describes her as a "licentious lesbian, only visited such [lesbian] bars." Another Jewish woman, Mary Pünjer (born in Hamburg in 1904), was arrested as "asocial" and "lesbian," according to Claudia Schoppmann. Like Jenny, Mary was gassed at Bernburg in 1942.[30]

While male homosexuals were prosecuted under article 175StGB, based on the original anti-homosexual law of 1871, paragraph 175 (not abolished until 1968 in West Germany), lesbianism did not fall under this law and was not considered illegal. Nevertheless, lesbians could be and were arrested in the category of asocial, and at Ravensbrück they wore black rather than pink triangles.[31]

Although there must have been nurturing lesbian relationships at Ravensbrück and other camps, the recollections that I heard from Jewish prisoners were always negative. Many of them were young women or teenagers from sheltered homes who did not even know what a lesbian was when they entered the camp, and they were shocked or frightened by the idea. Hannah Horon, who was later in Ravensbrück, remembered an experience in Auschwitz: "There was a woman, she wasn't Jewish, who waited for me when I came from work. And she said, come with me, and I give you bread, and I give you soup," Hannah recalled. "And she waited for me every day, and she only wants to give me something, I should go with her. Now, as a young girl at that time, I didn't know anything about that two women live together.... But when I found out, I said, what does she want from me, she wants to sleep with me, eh? So I refused the food from her, and I tried to get out, but she was after me for a while."[32]

Another survivor, Mina Goldstein, saw lesbians for the first time when she was in Ravensbrück and also did not understand their behavior. She told me she saw women running and laughing near the latrines, and was "stupid" and had to learn about it.[33] One survivor who was in Ravensbrück with her sister said she knew of some lesbian relationships. She also recalled she and her sister were once accused of being lesbians by someone who saw how close they were and did not know they were sisters.[34]

Survivor Elizabeth Kroó Teitelbaum went so far as to mistakenly describe Ravensbrück as a "lesbian camp."[35] "You could see that it's a lesbian camp, and you could almost tell who played what role," she told me. "You could tell on the people—the girls who were the prisoners. I guess they were there a longer time, and they were lesbian. It was known as a lesbian camp, and you could see who was the 'male' and who was the 'female' by their actions and by their holding each other. It was just known as a lesbian camp, and, frankly, I had a very personal, a very frightening experience with that," she recalled:

> Since we came from Auschwitz, everybody was shaven. I had very broad shoulders and sort of a masculine figure and hardly any hair, and this *kapo* [prisoner in charge of a group of prisoners] took a liking to me. She promised me chocolate and she promised me cigarettes and anything. She had a little hut of her own, supposedly. I have never been there, but I was told. And she promised me the sky from heaven, I should come and visit with her. Oh, just to visit. I got very frightened, because I saw what's going on in that camp. I had friends there from home, really friends, and from Auschwitz. You know, we went together, and you made friends easy. You were so hungry for some attention and some loving and some caring. And they knew what's happening. Unless there was an *Appell* [roll call] and we had to stand in line, when they saw her coming, they used to warn me. We had these bunks, three-layer bunks. I used to lie down on the bottom bunk, and they used to throw blankets over me and sit there on the bunk so that she did not realize that there is somebody under those blankets.

Gypsies

Gypsies, or Sinti and Roma, were also considered "asocial" and required to wear black triangles in Ravensbrück. They were subjected to official discrimination in Germany long before 1933, although there was no comprehensive law against them. In 1936 the Reich Interior Ministry issued guidelines for "fighting the Gypsy plague," which required photographing and fingerprinting them. Then, in 1937, "preventive custody," or concentration camp imprisonment, was authorized for Gypsies. Until 1942 only those who intermarried with Germans and were considered a threat to "racial purity" were targeted, and "pure" Gypsies were generally not arrested.[36]

Sinti and Roma women were incarcerated at Ravensbrück from the early days of the camp's existence. The first 440 Gypsy women were brought from Austria and Germany on 29 June 1939. At the end of 1943 the first large transport of Gypsy women and children arrived at Ravensbrück in very bad condition. There were then transports from Auschwitz-Birkenau on 15 April 1944 (473 women and children), 23 May 1944 (144 women and children), and 2 August 1944 (490 women and children). The women worked as slave laborers in the various industries at the camp and its satellite factories.

The testimony of Wanda P. is one of the few available from a Roma or Sinti survivor. She arrived in Ravensbrück from the Auschwitz-Birkenau family camp in the summer of 1944. Then twenty-two years old, she took the responsibility for a small Gypsy girl who had been separated from her mother, adopting her as her own. She was first put to work for Siemens, but the conditions were so rigorous and strenuous that for the first time she broke down and was unable to continue. She was then sent to work making straw mats inside the camp and also had to pave and smooth the streets in the camp.

Wanda was one of the Sinti and Roma women and girls from age twelve upward who underwent forced sterilization in Ravensbrück. In only four days during the first week of January 1945, Professor Carl Clauberg sterilized some 120 to 240 Sinti and Roma women and young girls. Some women were pressed to agree to the experiments with false promises of freedom in exchange for their own or their children's sterilizations. However, most of the women and young girls were sent to be sterilized by force without previous information, and many of them, mostly young girls, died from the procedure. A short time after the sterilizations, Wanda and other Sinti or Roma victims who survived were sent from Ravensbrück to Mauthausen. She was then taken to Bergen-Belsen, and after the camp was liberated by the British, she returned to her hometown of Hanover.[37]

THE GREEN TRIANGLE — CRIMINALS

This category is difficult to pinpoint. Some categories of "asocial" behavior later came to be defined as "criminal." In addition to these gray areas of what the Nazis considered unacceptable social behavior, some women at Ravensbrück were actual criminals. For example, they had been caught stealing or committing some other act generally accepted as illegal. These women were often placed as *kapos* in charge of the other inmates and were described in interviews with Jewish survivors and written accounts as unusually cruel and crude.

THE YELLOW TRIANGLE — JEWS

The experiences of some of the Jewish women who were part of this color-coded nightmare are told in detail in this book. Jewish women were in Ravensbrück from its very first days, arriving as political prisoners but also designated as Jewish. With the exception of a very short time in the fall of 1942, there was always a Jewish presence. However, the Jewish women were a minority within a diverse population that ranged from heroines to common criminals, from those who resisted as Communist atheists to those who did so because of religious convictions, from physicians and professors to uneducated peasants.

3

Olga Benário Prestes and Käthe Pick Leichter

O LGA Benário Prestes, a German Communist, and Dr. Käthe Pick Leichter, an Austrian Social Democrat, were Jewish political prisoners. They are remembered as great heroines for their resistance activities in Ravensbrück. Although they had different nationalities and political affiliations, Olga and Käthe sometimes worked together for the benefit of the other prisoners. For example, they collaborated on a clandestine newspaper and organized extra bread and margarine for women in the infirmary. Both of them were from well-off, assimilated, Central European Jewish families, became politically active at a young age, and served in high-level positions in their respective parties.

At the April 1995 ceremonies marking the fiftieth anniversary of the liberation of Ravensbrück, I had the opportunity to see the new Jewish memorial room in the museum space in the former prison block. Prominent among the Jewish women highlighted in this exhibit are Communists and Socialists who were arrested primarily as political activists, although the Nazis also took into account their status as Jews. Käthe Pick Leichter and Olga Benário Prestes's larger-than-life photographs are placed side by side in this exhibit.

OLGA BENÁRIO PRESTES

A German Jewish woman from an upper-middle-class Munich family, Olga Benário Prestes was born to Eugenie and Leo Benário on 12

Memorial panels depicting Olga Benário Prestes and Käthe Pick Leichter were placed next to each other in the exhibit memorializing Jewish prisoners. Created at the Ravensbrück memorial for the 1995 anniversary of the fiftieth anniversary of the camp's liberation. Photo by Rochelle G. Saidel.

February 1908.[1] Her father, a Social Democrat, was a prestigious lawyer who volunteered to represent poor factory workers fighting for fair work conditions. He taught Olga concern for the poor and oppressed. She became more radical than her father, joining the Communist youth organization in Munich at age fifteen. Soon afterward she became romantically involved with Communist leader Otto Braun and left home to carry out her revolutionary activities. When she was eighteen years old in 1926, she was imprisoned for the first time, along with Braun. She was released after three months of solitary confinement in Moabit Prison, and then in April 1928 she organized Braun's jailbreak. Her role in this mission made her famous—or infamous—and she and Braun fled to Moscow. While there, Olga was elected to the Central Committee of the Communist Youth International. She eventually broke off her relationship with Braun and was sent to Paris on a mission. When she returned to Moscow, Olga was given military training and named as a member of the Presidium of the Communist Youth International, the highest level in any Communist organization.

In 1934, at the age of twenty-six, she was chosen by the Comintern to accompany the Brazilian Communist leader, Luís Carlos Prestes, from Moscow to Brazil. Her mission was to help him in his revolutionary activities there, but his November 1935 revolution failed. They and other Communist revolutionaries were captured and imprisoned in Rio de Janeiro. In the meantime, she and Prestes had fallen in love, and she was pregnant.

This failed Communist revolution occurred five years after Getúlio Vargas had led the Revolution of 1930, and then become president of Brazil. His two-faced government was in some aspects "modern." For example, he instituted the secret ballot for elections, created a bill of rights for workers, and promoted employment through industrialization. On the other hand, his government was conservative and authoritarian, even totalitarian. São Paulo forces tried a counterrevolution in 1932, with the objective of reopening the Congress, where the state had a strong representation. Like the Communist revolution three years later, this so-called "constitutionalist revolution" failed.

At the time of the Prestes revolution, the Brazilian president had a friendly relationship with the Hitler regime. To retaliate against Prestes, in September 1936 President Vargas had the pregnant Olga snatched from her prison cell and brought to the port in Rio de Janeiro. She—a pregnant Jewish German member of the Communist Party—was placed on a German ship and sent back to Nazi Germany under armed guard. Upon arrival in Germany in October, Olga was brought to the Berlin prison for women on Barnimstrasse, and her daughter, Anita, was born there on November 27. Olga was told that as soon as Anita was weaned she would be placed in a German orphanage. However, at the age of fourteen months, the baby was miraculously rescued by Prestes's mother. Anita was saved, but Olga must have suffered beyond imagination. She never saw her child again. (Anita eventually returned to Brazil after the Vargas era and was reunited with her father.)

Only after Olga was transferred to Lichtenburg in February 1938 was she able to receive a short note from her mother-in-law informing her that Anita was alive and safe. At Lichtenburg, a medieval fortress that predated Ravensbrück as the main women's concentration camp, Olga was first placed in solitary confinement. She was in a dark cell in the basement for several months, with a cement bed, a straw mattress, and wood for a pillow. Her diet was bread and water, with warm food every third day. "The Gestapo had then not yet given up trying to get information from Olga on the activities of the International Communists in South America," according to one account. "For every interrogation she was brought to Berlin to Prince Albertstrasse. She was kicked, tortured, threatened with being shot, but she remained mute. The Nazis withheld information on the whereabouts of her daughter to pressure her."[2]

Later, in a collective cell, she was reunited with some comrades she had known in Berlin, as well as her beloved friend Sabo, Elisabeth Saborowski Ewert. She and Sabo, a non-Jewish political prisoner, were not only close friends but also co-conspirators in the failed 1935 Communist revolution in Brazil. They were imprisoned together in Rio de Janeiro and brought to Germany from Brazil on the same ship. The two women had been separated when the ship carrying them from Brazil arrived in Hamburg in October 1936, and they had not seen each other since then.

Olga was on the first transport from Lichtenburg to Ravensbrück, and she became a great heroine at both camps. She carried out many acts of resistance and worked to better the conditions of the other women, despite her own suffering. She was assigned as a *Blockälteste* (block senior), in charge of an unruly group of women whom she organized and taught the necessity of personal hygiene. The Ravensbrück memorial archivist has assured me in writing that Olga wore a red badge designating her as a political prisoner (along with the yellow triangle marking her as a Jew), and this seems likely. However, another source states that along with her yellow badge Olga received the black badge of the "asocial" prisoners, in order to "render it impossible for her to make contact with the Communists."[3]

Whatever the color of her badge, Olga managed not only to communicate with her fellow Communists but also to organize solidarity and resistance activities. As *Blockälteste* of Block Eleven, one of the barracks that housed Jewish prisoners, Olga made every effort to keep the women clean. Olga reportedly told her charges: "If we don't take care of our bodies the Nazis can do with us whatever they want. We are all in the same boat and if we want to be treated with dignity we need to keep ourselves as human beings and not as animals. I was instructed to be responsible for this block and therefore some things will be changing as of tomorrow." Olga was rapidly accepted as the authority and after two weeks the block was as clean as the circumstances allowed it to be. The women paid attention, took care of their hygiene, and every day more women took part in the morning gymnastics that Olga arranged. She also organized secret classes, including Russian and French lessons, and literature evenings.[4]

Olga even made a small secret atlas to teach other prisoners about geography and the war, and this amazingly detailed atlas is today in the Ravensbrück archives. In addition to her other work assignments, she was a slave laborer for the Siemens electric company at Ravensbrück. In January 1940, along with seventy-nine other women, Olga was sent to the prison bunker and remained there for thirty days. She had been among the prisoners kept for "security reasons" in closed barracks when *Reichsführer* Heinrich Himmler visited the camp. After one of the women in the barracks called out, "Heinrich Himmler, you are nothing more than a pederast, and a murderer," Olga and the other women were selected for the punishment bunker. She was whipped and on the verge of death, but when she was released she had to immediately return to forced labor at the Siemens factory.[5]

Thirty-four-year-old Olga was among those Jewish political prisoners gassed at Bernburg in the winter and early spring of 1942.[6] Although she is famous in Brazil and was considered a great heroine in the German Democratic Republic, her name is not well known in the United States.[7] Her last act of resistance was a letter to her husband and daughter, which they received many years later. Writing on her last night in Ravensbrück, knowing she would be sent to her death the next day, she told them:

> It is utterly impossible for me to imagine, my dear daughter, that I will never see you again, never squeeze you in my eager arms. I wanted so to be able to comb your hair, to braid your braids. . . . Above all else, I'm going to make you strong. . . . I've already gone back to dreaming, as I do every night, forgetting that this is to say goodbye. And now, when I'm reminded of this, the idea that I will never again be able to hold your warm little body is like death to me.

Brave and concerned about others until the end, Olga ended her letter: "I promise you now, as I say farewell, that until the last instant I will give you no reason to be ashamed of me."[8]

KÄTHE PICK LEICHTER

Dr. Käthe Pick Leichter is now honored as a heroine in Austria.[9] On the hundredth anniversary of her birth in 1995, the Austrian government issued a postage stamp in her honor. Her son Henry presented me with a first-day cover envelope when I met him in August 1998. He also shared with me an unpublished manuscript about his childhood, which gave me insights into Käthe's role as both a Socialist party leader and a mother.

Käthe Leichter was born in Vienna on 18 August 1895, the daughter of Josef Pick, a member of the Viennese cultural elite, and Charlotte Rubinstein Pick, the daughter of a banker from Bucharest, Romania. Käthe's "belief in socialism and her dedication to the cause was the strongest moving force in her life," according to Henry. "She was brought up under the strong influence of an immensely well-read father, a true liberal of the second half of the nineteenth century, with an unlimited faith in the forces of progress and justice."[10]

Even as a youngster, Käthe had a strong sense of social justice. "Very early she began to resent the injustices she saw around herself: the bad treatment of household servants by her mother and other relatives, the poverty she saw in the streets," Henry wrote. "All this led her to rebel against the complacency with which the ruling class (of which her own

45

family was a part) exploited or at least benefited from the social and economic injustice which prevailed around her." As a child, she sided with the servants against her mother, and at family gatherings "little Käthe to the horror of some of the richer relatives spoke up for the right of workers to organize and to go on strike."[11]

With her father's support, Käthe was admitted to the University of Vienna. However, women were not allowed to enter the Faculty of Political Science there, so she obtained her degree by transferring in her last year to the University of Heidelberg, Germany. She studied under sociologist Max Weber in Heidelberg and was deeply influenced by him. Together with other students she organized discussion groups on the topic of women's rights at the university. The women in her group talked about the works of John Stuart Mill, August Bebel, and Lilly Braun, and invited speakers from the Austrian women's movement such as Rosa Mayreder and Therese Schlesinger. To the great surprise of some of the women, Käthe went a step farther and invited male speakers as well. This was based on her desire to integrate women into the political movement beyond their own small circle, a lesson that some feminist activists today have not yet learned. It may also illustrate her ambivalent relationship to the women's movement.

She became a leading member of a leftist student antiwar group during her studies in Germany in 1917; the military authorities expelled her from the country and forced her to return to Vienna. Her father managed to negotiate her return to Heidelberg for forty-eight hours to take her final exams. At a time when it was unusual for a woman to receive an advanced academic degree, she was granted a Ph.D. *magna cum laude* in Social Sciences from the University of Heidelberg.

After receiving her degree, Käthe was deeply involved in the growing Austrian student socialist movement and through it met Otto Leichter, another activist. They were part of the left wing of the movement, the so-called *Neue Linke* (New Left), but remained with the Social Democrats when some members splintered off in 1918 to form the Austrian Communist Party. They were married in 1921, and in 1925 Otto joined the staff of the *Arbeiter-Zeitung*, the official paper of the Social Democratic party.

"In the early twenties there was a great movement, particularly among socialists, to shed the affiliation with the Catholic Church, to which some 90 percent of the Austrian population belonged, at least on paper," Henry Leichter wrote. "This was conceived as a protest against the dominant role which that church played through its close affiliation with the Christian Social Party. The movement also spread to other religions, and shortly before my birth, my parents formally left the Jewish faith."[12] Despite this renunciation and assimilation, the Nazis considered Käthe Jewish.

By the time her first son, Henry (then called Heinz), was born in March 1924, Käthe had already held a number of important positions. She had been secretary to Otto Bauer, the leader of the Austrian Social Democratic Party and, briefly, Foreign Minister of the new Austrian Republic. After the Social Democrats left the government, she went to work for the Chamber of Labor, where she founded and became head of the Department of Women's Affairs. She was instrumental in organizing a union of domestic employees, and was an activist, speaker, and writer for the party. She wrote articles for the party's theoretical journal, which were among the first to call for militant action against the advance of fascism. In 1929 she published a major study based on interviews with female workers, and the following year her *Handbook of Woman's Labor* was issued. In addition to her political and sociological work, she was also an accomplished pianist and violinist. Amid all of these activities, her second son, Franz, was born in 1930.

Meanwhile, the political situation had become dangerous for the Leichters and their associates. In March 1933, Austrian (Christian Social Party) Chancellor Engelbert Dolfuss dissolved the Parliament, introduced censorship, reintroduced the death penalty, and ruled by decree. The Social Democratic Party grew weaker as the political and economic situation in the country grew worse. In February 1934, at the insistence of Mussolini, the Austrian Fascist government banned the Social Democratic Party. A civil war broke out, and Käthe and her husband were forced to go into hiding. By the beginning of March they had escaped to Switzerland but then returned to Vienna and were deeply involved in the political underground. A year later, in March 1935, Käthe was jailed for four days and Otto was imprisoned for a longer time. In 1937 she took over the weekly *Information and News* publication of the "Revolutionary Socialists," and continued until 7 March 1938. She also wrote two illegal pamphlets, one entitled "*Was den Proletarierfrauen droht!*" (What is in store for the proletarian women!), and the other, "*Muttertag?*" (Mother's Day?), both of which focused on the rights of women.[13] Then, on 11 March 1938, Austria became part of the German Reich. The next day the SA came to arrest Otto Leichter, who was not at home.[14] A few days later he escaped to Czechoslovakia using a false passport.

"Why didn't my mother leave with him?" her son Henry asks. Answering his own question, he writes: "Part of the reason was probably that arrangements had to be made for us children, either to go with them or to follow them in short order. Another strong argument was that my father really was the more endangered of the two, was better known, and the Nazis had already come to look for him. But the main reason was that she had strong nerves and an unquenchable optimism which simply did not permit her to be scared, and, rather, led her not to recognize the danger she was in. . . . Thus she determined to apply formally for an exit permit and to make arrangements for furniture and personal belongings to be packed in order to accompany us."[15]

After some threats that included being forced to paint the word *Jude* on her window and hints of her imminent arrest, she finally accepted a false Czech passport that Otto had smuggled into Vienna through his contacts. Preparations were made for the housekeeper to take Franz, her younger son, out of the country, and Käthe and Henry left the apartment by climbing over the garden fence. He was supposed to stay with socialist friends while his mother spent the night with non-Jewish friends, and they had arranged to take the train to Czechoslovakia the next day.

On 30 May 1938, the day of the planned departure, Käthe called her mother from a public phone to say goodbye. A strange male voice answered, informing her that unless she turned herself in at her mother's apartment, her mother would be arrested. After sending Henry back to her friends, she went to her mother's apartment, was arrested, and sent to prison. Soon afterward the housekeeper, Irma, took Franz out of the country, having him pose as her son.

The day after Franz departed, the official passports and exit visas that had been requested for him and Henry arrived, and the boys were free to leave the country. Furthermore, the Gestapo called and announced that the boys had been given permission to visit their mother. Franz's absence was accounted for by filing a police complaint that he had been kidnapped. On 7 August 1938, Henry visited his mother in Gestapo headquarters, the Hotel Metropole.

Käthe maintained her brave attitude even when she had to meet her son under such horrible circumstances. "I have always been grateful to my mother for making this last visit with her so friendly and pleasant," he wrote. "I have the memory of great confidence, even cheerfulness, when she told me that, in three months at the latest, she would be free again and would join us abroad."[16] That evening he left for Switzerland by train and then joined his father and brother in Paris.

In the fall of 1938, Käthe was transferred to the *Landesgericht* jail and endured several months of solitary confinement. To survive the terrible loneliness, she began to write her memoir. After a trial in the summer of 1939, she was sent to Ravensbrück in January 1940. Rosa Jochmann, a non-Jewish Social Democratic resistance leader and friend who arrived at the camp a short time later and was with Käthe, tells of their encounters:

> Then I saw Käthe again in the camp. She knew I would hold the post of *Blockälteste* in the political block, and she immediately told me three things on the first day: "Don't forget that you are not a shop steward here, you always have to pretend to be following all commands, because the SS is always right, but you also have to do everything to sabotage

their work and to protect the inmates. You always have to pretend to be more stupid than our tormentors, because most of them are more than primitive. . . ."

We were not allowed to talk to the Jewish prisoners [such as Käthe] and were not allowed any contact with them, either, but we never obeyed that rule and were just careful not to get caught. On Sunday afternoons, when we had the least trouble with the SS, Käthe organized literary afternoons in Block Eleven, the Jewish block. Of course we had posted our friends outside the block. Old freedom poems and songs were sung, and we had many unforgettable hours that allowed us to forget our terrible hell at least for a short time. Together with Communist com-ᴵᵃᵈⁱ Dꞩ, Hꞩꞩᵗꞩ Bꞩꞩ∪ꞩꞩ, Käthe ꞩꞩꞩꞩᵗꞩd ꞩ ꞩꞩꞩꞩ ᵗꞩᵗꞩꞩd Sꞩꞩꞩ Sꞩꞩꞩ Iᵗ wꞩꞩ about two Jewish prisoners who escaped to a deserted island, and were shipwrecked.[17]

The play mocked the Nazis, but Käthe destroyed the written version and kept a fake innocuous play in her closet, in case of discovery by the camp authorities. Käthe organized all sorts of celebrations, according to her friend Rosa:

When we walked along the camp street on Sundays, we always asked Käthe to tell us something, for example about the French Revolution. "But I don't know any more than you do," she would say, and then proceed to give lectures on many Sundays about the things she didn't know "very well." She was self-confident, yet very modest and warm. She was always interested in what was considered the "lowest of the low," the prostitutes, thieves, murderers. Unfortunately, we had to destroy her sociological research into these topics when a block search was about to take place. She proved that these people were doomed to failure because of their circumstances: "It is not the fault of these people, it is the fault of society," she said again and again, and she was right.[18]

Käthe was forced to carry out hard physical labor, loading bricks onto ships on the Havel River. Another prisoner, Erika Buchmann, later gave an eyewitness account of the brutality of this work assignment, which she said was designated to the Jewish women: "They were forced to do the most difficult jobs and the tragic images of them when they left work, mostly weak, many of them old and sick, were unforgettable. Outside boats arrived fully loaded with bricks and building blocks and the strictest supervisor of the camp would receive the order to go to the boat with the Jewish commandos. Uninterruptedly the exhausted and nervous women felt the beating. Gloves were not distributed and in a period of a few hours their hands were injured from the stones and the coal, and bleeding from uncountable small wounds."[19] Among the poems that Käthe wrote at the camp, one was about her bloody hands. Her friends finally managed to have her transferred so she could stay inside the block and knit socks. Since she never learned to knit, other women would knit for her while she told them about the world, and how she thought it should be. They were all political Jewish prisoners who loved her and tried to help her. For example, they straightened her closet and made sure her bed was tightly made.[20]

Rosa Jochmann was an eyewitness to the beginning of the end for Käthe and some fifteen hundred women, mostly Jewish:

> In January 1942, a group of doctors entered the camp, and all Jewish comrades had to appear naked in the first row in front of the doctors. One of the doctors asked Käthe about her degree, and then said: "Oh, that is nice, they'll be able to use you at the new camp." Three times the trucks came in the middle of winter, and twice they had to turn around because the snow was too deep. Käthe said, "I am starting to get embarrassed. I feel like someone who always claims to go on a trip and never actually leaves." But then finally the trucks got through. On the evening before, Helene Potetz and I had been with our friends in the Jewish block, as usual. You can't imagine what that was like. It was as if they were aware of their fate. Only Käthe stayed calm and reminded everyone to pull herself together. We had worked with some friends in the clothing department to obtain warm clothes, so we could give them to Käthe and the other women. And we had agreed that Käthe would use another woman's identification number to get news to us, if at all possible. The number belonged to a Viennese Jewish woman named Bukowitz, who was not known politically.
>
> Then in the morning, as the *Blockälteste*, I was allowed out on the camp street, and Helene Potetz came along. We walked hand in hand, a silent mass, as we had walked twice before. I will never know if she understood that this was the end. She was so smart that I would rather think she pretended not to know, so we would feel better, to give us courage. She must have known she wasn't ever going to come back. Still today I see Käthe sitting on the truck, in the bitter cold, her eyes steadily set on us. Waving, she disappeared forever.
>
> Fourteen days later, all the prisoners' clothes came back, all the warm clothes we had organized for them, wool socks, a scarf, canes, glasses, dentures, just everything. And with the number for the Austrian woman named Bukowitz, we found a note: "Everything fine so far, treated well everywhere, traveling through Dessau. . . ." And that was where the words ended. The inmates working in the "Care Department" (*Fürsorgeabteilung*) walked in, as white as sheets. They had just sent fifteen hundred letters to relatives of the women. The entire transport had supposedly died of "circulatory debility."[21]

Herta Mehl Soswinski, the only Jewish political prisoner I know of who arrived at Ravensbrück before October 1942 and survived, remembered Käthe Leichter at the camp. Käthe had helped to make Herta's

Olga Benário Prestes and Käthe Pick Leichter

punishment order "disappear" when she fainted during a snow shoveling detail. Herta recalled the transport of Jewish prisoners who were sent out of the camp in March 1942:

> We did not know their destination, but it was strange that their prison uniforms, they had received new clothing before leaving, was [sic] returned to camp a few days later. We had arranged with Ruth, our table-elder, to send us some news, if possible, under the star of her jacket. She did so, and the girls from the clothing detail, informed by us, gave us the note. She wrote that she did not know where she was, but that they had been received by a group of physicians which even comprised a dentist. She could not write us any more because it was her time to get undressed. Thus, we knew just as much as before. Today, however, we know that the women were sent to Bernburg and were all gassed. The dentist was present in order to ascertain how much dental gold could be expected from the transport.[22]

Like Olga Benário Prestes, in mid-March of 1942, Käthe Pick Leichter was gassed at the Bernburg euthanasia facility. Their murders were part of the Nazis' organized extermination called "14f13." The first selections in Ravensbrück began in December 1941 and January 1942, and those selected were predominantly Jewish. Beginning in February 1942, as part of the euthanasia programs in the concentration camp under the code "14f13," they were sent to the Bernburg mental asylum, where they were killed in the gas chamber. In addition to those who were considered insane, weak, or incapable of work, women who had tuberculosis or asthma, healthy women classified as asocial women and criminals, and a large number of Jewish women (some of whom were not even subjected to a perfunctory physical examination) were selected to be gassed at Bernburg. According to inmates, about fifteen hundred to sixteen hundred female prisoners were taken to the gas chamber of the asylum in Bernburg after 3 February 1942.[23] Between that date and the construction of a gas chamber in Ravensbrück in December 1944, so-called black transports left Ravensbrück for the gas chambers of Auschwitz, Majdanek, Bernburg, or Hartheim. In this way, Ravensbrück was integrated into the Final Solution, the mass genocidal murder of Jews, as well as that of the Sinti and Roma, or Gypsies.[24] On 29 September 1942 Himmler ordered the remaining Jewish prisoners in Ravensbrück to be sent to Auschwitz, in order to make Ravensbrück *Judenrein*, or free of Jews. However, new transports soon brought other Jewish women to the camp.

Herta Soswinski, who was in Ravensbrück before Himmler's fall 1942 order and remembered Käthe Leichter's departure to Bernburg, survived to write an account of her ordeal.[25] Herta was arrested in Prague on 27 August 1940 because of her underground activities. After spending time in the Pankrac and Karlsplatz prisons in Prague, on 14 January 1942 she was transported to Ravensbrück. She traveled in a passenger train but recalled that the women were subjected to beatings and threatening dogs when they detrained in Fürstenberg. She was assigned to Block Nine, one of the two Jewish blocks at the time, and did outside work filling straw mattresses, carrying heavy cement, sacks, and digging ditches in frozen soil. At the beginning of October 1942, in compliance with Himmler's order, Herta was transported to Auschwitz. She continued working with the resistance there, managing to escape at the time of the January 1945 evacuations. Had she not escaped, there is a strong possibility that she would have been transported back to Ravensbrück, as this was the fate of so many Jewish women evacuated from Auschwitz. She settled in Vienna and married a comrade from the Auschwitz underground.

While we may never know the full stories of Olga Benário Prestes and Käthe Pick Leichter at Ravensbrück, both of these Jewish political prisoners who were murdered there left a legacy of intelligence, political integrity, and a sense of justice, as well as their altruistic concern for the suffering of the other women in the camp.

4

Resistance that Lifted
the Spirit

RESISTANCE during the Holocaust ranged from armed combat to cultural activities, along with trying to maintain a semblance of normalcy. While there could not have been armed resistance in Ravensbrück, there were acts of defiance against the war effort and the Nazi bureaucracy. For example, some of the women who worked at the Siemens factory sabotaged the production of V-1 and V-2 rocket components. There were also efforts at political resistance by prisoners who worked in the offices to keep secret records of arrivals, punishments, and deaths, and sometimes to "lose" an order for punishment. Most of the resistance, however, was aimed at keeping up spirits by sharing recipes, providing cultural enrichment, creating and offering small gifts, teaching, and helping each other survive. There is much evidence of women's kindness to other women in Ravensbrück, such as creating for each other drawings, embroideries, small gifts, greeting cards, and poems.[1] The prisoners also performed secret theatrical productions and taught educational classes. Birthdays and holidays were occasions when gift giving was particularly popular. Some women also made toys for children who were in the camp, especially at Christmas.

COOKING BY IMAGINATION

Re-creating recipes and discussing them or recording them in cookbooks was a form of resistance that was generally unique to women.[2] These

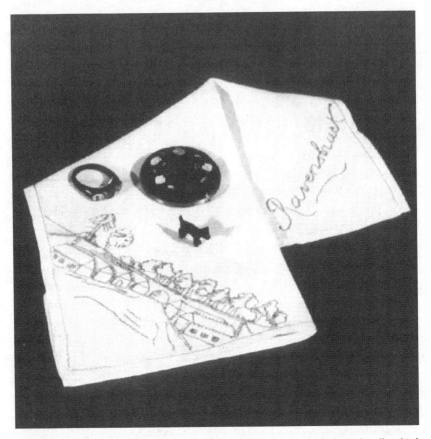

Small gifts that the women made each other to bolster their spirits, including a handkerchief that says "Ravensbrück." Collection of MGR/SBG.

women cooked with words—to bring back memories of home, assuage their constant hunger, and provide their campmates with food for thought in the true sense of the expression. They talked with each other about recipes and cooking, and sometimes they were fortunate enough to have a scrap of paper and a stub of a pencil to write down their recipes. I know of four existing recipe books from Ravensbrück, three belonging to Jewish survivors. (I assume there are more, especially among non-Jewish political prisoners who had more opportunities to create them.) One was created by Rebecca (Becky) Buckman Teitelbaum, a Belgian Jew who was in Ravensbrück for seventeen months, beginning in November 1943. Her nephew, Alex Buckman, discovered the recipe book in her Ottawa apartment in December 1997, when he was visiting while she was hospitalized at the age of eighty-eight.[3]

Becky was arrested in Brussels in 1943, after hiding her three-year-old daughter, Anny, in Chateau de Soliere, a convent-run orphanage. She was then sent to Maline for six weeks. Her husband, Herman, was sent to Buchenwald; a few weeks later, Becky was shipped to Ravensbrück. She was sent there instead of Auschwitz, because her husband was Hungarian by nationality, Buckman told me. At the beginning in Ravensbrück, "this little skinny woman" was forced to do heavy and difficult work in the latrines, he reported. Later, because she had office experience in a large department store in Belgium, she was given a much better slave labor assignment.

Becky had the relative good luck of being transferred to work in the office of the Siemens factory and stayed there for about two-thirds of her time in the camp. She sometimes had the night shift, which was not as stringently supervised as the day shift. She was then able to take paper from the office and cut it up to make her tiny recipe book. She sold food to get needle and thread to sew the pages into a book. The women in the barrack took turns talking about recipes, and Becky wrote them down. Although she could have been severely punished or murdered for creating her little books, Becky also produced two other recipe books (now lost) as gifts for comrades.

Becky's recollections about her cookbook were recounted when it was first displayed at the Vancouver Holocaust Education Centre:[4]

> Exhausted, cold and hungry they [the women in her barrack] would talk endlessly about the food they longed for, about family meals they had shared and the dishes they planned to make if they survived the war. . . . Each woman in turn would share recipes in a paradoxical effort to stave off hunger. It seems as though these oft-repeated recipes and stories about family meals served as a talisman, sustaining their humanity and hope in a time with little hope. In an act of enormous courage Rebecca hid away small pieces of paper and an indigo pencil and set about recording these recipes, so lovingly retold. In her clear, measured and even script [in French], Rebecca filled 110 pages.
>
> The pages are meticulously hand stitched as a little volume that can rest comfortably in the palm of one's hand. . . . The recipes themselves are quite extraordinary and elaborate as though only the most special of the recipes had the power to transport these women from their grim reality. Rebecca explains how upon the book's completion each of the women would take turns reading from its pages: *mousse au chocolat, gelée de groseilles, gâteau-neige, plat hongrois, oeuf hollandais, sabayon italien, soufflé à la confiture.*

As the Allies approached the camp at the end of World War II, Becky was among the more fortunate prisoners rescued to Sweden by the Red Cross.[5] However, her convoy was attacked during the evacuation, and shrapnel from an explosion injured her arm. Despite the wound, she continued to hold on to her small bag that contained her precious recipe book and even more prized letters she had received from Buchenwald from Herman, during her early days at Ravensbrück. She must have later fainted from the loss of blood, and her bag was left behind when she was carried from the truck to the hospital.

At the end of the war, Herman rescued their daughter, Anny, and their nephew, Alex, from the orphanage. He then discovered with the help of the International Red Cross that Becky was recuperating in a hospital in Copenhagen. Three months later, she returned to Belgium and learned that her brother and sister-in-law, Alex's parents, had perished in Auschwitz. After several months, Becky received notification that there was a parcel for her at the post office. When she opened it, she found the letters that her husband had sent to her at Ravensbrück and the little recipe book. Apparently the book had been traced and returned to Becky because her name was on the accompanying letters.

Becky and Herman became Alex's legal guardians, and in August 1946 she gave birth to a son, Abe, born in Brussels. In 1952 the family immigrated to Montreal, and in September 1953 another daughter, Shirley, was born there. After Herman died in 1992, Becky moved to Ottawa to be close to Abe. The recipe book was forgotten until Alex discovered it. He was surprised to learn that his favorite cake, "Alex's cake," which Becky made every Sunday, was in fact the *gateau a l'orange* in her Ravensbrück recipe book. Becky told him that she had never mentioned the tiny keepsake because she didn't think it was important. However, it is a rare and extremely important piece of evidence that documents how cooking by imagination became a form of resistance that kept up the spirits of groups of women in concentration camps.

Although there may be more, I know of only two other existing recipe books compiled by Jewish women in Ravensbrück. A notebook of recipes that belonged to thirteen-year-old Francesca Kwester-Stern was included in the exhibition, *No Child's Play* at Yad Vashem's Art Museum in Jerusalem. According to the scant information supplied by the museum and the exhibit coordinator, Francesca was born in Slovakia and sent to Ravensbrück in late October 1941 and spent eight months there. She evidently was deported there with her mother. "She overcame her agonizing hunger pangs by writing down recipes that she had collected from her friends," the exhibit's caption says. This caption is confusing, because it concludes with the information that, "In April 1945, she and her mother were taken to Sweden together with a number of other prisoners, in an ambulance of the Swedish Red Cross." If she indeed came in October 1941 and was in Ravensbrück for only eight months, she must have been rescued from another camp or later returned to Ravensbrück. No further information was available.[6] The story of the other recipe book by a Jewish woman, Eva Hesse Ostwalt, is told in a book published in German.[7] Eva was born in Cologne, Germany in 1902 and immigrated to the United States after World War II.

A recipe book written by Anna Maria Berentsen-Droog, a non-Jewish Dutch political prisoner, is in the Florida Holocaust Museum archive as part of the *Women of Ravensbrück: Portraits of Courage* exhibit. In an accompanying note to artist Julia Terwilliger, she explained one of the reasons the women wrote down their recipes: "If and when you are hungry you must all the time think of food." She arrived in the camp on 9 September 1944 and was liberated by the Swedish Red Cross on 24 April 1945.[8]

DRAWING BEAUTY AND HORROR

Creating art was another form of resistance, and some of the drawings done at Ravensbrück are so exquisitely executed that they stand on their own as works of art. The drawings were made not only as gifts to friends but also to record the horrors of the camp. There are pictures of bouquets of flowers, made to cheer friends, and drawings of the terror of everyday life. I have seen only one drawing actually done in the camp by a Jewish woman, a tiny pencil drawing by Becky Teitelbaum. Perhaps stricter supervision precluded most Jewish prisoners from carrying out this risky activity, or their drawings were lost, or they have not been publicly shown. After liberation, Jewish survivors such as Renee Duering and Ella Shiber made drawings of their memories of Ravensbrück and other camps.[9]

Rebecca (Becky) Teitelbaum left one small but exquisite pencil drawing of prisoners in the camp. This tiny sketch is now part of the collection of the Vancouver Holocaust Education Centre and was shown as part of the Centre's *Ravensbrück: Forgotten Women of the Holocaust* exhibit from February through May 2003. In addition to her drawing and recipe books, Becky also made a few sets of playing cards with flowers in the corners. She enjoyed designing the cards, and some of the Gypsy women in the camp would read them to tell fortunes, her nephew Alex Buckman reported.

Women who had been professional artists before their arrest were among the non-Jewish political prisoners, and Dutch survivor Aat Breur later became well known for her Ravensbrück drawings. Born on 28 December 1913 in The Hague, she studied in the art academy there. Her drawings from her days in the camp are today housed in the Rijksmuseum in Amsterdam. She and her husband, Krijn Breur, were part of a resistance group that attacked the Nazis with homemade time bombs, prepared falsified documents, and helped hide people who were in danger.

Aat and her husband were arrested in November 1942, and Aat expected to be held for only a short time. As she was still breastfeeding her infant daughter, Dunya, she brought the baby with her. Krijn was condemned to death and executed on 5 February 1943.

After nine months in prison in Scheveningen and Utrecht, in June 1943 Aat was deported to Germany and imprisoned in Kleve, Düsseldorf, and Berlin. She was then sent as a "Night and Fog" (destined for extermination) prisoner to Ravensbrück, given the inmate number 22981, and placed in Block Thirty-two. She was assigned to hard labor, but a comrade later helped her to find a job in the camp's bookbindery and there she was able to resume her drawing. Another friend, artist To Stolz, took Aat's drawings from the camp to Sweden when the Red Cross rescued her in April 1945. After liberation and a six-year recovery period from the tuberculosis she had contracted in the camp, Aat returned to her profession in Amsterdam. Her daughter, Dunya Breur, wrote a book, first published in Dutch and then translated into German, about her mother's experiences. The book is rich with reproductions of Aat Breur's sensitive drawings.[10]

Just as Aat Breur is a recognized artist in Holland and beyond, French (non-Jewish) survivor Violette Lecoq's drawings from Ravensbrück are known in her country and elsewhere. Violette was a nurse, not a professional artist, but she documented daily life in the camp in her drawings. She and her drawings became well known, because she brought them to the Ravensbrück war-criminal trials in Hamburg in 1946–1947 as part of her testimony against Nazi personnel at the camp. Violette was in the French resistance, working in an improvised hospital for Algerian soldiers who had been wounded fighting for France and carrying out other acts of heroism. She was betrayed, imprisoned, and then sent to Ravensbrück in August 1944. Like Aat Breur, Violette was designated a "Night and Fog" prisoner, condemned to death. Because Violette was fluent in German, she was assigned as the nurse of Block Ten and kept track of the daily atrocities that she witnessed there. Block Ten was designated for tuberculosis patients and for women who had been deemed mentally ill. Violette was rescued by the Red Cross in April 1945 and repatriated to France.

Her eyewitness accounts of the nurses' and doctors' brutality helped to convict them at the Hamburg trials. She testified against Nazi nurse Carmen Maria Mory, who murdered the "insane" women with injections, and she also gave evidence about a selection in November 1944, when 120 women were sent to the euthanasia installation at Hartheim. In addition, she recalled the sterilization of Sinti women in March 1945, performed by doctors Trommer and Triete. Besides testifying against these and other Nazi war criminals, Violette provided precise information to the Hamburg tribunal about the operation and location of the gas chamber.

While Aat's style of drawing is soft and gray, Violette's is stark linear black and white. Her drawings were published in France a few years after the end of World War II.[11] In addition to the works of Aat and Violette, drawings by other prisoners have also been preserved, and the Ravensbrück memorial has published a book containing artwork done in the camp.[12]

HANDMADE GIFTS OF FRIENDSHIP

Embroideries, as well as drawings, were popular gifts among the women. Using carefully concealed scraps and threads from the clothing factory or confiscated clothing, those who were fortunate enough to have a needle managed to make beautifully crafted gifts such as handkerchiefs, purses, and book covers. The Ravensbrück memorial has many examples of embroidered and hand-sewn gifts, and the Holocaust exhibit at the Imperial War Museum in London displays an embroidered scarf that had belonged to Dutch prisoner Jo Vis. She was in Scheveningen prison and then in Vught, before she was sent to Ravensbrück, according to information in the exhibit.

Creating a greeting card for a special occasion was another popular form of gift-giving and raising spirits at the camp. In addition to sewn items, the Florida Holocaust Museum has a now faded Easter card as part of their Ravensbrück exhibit. Dutch prisoner Clarin Smeenk made the small card with the drawing of an Easter bunny. She arrived in the camp on 9 September 1944 and was liberated by the Swedish Red Cross on 24 April 1945. The card was on Anna Maria Berentsen-Droog's slice of bread on Easter, 1 April 1945. The text is in English, rather than Dutch, and says: "Live to Learn, Learn to Live. Ravensbrück, 1 April 1945." Artist Aat Breur also made greeting cards with beautiful drawings of bouquets of flowers for her friends.[13]

While none of these embroidered gifts or cards was made by a Jewish prisoner, there is testimony that at least one Jewish woman was the recipient of such acts of kindness. Gemma LaGuardia Gluck, a Jewish prisoner held as a political hostage, recalled that the women in her block gave her homemade presents for Christmas 1944: "The most precious of the presents I received was a little album. It was put together from sheets of paper smuggled out of the camp office and bound in a piece of cotton print taken from the dressmaking shop. . . . The little album they had given me passed from hand to hand and everyone wrote in it something in her own language."[14]

Small three-dimensional carvings were also sometimes created as gifts. In the exhibit at the Imperial War Museum there is a tiny toy cello that Klara Rakos, a Hungarian Jew deported to Auschwitz in the summer of 1944, made for her friend Eva Hamburger, in a subcamp of Ravensbrück.

Some of the women even used the handles of their precious toothbrushes to make carved gifts. Examples of miniature toys made for children from these handles are on display at the Ravensbrück memorial. In addition, the women sewed dolls for the children out of scraps of cloth and even managed to crochet balls, which can also be seen at the memorial.

When Julia Terwilliger's artwork was displayed in an exhibit in Orlando (different from the Florida Holocaust Museum exhibit) in February 1997, an accompanying brochure emphasized the "courage it must have taken to create art and give gifts in that setting." This act of creativity and generosity "meant that one had to remember a different way of being that defied violence, terror and hate; and one had to acknowledge someone else when their own individual pain was so great. Gift giving, in these circumstances, took a kind of courage rooted deep in one's character that challenged annihilation. It was a courage that reclaimed one's humanness by connecting to past traditions of celebration and kindness. These gift-givers longed for friendship, family, food and drink, and the safety of their homes."[15]

Making and giving gifts—an activity that could result in severe punishment—was a forceful form of resistance that helped to sustain both the giver and the receiver. Sometimes even a gift that was not created with handiwork was especially appreciated. For example, Gemma LaGuardia Gluck recalled the bitterly cold day when she was shivering at roll call, and Lotti Lehman (Silverman) asked her what was wrong. When Gemma said that she had no underwear and was freezing, the younger woman insisted on giving her the underwear she was wearing. Gemma also recalled the generous gift that she received from Annamarie Thiel, a young German woman from Berlin, who had been arrested for helping her Jewish neighbors. She worked in the camp office and risked her life bringing Gemma and others copies of the newspapers destined for the camp officials.[16]

The involvement of Jewish women in this type of resistance at Ravensbrück cannot be fully documented. Virtually all of those who were at the camp in its early years (before it was "cleansed" of Jews in the fall of 1942) did not survive, and the many Jewish women who arrived during the last chaotic months had little or no opportunity to do much more than subsist and try to stay alive. However, given these limitations, there is documentation of resistance by Jewish prisoners in Ravensbrück who wrote poems, created and acted in plays, and taught classes.

POEMS, PLAYS, CLASSES, AND SONGS

Two Jewish political prisoners previously discussed, Dr. Käthe Pick Leichter and Olga Benário Prestes, made significant contributions to improving the morale and raising the spirits of their campmates. While other Jewish political prisoners who were at the camp in the early years may also have done their part to resist in this way, no records of their activities survived them. Since Olga and Käthe were so prominent among their peers both inside and outside the camp, books written about them based on their own writings and eyewitness accounts help to give us an idea of their involvement. The resistance efforts of non-Jewish women, some of which are mentioned here, have been well documented by survivors of national groups, especially the Polish, French, German, and Dutch prisoners.[17]

Käthe Leichter, who arrived in the camp in January 1940, wrote poetry and plays for the women.[18] Her poem *Kleiner roter Ziegelstein* (Little Red Brick) was created because she was forced to load bricks onto ships on the Havel River, and her hands were always bloody and infected. Another poem, *An meine Brüder* (To my brothers), was memorized by a young Communist girl and thus preserved. The poem is addressed to a universal brother in another concentration camp, with a refrain phrase, "I in Ravensbrück, you in Sachsenhausen, in Dachau, or Buchenwald." After asking the imagined brother whether he has the same concentration camp experiences as she, Käthe concludes with a message of hope:

Oh, my brother, once there will be the day when no roll call will keep us!
Gates will be opened wide and the great, the free world will embrace us.
And then we concentration camp inmates will walk on wide streets.
But the others are waiting for us.
And whoever sees us, sees the deep lines written on our faces by the suffering,
Sees the signs of our mental and bodily torture, which will stay with us forever.
And whoever sees us will see the rage flashing bright from our eyes,
Sees the rejoicing in freedom deeply imbedded in our hearts.
And then we march in rows, the last, huge column of people,
And the road leads to light and sun.
Oh, brother, are you also imagining that day, you also must think:
The day will be here soon!
And then we march away from Ravensbrück, from Sachsenhausen, from
Dachau, and Buchenwald.[19]

Schum Schum, the play that Käthe wrote and produced with Dr. Herta Breuer, had a clear anti-Nazi message. In addition to offering fantasy and a few moments of emotional and intellectual escape, it provided the women with opportunities for creative costume making. "Too bad that this play had to be destroyed, because it contained so many songs that made fun of the SS, and so much social criticism," Käthe's friend Rosa Jochmann recalled:

Too bad that this play couldn't be filmed. The most amazing jewelry was created out of toothpaste tubes, a bridal dress from scarves, even a top hat and tails for the groom, all out of paper. The bride, a Jewish girl from Holland, was a very young and beautiful girl, and the groom was an Austrian Jewess. . . . And the savages: the girls brought straw from the bindery, and we made little short skirts out of it. Our aluminum plates were polished all shiny, and hung from chains around their necks. It is impossible to describe it all. That day the SS didn't come, but later we were betrayed, and everyone was sent to the hole [punishment cell-block] for six weeks. . . . Käthe and her friend had planned ahead, though, and the play we had staged had been destroyed. At the same time, there was a second version of the play, which praised the SS and humiliated the Jews. That was the version Käthe had put into her closet. That was what saved us all, because if they had found the real play, we would all have gone to our final destination. As it was, the political commissary came to the cell, where thirty-two of us were in the hole, and laughed proudly: "So, you are beginning to learn, I see. You start figuring out that we are the superior race and you are the sub-humans."

Rosa added that all of the participants were sent to the gas chamber with the first transport.[20]

Olga Benário Prestes, who arrived from Lichtenburg in the spring of 1939, organized a small group to whom she read from Tolstoy's *War and Peace*. She used a moldy coverless copy of the second volume that one of her friends had found in the middle of a rubbish pile.[21] Her geography lessons on the progression of the war and her collaboration with Käthe Leichter on the preparation of a secret newspaper were mentioned earlier.

Gemma LaGuardia Gluck, who arrived more than two years after Käthe and Olga had been murdered at the camp, also tried to enrich the other prisoners' lives by teaching them. She recalled the English lessons she gave during her free time in the afternoon:

> These were the most gratifying hours I spent in Ravensbrück. Having no grammar book, I wrote one myself and made thirty copies for my pupils. I still have one of them. It is a hundred pages long. On the concluding pages I wrote several short prayers of my own composition and a number of proverbs.
>
> We had to study in secrecy, of course. If we had been caught, all of us would have been severely punished, especially the teacher. We used to post a lookout to signal us if any of the overseers approached. Paper and pencils were stolen for us by inmates who worked in the camp office.
>
> My students were girls and women of many different nationalities. Most of them were eager to learn English because they dreamed of going to the United States after liberation.
>
> There were two classes, one for beginners and a conversation class for the more advanced, those who had once studied English in school or had picked up some knowledge of the language in other ways.

I took pride in the fact that these women, from so many different walks of life, returned the affection I came to have for them. They were grateful for the things I was able to do for them and showed it in many ways.[22]

Singing was another cultural activity that could be defined as resistance by lifting the spirits. One singer that Gemma remembered, Frau Franzi Kantor from Vienna, was either Jewish or had been married to a Jewish man. She "organized Sunday concerts among the prisoners," Gemma wrote. "Imagine what it meant to all of us to be in a filthy, crowded block instead of in a beautifully decorated theater, looking at an emaciated prisoner instead of a prima donna in an evening gown. To see the singer we had to stretch our necks to find her sitting on the top of a three-decker bed. But we listened attentively to the wonderful melodies of Gounod's *Ave Maria* or Puccini's *Madame Butterfly*.

Most of the singers were French, according to Gemma.[23] "There was also Odette Garoby, the wife of a French sea captain from Algiers," she wrote. "On my first day in our block, when I was filled with misery and despair, I suddenly heard a beautiful voice singing *Swanee River*. To hear this familiar song, with the English words rendered in a charming French accent, was very comforting to me. . . . She was very chic and witty and could come up with a joke in the most dismal situation."[24]

Jewish prisoners made significant contributions to resistance that lifted the women's spirits in Ravensbrück. This was just one form of resistance at the camp, which also included stealing newspapers, keeping secret lists of prisoners, moving women's names to safer lists in the camp offices, hiding prisoners, sabotage, medical assistance, and collective childcare.

5

Joyless Childhoods

O F all of the Ravensbrück survivors who shared their stories with
me, the child survivors have the most heartrending recollections
of the camp. Some women arrived with children or gave birth
there, and surviving child prisoners have memories that suggest in some
ways, that the situation was worse for them than for their mothers. As
Sali Solomon Daugherty, who was imprisoned in the camp from age eight
to eleven, explained to me:

> I believe that when you enter "prisonhood," let's say, for any child at
> the age of eight, it is not the same as if an adult enters a concentration
> camp. Because when an adult enters a camp or prison, or being a pris-
> oner-of-war or being tortured under any circumstance, they have known
> another life before. They might already have had a very good youth.
> They might have had a loving youth, a wealthy youth, a poor youth.
> But when you are eight years old, then torture and prison and camps
> and rape become part of regular life. You have almost forgotten what
> it was before.

SALI SOLOMON DAUGHERTY

Sali's story is unusual because she arrived before any of the other Jewish
prisoners that I met. Furthermore, she was only eight years old upon
arrival and managed to stay alive in the camp for a long time—nearly
two and a half years. I had found her name in the Yad Vashem archives
in 1995, but only made an effort to find her five years later, when I discovered a wonderful photo of her taken after she was liberated to Sweden.[1]
Sali, who now lives in Jaffa, Israel, met me in my Jerusalem apartment

Unknown prisoner's drawing of a child in Ravensbrück, the daughter of Czechoslovakian prisoner Zdenka Nedvedova. Original in collection of MGR/SBG.

in December 2000 and shared with me her childhood memories of Ravensbrück. She was born in Amsterdam on 21 March 1933 to a Dutch mother, Rosetta Wertheim Solomon, and a Romanian father, Marco Solomon. Sali came to Ravensbrück by way of Westerbork, in either late

November or early December 1942, along with her mother and aunt. This was only a month or so after Ravensbrück had been made *Judenrein*, or free of Jews, and proves that there were Jewish women in the camp for nearly the entire six years of its existence.

Sali continued her explanation of why she thinks that the camp experience was different and more difficult for children than for adults:

> As I was five years old when the first bombs fell on Amsterdam, five or six maybe, something of that sort—I almost forgot—then suffering has become normal. You don't know what suffering is for a while. Because you are so young . . . when you're eight years old. So when I was in the camp there are facts that I remember: the jumping dogs that you try to explain; at four o'clock in the morning on bare feet standing *Appell* which is like the army; the screaming in the barracks, "*Aufstehen*" ["get up"] at two or three [a.m.] and unexpected hours.
>
> When I speak to people like you, who are doing something about it, these things come back as reflexes. I am hiding them. I seldom think about it. But these are definite reflexes that come back that are of course in the back of the head somewhere. And so I remember the dogs and the snow and that I was full of lice and that my hair was shaven. I remember that very well—in the beginning, on arrival. Later they let it grow back. And I remember that I had to work for Siemens—not directly in the Siemens factory, as I got older, because I was there three years.

Although Sali initially did not have many specific memories of her time at the camp, some things began coming back to her as we spoke. "The screaming and the hitting people—I remember that I saw all this," she said. "And people that were hit until they died on the ground." She clearly remembers the barrack she lived in. She and her mother were in the same barrack as Nomi and Chaja Moskovits, whose stories are briefly told in this chapter.[2] The mothers went to work and the children stayed in the barrack. Sali says that she helped to care for Chaja, who was only a baby.

Sali also recalls that she could go outside for about ten minutes at night:

> I remember that I was allowed to take a walk on a main thoroughfare in the camp. And I remember that I somehow made an acquaintance with a woman who was called Maria—I don't know how—on that road. Maria. She was a German but she was a Jehovah's Witness, and she took a very big interest in me in secret. Only that I remember by signs. And at the end there was nothing left to eat. We used to get one piece of bread a day like this, nothing more. And she was working in the kitchen, and she brought me a piece of bread almost every night, on that walk, like this. So I had two angels in the camp. The real *Waffen-SS* nurse who might have given me a shot to die, who never did it but

brought me marmalade. And this German—both Germans—that was
a prisoner, a Jehovah's Witness, she gave me pieces of bread. So this is
my story in the camp. Memories. I can only tell you memories.

Sali's memories about the kindness of the Nazi nurse are related to
the end of her stay in the camp, when she became very ill. "I was six
weeks in the *Revier* with yellow jaundice," she said. "And of course there
was no medication. But again one of these Germans said that it was very
good—that I remember—at that time I was eleven—to eat a lot of marmalade. And she would steal for me even though she was a *Waffen-SS*
nurse—she was a nurse in the hospital. She would steal for me from the
kitchen marmalade and gave me a lot of marmalade. And I guess I am
here today—I survived this."

Shortly before the Red Cross rescue operation began, Sali was sent
back to her barrack from the *Revier*. However, she was separated from
her mother during liberation:

The day of liberation, yes. We were waiting for hours. We hardly believed that we would be liberated, because the war had not been finished
yet. And while we were waiting, the Germans made us march in front
of the gas chamber. I remember the smoke coming out and people were
brought in and when they came out, on pushcarts, just like a dead ani-
mal. We were so skinny. We were all skeletons. Don't you think that we
were people. We were only birds. The whole group that was liberated—
probably one month later no one would have been alive anymore. We
were all that skinny. We all arrived sick, basically. All of us. Only I was
contagious—sick for others.

And we saw these skeletons come out on pushcarts. They would
probably just throw them away on garbage piles after they were dead.
. . . They were probably going to the crematorium with them. . . . So
this is very important. I remember seeing in front of me now a pushcart
and they were lying one with the legs this way and the other with the
legs that way. Like three girls sleep in one bed and you have no room,
one head there, one leg there.

Sali remembered how she and the women in her Red Cross convoy
were in danger even during liberation:

And I was put in one white Red Cross truck and my mother went in
another one. And they put me next to the chauffeur, who was a Canadian. And it was a three-day trip almost—I remember—until we arrived
in Malmö, Sweden. And I am sure that people have told you that many
of our people who made the concentration camps for three years and
four years died on that trip through the [mistaken] bombings of the
Americans. They bombed us, and my chauffeur—and there were very
bad attacks in the middle, I think near Lübeck—and he threw me out
into the woods and then he jumped himself from the truck. And he died.

And I survived, and in the forest I think I was picked up hours later by another Red Cross truck. So there were many people who did die on that trip of liberation.

Sali was quite ill when she arrived in Sweden. After she had been there for three days, she learned that her father had died at the end of the war. She was diagnosed as a carrier of tuberculosis and typhus, and placed in quarantine for six weeks. "They put this sharp lotion on me—that I remember," she said. "I was full of eczema from here to my toes. So I was not a healthy girl coming out of the camp." She was eventually re-united with her mother and lived in a small barrack with other survivors. She said that most of this period is "a blackout," but she remembers that she recuperated for several weeks in the home of a Swedish family on an island near Stockholm. She has a photo of Count Folke Bernadotte, the Red Cross official who led the rescue effort, and she thinks he gave it to her when he visited at that time.[3]

DUTCH SISTERS AND A BOY FROM POLAND

I met several other Jewish child survivors of Ravensbrück, including Nomi Moskovits Friedmann and Chaja Moskovits Dana, Sali's barrack mates, when I attended the fiftieth anniversary of the camp's liberation on 23–25 April 1995. Although I did not have the opportunity for in-depth interviews, some of the recollections they shared with me add to our knowledge of children's experiences at the camp. Chaja was just sixteen months old and Nomi was seven years old when they were deported from Amsterdam, along with their mother, Frida, and their eleven-year-old brother, Uriel. They arrived at Ravensbrück from the Westerbork transit camp in November 1943. Their father had Hungarian papers, and they were told they were being sent to Hungary to exchange for prisoners-of-war. The father, Cantor Ben Zion Moskovits, was sent to Buchenwald, and the rest of the family, to Ravensbrück. This seems to have been the case of other families who also had Hungarian papers, and a total of thirty children and an unknown number of women were in the group that came to Ravensbrück with the Moskovits family.

Even though she was only seven when she arrived, Nomi remembers that some of the Ukrainian prisoners in the camp were very anti-Semitic, and that they attacked the Jewish women for crumbs. Like Sali, Nomi said the children stayed with their mothers. She added that various mothers took turns watching the children while the other mothers worked. Some children's mothers died of disease or were murdered, and a rotating group of women took responsibility for the orphans' care. Nomi remembers a children's Christmas party in 1944: there was a tree and the singing of *Silent Night,* along with nearby guards and their dogs. The party was supposed to be in a park, separated from the mothers, she said, but some pipes broke or exploded and they never went there.

The family remained in the camp until February 1945, when they were taken to Bergen-Belsen. After Bergen-Belsen was liberated, the girls returned to Holland with their mother and brother, and discovered that their father had also survived and returned. On 19 November 1945, Cantor Moskovits officiated at the first postwar Jewish wedding in Amsterdam. He later also officiated at Sali Solomon Daugherty's wedding. The sisters grew up in Holland and came to Israel as young adults, where they both married Israeli men and now live in Netanya. When I met them in April 1995, their mother, age eighty-seven, was living in Amsterdam.

Simon Gerecht, another child survivor of Ravensbrück, also came to the 1995 camp ceremonies from Israel. He was born in Lodz, Poland, the son of Peretz and Manya Gerecht; his younger brother, Gershon, was born at the end of 1938. The family was transported from Pionki, Poland, to Germany by the Nazis and divided at Oranienburg. His father was sent to Sachsenhausen, and he, his mother, and his brother went to Ravensbrück. There were about three hundred Jews from Pionki on the train, he recalled. He was in Ravensbrück from August 1944 until January 1945, when he was sent with his mother and brother to Bergen-Belsen. Simon's brother died in Bergen-Belsen on or about 14 April 1945. His most vivid recollection of life at Ravensbrück is that of the women with no will to live who threw themselves at the electric fence. He also remembers that the Russian women "organized" food for the children. The Red Cross brought him and his mother from Bergen-Belsen to Sweden, and his father later found them through that organization. The family immigrated to Palestine in 1947.

STELLA KUGELMAN NIKIFOROVA

Many female survivors of Ravensbrück and other concentration camps have shared their poignant memories with me, but I find Stella Kugelman Nikiforova's story the most heartbreaking.[4] I met her in São Paulo, Brazil in November 1994, and saw her again at the Ravensbrück memorial in 1995, at the fiftieth anniversary ceremonies. On both occasions, I felt that the sad expression on her face was an outward reflection of her lifelong inner suffering. Stella was born in 1939 in Antwerp, the only child of Luis Gustavo Kugelman Griez, a Spanish Jew from Barcelona, and Rosa Klionski, a British Jew from London. They met while they were studying in Belgium, fell in love, married, and then Stella was born there.

Not only were Stella's parents Jewish but they were also members of the resistance in Antwerp after the Nazi occupation of Belgium in May

1940. They were arrested in 1943, along with sixty other families that had been carrying out acts of sabotage. Four-year-old Stella was sent to Ravensbrück with her mother. Even though she was so young, her documents listed her as a political prisoner, and, along with her mother, she had to wear a red triangle in the camp. This preschool "political prisoner" even had a number: 25622. She said she was dark and looked Spanish, and was taught to say in German at the camp: "I am Spanish." She was told never to tell anyone she was Jewish.[5]

Stella's mother died of tuberculosis within three months of their arrival at the camp. Stella was then cared for by a series of substitute mothers. The women hid her where the Nazis were afraid to enter, the barrack that housed women with tuberculosis or typhus. She remembers that after her mother died, a succession of women, one at a time, always took care of her. Whenever the woman who cared for her died, another took over. "It was always one woman, but the woman changed," she said. "It was a form of resistance—they were called the 'camp mothers.'"

As Nomi Moskovits Friedmann and others recalled with varying details, the prisoners were allowed to arrange a Christmas party for the children in the camp in December 1944. The women made small presents for them, even carving toys from their toothbrushes, and tried to make the day as joyful as possible for the suffering children.[6] Stella said that she remembers the party but didn't attend because she was sick with scarlet fever. She said that the women saved rations of bread and jelly and made "cookies," and they also tried to make toys. The women continued to care for Stella when she was ill, rather than sending her to the *Revier*. They knew she would be experimented on or murdered at the camp hospital, she said. She still remembers that during her illness a woman always sat near her to provide her with water.

In her memoir about Ravensbrück, Gemma LaGuardia Gluck commented about the Christmas party that Stella missed: "I was told that at Christmastime in other years no celebrations had been allowed and no presents permitted for the children in the camp. But in 1944, when I was there, Frau [Franzi] Kantor worked especially hard and got permission to have a Christmas tree made for the children. All blocks were allowed to contribute. How thrilling it was to see what beautiful things were made out of rags—dolls, dresses, aprons. Sketches were drawn by artists. Our block made balls, and so on. What ingenuity worked with the heart to make these children happy."[7] This happiness was, of course, relative, because soon after the party many of the children were shipped out of the camp and did not survive.

Stella, however, was at Ravensbrück until its evacuation. Her most vivid memories of camp life are of the last few days of April 1945. When the women were driven out of the camp on a death march on 28 April

1945, some of them were permitted to push Stella, age six, and other small children in wheelbarrows. She remembers hearing shooting as the women marched. During the night of either 28 or 29 April, there was terrible noise from bombing or shooting, and then the Nazis fled in the dark. The women found themselves free and disappeared into the woods. In the morning Stella woke up and saw that she and two other children were alone in the cart. There were no German soldiers or guards, nor any prisoners to care for the children. "It was horrible—I remember it well," she told me. "We all thought we would die. This was a moment when we thought there was no help. The women had all disappeared into the forest, and we three children were all alone, belonging to no one."

Stella was with the Russian women prisoners in the chaos of the forced march, and just as she was expecting to die in the wheelbarrow that morning, one of them suddenly returned from the woods. She was a doctor in the Soviet Army who had been a prisoner-of-war at Ravensbrück, and her actions prove that not all women were nurturing and altruistic. Fifty years later, Stella was still bitter about what happened next.

"If the woman had taken me back to the camp, my father would have found me," she explained. However, this doctor took Stella to the Soviet Union, and not until twelve years later did Stella have the opportunity to discover that her father had survived Buchenwald concentration camp. The doctor returned to the Soviet Union with Stella and another child in order to be "rehabilitated" as a heroic rescuer of children, rather than risking the possibility of being accused of treason for divulging secrets as a prisoner-of-war.

Because of this Soviet military doctor's action, Stella was liberated at the end of April 1945 but was soon incarcerated again in a different way. After clearing her own name with the authorities, the woman placed Stella in a cruel orphanage in an isolated area about three hundred miles south of Moscow. Although some of the survivors evidently made inquiries about Stella, she was never found and remained "lost" and alone until she was allowed to leave the orphanage at the age of eighteen.

After this second liberation, she looked for the woman doctor who had saved her and then abandoned her, and forced her to live twelve more years of misery. "I told her she ruined my life. She saved my life, and also ruined it," Stella said. "I found out that I had a father, and I could have been with him during those years. She told the truth and said she saved my life so she could be reinstated and have her papers back."

Stella had always thought that her father might be alive, and after her 1957 release from the orphanage, she started looking for him. She did not even remember her family name but found a camp survivor who knew it. This woman found a man in Antwerp who had been her father's friend, and through him Stella discovered that her father had immigrated to Brazil in 1952. He had remarried there and started a new life in São Paulo. When Stella visited her father for the first time in 1963, she was a twenty-four-year-old woman, and they had no language in common. Stella felt uncomfortable with his new wife and constrained by the unfamiliar language, climate, and culture. After six months she went back to the Soviet Union.

When I met her in 1994, she had returned briefly to São Paulo to take care of legal matters after her father's death. In the meantime, she had married the son of Dr. Antonina Nikiforova, a heroic doctor from the Soviet Army who had been imprisoned in Ravensbrück. At the time of our meeting, Stella had been married for thirty years but was planning to divorce. She had a son, then age twenty-five, and a daughter, twenty-one.

Stella never recovered from the tragedies of her life that began in Ravensbrück. She now lives in St. Petersburg, Russia, and has health problems that she said are the result of the severe beatings she received in Ravensbrück. She was officially declared an invalid and exempted from holding a job in the Soviet Union, because of serious headaches resulting from pressure on her brain. Stella seems not to know how to smile. I was present in April 1995 when she donated to the camp's memorial museum the pretty dress she had worn in Ravensbrück.

TOVA FLATTO GILADI

I met another child survivor, Tova (Guta) Flatto Giladi, quite by accident in New York City in December 1997. I had gone to Congregation B'nai Jeshurun on the Upper West Side to hear Israel Ambassador Naphtali Lavie lecture in conjunction with the publication of his newly published book. I had been acquainted with him for many years, because I had worked with his office when he was the Consul General of Israel in New York. I knew that he and his younger brother, who became Israel's Chief Ashkenazi Rabbi Israel Lau, had been in Buchenwald. I also knew that their mother, Chaya, had perished in Ravensbrück, although I did not have any details about her time in the camp or her death there.[8] Tova and her husband, Ben, were at the Lavie lecture, because they were old friends from the same hometown, Piotrkow, Poland.

Tova was deported to the camp from Piotrkow Trybunalski, Poland, where she was born on 5 November 1931.[9] Before the Nazi occupation, her father, Yako Flatto, had traveled to buy food to sell locally, and her mother, Sheina Judkiewicz Flatto, had helped him in the family store. She arrived at Ravensbrück in December 1944 just after her thirteenth birthday and was one of the older children at the camp. Fourteen was generally the cutoff age to be considered a child by the camp authorities, and therefore Tova was not sent out on work details. "The Ravensbrück experience was an experience that left a mark on my life, because this was the first place where I entered where people were totally dehumanized, that they were treated like animals, that they were constantly hungry, cold, beaten," she said.

When the Germans entered her hometown in 1939, she was seven years old and had completed first grade. She remembers the restrictions imposed by the Nazis as gradual and insidious. Tova's father was protected from deportation after he began working in a Nazi factory, but her mother, "a very capable lady," was unable to do factory work because of her young daughter. One day a local policeman told her mother, "Mrs. Flatto, you are standing here in your business, and the ground is burning under your feet. You don't realize it." After this warning, Tova and her mother went into hiding in an attic with a large group of people.

Later, the hiding place was discovered, and the group was rounded up and herded into the local synagogue. Tova's mother bribed a policeman, and they were able to run back to the ghetto. Tova and her mother were not registered workers and had to remain in hiding. "Once I hid in a closet, a wardrobe closet," she said. "They were looking for people for work, and they were touching my shoes. And I made pee-pee for fear, and they thought there's a pair of shoes in the closet." Afterward Tova and her mother were hidden under a staircase, with huge rats. "We were afraid to sleep," she said. "My mom was watching me [so that] they shouldn't eat me alive."

Because of the impossible conditions, they came out of hiding and registered, and her mother began working, sorting goods that had been left behind by other Jews. After three weeks there was another roundup, and Tova and her mother were again sent to the synagogue. She was separated from her mother and terrified. "I was so afraid of this dog," she said. "He was eating people alive. It was a terrible dog. And then I said to myself, 'Oh, God, my God, it's the end to the world. If my mom knows that they will kill us here, and she left me behind, this is already the end of life.'" Five hundred Jews were shot, but she was saved and sent back to the ghetto by a German who may have been bribed by her uncle.

Eventually Tova and her parents were put into cattle cars, where the men were separated from the women. "The conditions were very bad, because we were crowded and there was not enough to eat and not to drink," she said. "And the winter was just unbearable. This was the winter of 1944. I think it was the coldest winter that I could ever remember in my life." The cars with the men were detached from the train at Buchenwald, and the women continued on to Ravensbrück. "I was in Ravensbrück with my mother, and I was too weak for that kind of work, because they were carrying potatoes and all kinds of vegetables, and there

[were] such boxes, deep boxes made out of wood, and two women were carrying one side and the other," Tova said. She continued:

> So we were there. We didn't know where we had come. When we arrived, they took us to a place, and we were sure that they're taking us to be gassed, because they took everything away from us and they put us into showers. . . . My mother told me to swallow—there were some coins, like dimes, gold Russian coins. So she gave me to swallow three coins like this and a diamond out of the ring, and she swallowed some. When we went there, they took everything away, but that what was swallowed, they could not. See, in those days they weren't so sophisticated that they should put X-rays through you. So we went to this bunk. There were bunks, and in this place there were all kinds of nationalities. There were German ladies that were against the regime, political. There were prostitutes. There were people that, instead of going to jail for robberies, women, they were there. And we were put on bunks that had just a blanket—just blankets, nothing else. Two people had to share one bed, one bunk, and there were rows of people, so, let's say, such a row could be six women.

Once in her barrack with her mother, Tova had to retrieve the coins and diamond she had swallowed:

> I remember when I came they had still nice toilets there in Ravensbrück, in the German camp. So I had to find those things my mother gave me, and they were knocking on the door. You had only so much time to shower or so much time to be in the toilet. And if [the overseer] just doesn't like you for any reason, she was beating you. This was a pleasure for her. It was just, they treated us like animals. And we had no names. Everybody had a number. Each one, the ones that they were there longer, they learned some tricks, so they took it out on the new ones that didn't know anything
> So the Ravensbrück camp was a camp of a lot of beating, mistreating, those cold hours in the outside. They told us to shower in cold water and run from one building to the other naked in the coldest time of the year. The people that took care of us were SS ladies. I will never buy a cape in my life, because they were wearing capes. When I go down the subway sometimes and I see a woman in a cape, I get such a shiver. . . . They're not successful in private life, and they were very mean to us and they were very sadistic. As a young child, I saw behavior of people were so, they brought us—because, you know, a human being could be brought to a situation of a beast. In the beginning, they gave you small portions of bread. So some people were hungry and they ate everything at once, and some people tried to leave a tiny piece for later. So somebody could come and take it from your mouth with your teeth, because they dehumanize us against one another.

Unlike many of the women and some of the children, Tova did not have her "beautiful blonde hair" shaved. However, her mother was concerned about lice and cleanliness, and so received permission from the block elder to use a knife to cut Tova's hair in the barrack. "There were no circumstances to keep it—cold water and lice and all that trouble," she said. "I was envying the ones that had short hair. It was easier to handle it." Tova recalled:

> The women went to work, and the children stayed [in the barracks]. But the worst thing that could have happened was those head counts. They took us. They woke us up very early, and they made us look like crazy. To a tall woman, they gave a short coat. To a short woman, a long coat. Wooden shoes. It was just terrible. And there were not enough clothes, and we were freezing, and we were standing for hours. So then they'd count the women that they had to go to work, and the children [went] back [to the barracks].
>
> One day someone told my mother that they might come for the children, so she was so afraid and she took me to work. She took me to work, and they told me to carry this [wooden box]. But they had a method that they took more women for a certain work than they needed in case somebody dies on the way or in case they beat somebody to death. So they needed a certain amount of women. So there were some women going in the back in case they needed to exchange someone. So when I was carrying this [heavy box], I couldn't carry it. I was afraid my mother was going to be beaten, too, not only me. They saw that I am too small, so they took somebody from the reserve and they told me to go back. So after this, my mother said, "There's nothing you can do."

Tova and her mother were in the camp for about three months. "They gave us once a day soup that was like water, with certain vegetables," she recalled. "It looks like poison ivy that was cooked, full of sand. And in the beginning, they gave us a slice of bread." Her mother was beaten for trying to steal some potatoes to augment their diet. "She put two potatoes in her coat, and [the overseer] found them. So for those two potatoes, she was lucky, because some people they shaved their heads, too, that they should all know what terrible thing they did. So for those two potatoes, she was beaten terribly." In February 1945 Tova and her mother were sent to Bergen-Belsen.

JUDITH ROSNER GERTLER

Judith Rosner Gertler, another Jewish child survivor I met by chance in New York City, was eleven years old when she arrived in Ravensbrück directly from Hungary on 7 January 1945.[10] An only child, she was born in Mukachevo on 20 December 1933, the daughter of Marion Klein Rosner and Zoltan Rosner. For six months before her arrival at

Ravensbrück, she and her mother were in a confinement camp in Hungary. Her mother was shot on the death march from that camp to the Austrian border, so Judith suffered the loss of her mother before she arrived at Ravensbrück. Her aunt, her father's younger sister, was also with her and served as her surrogate mother in the camp.

When Judith's group of women and children reached the Austrian border, they were put into railroad wagons, she recalled. When the train finally arrived at the camp, after days of delay in Berlin, female guards came to take the group off the train, she said. "I don't know how many there were, but they came with the dogs and right away got the dogs on us barking and they screamed and they yelled and they started to hit." She remembers that they used whips, while screaming in German, "*Schnell, schnell, schnell*" (fast, fast, fast).

"It must have been like three, four in the morning, and they herded us into the showers," she said. "It was snowing. That part of Germany is very cold in late winter. It was very, very cold, windy." The women worried in the shower that they would be gassed there, she recalled. Afterward, the guards took away all of the women's clothing and meager possessions. "They gave us other clothes that had an X on the back cut in, or it was [painted] with white oil paint. They gave us some clothes, and they let us keep our shoes. They didn't have children's shoes. We were put in certain barracks. They had us sleep four in a bunk."

"The experience was terrible, and life there was very hard," she continued. "The day was very short, and the nights were very long and cold. The children didn't go to work, but the women had to go every day." Like Tova Giladi and others, Judith remembered that the children were required to join the women for the daily roll call. "Every morning, at three o'clock, they would wake us up and start giving out the black 'coffee,'" she said. Afterward, there was roll call, before the women went out to work. "And the counting," she recalled, "the counting never ended. They never found how many missing, how many remained dead, how many couldn't get up. And you had to move from one place to another. If the lines were not straight, they couldn't count. They didn't add up. It lasted like two, two and a half hours."

The counting was accompanied by constant beating, Judith said. "When we walked out from the barracks, everybody got one over the head. This was by the inmates. These people were in charge. They put inmates in charge of every room and every barrack. A barrack had like four rooms, and they were chasing the people out. They didn't want to go out into the cold. It was terribly freezing temperature. We didn't have good clothes on, and we knew what's waiting for hours to stand there. So everybody was like holding back. They didn't want to go. And they were chasing us and hitting us all the time," she said.

"When we got out, there were more of the Germans out there. They never came in, the Germans, because these people in charge, they were responsible for the count. So they were trying to get out everybody, but there were so many dead during the night. Then they had to go and bring out the dead people and have them lined up to make the count."

When the roll call ended and the women went off to work, the children went back to the barracks to pass the long hours of the day. "We tried to keep occupied with our whatever it is," Judith said. "We were talking about breakfast and imagining what we would have eaten if we would be home. Then maybe we were delousing ourselves, and then we were having lunch' and make li li ... everything, and trying to keep some kind of a conversation."

The women returned from work when the short days began to get dark and then went to bring the children their soup. There were no lights in the barracks, Judith said. "All the windows were broken in the barracks. We had no blankets. We were covering ourselves with the coat that we had, and if you took off your shoes, you had to make sure you put it under your head, because otherwise they would steal. If you had to use the bathroom during the night, they wouldn't allow you to go in shoes. It was filthy, it was overflowing. You had to go in your stockings there. By the time you came back, it was frozen on you. So it was a miserable day and a more miserable night, because the night was so long and cold and you couldn't keep warm."

Judith's aunt came down with typhus and was sent to the *Revier*. Judith remembers that she was terribly lonesome and frightened that she would be sent away alone. "At the end of March, a few times they wanted to send me in the transport, and every time I kept saying, 'I cannot go because my mother is in the hospital.' I called her my mother because that was my only attachment to somebody. And they somehow listened to me. They didn't bother me." Her aunt had a mild case, and managed to recover and leave the *Revier* after she realized that Judith was waiting for her.

Soon afterward, at the end of April, the Russian Army was approaching and the Nazis decided to evacuate the camp. Judith and her aunt then embarked on a grueling death march, which is detailed in chapter 12.

Upon her return to her hometown of Mukachevo (formerly Munkács), Judith learned that her father had survived. She stayed in a sanitorium for six months to recover from lung disease, and then in 1946, at age twelve, Judith decided to go to Israel alone. The trip itself is a long story of illegal immigration that includes incarceration on Cyprus by the British. After ten years living in Israel, she met her husband, Harry Gertler, on a visit to the United States. They were married on 21 June 1959, and their son, Marc, was born in April 1960. Judith now lives in Brooklyn, New York. Her father died in Israel in 1980.

WATCHING CHILDREN SUFFER

Perhaps the eyewitness recollection of Gemma LaGuardia Gluck best describes the situation of the children: "The little ones, of whom at one time there were perhaps five hundred, added a note of special horror and tragedy to the atmosphere of the camp. They looked like little skeletons wearing rags. Some had no hair on their heads. Nevertheless, they behaved like children, running around and begging things from their elders. They even played games. A popular one was *Appell,* modeled on the camp's daily roll calls."[11] This scene of the children acting out the roles of victims and perpetrators is painful to imagine. Like children everywhere, they played games of make-believe that mirrored the reality of their surroundings. Most of them were sent on to other camps and did not survive. Sad as they are, the children's stories recounted here are those of some of the more fortunate Jewish children of Ravensbrück.

The suffering and murder of the children was not only tragic for these young victims of the camp but also added to the misery of their birth mothers, surrogate mothers, and other sympathetic prisoners. The statistics on the arrivals of children and the births (usually followed by death) of babies are incomplete, and we will never know the full extent of the horrors inflicted on children and newborns.[12] I have never found an explanation for why the Nazis sometimes allowed young and unproductive children to stay alive in Ravensbrück.

6

A Year of Comings and Goings, 1944

THOUSANDS of Jewish women arrived in Ravensbrück in 1944, especially those caught in the Nazis' last major roundup of Jews in Hungary in the summer and fall of that year. Along with some women from Hungary, a Polish Jewish woman arrested while posing as a Christian (in the aftermath of the Warsaw uprising) and a Jewish woman turned in by a neighbor in Bratislava tell their stories here. In a series of seemingly arbitrary transfers that must have been traumatizing, by the beginning of 1945 all but one of these women had been sent to another camp.

MARGO WOHL GUINESS

When I met Margaret Wohl Guiness (known as Margo) in California in 1998, she could not walk without crutches but was remarkably optimistic and positive. Her disposition not only belied her physical problems but also her haunting experiences during the Holocaust. She arrived in Ravensbrück in August 1944 and was transported to Dortmund in November, and then to Bergen-Belsen.[1] "If I was made of glass, you could see the scar tissue inside," she said of her experience in Ravensbrück. She was arrested in Budapest, where she and her older sister, Bozena, had been living in a pension and posing as Christians. Daughters of Theodor Wohl and Anne Ritter Wohl, they had fled to Budapest from Kosice, Czechoslovakia, after the Nazi takeover. Then fourteen years old, Margo

Das Zelt (The tent). Drawing by an unknown prisoner artist depicts women forced to subsist in a tent at Ravensbrück in 1944. Photo from the first Ravensbrück Camp Museum. Collection of MGR/SBG.

had the false identity papers of seventeen-year-old Maria Karolchik. She and her twenty-eight-year-old sister were able to pass as Hungarians because they spoke the language fluently. "When my sister took me with her to Budapest, to Hungary, and we ran away from home and the deportations were taking place, I was still secretly playing with dolls," she told me. "I was probably a very immature little girl." She said that even her sister was young and naive, although at the time she "seemed like a very mature lady." Margo worked in a drugstore and her sister had a job as a bookkeeper.

One day in June 1944 when the sisters returned to their room, the Gestapo was waiting for them. "The people were playing cards in the salon, and instead of alerting us, they let us walk in almost to the jaws of the lion," she recalled. "We didn't have a chance." The Gestapo had ransacked their room and found a second set of false papers, which her sister had sewn into the lining of her purse. "They took us to their headquarters, and they arrested us on suspicion of espionage," Margo said. "But then they couldn't prove anything either way, so then they thought that we were Jews trying to escape and trying to hide. So it was either one or the other."

The sisters were taken to a prison for common criminals, where one floor was reserved for the Gestapo. Their separate interrogations took place both at the prison and more intensively at Adolf Eichmann's headquarters. "They would burn me under my chin with cigarettes, and I think I have a scar here, because it turned malignant—that burn, which left a scar. It had to be taken off. I am full of scars, all kinds of both mental and physical," she said. "I was very worried about betraying my sister, because it was very tempting to tell them the truth and stop the beating. But I pretended that my tongue was burned and I couldn't speak."

In August the sisters were deported to Auschwitz, where Margo continued to claim she was seventeen. The next day, along with about one thousand other women, they were selected for transfer to Ravensbrück. It had never been proven that the sisters were Jewish, and she remembers that most of the women in their cattle car transport were non-Jews. At Ravensbrück the sisters were not designated as Jewish.

Margo's memories of the trauma of her arrival at Ravensbrück are still vivid. "I remember being promised that all our belongings would be returned to us," she said. "And again, we were given a shower and given these terrible-looking prison uniforms that really made us look like circus people. For example, my sister, who was taller than I was, was given a very short dress and I was given a very long one. So we exchanged to make it look a little bit better. But no undergarments, no outer garments were given, and like within a month, by September, the weather had turned cool, really cold, and all I remember was always my teeth were chattering. My teeth were chattering."

Like some other survivors, Margo spoke of disassociation as a means of coping with the unbearable circumstances of camp life. She believes that her ability to mentally disengage herself from the cruel reality helped to keep her alive. "And during those endless roll calls, when people who were dead or alive—they all had to be there—I remember in my head I was always home," she said. "I was either practicing the piano or ice-skating. And I understand that this kind of disassociation from this terrible circumstance is what saved my sanity and saved my life, that I was able in my head to disassociate from whatever was going on, because my memories from home, which had been very recent, were so warm."

Margo worked in the Siemens factory and remembers that working there was better than returning to the main camp. "We were really always ankle deep in mud, it seems to me, and I was always freezing and shivering," she said. "A lot of it could have been because of the lack of nutrition, because the nutrition was so terrible and so little." Although she was only fourteen, Margo had remarkable intuition for survival. "I had made up my mind in Ravensbrück that I will defy them," she said. "And so whatever work was available, even when we came back after twelve hours of work, I would volunteer for additional work. I would work in the kitchen, where they were preparing the food for the guards, for the

German guards. And so occasionally a little additional food was to be gotten from that expedition." Margo made clear that her reason for "volunteering" had the purpose of obtaining additional food, as she felt, "that was the only route to survival. There was no other."

Margo also recalled another way she tried to survive—by keeping as clean as possible: "As winter set in, as the cold weather set in, our facility was very meager to cleanse ourselves," she said. "I'd roll in the snow to cleanse my body, and I'd gotten used to it on a daily basis. It's an interesting thing how many things you can get used to in life, where the cold didn't bother me anymore. I got used to it. That was the only way I could see to cleanse myself and cleanse my clothes. That particular winter set in very early. I think already by the end of October, November, winter had set in, and we had snow on the ground. It happened to be a very cold year. That's all I remember is always freezing."

Even though Margo seems to have known how to care for herself, she gives her sister credit for getting her through the ordeal. "I attribute, definitely, my own survival to my sister, who always talked to me about the fact that this cannot go on very long and this is a temporary situation and it will all end," she said. "And somehow Bozena was like a mother. I always believed what she was telling me. And so I did the best that I could to disassociate from whatever was happening." However, she added a somewhat contradictory statement about a time when her sister's own struggle to survive diminished. "I must say that my sister, Bozena, who was always very courageous at home and very intelligent, in Ravensbrück she gave up," Margo said. "She gave up. She became very resigned to the fact that we are not going to make it after all, because it didn't look like any of us would make it, you see. I mean, the camp was administered with such precision, with such cruelty, with such discipline that really—it was very interesting. When this woman, this SS woman, said that, 'You will never be free. You will always be our slave. . . .'"

Dr. Karl Gebhardt selected her for a "medical" experiment in November, Margo said, but she and her sister managed to get on a transport to another camp, Dortmund. She remembers Dortmund as a factory camp, with about two thousand female prisoners who worked for the munitions factory, manufacturing V-2 rockets. Her sister worked in the commandant's office, and she worked where the food was distributed to the prisoners, "which was a marvelous opportunity for me to eat and to smuggle additional food into the camp." Her sister planned an escape, but a third woman they had asked to join them left them behind.

After bombs destroyed the factory's roof, they were evacuated to Bergen-Belsen. Margo was then ill with typhus for six weeks. "I remember one day hearing tremendous commotion outside the barracks, and I pulled myself up to the window and I saw umbrellas coming down from the sky, because I'd never heard of paratroopers," she said.[2] "By that time, I told my sister what I had seen, and she was convinced that I was hallucinating, that I was actually—because I had so much fever." Margo and her sister were taken to Sweden by the Red Cross, and Margo describes as "the saddest loss" and "the darkest area of my life" the fact that her sister was so ill that she died there.[3] None of Margo's family, which included two brothers and another sister, survived. She came to the United States, married, and now lives in California. Her ability to write about her experiences and her losses helps her to cope.

Like Margo and her sister, Olga Weiss Astor and her sister, Etelka, were arrested in Budapest.[4] They were rounded up from a ghetto house in September 1944 and taken to Ravensbrück. The daughter of Israel Weiss and Sarolta Kahan Weiss, Olga was born in Miskolc, Hungary on 19 September 1924. In addition to her sister, she had four brothers. She attended *Gymnasium* and had wanted to be a pharmacist, but her father decided she needed a practical skill and apprenticed her to a tailor. When the deportations began in Budapest, a Christian woman promised to hide Olga and her sister. Their brother, Samuel, had escaped from a forced labor camp and appeared in the city just before they were to go into hiding. Since they thought he was in more danger, Olga sent him to use their hiding place. The sisters were then among those rounded up the next morning. "So we were chased out, and the march started," she said. "We had to go with our hands up, and there were lots and lots of people, the good citizens of Budapest, nice Hungarian people who love Kodaly and Bartok, and they spit on us, and, oh, they clapped, it was a joy for them."

She arrived at the camp at about the time of her twentieth birthday, and remained there until she was transferred to Burgau, a subcamp of Dachau, in January 1945. Her journey to Ravensbrück began with a forced march all the way to the German border, with a stopover in a brick factory. "That is an unforgettable place," she recalled. "The floor had some wood planks, but there were big spaces between each plank. . . . By the time you came out you only knew that you were red from the brick color because you looked at somebody else. You didn't have a mirror. So if she was red, I was red."

The women marched under the guns of Hungarian Nazi collaborators, and were forced to lie down in the fields in the rain. Sometimes people had to dig ditches, which became their graves. As the women continued on their march, they were burdened by their possessions and dropped them along the way. When they finally reached the border, they were put on a train headed for Ravensbrück. At this time Olga and her sister met and became friends with another pair of sisters from Budapest, originally from Romania, Esther Tuvel (later Shuftan) and Sara Tuvel (later Bernstein).[5]

Like Margo, Olga vividly recalls the group's arrival in Ravensbrück. "We still had clothes on that fit," she said. "We were still a *mensch*—we still were people. We still had our hair. We were recognizable as a human being. When we arrived in Ravensbrück on that train and the SS guard was waiting for us with dogs and these machine guns and '*macht schnell, macht schnell*' [make it fast, hurry up], we had to go really fast off the train." Olga said she will never forget her first impression of the camp. "They marched us in, and we saw walking skeletons wearing striped clothes," she said. "I cannot forget that. And I said to myself, 'No, I am not going to look like this. How can I look like this?' You see, we didn't know—I mean, I think youth was on my side, on everybody's side there. Youth was there, and an ability to take yourself out of this situation."

Olga continued, using the same "circus" language as Margo to describe the clothing she received. "The first thing they did, we had to go to the shower," she said. "Thank goodness water came out of that shower. Then everybody was shaved. Every bodily hair was removed, and it just so happened that tall girls got short clothes and short girls got long clothes and looked like clowns, and when you came out of that shower, you didn't recognize your sister or your best friend because hair is something—when you lose it, you're gone. That was terrible."

Olga also remembered the severe overcrowding. "First, when we arrived in Ravensbrück, it was so overflowing that they didn't have room in the barracks," she said. "Even though a barrack that would hold, let's say, two hundred had there two thousand or twenty-four hundred. We were four to six to a bunk bed without a mattress, like forks or spoons you put together. If one moved, everybody moved. If one turned, everybody turned." The women were chased out of the barracks at around two o'clock in the morning, she recalled. "I don't care if the snow was six feet tall or the sky was breaking apart, we had to stand there and in perfect order. I mean, you were not to move your head. You were not to move this way or that way. And the SS went and counted you."

Olga first worked sorting clothing, and then shoveling coal. Like Margo, Olga used an intuitive psychological skill to cope with her ordeal. She explained it by referring to the common expression, "I was beside myself." "It was so interesting that I was marching in Ravensbrück and the *kapo* stayed there with this stick," she said. "I was beside myself. You know, I did not march. That was not me. I saw myself next to that person. Isn't that interesting? So that whenever somebody says, 'Oh, I am beside myself,' you really can be. It just depends how much trauma you have. It was unbelievable."

In addition to the harsh work conditions, Olga described her constant hunger. "The hunger—do you know what hunger is?" she asked me. Answering her own question, she said, "I don't think you do. No. You don't know what hunger is. You think Yom Kippur you're hungry? Are you kidding? You know what hunger is? When night after night, you dream—if you call it a dream—that there is a slice of bread here and your arms are cut off, you cannot reach. That's hunger. That's what I had every night."

Like other women who were in the camp, Olga recalled the indignities of the latrine. "Everybody had dysentery," she said. "You could only go to the latrine at certain times. Now, you know, nature calls and you have to go, when you went to the latrine, the SS stood and watched you with the gun." Once Olga decided not to wait for permission. "I remember one night I crawled through the window. I had to go. You couldn't go. You couldn't say, 'I have to go to the latrine.' No way. You only go at certain times. That's it. And I crawled through the window, and I squatted down right there and then, outside, and bombs were falling over Berlin, and it was the most beautiful sound in the world. That was music to my ears."

Olga also spoke of the women being forced to march wearing wooden shoes. "And then the snow gets on it. You know, it sticks to wood. In the winter it was frozen, and it was snow, and the snow gets onto the shoe and it doesn't want to leave it, and you walk like this." However, no matter how difficult it was to walk and "no matter how sick you were, no matter how bad you felt, no matter how—your best bet was just to go out." Sometimes, "you died right there on the march to work."

After Olga's bread was stolen, she stopped saving it:

> I ate it right there and then, and to hell with the rest of the twenty-four hours. Because once I saved up my bread to exchange it for a sweater, because I was terribly, terribly cold, and there were Gypsies, also, Gypsies. I don't know where they got the sweater. Maybe it was their own. And in that place where we were gathered for counting, I approached one woman, and I told her that I have two pieces of bread and I would like a sweater for it. She says, "Tomorrow." So, tomorrow I looked her up. "Where is the bread?" "Here." She grabbed the bread and ran. To me, that was enough for me forever to never, ever again put even a crumb under my head. If you had something, you put it under your head. But then I just ate it up as soon as I got it, and that was it. In those days I didn't have a problem how to lose weight.

One of her most memorable experiences was the day she said she "got crazy" and told her sister she was not going to work:

> So I thought I will hide out behind the latrines. And to my "good fortune," I am hiding out with the gray blanket over me, and then they

come. This is probably the first time in camp history that they clean the latrines. They had those big hoses with the water, you know? And here I was running like a wet rat, you know? They hosed me out of the latrine, and I tried to get back. I don't know, I worked my way into one of the barracks where there were—they were not gone to work that day— why I wouldn't know, and they all had the gray blankets, so I blended in real nice. But that was not the barrack where I belonged, and I wanted to know how do I get to my barrack because my sister is there. The girls there told me that they were transferred to another barrack. So then I found them in Barrack Twenty-one. But I never—from then—I never, never, never stayed around, because that was more dangerous than going to work.

This horrifying memory of the latrine reminded Olga of the expression "latrine news," the term used for any rumors or information that reached the women. "You went to the latrine when you were allowed to go and you found out something," she said. "So one day the news was that President Roosevelt was paying for each prisoner, I don't know, let's say a dollar. What do I know how much? And we will be liberated soon, and the Red Cross will come to pick us up. And lo and behold, that day we saw a Red Cross car in the camp, but they didn't come for us. They didn't come for us."

Conditions became so harsh that "the living envies the dead," she said. The hope that her other family members were quickly murdered made her "happy," because they would not have to live through the horrors of the camp. "I have never heard so many *Shema Yisrael* [prayers] in my life—and I come from a very religious family—that I had heard in camp," she said.

Olga has one vivid memory of Ravensbrück that I have never heard or read in other survivors' accounts or in documents. She recalled an especially cruel treatment for the Jewish prisoners to mark the celebration of Christmas. "I will never forget, as long as I live, Christmas Day 1944," she said. "We were marched out. We didn't go to work [on] Christmas, and the Jewish prisoners, only the Jews, they were marched out naked, and we had to stand naked outside [for *Appell*]. Because we were killing Christ. We killed Christ, as if they were so holy, you know? I will never forget it."

Soon afterward, in January, Olga and her sister were sent on a transport to Burgau. She remembers the horrors of that trip:

And the nights were the worst, the nights, because then you heard— especially when they transferred us on trains in the cattle cars, and there were at least 120 in the cattle car. We went from Ravensbrück to Burgau in cattle cars. We were on that train at least ten days. It was locked from the outside. There was a pail there and no food, no water. The train, of course, had some holes, and it was winter and it was snowing or

Year of Comings and Goings, 1944

raining. . . . But the train stopped, the SS opened up the trains. We should throw out the dead, which was actually a blessing, because then we had more room in the train. You see, you were sitting like this, and you couldn't do anything. That's how you were. Or if you were standing there, you couldn't fall down because you were so tight. And when they opened the doors, some people at the train station, as if they were waiting for this train to come, they were women, *babushkas* [head scarves] on, but they were not prisoners, they were civilian people, regular people. I say "regular" people. I was irregular in those days. Anyway, they threw bread into the train, and, I don't know, they handed down a pail, and they got some water, but they threw bread in the train, but it was the worst thing they could do, because we killed each other for it. You see, it wasn't enough. So you throw in the bread for one hundred people, you tear each other up to get a crumb. Now, these were the train rides, and the trains were absolutely terrible, the nights on the train.[6]

When the Allied troops came closer to Burgau, Olga and her sister were with a group that was sent to Dachau. However, Dachau was already extremely overcrowded and refused the transport, which ended up in the subcamp of Allach. On the short trip between Dachau and Allach on 29 April, Olga received a wound from which she still suffers today. "We had to stand five in a row, you know, and then the guards got the machine guns and started shooting, and that's where I got the bullet in my left hip," she said. "But that's running ahead of my time." We will pick up Olga's story again in chapter 14, which deals with the aftermath.

ELISABETH KOEVESI PAVEL

Two other survivors who arrived from Hungary in 1944 came from cities outside of Budapest. Elisabeth Koevesi Pavel was born on 24 September 1918 in Ungvar (now called Oroshaza), Hungary. She arrived at Ravensbrück in November 1944 and remained until 13 January 1945. She was the only child of Ernoe Koevesi and Eva Herskovits Koevesi. After the family moved to the ghetto in 1944, she and her parents lived with her aunt and cousin in a small apartment with one room, a kitchen, and an outdoor toilet. On 20 October her father was taken away, and three days later Elisabeth had to report at a collection point in a local sports arena. Her father never returned, but her mother survived.[7]

Elisabeth, her cousin, and two friends reported together and then were sent on a forced march. "We walked through the country," she said. "We stopped at certain places for the night. There was one time when we were in the open. There was one time when it was raining." Along the way, Elisabeth's group once had to dig trenches for the army. When they reached the German border, they were brought to Ravensbrück in what

87

she described as "empty wagons" (probably open railroad cars). She remembers the group's arrival and said that outside the gate the camp was "clean" and "beautiful." However, the scene was different once the women passed through the gate.

They had to undress and give up all of their belongings, but their heads were not shaved, she said. "At first we were laughing how we looked in our outfit. . . . They had the star in the back.[8] Light clothing. And I'll tell you something. . . . I think when we went from Ravensbrück, then I got frozen." Elisabeth's work at Ravensbrück was unloading boats and wagons, and putting the cargo into a storage depot. She, her cousin, and the two friends were still together at this time. When she was shoveling coal, someone accidentally broke her glasses and they were not replaced until after liberation.

In January Elisabeth was sent to work at Venusberg until April, and then to Mauthausen, which was liberated by the United States Army on 5 May 1945. She returned to Budapest in June and was reunited with her mother. Four years later she married Jakob Pavel, who had been in a forced labor camp. They, their two sons, and Elisabeth's mother immigrated to the United States in 1957.

ILONA KLEIN FELDMAN

When Ilona Klein Feldman arrived in Ravensbrück in November 1944, overcrowding was so serious that, like thousands of women, she was first placed in the infamous tent, an experience that most women did not survive. She was born in Nyirtura in the province of Szabolcs, Hungary on 13 October 1925, the daughter of Ignac and Ida Klein.[9] She was deported on 22 May 1944 and sent to Auschwitz. Later that month she was sent to Frankfurt, and then to Ravensbrück. "It was so big to me—like Auschwitz," she said. "It was a very cold day. They didn't have any place for us in the barracks. They took all of us to a big tent. We had to walk and we were very cold. We went to the tent—it was terrible—no floor, just bricks, and no beds. Outside it was snowing and we were in the tent. We didn't have anything to cover ourselves. We were cold, hungry—the people got sick there quick[ly]. We had already some dead. I don't remember how long we were in that tent. But after a while they found some place for us in the barracks." Ilona was placed in a barrack that had a mixture of non-Jewish prisoners, including women from Germany, Poland, and Russia. She said the Polish women, among whom she had a place in a bunk bed, treated her badly, but then the Russian political prisoners "adopted" her and she moved up to their bunk.

"Sometimes they took me to work," she said. "Not always—they didn't have work for everybody. There were basements where they kept potatoes, carrots, and beets. We had to bring it from one place to the other. It was hard. We were already very weak and starving. It was very cold—we didn't have a coat or a jacket. We had to carry—two of us—on a wheelbarrow—the vegetables. Some people collapsed many times. I wished it should happen to me, too, because then I didn't have to do it." In mid-February 1945, Ilona was transferred to Bergen-Belsen and liberated in April by the British Army. She married Ferenc Feldman in December 1947, and they had two sons. The family immigrated to the United States, and Ilona now lives in Chicago.

DORIS FUKS GREENBERG

Because the Nazis took over Hungary in March 1944 and then began deporting Jews to concentration camps in Germany and Poland, it is understandable that many Jewish women were brought from Hungary to Ravensbrück that year. However, it was not the norm for a Jewish woman to arrive at Ravensbrück directly from Warsaw that fall, a year after the Warsaw Ghetto was liquidated. Doris Fuks Greenberg was an exception, because she had been living as a Christian with false papers. The daughter of Henryk and Gucia Rosenfarb Fuks, Doris was born in Warsaw on 4 March 1930, five years after her sister Marysia.[10] She was rounded up as a non-Jew with thousands of Polish Christian women after the Warsaw revolt in August 1944.

At the time of the German invasion of Poland in September 1939, Doris and her sister were students. "When they defined the ghetto, where it is, and our street was outside of it, we had to move," she said. "And that's when all the bad stuff started. . . . Since that time we had to move a few more times, because every now and then they made the ghetto smaller. They excluded a part. As they excluded, we had to move out somewhere else. So we had moved a few times."

Doris's parents and sister were deported from the ghetto, but she remained with her aunt, a grandmother, and two uncles. One of the uncles had a non-Jewish wife who managed to rent an apartment outside the ghetto, and Doris and her remaining family were smuggled out of the ghetto, one by one, before the Warsaw Ghetto uprising in April 1943. "But it was also a short-lived thing, because somebody must have noticed and told on us," she said. "One night some agents came in, Polish agents, and they found us." They stole the family's possessions and made them promise to disappear by morning.

Afterward the family members went their separate ways. Alone at age thirteen and a half, Doris secured false documents and at first worked as a maid near Warsaw. "Then one day I had to leave," she said. "Apparently some news leaked out, and the priest saw me in church and he invited me to talk to him. He gave me a pocketful of nuts and candy, and told me that he knows who I am and that it would be nice for me to leave for a couple of days, because he feels we're going to have some guests, uninvited guests. So I understood, and I left."

Doris had become friends with another Jewish young woman who was passing as a non-Jewish Pole in Warsaw. "She got a job as a cook in a restaurant in a suburb of Warsaw," Doris said. "So she invited me because her bosses needed a helper for her. So she suggested that I come, and I got a job being the cook's helper." At the end of the Polish revolt, in September 1944, Doris and her friend were rounded up with the other local residents and put on a train headed for Ravensbrück. "The whole population was evacuated," she said. "We were running in the middle of the streets and we could see that the buildings were still smoldering. Some stones, some bricks were falling. That's how we came together to the concentration camp. We traveled together."

Doris recalled her arrival at Ravensbrück, which must have been in early October 1944:

> We were separated before we entered the gates, into different groups. There were some tables with papers where I think somebody put your name and gave you a number.[11] This was the part—we couldn't see that until we got close to it, because the lines were enormous. We could see where the people walk in, like straight ahead to the building, quite a lengthy building. People were walking in there. But we were in the line, and when we got closer to that table, somebody was putting our name and then giving us numbers, I think. Or the numbers, we got them after the bath. But we gave our names. I think that at that time they would put the number on and then later give them out. It was only somebody writing our name and then next to it probably a number, because when we got out, we got the numbers.

Doris remembers that her friend had poison, and said to her, "Look, we see people go in, we don't see anybody that we know coming out, maybe it's time to take the poison." However, Doris, who described herself as "such a chicken," responded: "Look, if we're going to die, so another few minutes. Maybe the Germans will find a poison and test it, try themselves. Why hurry up?" After the women had their hair clipped, they were given a shower.

"That was a relief," Doris said. "We came out of the shower. The clothes that were left, any belongings or whatever we had, we don't see it anymore. We get handed the stripes. I got a dress that you could put a refrigerator in it, and I was a kid, and some tall women got a dress that I couldn't fit in." Like others who resolved this problem in the same way, Doris switched her dress with another woman. "That dress that I got was just barely covering," she said. "But they gave us also a jacket. The jacket for me was almost as long as the dress. Better than nothing. Then they gave us underwear, a pair of underpants. You should have seen that. They reached to my knees. You know, if it wouldn't be so sad, it would be very funny," she remarked. "But we were given those clothes and wooden shoes, just a sole with one stripe. We never saw our things again."

"And they gave us a red triangle with the letter *P* on it," she continued. "We had to put here the white strip with a number, and above it the red triangle with the letter *P*. That was our name. From then on it was the number." Doris's number was 74073. Although she recalls that many women's heads were shaved, she was spared this trauma. "They seemed to say that they were checking, and whoever had no lice wasn't shaved, but I don't believe that all those people had lice. No, I don't believe that. If anybody would have, it would have been us, because we had no place to wash or no—so I don't know why."

Doris recalled what happened next. "Then we came out from that building and we then understood what's happening," she said. "We didn't see people coming out, those people who came in, because they looked different. When they came in, they are people wearing clothes, having their hair and holding a pocketbook or something or some of their belongings. We were underway maybe a week or ten days, but in the train, everybody had whatever everybody had. So when we walked in, we looked like human people. When they walked out from the building we just saw people in those striped dresses, no hair. You couldn't recognize a face. Somebody came to us when we're in the line and says, 'Hi.' We didn't know who it was."

Once Doris arrived at her assigned barrack, she saw Yiddish writing on the walls. Her friend, who could read Yiddish, read the names of people and messages such as, "Tell others what they did to us." "Don't let the world forget." Another vivid memory of Doris's short stay at the camp was the day she saw "a truckload of dead bodies, skin and bones." She also remembers hearing screams. Doris and her friend stayed at the camp for a very short time, perhaps no more than a week. They were then transported to a subcamp called Neubrandenburg, where they worked in a factory that made airplane parts.[12]

On 8 March 1945, Doris was sent from Neubrandenburg to Kühlungsborn, a small town in the north of Germany near the North Sea. As she and her friend were still posing as non-Jewish Poles, she was assigned to work for a German family, and her friend was sent to a nearby farm. Doris said she was not treated badly and was required to clean the house, help with the cooking, and gather kindling wood. On about 5 May the Russians arrived, but they assumed that Doris was a Nazi collaborator. She ran away to the farm where her friend was working, and when a group of Russians arrived at the farm, they used her friend as a translator. The two young women obtained forged Russian papers that enabled them to reach Berlin. Once there, Doris finally convinced the Jewish communal organization that she was Jewish, and then was sent to the Bergen-Belsen Displaced Persons camp in the British zone. Afterward she immigrated to the United States, and in the 1990s was living in Stamford, Connecticut.

SUSAN JAKUBOVIC KORNHAUSER

Susan Jakubovic Kornhauser, the daughter of Leopold and Karolina Reissman Jakubovic, was born on 14 June 1928, and grew up in a middle-class family in Michalovce, Czechoslovakia.[13] When the Russian front approached around the beginning of 1944, the remaining Jews were forced to leave, and her family moved to Bratislava. Her father's position in the finance department gave them protection until September 1944, when all exemptions for Jews ceased. The family was hidden until December 1944, when a neighbor reported them, and they were captured by the Gestapo. The men and women were separated, and Susan and her mother were sent to Ravensbrück. They arrived there on Christmas Eve, during the last week of 1944.

Like the other women who described their arrival, Susan's biggest fear was entering the shower. "And they took us to the showers," she said. "We were scared of those showers, because from the stories that we heard prior to it, we knew that the showers weren't really showers, that those were gas chambers. So we really didn't know whether these are showers or gas chambers. But those were showers they gave us. They took all our clothes away and they gave us new clothes. The only thing that we were left with were our shoes, and they didn't shave our head anymore." She continued:

> From there, we were moved to a quarantine block, which was Block Number Twenty-three. I was there with my mother all the time. My mother got already sick there. Me, I was always an overprotected child, and our roles were reversed, because at that point I was the adult and I had to take care of my mother. I was fourteen. We stayed in that block, I believe, one week. This was a quarantine block. I met there a Polish Jewish doctor who was very kind to me. And she saw that Mother was sick, so she told me that she will transfer us to a Block Twenty-one, which are mainly sick people there. I was petrified when I heard the word "sick people." I was scared that they would send us to gas chambers, me or my mother or both of us.[14] She told me I shouldn't be scared, nobody would take us to the gas chambers, but the only advantage is

in this block that nobody has to stand *Appell*, and that will be very helpful for my mother. Maybe she would be cured there.

Susan and her mother were transferred to the other block, and she discovered that she had been given good advice. However, she was given a horrifying work detail. "We stayed there almost to the very end," she said. "My mother was better, better, worse, but we really didn't have to stand *Appell*. I was taken to work from that block, which I didn't mind, but the work I was given, because it was a block of sick people, many people died on this block, and the corpses were piled up in the washroom," she said. "I was a young girl, so the work I got to do was to carry these corpses. When I got this job, the first day I was crying terribly. I couldn't control myself," she recalled. "As days went by, one becomes numb. Later on I didn't feel any pain or I didn't have any feeling towards what I was really doing. So this was the only thing that I was doing in Ravensbrück."

Meanwhile, Susan gave up a precious possession to try to improve her mother's health. "I had very nice boots, beautiful boots," she said. "The *Stubova* [room senior] liked my boots, and she told me, if I give her the boots, she will provide food for my mother. So I gave her the boots, and she really gave me a little bit more food for my mother, so she was able to survive maybe until the end of March." However, by then Susan's mother was so sick that she was no longer conscious. "I kept her on the block as long as I could," she said. She didn't want her taken to the camp hospital, but it was impossible to keep her in the barrack. "The *Stubova* promised me that I would be able to go and visit her," she said. "Unfortunately, there was nobody to visit my mother when she died, but I don't know exactly when."

Susan was alone after her mother's death, and she was in the precarious position of losing her reason to live. However, she was fortunate that a woman who had come on the transport with her took over as a surrogate mother. Susan said she was extremely kind "and somehow she took care of me." By then many women were being sent on to other camps, because the front was coming closer. "So there were constantly selections for transports," Susan said. One day, "they said that they are selecting people for a transport, only a few young women, but they shouldn't be Jewish. Jews they are not taking. We had a Star of David on our uniform. So this woman is telling me, 'Obviously this must be a good transfer if they are not taking Jews. You know what? We will remove our Star of David, and we will go and stand in the line where they are selecting the people on this transport,' and this is what we did."

Susan and her new protector were sent to a labor camp in Bohemia, and she believes she was there for only about two weeks. She was liberated by the United States Army in May and then returned to Bratislava.

She married Emanuel Kornhauser in 1948, and the couple left for Israel a year later. Then, in 1958, they and their two sons immigrated to Toronto, Canada.

OTHERS WHO ARRIVED IN 1944

The recollections of Margo Guiness, Olga Astor, Elisabeth Pavel, Ilona Feldman, Doris Greenberg, and Susan Kornhauser can give us some idea of the unimaginable suffering of the thousands of Jewish women who entered Ravensbrück during the last months of 1944. They also demonstrate how other women, especially family members or close friends, helped to ease the constant horror. Their stories were chosen because they were the most detailed, but other women who arrived at this time also shared a few memories with me. For example, Blanka Adler Kahan, who was born in Budapest in 1915, arrived by way of Auschwitz-Birkenau in May 1944 and was sent later to the Malchow subcamp. She said in a phone conversation that she was a puppeteer and performed in Ravensbrück. However, she was too ill and depressed to share her complete story. Another Hungarian survivor, Edith Gabor Vidos, who was born in Budapest in 1925, was in Ravensbrück for less than a month, in December 1944. And Alice Strum Birnhak, who was born in Kielce, Poland, on 15 June 1922, was sent from there to Auschwitz in August 1944, and then to Ravensbrück in October. In December 1944 she was also sent on to Malchow.[15]

The stories of three other women who arrived in 1944, Basia Zajaczkowska Rubinstein, Mina Lewkowicz Goldstein, and Ester (Eliz) Weisz Grun, along with the continuation of the testimonies of Margo Wohl Guiness and Olga Weiss Astor, will be recounted in the next chapter, which deals with slave labor at Ravensbrück.

Gefangenen-Stärkemeldung

vom _21. 5. 39_

	•	Rapport-Meld.	Zugang	Abgang	Juden	Kranf-Meld.	Zugang	Abgang	Insgef.
Schutzhäftlinge polit.	84				30				114
J.B.B.	388								388
Rassesch.	8				91				8
Schulungshäftlinge	2								2
Abschiebungshäftlinge	13		2		3				16
Vorbeugungsgef. Krim.	118				1				119
Total	229				11				240
Stand (morgens)	837				137				974
+ oder ÷	÷			+oder÷	÷				
Stand (abends)	837				137				974

Davon waren:	rückfäll. Schub-häftlinge	mehrm. in Schub.	im Revier	im Kranken-haus	Arrest	Einzel-haft	Trans-port	Urlaub	be-schäftigt	ver-fügbar	ins-gesamt
Schutzhäftlinge polit.	3	8	2			3	4			75	84
J.B.B.	4	43	1		3	2	1			381	388
Rassesch.										3	3
Schulungshäftlinge										2	2
Abschiebungshäftlinge							1			12	13
Vorbeugungsgef. Krim.			1			2	1			114	118
Total			2		1		3			223	229
Juden	2	4	1			2	5	1		128	137
Insgesamt	9	55	7		4	9	15	1		938	974

Lampepts

Auffeherin

Druck · E. Schulze, Dresden

Camp list accounting for prisoners, 21 June 1939, showing how Jewish prisoners (middle column, titled *Juden*) were always separated, even when listed in another category. Collection of MGR/SBG.

SS propaganda photograph of *Reichsführer* Heinrich Himmler reviewing female overseers at Ravensbrück, *SS-Propaganda-Album des Frauen-KZ Ravensbrück*, 1940–1941. Collection of MGR/SBG.

SS propaganda photograph of Ravensbrück concentration camp barracks, *SS-Propaganda-Album des Frauen-KZ Ravensbrück*, 1940–1941. Collection of MGR/SBG.

Exterior of prison cell building and crematorium. Note the heavy roller that the women prisoners were forced to pull in order to smooth the roads. Photo by Rochelle G. Saidel, 1995.

Interior of the crematorium at Ravensbrück. Collection of MGR/SBG.

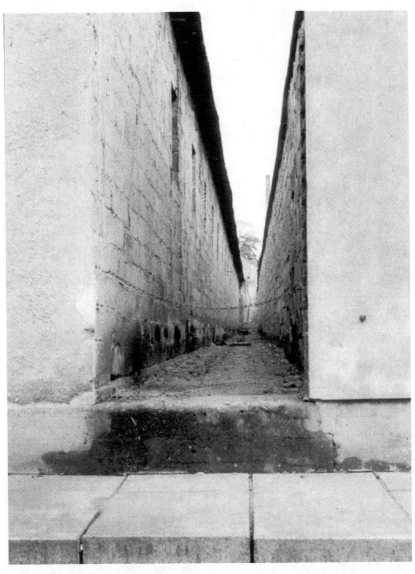

The shooting corridor at Ravensbrück. This was one means of murdering prisoners. Collection of MGR/SBG.

Corridor of the cellblock building, where women were held in solitary confinement. Collection of MGR/SBG.

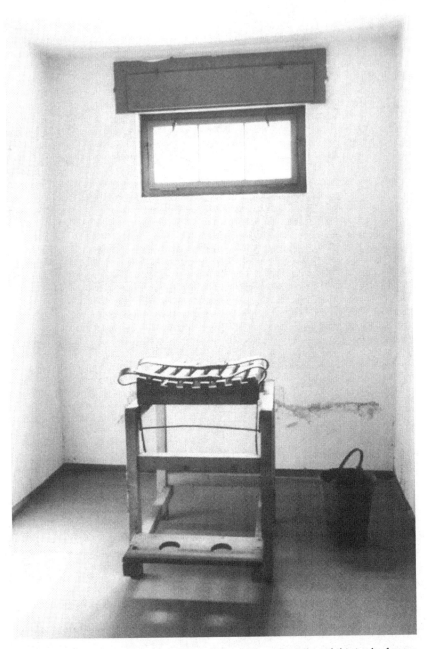

Rebuilt beating table used to torture the prisoners. Photo from the exhibit in the former cellblock building. Collection of MGR/SBG.

German Jewish political prisoner Olga Benário Prestes, murdered in 1942. *Frauen aus Ravensbrück, 1995.* Calendar, published by SBG/MGR, Edition Hentrich, 1994.

Austrian Jewish political prisoner Dr. Käthe Pick Leichter, murdered in 1942. *Frauen aus Ravensbrück, 1995* Calendar, published by SBG/MGR, Edition Hentrich, 1994.

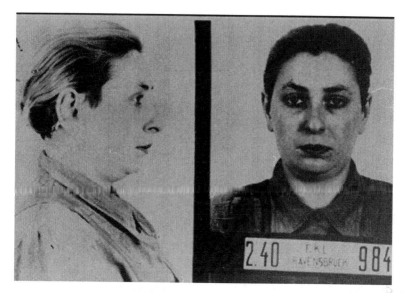

Nazi police file photograph of Jenny Sara Schermann (sometimes called Henny), a Jewish prisoner at Ravensbrück, who was accused of being a lesbian or "unnatural fornication" and condemned to death by gassing at Bernburg. Used with permission of Staatsarchiv Nürnberg (photo NO-3060), photo courtesy of the United States Holocaust Memorial Museum, Washington D.C.

Ravensbrück scrip that survivor Mina Lewkowicz Goldstein "earned" working as a slave laborer in the camp textile factory. Goldstein collection, United States Holocaust Memorial Museum, Washington, D.C.

SS propaganda photograph of Ravensbrück prisoners working outdoors. *SS-Propaganda-Album des Frauen-KZ Ravensbrück*, 1940–1941. Collection of MGR/SBG.

SS propaganda photograph of women prisoners working in a straw factory in Ravensbrück. *SS-Propaganda-Album des Frauen-KZ Ravensbrück*, 1940–1941. Collection of MGR/SBG.

Count Folke Bernadotte, head of the Swedish Red Cross. Photograph given to child survivor Sali Solomon Daugherty in Sweden. From the exhibit *Women of Ravensbrück: Portraits of Courage,* Florida Holocaust Museum, St. Petersburg, Florida.

Prisoners in last days of Ravensbrück, with Xs on their backs. From the exhibit catalogue, *Ich grüsse Euch als freier Mensch* (I greet you as a free person), 1995, edited by Sigrid Jacobeit, MGR/SBG. Courtesy of MGR/SBG (no known provenance).

Ravensbrück survivors at the time the camp was liberated by the Soviet army, end of April 1945, according to the United States Holocaust Memorial Museum, the *Federation National des Deportes et Internes Resistants et Patriots* (National federation of deportees, resistance prisoners, and patriots) in Paris, and *Suddeutscher Verlag*, a publisher in Munich. Because a caption that accompanied this photo taken by R. Karmen described it as "Ravensbrück, in Pomerania," perhaps this is one of the subcamps. Permission of Sovfoto/Eastfoto, New York.

Bozena Wohl, the sister of Margaret Wohl Guiness, shown with a nurse after her liberation to Sweden. Bozena died in Norköping, Sweden, of illness related to her suffering in Ravensbrück. Photo courtesy of Margaret Wohl Guiness.

Female guards and overseers employed by the SS at Ravensbrück on trial for their crimes, Hamburg, 1947. First row, *left to right*: Dorothea Binz, Margarete Mews, Greta Bösel, Eugenia Von Skene, and Carmen Maria Morey. Second row, *right*, Vera Salvequart. Collection of the *Dokumentationsarchiv des Österreichischen Widerstandes*, Vienna.

A proposed shopping center that was not allowed to open on the grounds of Ravensbrück, after an international protest. Photo by Rochelle G. Saidel, 1995.

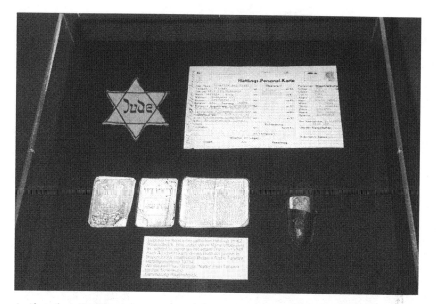

Artifacts from Jewish prisoners at the exhibit created for the 1995 ceremonies marking the fiftieth anniversary of Ravensbrück's liberation. Photo by Rochelle G. Saidel.

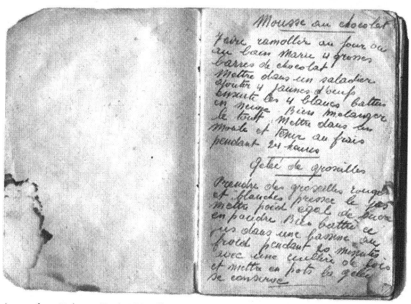

A page from Rebecca (Becky) Teitelbaum's recipe book, showing her recipe (in French) for chocolate mousse. She wrote the 110-page (4.5″ x 6″) book in Ravensbrück between 1944 and 1945. © Vancouver Holocaust Education Centre 2002, reproduced with permission of the Vancouver Holocaust Education Centre, Canada.

Cantor Estrongo Nachama of the Berlin Jewish community leads a memorial service at the fiftieth anniversary of Ravensbrück's liberation, 1995. Photo by Rochelle G. Saidel.

7

Women at Work

THE RECOLLECTIONS of Jewish women who were employed in the factories or had outdoor assignments provide a glimpse of the suffering and inner strength that accompanied their slave labor in Ravensbrück. The prime employer of Ravensbrück slaves was the Siemens electric company (known as *Siemens und Halske*), one of the foremost industrial exploiters of concentration camp inmate labor during the Nazi era and today one of the largest electric companies in the world.[1] Like other major German businesses throughout the greater Third Reich, Siemens used concentration camp prisoners to produce armaments and other merchandise for the war effort.

THE SIEMENS FACTORY

Siemens built a factory in a separate camp adjoining the main Ravensbrück one in 1942 and "hired" the women to make electrical components for V-1 and V-2 rockets. At first all of the slave laborers were marched the short distance to the factory every day and returned to the main camp after their shifts. However, by late 1944 Siemens had separate barracks for some of the prisoner-laborers, located next to the factory. Although conditions were supposedly somewhat better than in the main camp, the women in the Siemens auxiliary camp also suffered from hunger and inhuman conditions. Breakfast was artificial coffee, followed by bread and a big spoon of cabbage once a day. When a woman became ill, she was brought back to the main camp, usually murdered, and replaced.

95

Women on Their Way to Slave Labor at the Siemens Factory. Drawing by an unknown prisoner artist. Photo from the first Ravensbrück Camp Museum. Collection of MGR/SBG.

Margo Wohl Guiness

Margaret (Margo) Guiness, whose arrival from Budapest in August 1944 was detailed in the previous chapter, was among the survivors who told me about their slave labor for Siemens. Claiming to be older, Margo was only fourteen when she worked in the Siemens factory. "We worked on a very small component—electrical component," she said. "I understand that they used them for submarines. It took very nimble hands and very good vision, and all of this we had." She remembered how hard it was to alternate day and night shifts every week. "This was the most difficult, because by the time we were able to get accustomed to sleeping in the daytime, every week our shift changed," she said.

Margo's barrack was in the main camp. "A group of us, we would march [to the Siemens factory]," she said. "We had to sing on the way. I remember going on a route, and there was a lake. And then I remember seeing that church steeple, and I thought, 'My God, what kind of world is this, where people are praying while we are treated like that?'"[2] Margo was transferred to Bergen-Belsen in November 1944.

Basia Zajaczowska Rubinstein

Basia Zajaczkowska Rubinstein, another Siemens slave laborer, has unusual recollections because they were provided in two stages, nearly fifty years apart. In addition to the sketchy information she shared when I met her in 1995, I obtained the transcript of much more detailed testimony that she gave on 12 December 1945. When I met her at the fiftieth anniversary of the camp's liberation, she told me that she had worked at the Siemens factory. Born in Kielce, Poland, on 15 February 1926, Basia said that on 20 August 1942, twenty-one thousand Jews, including her family, were sent from there to Treblinka.

The Jews who were thirteen to twenty-five years old were sent to work rather than to Treblinka. Basia witnessed how younger children were put into an old house in town and shot, she said in 1995. She married Morris Rubinstein in the Kielce ghetto in November 1942, when she was only sixteen. From Kielce, Basia and her husband were taken to Pionki, a work camp; they hid in the forest when it was evacuated in July 1944. One day, while still in hiding, they heard dogs and Nazis. A Ukrainian soldier who went into the bushes to urinate saw Basia's feet when he bent down to pick up his hat. He said, *"Shalom,"* and then took them at gunpoint, she told me.

From the Pionki area, Basia was taken to Ravensbrück in October 1944 with other Jewish women. When they entered the camp, she hid her friend's four-year-old son, Michael Kaplan, under her skirt, because the boy's mother was hysterical, she recalled in 1995. In the camp, Basia worked with non-Jewish Polish women. She remembered many suicides by the German *Mischlinge,* women who were part Jewish. At one point the camp guards said they wanted "volunteers" for medical experiments. She saw those "volunteer" women when they returned, bleeding from the experiments; Basia was saved from them because she said she was Jewish. The experiments were performed only on Christian Polish women, she said.

Basia remembered people freezing and dying during the long roll calls, which could last from two until five o'clock in the morning if someone was missing. She worked both day and night shifts for Siemens. When the Red Cross arrived in April 1945, the women from the Siemens camp were brought back to the main camp. After about a week, the Polish Jews were told they could go to Sweden, and she left the camp on a Red Cross white bus on April 18.[3]

Four years after talking with Basia and her family at the camp memorial, I visited Lund University and discovered an interview with her (in Polish) conducted on 12 December 1945.[4] In her 1945 testimony soon after liberation, Basia gave many more details about Kielce, Pionki,

Ravensbrück, and Siemens. She also provided more information about the liquidation of the Pionki factory and her capture, although in this early testimony, she did not mention being discovered by the urinating Ukrainian.

"In July 1944 the front got nearer and we even heard explosions," she said to her 1945 interviewer. At this time there were no raw materials, and the work in the Pionki factory stopped. After a week with no food or water, her husband was among two hundred men chosen to carry out the liquidation of the factory, and the rest of the prisoners were sent to Auschwitz. "I hid in the toilet. I thought that my husband would return from the factory and we then would be together again," she said. "My husband did not return, but I managed to get to him. . . . We decided to run away. We escaped into a forest. After two weeks we were discovered and sent to Oranienburg. The men were left in Oranienburg, the women were sent to Ravensbrück. We were twenty-five people all together."

Upon arrival at Ravensbrück, Basia was given a shower, her hair was cut, and she received flimsy clothing but no underwear, and wooden clogs. She was designated as Number 72316. After a month in the main camp under "horrible conditions" with four women to a bed, Basia wanted to be transferred to a labor subcamp. "I thought it would be better in a [labor] camp," she said. "Most of all I wanted to get some clothing. It was cold and I had no underwear. In exchange for bread, I 'bought' myself underwear and stockings. I had not eaten any bread because I bartered it for clothing. The inspection lines were very long. Wind tore into my head. I had no hair. It was forbidden to wear a kerchief on the head—I was beaten for that." In December Basia was assigned to work in the Siemens factory and transferred to the adjacent barracks. She described the situation there:

> The camp was fenced with electric wires. It was a small camp, with four barracks. The fifth barrack housed washrooms and latrines. Hygienic conditions were bearable. We could wash up any time after work. The living blocks were all kinds of sizes. In the blocks there were two-tiered beds. Everyone received a bed, a sack stuffed with straw, and a blanket. The blocks were sufficiently clean. The food was better than at Ravensbrück. Initially we received thirty dkg [10.5 ounces] of bread, and later the rations were cut to eighteen dkg [6.3 ounces], but the soups were good enough, sufficient quality and clean.[5]
>
> We were roused at four in the morning, we received coffee, and at five A.M. was roll call. We started to work at six A.M. At noon we had a recess for lunch. We ate in the camp near the factory. At one P.M. we started to work until six P.M. At six P.M. there was again roll call, not too long, and we were free. There were also night shifts. Every two weeks we worked at night. The shift started at seven P.M. and ended at six A.M. At twelve midnight there was a half-hour recess. Night shifts were very

98

difficult because of insufficient light. We had to strain our eyesight. Overall the work was not heavy, [but] it demanded a lot of attention. It was precision work. A quota was demanded. Whoever did not produce the demanded quantity was punished. There were also awards but we did not use them. Supervisors watched over us during our work. We were not permitted to rest. If the female supervisor thought that we did not work hard enough, she would hit us.

This detailed report of Basia's work regime at Siemens, made within months of her liberation, confirms her own recollections and those of others offered some fifty years afterward. She also recalled the rigid rules for using the latrines, and the harshness of the SS supervisors. "They did not permit us to go to the toilet," she said. "There were certain hours assigned, twice a night we could go to the toilets in groups. This was a tragedy for us. As a result of cold weather the girls had bladder problems. Many had stomach problems." Basia also spoke of the supervisors. "The supervisors were not good toward us," she said. "They always criticized us that we did not work well despite all our efforts. The civilian supervisors had a better attitude toward us. Because of political changes they improved. They explained to us that they themselves were forced to work, they were also supervised, and they did not receive even enough food. The SS supervisors were the exact opposite. When things on the war front were not going well, they harassed us more."

In contrast to the treatment by the supervisors, Basia said that relations among the prisoners were good, despite their diverse backgrounds. "They were all nationalities, Dutch, Belgian, French, Czech, Polish, German and Jewish, Hungarian, Russian, Yugoslavian," she said. "German prisoners had privilege. One German woman, a [prisoner] block supervisor, had treated us badly."

While the rules of Ravensbrück stipulated that the women did not have to work on Sundays, Basia's testimony reveals that this was not always the case. "Sunday the factory did not work, but we worked in the commandant's garden, so that we never had a free day," she said. "The camp commandant was not terrible. Sometimes he listened to our complaints. He was also sometimes capricious. One Sunday while working in the commandant's garden one of the girls smiled to another. The camp commandant claimed she laughed at him." None of the prisoners' explanations resolved the situation, and they were all punished. "The whole camp did not receive food for one day and a half," she said. "The infraction of one prisoner brought punishments on the whole camp. Once when we went to wash our filthy hands during work, the supervisor reported us to the commandant and the whole camp was punished."

Basia confirmed that women in the Siemens camp "underwent a selection," and those no longer able to work were sent back to the main camp, most likely targeted for extermination. "They picked out older people that had injured legs and other disabilities," she said. "Or they were too weak to work. Those who had been selected out were sent to the crematorium in Ravensbrück. In Siemens we had no medical services. Only at the end, they established examinations for the not seriously sick. Seriously ill were shipped to Ravensbrück [the nearby main camp]."

One could feel the end of World War II approaching, according to Basia:

> In March there were noticeable changes in the camp. Work in the factory limped along. There were shortages of raw materials. There were murmurs about the approaching war front. On April first we were awakened during the night. We were let out of the [Siemens] camp and taken to Ravensbrück. In Ravensbrück it was chaos. There was no food. We received Red Cross parcels. We felt the end. The parcels did not do us much good; many got sick. We did not go to the factory anymore. On 24 April 1945 an order went out that all Polish Jewish women be registered. We were placed in a penal block. We were not given anything to eat. No toilets. We were beaten mercilessly during the inspection. We thought we'd be sent to the crematorium. Rumors went around that we'll be liberated. We were constantly harassed so much so that we did not have faith in anything.
>
> On April 26 we were led out of the penal block, the guards tore off our numbers and triangles, we were given Red Cross parcels. We were led out of the camp. We did not know where we were going. Outside the camp the white buses of the Swedish Red Cross were waiting for us. We were free. We did not believe it. We wanted to reassure ourselves. We wanted to talk to the driver and even at that last moment, the supervisors shouted that we were not allowed to talk to the drivers.

Basia was reunited with her husband after her recuperation in Sweden. They immigrated to the United States, settled in Lincolnwood, Illinois, and had two daughters, Joyce and Ida.

WORKING WITH TEXTILES

While the women who worked at the Siemens factory were forced to contribute to the war effort by producing electronic parts, other women at Ravensbrück slaved at less technical but nevertheless important war-related labor. As Ravensbrück was one of the Nazis' main depositories for confiscated clothing and furs, an industrial court in the rear of the camp included a factory for remodeling leather and textiles, a subsidiary of Dachau Enterprises. There was also a tailor shop that produced the prisoners' striped uniforms and uniforms for the SS, and fur coats for the *Waffen-SS* and the *Wehrmacht*. In another shop the prisoners wove carpets from reeds. The women usually worked for twelve hours a day, under conditions of extreme exploitation. Prisoners were beaten if their production was not considered sufficient. If an article of clothing was not sewn properly or a needle or machine broke, the guards often smashed the prisoners' heads onto the machines until blood flowed.

Mina Lewkowicz Goldstein

Mina Lewkowicz Goldstein, one of the women who worked in this industrial complex, was born in Lodz and now lives in Los Angeles, California.[6] She was taken directly to Ravensbrück from the Lodz Ghetto on 22 October 1911. She was allowed to take a bag of clothing from the ghetto and even brought some photos of her family wearing yellow stars on their garments. She had been one of 550 factory workers on a list in Lodz, which she describes as "something like Schindler's list." She was under the protection of Hans Biebow, chief of the *Gettoverwaltung* (ghetto administration), who was condemned to death and executed as a war criminal in 1947 (unlike Schindler, who was honored).[7] Mina's place on this list enabled her to stay in the Lodz Ghetto after its residents were deported to Auschwitz at the end of August 1944.

"Biebow was cunning. He understood the situation," according to Dr. Michal Unger, an expert on the Lodz Ghetto. "Biebow tried to make an alibi for himself. There were three groups of Jews left after the evacuation of the ghetto. He kept one group of about six hundred Jews to clean up the ghetto. The second group of some five hundred or more people were metal workers. They were sent to Auschwitz with their children, did not have to face a selection, and then were sent on."

The third group was evidently the one that Mina Goldstein was in. "In 1944 a Jewish engineer from Prague had developed a process for prefabricated houses, and a plant was established in the ghetto," Unger explained. "Biebow wanted to establish a factory for lightweight walls in Oranienburg, after the ghetto was liquidated."[8] According to Mina, Biebow decided to take her group to work at Oranienburg, and the women were sent first to nearby Ravensbrück for clearing, while the men spent three months building barracks for the group at Oranienburg.[9] The women were then supposed to rejoin the men at this special work camp.

Mina was twenty-two when she arrived at Ravensbrück with her mother, and she was first placed in the Gypsy barracks. Her first job was to cut down trees, and she said that the authorities wanted to make her the forewoman. However, she was frightened of the responsibility, and thought she was too young to be in charge. She heard they were assigning people to do sewing and thought that at least it would be warm in the clothing factory. This factory made new uniforms and gloves for the SS and military, and later also made uniforms for the prisoners. The factory where Mina worked was part of the complex of sewing and leather shops. Construction of this so-called *Industriehof* (industry courtyard) began in 1940, and it was then enlarged and housed the SS-owned *Gesellschaft für Textil- und Lederverwertung GmbH (Texled)*, a company for manufacturing textiles and leather. Women also worked in an SS company that belonged to the *DAW—Deutsche Ausrüstungwerke* (German equipment factory). During the second part of 1942, four thousand to five thousand women worked there. These workshops continued until 1945 and had departments for storage of confiscated goods, sewing, repairs, weaving, and making items from straw.[10]

Mina worked during the night shift in the textile and clothing company at Ravensbrück, which was in a separate attached camp with its own barracks, in the *Industriehof*. She said there were only nine Jewish girls and women among the hundreds of workers there. The slave laborers received special Ravensbrück "money" there, and she was able to save one of these rare "*Reichsmark,*" which she has donated to the United States Holocaust Memorial Museum. "All you could do with this money was buy some frozen vegetables such as kohlrabi from a barrel," she said. "It was cut in small pieces. If there were no vegetables available, the women kept the money—there was nothing else you could do with it."

Mina said she maintained a low profile in the *Industriehof,* and no one generally bothered her. She remembers, however, that there was a French Jewish woman whose job was to iron collars. An SS man repeatedly hit her in the face, and she answered him back, so he kept on beating her. The factory was heated and warm. The women on the night shift were given a half-hour break from work during the middle of the night, probably because the SS-auxiliary women who watched them needed a break. They went to the bathroom and were able to get hot water for washing themselves from the steam-table pipe. Mina took the water once a week so she and her mother could wash. In order to receive this water, the women had to give up one slice of bread, which, along with a slice of salami, was their entire meal.

At first her mother worked with her, but then there was a selection and her mother was sent back to the main camp. Mina didn't want to stay without her mother, but she did go back to the factory. Her mother came to visit her and stayed in bed with her during the day; the barrack *Älteste* then kicked her mother out. The women from her Lodz group were finally cleared to leave Ravensbrück for Oranienburg during the first part of February 1945, perhaps 8 February, according to Mina. She refused to go because her mother had not been cleared, and two days later her mother died of starvation. Mina was ultimately rescued to Sweden.

Olga Weiss Astor

Olga Astor, whose background and 1944 arrival at Ravensbrück were described earlier, worked with textiles in a different way at the camp, sorting clothing that the Nazis deposited there. Regarding the clothing-sorting operation, Olga described huge open fields that might have been pastures. "And they were piled mountains of clothes and shoes, toothpaste, everything [the Nazis] stole from other places, from other countries," she said.[11] "I mean, you were crawling on that, you know? And you had to separate or something. And some of the girls got the idea that, 'Well, this is a good thing. We could get dressed here. We could put on some warm clothes.' Because we just had a thin nothing, and this was December or November or October, and if you are emaciated, then it's very cold. . . . Some of the women thought that this would be a good opportunity. We can put some clothes on that we find, some sweaters, some mittens, something, and put the old clothes over it."

She said that some of the women left for work on the clothing hill looking very thin, and returned appearing to be much fatter. Olga, however, never put on any layers of clothing, because she had too much fear of being beaten. "I went out skinny and I came back skinny," she said. "But there were some kids who got toothpaste and then they put on some new clothing and made crosses in the back with the toothpaste [to imitate the requisite white Xs painted on the back of the prisoners' clothing]. You didn't fool them. You found shoelaces, and if you put shoelaces in your shoe, then they knew immediately that you stole them, because they took everything away from us. We didn't have toothpaste. We didn't have toilet paper . . . or a toothbrush or anything."

Olga's slave labor assignment was later changed to shoveling coal. "The coal was already on the ground, and we had to put it into those carts and push it on the railroad tracks," she said. "When they ran out of what work to give us, then we carried one mountain from here to there, and they beat us to *macht schnell, schnell, schnell, schnell* [make it fast, fast, fast, fast]."

WORKING OUTDOORS

Ester Weisz Grun

Ester (Eliz) Weisz Grun, who worked outdoors at the camp, described her beatings and extremely heavy slave labor in subfreezing weather. She arrived from Auschwitz in December 1944 and says of her time in Ravensbrück, that it "was one of the most horrible experiences I had to go through in my young age, and to be able to survive it, it's a miracle."[12]

She was born in Satoraljaujhely, Hungary on 13 March 1923 and raised in an Orthodox household by her parents, Herman Weisz and Regina Weider-Aushitz. Her mother and older sister were murdered when they arrived in Auschwitz in May 1944, but her younger brother survived Theresienstadt. Her father and her other brother were sent to a work camp in 1940, and she did not hear from them again until after World War II.

In April 1944 all of the Jews in her town were forced into a ghetto. "We were just pushed together the worst way, like sardines, and we just had to share with families whatever rooms there were available. There was no privacy," she said. The next month the Jews were "pushed into the cattle cars where the filthy, dirty horse manure, cow manure [were] on the floor inside of the wagons, and we just had to go in like animals, and we did not know where we are going. We were not told about that until we found out the big sign of Auschwitz, the gate of Auschwitz, the gate of hell." Ester never saw her mother or sister again. She remained at Auschwitz-Birkenau until December 1944 when she and about one thousand young women were put into cattle trains; they traveled for several days without food or water, night and day, without knowing where the train was going.

Ester's recollections about entering Ravensbrück were similar to those reported by Basia Rubinstein and other women who arrived in late 1944. However, in addition to the assignment of numbers and flimsy, inappropriately sized clothing, the shearing and shaving, and the showers, Ester mentioned routine slapping that began with her arrival and continued afterward:

> There was a very tall, like a middle-aged woman, very tall. She must have been probably like five feet, ten or eleven inches, singly going beating every one of us. Like an animal. You cannot imagine how a woman—this is not an SS—this was somebody chosen who perhaps was trained how to beat up every one of us. Slapping, I never forget. That room was dark, because we arrived at night.
>
> Well, we were pushed like herrings together, and this woman is just going to every head, slapping, and I see the stars as she is slapping me, she was so strong and powerful. We were crying. We were screaming and crying. It hurt us. It was painful the way she was slapping our face. She was the only one who went through over a thousand heads, a thousand people. Slapping. For hours we heard nothing but slap, slap, slap, left to right. Like an animal, like a wild beast. In that concentration camp, in Ravensbrück, there were a lot of Gentile Polish people, and she was one of them. She was not Jewish.

Even after her experiences in Auschwitz, Ester could not comprehend the manic cruelty of the woman she described:

> She could have killed us, it's like I said, you know, like quietly, [to] whoever stood next to me—we became very close with a few of them who

were very close to each other. I said, "Why is this woman doing this? Why is she hurting us so terribly?" We were silent, and the only thing you heard in the dark was slapping, slapping both sides. She was an expert in slapping. The very first night, this is the way they welcomed us in Ravensbrück. Ravensbrück was another Auschwitz, another hell that I sometimes, when I think about it and everything is coming back to me, I almost feel that Ravensbrück was worse than Auschwitz. The SS were animals, and the people who were trained to be like an SS, and they had authority. They were beating us and kicking us. Every SS woman and every SS man was specially trained in that area of beating. They were so abusive. They humiliated us like the worst way—for no reason.

Ester said that at other times the women were beaten over the head in groups of about two hundred by SS-auxiliary women, using leather clubs that were approximately two inches wide, two inches thick, and fifteen inches long. "This was a routine," she said. "This was the treatment every single day by them. They would just separate a couple hundred of us. And another one would separate a couple hundred and put them into another room." She described the beatings, which took place after the morning roll call, or *Appell.*

"Then the SS would say, 'that room,' and we would go into that room, and then they had their kick," she said. "They were sick people, and the only thing they were interested [in was], how much can they beat the life out of us. I remember one morning, because I was tall enough, if you were shorter you had a better chance not to be beaten up that badly, because you were sort of lost in between the taller people. But I was tall already, like five feet, five inches, and I got the beating practically daily." One day Ester collapsed during the ordeal. "She hit my head so badly that I got a concussion," she recalled. "I was between all my people on the floor, and they just let me be down there. I shouldn't get more beating, until I regained consciousness, and then we got asked to get out."

In addition to beatings, Ester described other kinds of suffering in the barrack. "It was horrifying. We were on top of each other," she said. "But we were pressed together so very, very tightly at night for sleeping, and you would see the mice and the rats that were horrifying. The filth, the disease, it was covering all of us, and this is why in Ravensbrück we had so much death, because the people could not survive. The conditions were absolutely horrifying. Everybody got sick, except me. There was no such a thing, nursing or hospitalization. They just died right next to me daily, and at night, you know, you wake up and you will see a dead body right next to me. The following night it happens the same thing, because of the horrifying disease and the condition. The disease spread, it was all in the air."

She also remembered the meager rations the women received, even after a day of hard labor. "In the evening when we were taken back to

our room and we had to gather in line, and we got a little soup, a little
lukewarm water and maybe three or four tiny vegetables would swim in
that little mug, and that was our main dish," she said. "In the morning
we would get this terrible bun, slice of bread, which must have been like
a quarter of an inch thick and maybe two inches wide and three inches
in length, and that was our whole meal for the day." Ester described her
grueling outdoor slave labor:

> In Ravensbrück I had to work very, very hard. I was chosen—after the
> beating, I was chosen once for a few days to cut [a] huge tree into logs
> for firewood. Just by taking a guess, this tremendous tree must have
> been at least thirty inches in diameter. I had a partner, and we were
> given a very long blade of saw, and I can't even tell you how long it
> took us to really cut this big tree through to make it into certain length,
> like twenty inches, and then cut them up for firewood. This was [wear-
> ing] like one layer of clothes and [having] no food, outside probably
> thirty-five below zero, the month of January, because all concentration
> camps were created in the forest, far away from the cities that nobody
> should know where we are existing. And I did that for a few days.
>
> If they would beat me, then they would lose me. I wouldn't be able
> to do anything. So they just let us do whatever we were able to accom-
> plish, and believe me, we made sure that we followed up, not to mention
> that by then we don't have much strength. We were frozen, because it's
> bitter cold outside, and just one layer of clothes on our body didn't mean
> too much, but we survived it.

Ester always worked outside, and one task she was forced to do was
moving bodies from one place to the other. "I had this horrifying job one
day that I was chosen to take out the beautiful lady who died next to
me," she recalled. "She was a doctor, and she didn't live long. I was
chosen to take her out, which was very, very hard on me, but I had to
do it. I had no choice, and another girl, we were told to take her into
the cellar. There was a cold basement where they were collecting the dead
bodies, and I took this beautiful lady into the cellar with one of my
friends." She spoke more about her work moving the bodies. "From there
on I was chosen many days to remove the dead bodies," she said. "The
two of us, because a dead body is a dead body, and it's very heavy. There's
no way one person can do it. So we did it, the two of us, and then SS
would arrive with a truck. We had to fill in the truck with this beautiful
dead body that I never will forget. They were taken on top of the mountains. In the forest there was a huge hole dug up, and that's where we
had to put the body."

In addition to cutting down trees and carrying dead bodies, Ester
sometimes had to remove unused vegetables with a huge wagon. The

vegetables were taken from the kitchen, and dumped in the forest. However, Ester was then assigned another task, which she described:

> And then one night I was taken for *Nachtschicht* work, which is a night work. You would never guess what it is. Even myself, I still can't believe what I had seen. The Germans took everything out from every Jewish home that you have to visualize, whatever value was in a home, and that we left there. Here we are, a few of us were chosen to be taken outside in the middle of the freezing night, and there were hundreds and hundreds of open trains, wagons, and in these wagons they had the most magnificent Persian rugs by the thousands, not hundreds, but thousands.
>
> Loaded, and this is all open, so you have to visualize that with my poor body, with another one, we were chosen, two girls, that we have to pull out of the snow and heavy icing, because daily, daytime, the ice and snow would melt, overnight it's freezing cold and it would freeze, we have to pull these rugs one by one out of the wagon. They had enormously huge storage, and we had to make sure that every rug that we pulled out of the icy snow we were rolling it up and put them into storage on top of each other. Night. We were chosen only doing this at night. Oh, many, many nights I did it. Just rugs. And rugs, I don't know if you can visualize the weight of a size of a rug like perhaps fourteen by twenty, or sixteen by twenty-five [feet]. They were all big sizes. There was a very well-built storage for it, yes. . . . We had to roll them up inside and then put them on top of each other. You couldn't protest.

Meanwhile the daily beatings continued, and Ester recalled them in detail. "You know, I'll never forget where, with the beating, that you should see how we looked after the beating," she said. "Most of us got a concussion, and when we were looking at each other—there were no mirrors to see my face, how I look, but I looked at the one who stood next to me and I'm looking at you. I see her, her name is Rebecca. Rebecca had black eyes, and up to here, she was black and blue. She was swollen, the face was swollen like that. She looked at me, she says to me the same thing. She says, 'Ester, you are black. Your eyes up to your nose down to here, blood-clotted.' And my head was swollen. I felt the pressure, the terrible pressure all through my head."

Raised to be a very observant Jewish young woman, Ester prayed in Ravensbrück. "Before I went to bed, before I closed my eyes, or in the morning, or when I would stand out under the sky, under the stars, I would pray. I would talk to God and ask Him for help, and many, many times, most every single day," she remembers. "I said to God, 'If you see what goes on here in this terrible concentration camp with these horrible Nazis, the way they are treating us, just look down and do something.' . . . I kept my religion. I was praying every day." One day Ester's prayers were answered: "Then finally one morning, when we had the head count, there was one SS woman and one SS man who pulled out from the line sixteen young girls, and I was among them. . . . So all of a sudden these two people were taking charge of us. This huge big iron gate opened up, and we left Ravensbrück behind us."

Ester believes it was a miracle that she was able to get out of Ravensbrück alive. "God had given me the chance to be removed from the horror, to be removed from hell and taken to another concentration camp, which was also hell, but somehow whatever I had to do physical at least I was able to do," she said. She was transferred to Meuselwitz, a little-known subcamp south of Leipzig.

Ester's description of her bruised and swollen face, like the other women's recollections of the suffering they endured during their slave labor, is a reflection of the fact that the women were not spared harsh working conditions because they were female. They may have been assigned specific tasks, such as delicate handwork in the Siemens factory and sewing work in the textile industries, because the Nazis thought that women could do these jobs better than men. However, the assignments were not given because the work was lighter than men's labor. On the contrary, their work was extremely difficult. It included heavy physical labor, job-related injuries, and cruel treatment by guards and overseers, and was sometimes overwhelming to the point of death.

8

Gemma LaGuardia Gluck:
A Jewish American

ATEGORIZED as a special prisoner in Ravensbrück, Gemma LaGuardia Gluck was exempt from the strenuous slave labor required of the other women. She was born and died an American citizen but was officially Hungarian during her time in the camp. As the sister of then New York City Mayor Fiorello LaGuardia, she was incarcerated as a potential exchange hostage. Gemma was Hungarian because she had been required to relinquish her U.S. citizenship when she married her Hungarian Jewish husband, Herman, in 1908. She regained her citizenship from the United States after she was liberated and learned that her husband had been murdered by the Nazis.[1]

GEMMA'S MEMOIR

Gemma wrote a memoir about her experience in Ravensbrück and its aftermath soon after her return to the United States in 1947. However, it remained unpublished until S. L. Shneiderman sought her out in her Long Island City, New York apartment in 1961. A prolific journalist and author in English, Yiddish, and Polish since the 1920s, Shneiderman had returned to New York after covering the Adolf Eichmann trial that year in Jerusalem. Eichmann, the Chief of the Jewish Office of the Gestapo who implemented the "Final Solution of the Jews," was sentenced to death on 2 December 1961 in Jerusalem for crimes against the Jewish people and crimes against humanity, and executed in Israel on 21 May 1962.

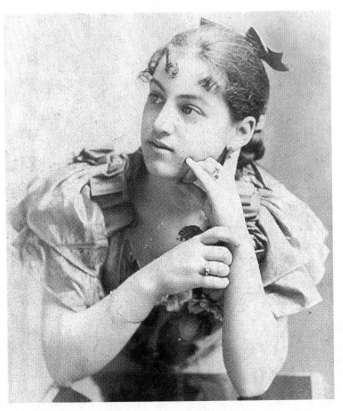

Gemma LaGuardia Gluck as a young girl. Collection of The LaGuardia and Wagner Archives, LaGuardia Community College/The City University of New York

In connection with the trial, Shneiderman had been given a document about Gemma and her imprisonment in Ravensbrück. When he discovered that Gemma was still alive he visited her; she shared with him her memoir. By then she was almost eighty and partially paralyzed from a stroke. With Shneiderman's able editorial assistance, the memoir was expanded and then published as a small book later that year.[2] On 1 November 1962, Gemma died at Elmhurst Hospital in Queens, New York. Shneiderman, whose impressive writing career spanned more than sixty years, died in 1996 at the age of ninety.

While I had no personal connection with Gemma, I did coincidentally talk with Shneiderman about another project. He was involved for many years with Jewish communal issues, including the effort to create a Holocaust memorial in Riverside Park in 1946. I spoke with him in 1990 when I was writing my doctoral dissertation (later a book) on efforts to memo-

rialize the Holocaust in New York City.[3] At that time he gave me impor-
tant leads on where to find documentation on the early proposals for
Riverside Park. Later, after I learned of his participation as the editor of
Gemma's memoir, I visited with his widow, Eileen (Hala), and their son,
Dr. Ben Shneiderman in Ramat Aviv, Israel. Eileen recalled meeting
Gemma while her husband was working on the book, and her comments
about this firsthand contact made Gemma real and alive for me.[4]

Many people are not aware that Mayor Fiorello LaGuardia and his
sister Gemma had a Jewish mother. Gemma was born in New York City
in 1881, the daughter of Irene Coen, a Jewish immigrant from Trieste,
and Achille Luigi Carlo LaGuardia, a Christian from Foggia, near Naples.
Her parents had married in Italy a year earlier and sailed to New York
on their wedding day. While Gemma was never a practicing Jew, she was
Jewish both by *Halachic* (Jewish religious) and Nazi standards.[5] Gemma's
brother Fiorello, a year younger than she, became famous as the mayor
of New York City from 1934 until 1945. He was also a U.S. congressman
from 1917 through 1919 and from March 1923 to March 1933, and
held many other distinguished public positions. Gemma's relationship to
her illustrious brother was both the cause of her arrest by the Nazis and
the reason she was able to survive her ordeal.

The LaGuardia family moved around quite a bit within the United
States as the children were growing up, because Achille was a bandmaster
in the U.S. Army. The family also traveled to Europe during Achille's six-
month furloughs every three years, and when he retired he decided the
family would live in Trieste. He opened a tourist hotel in nearby Capo
d'Istria, and there Gemma studied Italian and German. After Achille died
in 1904, Fiorello, then the American Consul's agent for immigration in
Fiume, brought the family to live there. He and younger brother Richard
then left for America, and Gemma and her mother remained in Italy.[6]

GEMMA IN BUDAPEST

Gemma taught English in their apartment, and one of her students, Herman Gluck, eventually asked her to marry him. The ceremony was performed by a rabbi "out of respect for my husband's religion," she wrote.[7]
After a short time, Herman, Gemma, and Gemma's mother, Irene, moved
to Budapest, where Gemma gave birth to two daughters, Yolanda in 1911
and Irene in 1918.[8] The family had a comfortable home and enjoyed a
good life.

This good life, which had been somewhat affected by the onset of
World War II, changed abruptly after the Nazis fully occupied Hungary
in March 1944. Hitler had issued a secret order on 12 March, explaining
the need to invade Hungary, and then on 15 March invited Hungarian

Regent Miklós Horthy for a discussion on 18 March outside of Salzburg. Even before Horthy returned to Budapest on 19 March, German forces had invaded Hungary without firing a shot. The Special Operational Commando Hungary, previously organized by Adolf Eichmann in Mauthausen concentration camp, arrived in Budapest on the same day to implement the deportation of Hungary's almost eight hundred thousand Jews. A Central Jewish Council was formed as soon as the Germans arrived, and all other Jewish organizations were outlawed. Ernst Kaltenbrunner, head of the *Reichssicherheitshauptamt—RSHA* (the Reich's Main Security Office), placed two Hungarian known anti-Semites, László Endré and László Baky, as chief aides to Minister Andor Jaross for issues related to the Jews.

The first major effect on the Gluck household was that Herman lost his position at the Allgemeine Credit Bank, because he was a Jew. On 31 March an order was issued that Hungarian Jews had to wear yellow badges as of 5 April. After a 7 April meeting held in the Ministry of the Interior, orders were sent to prepare for deportation of the Jews. The some 185,000 Jews of Budapest, about twenty-five percent of the country's Jewish population, were not included in this first stage of deportation to Auschwitz. By 9 July, 445,402 Jews had been deported from the other areas of the country, including the suburbs of Budapest.

Within Budapest a census was ordered on 3 May, in preparation for subsequent deportations. Then, on 15 June, the Ministry of Interior ordered the Jews to leave their apartments and move into those marked with yellow stars. Horthy tried to halt deportations in July, and on 25 August, Eichmann's effort to renew them was prevented both by Horthy and by an order from Himmler. Nevertheless, some deportations were carried out in September. Horthy was forced to resign on 15 October, after a coup by the Hungarian right wing aided by the Germans. Ferenc Szálasi, head of the anti-Semitic Arrow Cross, became prime minister and remained until the Red Army conquered Hungary. The Russians entered Budapest in mid-January 1945 but did not completely drive out the Germans until early spring.

At the time of the 15 October 1944 coup there were nearly two hundred thousand Jews living in Budapest, and Eichmann returned two days later to begin massive deportations. The first group of twenty-five thousand set out on a death march on 8 November, marching toward the Austrian border and away from the approaching Russian troops. Many of those Jews not sent on death marches were placed in hard labor battalions, building fortifications. By the time Hungary was liberated in early April 1945, some 119,000 Jews remained in Budapest.[9]

This brief background and chronology of the deportation of Hungarian Jews clearly indicates that the case of Gemma LaGuardia Gluck was not "routine." While some Jews were arrested in Budapest earlier, the masses of Budapest Jews were not deported until Eichmann returned in October. The stories of four Jewish women's deportations before October in Budapest were recounted in chapter 6. Margo Guiness and her sister, suspected as possible spies and not proven Jewish, was arrested in June 1944 in Budapest, and Olga Astor and her sister were deported from a ghetto house in September of that year. However, Gemma was arrested even earlier, before there were mass roundups in the capital or the Ministry of Interior had ordered the Jews to leave their apartments and move into those marked with yellow stars.

On 12 May 1944, Hungarian officers arrived at her Budapest home with orders from the SS to search for an undetermined "suspicious object." For three hours they tore the house apart, finally revealing they were looking for a short-wave radio transmitter. Their excuse for the search was that Gemma was allegedly communicating via such a transmitter with her brother, Fiorello, in New York City. They finally left, after stealing all the provisions Gemma had stocked in the pantry.

On 7 June 1944, when Jews outside Budapest were being deported but the Jews in the capital had not yet been ordered to move to specially designated buildings in the city, Gemma LaGuardia Gluck was arrested by four German officers.[10] She was told she would be interviewed at the police station and could then return home, and her husband asked for and received permission to accompany her. She thought the arrest might have been related to an article in a local Nazi newspaper a few days earlier, that asked how the Hungarians could permit the sister of Mayor LaGuardia, "Hitler's greatest enemy," to live in Budapest.[11]

However, her case had been discussed at much higher levels. A document submitted at the trial of Eichmann in Jerusalem in 1961 by Gideon Hausner, the attorney general of the state of Israel, was written by Eberhardt von Thadden, Nazi Foreign Office expert on Jewish affairs, and addressed to the German Legation in Budapest. The document reported on his efforts at a meeting with Eichmann in Budapest on 23 May 1944 to persuade him not to send Gemma to an extermination camp but instead hold her as a hostage.[12] A letter dated 14 July 1944 to von Thadden from the office of the Chief of the *Sicherheitspolizei und des Sicherheitsdienstes—SD* (Security Police and Security Service of the SS) clearly states that "Gemma Gluck is the sister of Mayor LaGuardia in New York," and "at the instruction of the *Reichsführer* [Himmler]" she was brought to Ravensbrück "as a political hostage." She is described as Jewish, a "first-degree *Mischling* [product of a mixed Jewish-non-Jewish marriage] by race," and married to a Jew.[13]

The couple were first taken from their Pest home to a prison in Buda and placed in separate cells for five days. They were then put into a second-class train compartment, heading for an unknown destination and escorted by two SS officers. Herman had correctly noted that they were on a train to Vienna, where they arrived late at night. A second train took them to Linz, and from there they were brought to Mauthausen concentration camp on 16 June. After about a week at this location, Gemma was informed that she could no longer stay at a men's camp, and she was again taken to Linz. From there, she was sent to Berlin on 29 June, accompanied by two guards. After she was registered at the Gestapo prison on Prince Albertstrasse, she was driven to Ravensbrück on 30 June 1944.[14]

GEMMA IN RAVENSBRÜCK

Like other survivors who arrived at the camp before its overcrowded and deteriorated last months, Gemma recalled that the approach was "pleasant and picturesque," with flower beds, "dark patches of pine woods and a calm blue lake." However, "the landscape changed suddenly as the high concrete walls of the camp and its barbed-wire fence loomed on the horizon."[15] And like other survivors, she described her terrifying entrance routine: showering, exchanging her clothing for an ill-fitting uniform and shoes with wooden soles, receiving her number (44139) and color-coded triangle, and being assigned to Block Twenty-four, the quarantine block. Her special status soon separated her from the other women, and she remained in the quarantine block for only six days, rather than the requisite month.

On 4 July, the camp commander ordered her taken to Block Two, which, along with Block One, was considered an "elite" block. She was told she could thank her brother for her status as a *Sonderhäftling,* or special prisoner. While she was given the same terrible food that all prisoners received, her privileges exempted her from working twelve-hour shifts and allowed her to have a bed to herself and daily one-hour afternoon rest periods. Her daily ration consisted of a breakfast and supper of black coffee and a piece of "terrible black bread which many times had great holes gnawed in it by rats," and a dinner of turnips cooked with potato peelings.[16] During the early months of her arrest the women also received imitation honey or marmalade, and a potato "cheese" and a piece of sausage once a week, but during the last months, they received only one quarter of a loaf of bread. At the end, this bread had to be divided among five or six women, rather than four.

Although Gemma was not required to work twelve-hour shifts at hard labor, she had two jobs at Ravensbrück. She was appointed the supervisor for receiving packages for her block, mostly Red Cross packages sent to non-Jewish French, Polish, and Czech prisoners. In addition, she volunteered to serve as a dining table supervisor, or *Tischälteste*. Although the tables were generally arranged according to nationality, she was granted permission to choose an international group of women to sit at her table. She had thirty-four women from twelve different countries, including Russia, Czechoslovakia, Poland, Norway, Yugoslavia, Italy, France, and Hungary. The women also practiced several religions, and included twelve Jehovah's Witnesses. They ate in two shifts, with the laundry workers eating at noon and the office workers arriving half an hour later. Gemma's job was to divide the bread and soup into thirty-four equal portions, and to clean the dishes and cupboards. She was also required to make a monthly inventory of the women's clothing. She said she did the work with love for her "children," and they called her *Mutti,* the German term of endearment for "mother."[17]

On 7 April 1945, a week before she was sent away from Ravensbrück, Gemma was appointed to hand out the Red Cross food packages that had arrived from Canada. For the first time, Jewish women were included in the distribution. Gemma recalled that "at times I thought my heart would burst within me to see these women in such condition, ill, thin, dressed in rags, some were like walking skeletons, some the shadows of beautiful women, some so weak that when I handed them the five-pound packages they fell to the ground."[18]

Gemma's relatively unrestricted movement as a special prisoner gave her the opportunity to serve as a witness to events in Ravensbrück. "When I entered the camp, I thought to myself that some day I must describe all these horrors for the whole world to know how these women had suffered," she wrote. "Therefore, without arousing suspicion, I went everywhere and looked at all that was possible and listened to what was happening. . . . I purposely went to see a woman after her first beating. I'll never forget this scene and I didn't have the courage or strength to see her after her second or third beating."[19] According to her observations, "the Jewish women had the worst and dirtiest work to do. Their block was the most unhealthy and dirtiest, with no electric lights. They were treated like animals and not like human beings."

Gemma's private bed near a window in Block Two also gave her the opportunity to observe the crematorium. "As I could sleep little, I watched the grim flaming smoke pouring out of the chimneys of the crematory," she recalled. "And oh, the terrible odor. We could force our eyes shut, but we could not keep the stench of death away from our nostrils. When we were awakened at four A.M., the first thing we saw was the flaming smoke, the first thing we were aware of was the smell."[20]

Gemma's special status kept her from being condemned in a selection during the first few days of April 1945. All of the women had to participate barefoot in a special roll call, and doctors from Berlin examined the prisoners to see which ones were too sick or weak to walk. This was in preparation for an anticipated death march from the camp as the Allies approached. A woman in her sixties, Gemma was very old by concentration camp terms and most likely could not have survived had she not been a special political hostage. Evidently the Berlin doctors had not been apprised of her privileged status, and she was required to walk in a line in front of the doctors. She, along with many others, did not pass inspection and was selected to be sent to the gas chamber. However, her block overseer spoke to Fritz Suhren, the commander of the camp, reminding him that she was the sister of New York City's Mayor LaGuardia. Thus, she was saved, and wrote: "The camp personnel director told me afterward that I was kept from the gas chamber because they were fearful that some harm would come to the Germans in New York in reprisal."[21]

During her time in Ravensbrück, one of Gemma's greatest worries was the fate of the other members of her family—her husband, daughter, son-in-law, and baby grandson. She did not learn until a few days before her liberation that her daughter, Yolanda Gluck Denes, and her grandson, Richard, had been in the camp since August 1944. Yolanda and the baby, just five months old when he arrived, had been kept in solitary confinement in a cell on the other side of Block One. Yolanda was never allowed to see or speak to other prisoners, and she had no idea that Gemma was also there.

In late spring 1945 a prisoner who worked in the personnel office told Gemma that she had seen a record of a Hungarian woman and her baby son who were being kept incommunicado in the camp, and the description matched that of her daughter. Soon afterward, another prisoner showed her a receipt for a Canadian Red Cross package, signed by Yolanda Denes. At the sight of the signature, Gemma screamed and fainted. A few days later, Kommandant Suhren sent for Gemma and asked her if she knew a woman named Yolanda Denes. She replied that Yolanda was her daughter, but protected her informant by not revealing that she knew she was among the prisoners. On the afternoon of 14 April 1945, Suhren brought mother and daughter together. They were told they could embrace each other and that they were free to stay together. The next day they were to be sent to Berlin, probably to be exchanged as hostages, but the Russians arrived in the city before this could happen.

GEMMA'S LIBERATION

At 3:30 A.M. on 15 April, Gemma, Yolanda, and now fourteen-month-old Richard were taken out of Ravensbrück. The baby's head was so wobbly that he could not support himself to sit up. He was unable to grasp anything with his hands, and he had no teeth. "My first thought was: 'where am I going to bury this baby? He won't live,'" Gemma wrote.[22] Even as the family went through the Ravensbrück gate, Gemma feared that, like countless others, they would be shot from behind. However, they were allowed to leave and then taken to Berlin in a second-class train compartment.

Their plight was far from over; they were brought to the Gestapo prison on Prince Albertstrasse and put into a cold basement room in solitary confinement. Their only food was from the Red Cross packages they had brought with them, and they had to suffer through nightly air raids and crowded, damp bomb shelters. After five days, they were taken to another prison on Kaiserdamm, in the Charlottenburg section of Berlin. When the Russian soldiers entered the city a few days later, the prison doors were thrown open and all of the prisoners, including Gemma and her family, were freed. "May God forgive me," she wrote, "but at that tremendous moment I rather would have remained within the prison walls than to get our freedom in such a manner."[23] She and her daughter had no money, no identity papers, and no idea where to turn for help.

After spending eleven days and nights in an air raid shelter, they were able to come out on 2 May 1945, the day after the Russians conquered Berlin. The three of them were in terrible condition, and they were invited to stay for a while in the damaged home of a woman who had been in the shelter. The mayor of Charlottenburg then discovered their identity and invited them to his home, where they had much more luxurious surroundings. However, Gemma realized after a few weeks that the mayor and his wife were keeping her as a hostage. The Russians had dismissed the mayor from his position, and the couple wanted to use Gemma to reach the American zone and influence the Americans to protect them. They tried to force Gemma and her family to flee Berlin with them, but she insisted on staying until she found out about her husband and her son-in-law.

Gemma and her family moved to the home of the Taroschowitz family, where they were helped by the Anti-Fascist Society that had been organized to help concentration camp survivors. She was interviewed on radio about her experiences at Ravensbrück, and she asked—to no avail—on the program if anyone knew the whereabouts of her husband or son-in-law. When British, and then American, troops entered Berlin, Gemma was able to get a message to the American authorities, asking them to inform her brother that she was there. She was almost immediately overwhelmed by help from American officers, soldiers, and news reporters. A U.S. Army captain, Kathryn Cravens, arranged for her to make a radio broadcast to New York and to speak with her brother via the radio. Mayor LaGuardia promised he would do everything he could to bring them to the United States, but that he could not make exceptions and her daughter would have to wait her turn in the immigration quota.

Gemma wrote to Fiorello from Berlin on 15 July 1945, telling him that she was living in a "good room" and that the American Red Cross had contacted her. She asked him to "try to find our husbands and get us soon over to the United States of America (but I should like to come with a ship and not with an air-plane as I fear my heart is too weak and I think a sea-voyage would do me good)." She did not provide details of her ordeal, stating that, "I don't want to write about what we went through, this I shall tell you all when we shall be together." Writing of her grandson, she added: "Richard is a real sweet and good baby. He was the one who kept us alive, as I can assure you in one year's imprisonment one got such moments where one lost courage and the thoughts of that baby kept up my spirit."[24]

Gemma and Yolanda stayed in Berlin for months with no news about their husbands or their immigration status. Corresponding with Harvey Gibson, president of Manufacturers Trust Company in New York, Fiorello sent Gemma money and checked on her through the American Red Cross.[25]

GEMMA'S RETURN TO THE UNITED STATES

On 31 October 1945, Fiorello wrote to Gemma via the Red Cross: "This is the first opportunity I have had to get a letter to you through proper legal channels. The regular mail is not yet opened from the United States to Germany, hence I could not write to you and I would not do anything to violate the law." He expressed his "anxiety" for Gemma's "welfare," but made it clear that he would not use his influence to do anything extraordinary to help her get to the United States. He wrote:

> Your situation is extremely difficult. No exceptions can be made. If any different treatment were applied to you, it would cause hundreds of thousands of demands for the same treatment. The publicity which you obtained [on the radio] and the fact that I might be known, makes it all the more difficult. But let me repeat, your case is the same as that of hundreds of thousands of displaced people.
>
> I will provide for you and do the very best that conditions will permit. You must be patient. . . . You have lost your citizenship, therefore that is something that cannot be remedied. Notwithstanding, out of kindliness, help has been given to you and will continue to be given to you. . .
>
> I learn with a great deal of disappointment that displaced nationals in Germany cannot be sent anywhere. I am trying my best to have you sent either to Sweden or England or Portugal or Italy. There are many insurmountable obstacles. Again, if they do it for one they will have to

do it for hundreds of thousands. I will try my best. I will then be able to provide for you and you can get an apartment, and of course, living conditions will be so much better.

As to your returning to the United States, I am doing all I can, but I cannot get Yolanda and her child in. You do not want to leave them alone. Unless the law changes, this may continue for some time. If it can be done, it will be done.

He concludes the letter by expressing his belief that she should be "realistic" that her husband and son-in-law are probably not alive, although "there is always hope until definite information is received." He acknowledges that conditions are terrible in Germany, and that he will do his best to either get her to another country or to continue to provide for her in Germany. He then adds: "Be very careful in the statements that you make."[26]

True to his word, Fiorello managed to obtain an invitation to Denmark for Gemma and her family. When he could not reach his sister through normal channels, he carefully asked General Dwight D. Eisenhower to pass on his letter to her informing her of the good news. He wrote to Eisenhower:

> I have found some difficulty in getting a letter to my sister. If no violation of rules is involved, I would greatly appreciate it if the enclosed could be delivered to her. Of course, you are free to open same. I can assure you that there is no violation of any existing rules in the contents.
>
> I received word from the Danish Minister that arrangements have been made for Gemma's entrance into Denmark. I am very grateful for this. However, if it is possible to get her into the Italian Section of Switzerland or into any English speaking country, it would be much better because of the language.[27]

The letter from Fiorello to Gemma explained that he was sending her and her family to Denmark where they could arrange for visas and other permits, and then travel to New York as private passengers. Since he had been appointed the head of UNRRA (United Nations Relief and Rehabilitation Administration), he did not want his family to be among the first displaced persons entering the United States. Around the time that the arrangements for Denmark were being finalized in April 1946, Gemma learned that her husband, Herman, had been killed in the hospital at Mauthausen. Another prisoner, Dr. Joseph Podlaha, testified at a war crimes trial that he had witnessed the death of Herman Gluck, the brother-in-law of the mayor of New York. They then found out that Gemma's son-in-law had died of starvation at Mauthausen.

In May 1946 Gemma and her family moved to Copenhagen to wait until their papers were in order. Fiorello visited them when he made a

UNRRA tour in September. Although Gemma had relinquished her U.S. citizenship to marry Herman in 1908, she easily regained it after his death was certified. Yolanda, however, had only Hungarian citizenship, and Fiorello continued to insist that his family should not receive preferential treatment on entrance lists.

On 2 April 1947 Gemma wrote to Fiorello the "good news" that Yolanda had received her quota number 801-802, and that she had already received a "Provisory Passport," valid for departure until 1 July 1947. She gave him information about booking a ship to New York and asked him, "Please Fiorello dear write all clearly how and when we shall travel and give us all directions." She complained of muscular rheumatism that had kept her in bed for twelve days, adding: "I was so angry as in the camp I wasn't ill and here the whole winter I was O.K. and as spring comes I get ill."[28]

Finally, on 1 May 1947, Gemma received a letter from Fiorello that everything was in order. A week later she received notice that passage was available on a ship leaving in two days. Gemma, her daughter, and grandson arrived in New York on 19 May 1947.[29] "It is a bitter thing to have nothing in one's old age," she wrote. "One is almost too weary to start a new life."[30] However, despite the loss of her home, husband, and sheltered former life, she was able to overcome despair and move forward at the age of sixty-four. Gemma also had to face another tragic situation soon after she arrived. By then, Fiorello was gravely ill with cancer, and he died in New York City four months later, on 20 September 1947. Gemma continued to live a quiet life in New York, residing in a small apartment with her daughter in a municipal housing project in Queens. If Shneiderman had not accidentally learned about her and helped her bring her memoir to fruition, her important eyewitness testimony documenting her time in Ravensbrück would probably have been lost.

9

Jewish Evacuees Arrive from Auschwitz

WHILE Gemma LaGuardia Gluck's status as a political hostage makes her story of survival unique, the largest number of Ravensbrück's Jewish survivors arrived after Auschwitz-Birkenau was evacuated in January 1945. After surviving that camp and a murderous death march, and then riding in open railroad cars in sub-zero weather, these women were extremely weak when they reached Ravensbrück. Arriving toward the end of the camp's operations when conditions were at their worst, most stayed only a short time before moving on to one of the camp's satellites. Because of these circumstances, some of these survivors have limited or no memories of their experiences at Ravensbrück. However, others have vivid recollections that contribute to an understanding of the camp's last chaotic months.

In survivor registries and testimony archives in the United States, Israel, and Europe, most of the Jewish women who list Ravensbrück as one of the camps they endured are those who arrived with this late group. Therefore, among the women who agreed to be interviewed or share unpublished memoirs with me, the majority came from Auschwitz in late January or early February 1945. Most of those who entered the camp before 1944 did not survive.

The number of Jewish women who arrived from Auschwitz in 1945 is unknown, but it is estimated in the thousands. For example, Lidia Rosenfeld Vago, whose story is recounted here, has kept track of the

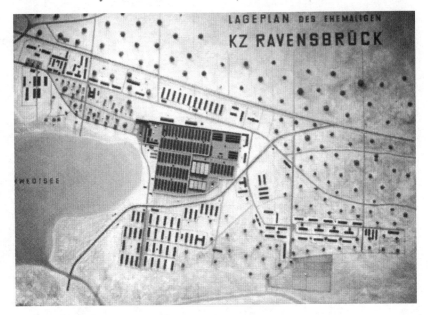

Model of the Ravensbrück concentration camp. Collection of MGR/SBG.

survivors from her group, the *Union,* the munitions factory at Auschwitz. She told me that thousands of Jewish women were sent from Auschwitz to Ravensbrück. She believes that all of the eleven hundred women who were slave laborers with her at the *Union* were sent on the death march toward Ravensbrück. Many of them did not survive the trip.[1]

Mina Lewkowicz Goldstein, whose work in the textile industry at Ravensbrück was detailed in chapter 7, had been sent to Ravensbrück from Lodz in October 1944. She remembers the arrival of the women from Auschwitz in January/February 1945.[2] Her barrack was in the separate *Industriehof* work camp, which had a gate and required the permission of a guard to enter or leave the main camp. One night when she left the work camp to get a new needle for her sewing machine, she saw women who had just arrived from Auschwitz and were spending the night sleeping alongside the wall in the snow. She didn't then know who these women were. They asked for water, but when she tried to give it to them, the guard beat her. Then she saw a woman who had been very beautiful in her ghetto. "She had been famous in the Lodz ghetto and now she had diarrhea and was begging," Mina said. She went to get the woman some chocolate from a Red Cross package, but when she returned, the woman was gone.[3]

Jewish Evacuees Arrive from Auschwitz

ROSE FROCHEWAJG MELLENDER

Rose Frochewajg Mellender is a Jewish survivor who recalls details of her arrival from Auschwitz. Born in Bedzin, Poland, in 1924 to Leib and Kayla Przyrowska Frochewajg, she had three sisters and a brother.[4] She was able to survive selections in the ghetto until 1943 because she had a job sewing buttons on army uniforms. However, when she and her family were discovered hiding in the ghetto in December 1943, Rose was sent to Auschwitz. "They put us in cattle wagons. No water, no facilities where to urinate or anything," she said. "They were shooting at the wagons and killing, and if you cried for water, they killed you, so you didn't say anything. You survived. It took two days and two nights."

One day in January 1945 when Rose returned to her Auschwitz barrack after work, she and the other women were ordered not to get undressed because they were going to march. "They chased—it was snow, it was cold," she recalled. "They said, 'we can't even give you bread, because we gave already to the others. There is no more bread for you.' . . . I made a mistake, because my friends stayed on, they hid under the bunkers, and they stayed on because there was a rumor that at night or [in] two, three days, the Americans or the Russians are on the way." Rose's cousin told her not to listen to her friends, because she thought they would have a better chance of surviving if they left the camp. "So I went with her," Rose said.

Rose was saved from starvation on the death march by a German man who knew her from home. He had been arrested for helping Jews. "He gave me two breads, two-pound breads, a little salt, and a little sugar, and some margarine," she said. "He says, 'I'm a German. I will always get it, but you will not get it and you will die.' And that's how I survived with my friends, my cousin. I helped everybody. With those two breads, we used to cut a piece, a piece every night. He was sent like an angel to me."

"When we came to Ravensbrück, it was that deep in mud," Rose continued, gesturing at knee level. "Terrible. There were the worse conditions you ever saw. They put us . . . in stalls, where cows used to be, or whatever, and on straw and in that mud. That was Ravensbrück." She recalled details of her entry and the first days in the camp:

> It was in the evening. We were hungry and cold, frozen, and they put us on that straw in mud, like. They said, "In an hour they [are] going to start taking your numbers and we will put you in a place where you'll be able to sleep, go to sleep." We were there like two days in that mud, without food, without anything, nothing for two days. They just left us there, closed it and they said, "If you have to go there is a big pot, go there. But don't make number two, make number one." What those people did that had to make number two, they were afraid. Don't ask.

123

If they made number two, they beat the hell out of them. So you had to hold for two days.

After the next day, at night they start dispersing you. They came and they put you into a barrack. It was called a barrack. There were already old-timers, Russian and Ukrainian . . . and we knew that the Ukrainians, forget it, worse than the Poles. They just were no good. They were out to take everything what we had. So we were afraid to take off the stuff, because they told us—somebody said—don't leave anything, because they would take everything. If you fall asleep, don't be surprised, you're not going to have your shoes on. The coat, like the sweater—so you were afraid to take it off. They used to take at night when you slept, they took your shoes and you walked in socks the next morning. They took my shoes off. They took my scarf. They took my shoes. It was the worst. We were there like a couple of weeks, not working, not doing anything. They had to think what to do with us, where to bring us.

They were making our life miserable. You weren't allowed to say that you were sick or whatever, because right away they took you away. Terrible. You had to stay for a little soup, you had to stay ten hours and if it was out, you didn't get it. You didn't eat.

Rose said that her cousin was a great help to her during her ordeal. "She used to give me food," she said. "She used to give me her socks. She used to knit. She used to unravel her sweater or her scarf, and made me gloves. I'm telling you, she helped me so much. She was a woman in her fifties, probably. Yes, in her fifties. At that point I was seventeen." Rose had other friends at the camp, and they tried to help each other, she said. "We used to exchange, like I didn't like—as much as I was hungry, I hated—they gave Sunday, they gave rice with sugar, but they put in so much sugar, they didn't give you should taste good. You just felt the sugar and not the rice. So I couldn't eat. So whoever liked that used to give me a little salt for it or a piece of bread, and I gave them that. So you did this with friends. And you slept with friends."

Rose also recalled the lice and diarrhea that plagued her and the other women: "Lice—boy, I'm telling you!" she said. "You put your hand in them you took [them] out by the dozens. So one used to clean the other and look where you have them and wash you off with hot water and gasoline, a little bit we got. We used to take care of it. . . . As a matter of fact, when I came out from camp, so I thought, oh, my God, we'd be sick. . . . Whoever did not watch out and ate died, got diarrhea and died. I said, 'I don't want to eat. I'm going to watch it.' I ate little by little. Never got sick. It was fine."

The only sickness she suffered at Ravensbrück was severe diarrhea. "I tore the lining from my coat and I cleaned myself with it. And I took my sweater, because I threw out the underpants and I made underpants . . . I tied up the sleeves. You learn how to survive," she said. One day

Rose heard an announcement that the transport that just came was going farther, "to a very nice camp." "So, we thought, 'Ah-oh. God knows where we're going,'" she said. And she soon discovered that her next destination was the satellite camp of Malchow, a little-known camp that will be described later.

I. JUDITH BERGER BECKER

I. Judith Berger Becker, another survivor who came on the death march from Auschwitz, was introduced in chapter 1. The daughter of Pepi (Penina) Lieder Berger and Ephraim Fritz Berger, she was born in Stettin, Germany, in 1928. Along with thousands of Polish Jews, she, her siblings, and her mother were exiled from Germany and sent to the Polish border at the end of October 1938. She estimates that she arrived at Ravensbrück from Auschwitz in early or mid-February 1945.[5] "And of course when I say 'death march,' I really do mean death march," she said. "We had I don't know how many [dead]. In our wagon, there were at least ten or fifteen dead women, and these were people who had survived the march. But we had no food. We ate snow. The wagons were open."

"When we came into the camp, the camp [was] totally gray," Judith continued. "The overall impression was just an expanse of gray, and the *Appellplatz* [roll call area] was all mud, and there were these planks running along left and then straight across to the end of this particular camp, and then on the right-hand side in the corner was this pitiful orchestra playing—the women's orchestra—as we came in."[6] With the exception of a few women who were allowed to stay because the *kapos* [prisoner-overseers] were acquainted with them, the group was sent on to another camp. Judith called this the *Totenlager*, the death camp, but it most likely was the *Jugendlager*, the so-called nearby youth camp that indeed became a death camp. She remembered passing through the main camp until her group reached this destination:

> There were hardly any people walking, there was illness—horrible. . . . Just mud and these gray barracks. People were actually lying in the doorway of the barracks. They couldn't move—apparently they had been starved. But they kept chasing us farther, until we came to an area that was apparently known as the *Totenlager*. Now every camp had an area where the dying and the ones who were going to be killed next were being kept. . . . And we were driven into a barrack and the barrack had nothing in it. There were no bunks, there was nothing in it, it was just the barrack. And everything was closed—there was one door and they locked it after they pushed us all in, and the windows were closed, and the windows were just up on top, like windows you see on a wagon train, and as it turned out the *kapo* group among us, who had been with us throughout the death march, they

were strong and very assertive, and they were organized. So they immediately took over a certain area of the barrack and they guarded it from anyone else coming in. But the total space was not adequate, it was half the space required for everybody to stand.

Judith estimates that there were about a thousand women in a barrack that should have held a maximum of 150 with bunks, or five hundred standing. She recalled:

As it happened I was also together with my mother, Pepi Berger, and my sister, Marlit. And we had sworn to stay together—either die together or stay together. And so we were together. And in this crush—my sister is two years younger than I am—and in the crush she wound up being up there [with her feet off the ground]. And I wanted—and my mother couldn't stand up. She didn't have the strength to stand up. So I was trying to make room for my sister to come down from the air and my mother to sit down. So in order to do this—I was—like everybody else—I was using my elbows to create a bit of space. And in the process I knocked the glasses off another girl who was probably my age. She was trying to do the same thing for her mother. She also had a mother.

And my mother who was remarkable in that respect, she got on my case. And she screamed at me. She said, "How dare you break this girl's glasses? Do you know what it means for her (this was 1945) to have glasses? And here you knocked off her glasses. You find her glasses!" So meanwhile this other girl and I are trying to dive down and find her glasses. Well, when we did find her glasses, one of them was broken, but the other one I was able to retrieve and give her and she kept the other one, too, because she had more vision with a splintered glass than she would have had without it.

And my mother carried on, she shouldn't wear these glasses with splintered glass—that it would hurt her. So at that point, when mother had said, "show some humanity," the two of us—two teenagers—we were like two bulls trying to fight for space—we organized ourselves that we were going to take turns sitting and standing. So the two mothers would sit and we would stand, always pushing the crowd aside. But this didn't last very long because we didn't have the strength to do that. And sooner or later we were overwhelmed by people just falling on top of each other. And—no food.

On the second day of this ordeal, Judith's mother realized they would die if the situation continued. She decided that Judith should resolve this problem:

She always used to give "cute" commands to me. So she says, "you see that window—go and open the window." So I did, I literally dove over people in order to get to the window, and I stood on somebody—I had no idea who—and I got to the window and I opened the window. And it was very cold air coming in, it was winter, and I could see out and I saw the snow. So my mother said, "what did you see?" And I said, "I see snow." So she says, "rip out the window." I say, "how am I supposed to rip out the window, how can I do it?" She says, "I don't care, just rip out the window." So I got two or three people who were close to the window to help me, and we ripped out the window, so air was coming into the room. Then my mother says, "Now, let's climb out of the window." So sure enough, she dove over, and the other one dove over the people, and on my shoulders they stood and they managed to crawl out of the window, and they fell out of the barracks. And outside, my mother said, "Now strip, and start rubbing yourselves with the snow." Because, she said, our circulation is going to go first, because we just couldn't move, it was an impossible situation.

So that's what we did, there was fresh snow, and we ate the snow, and then we rubbed ourselves with the snow and did exercise, and then the guards came with the guns. So when they saw us, they thought that we were putting on a show for them, you know, women, undressing, so they started to laugh. So my mother says, "Don't pay any attention, just do what you have to do," and in the meantime, other women were coming out from the same window, they saw that it was possible. So when they came out, we made our way back in through the window, and the guards started eventually shooting. . . . So some people died in the process.

We managed to get back in. However, we realized that even this couldn't last. So the following day they asked for people to volunteer for a detail, a work detail. So I knew always that if you go to a work detail, you get food. You always get something. So I said to my mother, "I'm going to try to make it to the door," because you had to go to the door in order to get out. And I was very far from the door, and I saw that I was never going to make it. There were too many people to dive over. Because then somebody would push you around, and you'd have to straighten yourself out, it's impossible. So she said, "Go out the window, and see if you can get to the door from there." And that's what I did. So I thought, oh, boy I really made it.

Judith thought that her misery had been somewhat relieved, but she had no idea of the shock that was in store for her:

They had about eight of us, and they marched us to a place, and they gave us the canteens. They took us to carry three or four urns, that means two to an urn, and these urns were very heavy, and it was snowing outside, there were no roads, it was very difficult going, and some of the girls just couldn't do it, and some of the coffee spilled on their hands, but thank God the distance wasn't so terribly far. I thought they were going to take us to our barrack, to give us coffee, but that wasn't the case, they took us to another barrack, and here, we met these women that I would like to find out more about.

Judith entered the barrack, pulled in by the group of women who lived there:

> Once I got into the barrack, [the women] blockaded the entrance. And they started making horrible sounds, they were making animal sounds, and they opened their mouths, and they kept pointing, pointing, pointing, it was . . . coming from a daylight environment into a dark barrack . . . you know, the barrack was dark, basically, I didn't understand what was going on. I didn't see. Until they just wouldn't let go, and they kept holding on to me, and this, and this, and this, and then they made gestures on their pubis, and it turned out that all of the women in that barrack had had their tongues cut out.
> They were all of the same age, approximately, they were all of the same stature, they were all petite, pretty women, young, I would say, it's hard to estimate, but I would say no more than the early twenties, and they had hair, they were not shaven, they had hair, which is significant. . . . And they were gesticulating sexual overtones, "and here," and making horrible, horrible, noises. By the time I understood, or thought I understood, the German guard was already whipping me, and I had to go out. . . . But I've never found out who these women were. . . . I mean the brutality, to cut out their tongues so that they couldn't report, in other words, they were using every opportunity to tell somebody, they probably were killed, I don't know. . . . I may very well be the only one who can report about it. . . . We were never taken there again.

As far as I know, Judith is indeed the only one who ever reported about the tragedy of this group of women, and there is no further information.[7] Judith, her mother, and sister were in Ravensbrück for a month or less, and then shipped on. They all survived, and Judith today lives in Jerusalem. At age one hundred in 1998, her mother, then Pepi Schreier (the surname of her third husband), was considered the oldest living Auschwitz survivor by the Conference on Jewish Material Claims Against Germany.[8]

HANNAH CUKIER HORON

Hannah Cukier Horon, like Rose Mellender, Judith Becker, and other women I spoke with, had intense memories of the death march from Auschwitz. "It was January 1945," she said. "I will never forget this, they put us on a—not a regular train—on those . . . with no window, a window on top there, each one." Upon arrival at Ravensbrück, there was no food available, she recalled. The women survived on little else than melted snow. "We came to Ravensbrück in January, and the barracks weren't ready for us," she said. "So they left us in the gutter, sleeping, peeing, and everything, overnight. In the morning, we were frozen to the street, we couldn't even get up."

The women received no food when they arrived, she said. "The only food we got, if the Germans ate [from] a can, and were nice enough to give us the can to lick, we used to put . . . some of them we used to urinate. And some of them we put a hand through the little window, and took the ice . . . you know, January in Europe, there is ice, snow. So we put in the snow and let it melt, and this was our liquid that we used to drink." She stayed at the camp and worked until April, but cannot remember what her job was.

Contrary to most survivors, Hannah insists that once she began to receive food, it was better than in Auschwitz. "In Ravensbrück, there was something in the soup, what everybody wants, from the bottom, because it was thick," she said. "It was not watery. Whatever was there, it was potatoes, or barley. I don't know—it was something, not leaves, at least." She believes that in Ravensbrück the guards were a little more lenient, because they knew that the war was coming to an end. "They were fighting on the front, and we didn't get bread every day because they didn't have enough," she said. "They didn't have people to bake the bread, they didn't have enough flour, so the first thing was to the soldiers in the front. You know what, in the end, we got stale, old bread, they couldn't give to them, so they gave to us." She was there until she was rescued and taken to Sweden by the Red Cross in April; her experience in Sweden is detailed later.[9]

LEA GELBGRAS FERSTENBERG

Lea Gelbgras Ferstenberg, another Jewish survivor who arrived on the Auschwitz transports, was born in Warsaw, Poland, on 25 December 1920.[10] She was the youngest of Hanoch and Pnina Gelbgras's four children, and her mother died a year after she was born. After the war broke out, Lea was a storyteller for children in the Warsaw ghetto. She was deported to Majdanek on 27 April 1943. Two months later she was sent to Auschwitz, where she was assigned to slave labor in the *Union* ammunition factory. She was in Ravensbrück for about two to ten days, before being sent on to the satellite camp of Neustadt-Glewe. "This was very short. But I tell you one thing, being short, every day was too long," she said.

Lea recalled the end of her time at Auschwitz on 17 January 1945, and the subsequent death march to Ravensbrück. "Suddenly there was a lot of bombardment and we were hiding," she said. "Hiding. Hiding behind the machines. Where could you hide? I didn't have shoes." Someone gave her shoes before the women left the camp, and she and others took extra clothes from the storage area. During the forced march at gunpoint the women were always hungry. "Our group didn't get bread, because bread was distributed in the morning and we went in the night," she said. "But we met some guys and they were throwing bread to us, guys from the camp. . . . When we were walking together on the march, mostly, you see, you wanted to be with the people from the same group, like our Warsaw group—we were together. You'd be surprised that we were even singing because—to give ourselves courage. But, of course, when you walk, walk, you saw on the way people, they were shot and killed."

She recalled her arrival and her stay at Ravensbrück:

> That looks to me like a field of dead people, just moving, like mario-
> nettes, puppets. . . . That wasn't exactly like in Auschwitz that you were
> selected to die in crematorium in the gas chamber. There was more, how
> I had the impression, that they knew that you have to die there, because
> there was no food—was not organized. You see, in Auschwitz—that
> what I jokingly say to you to compare the two hotels—in Auschwitz
> you knew that you'd get soup, that you'd get a portion of bread. You
> knew that you'd get some coffee, something in the morning. There [in
> Ravensbrück] you really didn't know where you are suddenly. Besides,
> that was the time that was lots of bombardment. The airplanes were up
> there. So if even came the time that they have to serve our meal, no,
> they didn't. Sometimes in the night, eleven o'clock in the night, they
> were calling us, "Come to eat." People were tired, you know, from hun-
> ger and from expectation. That's what the impression Ravensbrück
> made on me. I saw many, many woman so emaciated, so looking close
> to death. That's what I remember from Ravensbrück.

Lea said she was neither forced to work nor beaten. She felt she was simply in a holding situation, before she was sent on. "We were nothing. We just were nothing," she said. "We were waiting. Waiting. Waiting to go someplace. So some people went to Malchow, some people went to Neustadt-Glewe. In Neustadt-Glewe, we were lucky because we were liberated."

LIDIA ROSENFELD VAGO

Lidia Vago, the survivor who has done considerable research on the women shipped to Ravensbrück with her from the *Union* munitions fac-tory, was born on 4 November 1924 in Gheorgheni, a small town in the Carpathian Mountains.[11] Her father, Dr. Endre Rosenfeld, was a gen-eral practitioner and her mother, Dr. Jolan Harnik, was a dentist. This area of Transylvania belonged to Romania until 1 September 1940, and then became part of Hungary. As mentioned earlier, the Germans took over in Hungary on 19 March 1944, and, with the help of the Hungarian authorities, they began deporting the Jews outside of Budapest. Lidia, her mother, and her sister Anikó arrived in Auschwitz on 10 June, and her mother was sent immediately to the gas chamber. She and her sister were there for seven months, working in the *Union* until the massive evacuation on 18 January 1945.

In an unpublished manuscript that she shared with me, Lidia wrote:[12] "The *Kalendarium* [calendar, or chronicle of the camp] mentions a transport of women from Auschwitz including 520 Polish women, entering *K.L.* (concentration camp) Ravensbrück on 23 January. I don't think we were among them, a mere five days after leaving Auschwitz. 166 Polish women are also mentioned on 24 January. We were most probably included in the entry of 27 January. Translated from the German edition: 'A transport of two thousand female inmates arrive, and at the beginning of February, the last transport with approximately three thousand women from the *K.L.* Auschwitz comes in. They made the journey from the *K. L.* Auschwitz to the *K. L.* Ravensbrück partly on foot, having needed two weeks for three hundred kilometers.'"[13]

Lidia described the arrival of her group at the camp:

> As soon as we had reached our destination one evening, the half-frozen dead-on-their-feet women tumbled out of the railroad cars. However, the catatonic lethargic masses were revitalized by the blinding searchlights signaling an ongoing real selection at the gate. . . . Of course, we had no idea where we had arrived.
>
> The women were not required to undress, but anyone who appeared to be a "*Muselmann*"—a walking corpse—was singled out. The others were ordered to discard any items of clothing they were carrying, but could keep what they were wearing. . .
>
> A pathetic sight caught my eye: a woman in front of us was smearing something red on her pale lips. She had probably bought a lipstick in Auschwitz just for such a purpose.

Lidia was worried that her sister Anikó would not pass inspection because she had a festering and rotting infection on her hand. "Anikó somehow managed to conceal her infected hand with the sleeve of her coat and her empty bread satchel," she recalled. "She slipped through, and got a new lease on life." However, her condition began to deteriorate after their arrival in Ravensbrück. Lidia described her first night at the camp as the "most dreadful, horrifying, harrowing experience of all our camp life." It was worse than the four-day trip to Auschwitz, the shock of her first day in Birkenau, learning of her mother's murder, and participating in the death march and freezing train ride to Ravensbrück, she said, because she felt that time was running out and the end was approaching. Lidia described the chaotic situation:

> We could not see where the large soup buckets were set up, but sensed the direction from the surging crowd, and were swept along in the stampede. No power on earth could have aligned us in rows of five, which

had become second nature to us in Auschwitz-Birkenau. Not even a volley fired above our heads would have done the job. There were no SS men or women there, just starving Jewesses fighting it out. Anikó and I held each other tight by the hand or arm, so as not to fall and be trampled upon, or lose each other in the throng, and we also had to protect Anikó's infected hand. We had only one tin cup or a small bowl for both of us, tied around my waist with a string, and I also clutched it with a firm grip, because not everybody had a cup or a bowl, and without one, there was no hope for life. I don't remember the great climactic moment when a ladle of soup was splashed into our cup, and I don't think we managed to get a second helping because we had only one cup.

Lidia and her sister were first sent to the infamous tent (*Zelt* in German), which was often a death sentence. "The 'Zelt' was an enormous tent crammed with women 'up to zero place,' as the Hebrew figure of speech would describe it," she said. "We were among the last to be jostled in, and several hundred other newcomers spent the rest of the night on the frozen snow outside." She described her time in the tent:

> It was better to be seated close to the entrance, because it was safer than sensing the constant danger of being crushed to death in the middle of an uncontrollable mass of humanity fighting for a few centimeters of *Lebensraum* [living space]. Lying down was not possible, not even sardine-style, so we all sat on our feet pulled up sideways under our bodies, tightly squeezed together, as we had been sitting in the cattle car on our journey to Auschwitz. Here was a difference, though: no rucksacks and bundles to sit on, and no tiny biscuits with hard quince jam to munch at.
>
> There could not be any spot of unfilled space left on the ground for feet to step down while jumping over the bent, resting bodies, in a rush toward the toilet—'*Kuebels*' [buckets] at the entrance. I remember being awakened in pain and nausea from a slumberous state of half consciousness. By the time these skipping bodies reached us in the front rows, they were not able to contain themselves any longer. . . . I don't remember how many nights we spent in this appalling circus tent.

Meanwhile, the abscess on Anikó's hand became life threatening and needed treatment, despite the risk of seeking medical help. An SS-auxiliary *Aufseherin* [Nazi female overseer] had even noticed the rotting smell coming from the hand. Anikó was admitted to the infirmary of the *Revier*, and her hand was immediately operated on. Lidia was not allowed to accompany her, but Anikó later told her that the operation was performed under general anesthesia, and when she came to, her hand was bandaged. "Who understands why they didn't 'put her to sleep'?" Lidia asked. "Fortunately, there was no logic at all in the death camps."

With their faces and hands gray from dirt, Lidia and her sister were finally allowed into a washroom, she recalled:

There were several taps around a cylindrical column, with a basin running around underneath. If it hadn't been for the filth and overflowing basins, even the ice-cold water would have been a real pleasure after being glued into our garments for two weeks. I washed Anikó, because she was not able to undress and wash herself, and she was apathetic, losing her will to live, in spite of the salutary relief of the operation. "I want to go to mother" was practically all she was ready to communicate.

We became suddenly infested with lice in our clothes and short hair. They were sucking our blood incessantly, like the bedbugs in Birkenau. I had to delouse both of us whenever we had nothing else to do.

After some monotonous days of utter hopelessness, as if we had been forgotten, we were shaken up by some administrative interest in us: registration. We were not scared that it might mean a selection, because we rationalized that if they had brought us to Ravensbrück to liquidate us when time had run out in Auschwitz, they could have done it *en masse* upon our arrival. So, it was reassuring to be registered, because it could only mean transport to a work camp. After all, the war was going on, and slaves were in demand inside Germany. I don't remember if we had to undress, but we kept our clothes. One by one, we entered a room that looked like a clinic. Something was registered, probably our personal data, including our tattoo number.

Lidia remembers something unusual that happened at this point in the registration and medical examination. No other survivor has mentioned it. "An apparatus, which looked like a weighing machine, but was a measuring machine, stood by the window," she said. "I was ordered to stand on it, and somebody adjusted a small sliding board to the top of my head, reading my height from the fixed measuring pole. Three months before the collapse of the Third Reich—and they knew it—why were they curious to know my height?" she asked. "Then we received a slip of thin white cloth with large numbers in blue print," she continued. "Mine was 99626 and Anikó's, 99627. I have kept mine. I can't remember how these numbers were attached to our clothing, because we had no needle or thread. The same number was also written on a small slip of thick pink colored paper."

After the registration process, Lidia and her sister were sent to a block with tiered bunks. She believes it was Barrack Thirty-two, which she said was rumored to house women designated for an impending transport to a work camp. Meanwhile, Lidia and Anikó were ordered to the *Jugendlager* to work stuffing straw mattresses, and she remembered that experience. "There were a few small blocks there, and as we were not severely guarded, I opened a door, out of curiosity," she said. "A large room was crammed with old women sitting on the floor. I asked them where they came from, and one of them said, 'Budapest.' . . . I hastily left the room, and opened the adjacent door. It was a very small room containing several naked corpses. . . . We filled the straw mattresses only for a few days, and returned to the main camp in the evenings. In the two or three days that we were working in the *Jugendlager*, we received an extra bowl of soup, but even so, we were starving and getting weaker by the day, as the first half of February passed."

Soon afterward, Lidia and her sister were designated to leave Ravensbrück, but the circumstances could have been fatal. When the roll call preceding their transport was underway, Anikó was in the *Revier* having her bandage changed. Lidia recalled the terrifying situation:

> The fact is that I had to stand somewhere in a row of five, and Anikó was not there. I just stepped into one of the rows where one was missing. The officers who were doing the sorting started out at the end of the rows opposite the direction of the *Revier*. Fortunately, the procedure was rather slow, and I was desperately trying to gain time by moving backward, to the left, behind the rows of five. But as I could not leave my row truncated without a fifth woman, I had to search for and implore lonely women from other rows to the left to change places with me. This was not an easy task. . . . I can only imagine what punishment I would have got if caught in the act of manipulating the once lined-up rows of five.
>
> After about half an hour's nerve-racking "row-jumping," Anikó appeared at long last, running toward our column. Somehow we managed to fall in line, and we were earmarked for the transport to Neustadt-Glewe, which was to be our third and last concentration camp for two and a half months.

Lidia and her sister arrived in Neustadt-Glewe on 16 February and were liberated on 2 May 1945. She later married historian Bela Vago and has lived in Petach Tikvah, Israel, since 1958.

LILLY EISLER, VIOLA EISLER BARAS, AND EDITH EISLER DENES

I met only one other family of Ravensbrück survivors who, like Judith Becker and her mother and sister, had the unusual good fortune to survive their ordeal together.[14] Lilly Eisler, then age thirty-six, and her daughters Viola Eisler Baras, then sixteen, and Edith Eisler Denes, then fourteen, were taken to Auschwitz in April 1944 from their hometown, Munkács (now Mukachevo), when it was part of Hungary. They worked together in Auschwitz sorting the clothing of people who had been gassed. Viola said of their time in Ravensbrück: "For us, whatever we did after was a relief. We were sorting the clothes from the dead people [in Auschwitz]. . . . Because those people who worked what we did . . . they used to say that every three months they used to kill them and get new ones, so in case anyone stays alive, they shouldn't have a story to tell."

Both Viola and Edith recalled the death march out of Auschwitz. Viola remembered, "We walked and walked, and those people who stayed behind, they just shot them. So we had to leave them there, nobody could help them. They stayed behind. So we just pushed and pushed. I don't know for how many days we walked. Edith spoke of the train ride, after the forced march: "And then, I remember it was a train. I remember it was snowing and it was open, and the snowflakes came down and we had very dry bread. And my mother said, 'put a little like sugar, the flakes, and then it will taste better, the bread.' It was so nice to have the little flakes on the bread—it made it a little tastier, like sugar." Viola and Edith didn't remember much about their almost two months in Ravensbrück, and Lilly said it was too painful for her to try to remember. However, both sisters remembered that they and their mother had to dig ditches. "Once my mother was almost fainting, she couldn't do it, so a German—he wasn't an SS—a German soldier who watched us—took it over and worked instead of her to finish her job," Edith said.

The family was sent to Neustadt-Glewe at the end of March, and Viola's most vivid memory is of food. She said that they received milk there, although she does not know the source, and liberating soldiers gave them chocolate. Eventually the Russian Army sent them back to Budapest. They finally reached Mukachevo (Munkács) and later were reunited with their husband and father, Jacob.

As it was so unusual to meet a ninety-three-year-old mother and two daughters who survived together from the beginning to the end of their living nightmare during the Holocaust (and fifty-six years later were still living next door to each other in Tamarac, Florida), I asked them to tell me how they helped each other during their ordeal. Viola did not provide details but summed up her answer by saying that without their mutual support, they probably would not have made it. Her explanation was simple yet profound: "If I had something, they have. If they had something, I have." Edith added, "I think that's the reason we stayed alive together, because we were the three of us." And their mother, who had remained quiet throughout the discussion, finally spoke up: "I can tell you that God was very good to me."

OTHER JEWISH WOMEN FROM AUSCHWITZ

Like Lidia Vago and her sister, Lotte Brainin, a survivor from Vienna, was also in the infamous tent when she arrived in Ravensbrück from Auschwitz. She wrote to me briefly about her experiences.[15] "A large group of Jewish women prisoners came together with myself from Auschwitz to Ravensbrück and were taken to the infamous tent in the camp under extremely dreadful conditions in the very harsh winter of 1945," she recalled. "I myself came out of the tent very soon through the help of a non-Jewish girl prisoner, whom I had known in Vienna before the war. From Ravensbrück I was sent to the so-called Youth Camp [*Jugendlager*] in Uckermark, which was in fact a *Nebenlager* [neighboring camp] of Ravensbrück and turned out to be again an annihilation camp. There many women, Jewish and non-Jewish, were murdered by the Nazis until the liberation of the camp by the Soviet Army," she said.

One survivor whom I never met, Jacqueline Schweitzer Gropman, communicated with me via her son, Larry Gropman.[16] Her story is unusual, because she is the only Jewish survivor from France that I came across in the group of women who arrived from Auschwitz. Unfortunately, she was terminally ill when her son contacted me, and she died of cancer in the fall of 1996, before I had a chance to talk with her. Jacqueline was born in Paris in 1924 and managed to live within the city for four years during the Nazi occupation of France. She was arrested by a French policeman who noticed errors in her forged identity papers in July 1944 and then turned over to the Gestapo. She was deported to Auschwitz and then sent on to Ravensbrück in January 1945. After three weeks in the camp, she was transported to Malchow. She returned to Paris by the end of May 1945, but could never forget that she had been arrested as the result of a French policeman's collaboration with the Nazis. Jacqueline immigrated to the United States in 1946, married, and had two children. After her husband died, she moved to the Detroit area in 1984 to be near her son.

Other Jewish women who wrote or spoke with me briefly about their arrival from Auschwitz in January/February 1945 include *Union* members Erna Ellert of Ramat Hasharon, Israel, Renee Duering of Daly City, California, and Dr. Lore Shelley of San Francisco. In her book on the *Union,* Dr. Shelley recounts the stories of a number of survivors who arrived in Ravensbrück.[17] The stories of Rachel Rozanbaum Hocherman and Rosa Korman Fajerstajn, who also arrived at this time, are told in later chapters.[18]

Although the thousands of Jewish women who arrived from Auschwitz came toward the end of World War II and were at Ravensbrück for only a brief period, their testimonies confirm that there was indeed a sizable Jewish presence in the camp. They also demonstrate how the close relationships between family members or friends helped some of the women to overcome untenable circumstances and stay alive.

10

Late Arrivals from Other Camps

WHILE most of the Jewish women sent to Ravensbrück during its last months were from Auschwitz-Birkenau, some came from other camps. For example, Fela Szyjka Kolat and Manya Friedman arrived from a work camp in Gleiwitz, and Gloria Hollander Lyon was in many other camps before Ravensbrück. Their stories broaden the picture and demonstrate that late arrivals came not only from Auschwitz.

FELA SZYJKA KOLAT'S ARRIVAL FROM GLEIWITZ

Fela Kolat, the daughter of Chaim and Bluma Szyjka, was sent to Gleiwitz from her hometown of Sosnowiec, Poland.[1] Fela was a slave laborer in a factory that made soot for rubber in Gleiwitz, a camp that became a subcamp of Auschwitz in May 1944. "I never complained about the conditions [in Gleiwitz], because we had four pieces of soap for the whole month, and we had nice warm water," she said. "We had two jump suits, [so that] one could be washed. We washed every day. One was dry, and after work they delivered—in the morning they gave us—not coffee, but something black, a liquid, and a portion of bread—a piece margarine or a piece marmalade, and for the soup, they gave us—naturally it was a lot of sand in it because it was spinach and other vegetables, and some potatoes. . . . It was more for a cow than for a person. But the main thing, I was not exactly to say hungry. It gave me some nourishment. . . . And this went on, like I said, until the day, January 1945."

Fela and her group of slave workers were sent to the Gross Rosen concentration camp on about 20 January, but there was no room for them and they were then sent back to Gleiwitz. "The trip, like I said, we walked one day, and then the order came to go back, there was no room in Gross Rosen, so we walked back to Gleiwitz," she explained. "We walked and walked, and the blanket was heavy, and my legs were not going, and we reached at night a barn, and there on the floor we rested. What's gonna be next I don't know." Fela recounted what happened after the group returned to Gleiwitz:

> They put us on a train that was open—not a closed—open train. So they pushed together one hundred fifty girls [in] what was room for maybe seventy-five. There was really no room to bend down, to sit down, nothing. And it was January. It was snowing. So they, we traveled. They really didn't know where to take us. But I remember passing by Czechoslovakia, and the people in Czechoslovakia were very kind, because they tried to run with pails of water, and some threw bread, whoever caught, caught. And the bread [that] they gave us when we started out, I don't know what happened because I didn't have it. Because we slept in the bunk, if I had it, it was in the train, when you are up all day, sometimes your eyes close and whatever you had in your hand, it disappears. So we had no bread after this.
>
> It took two weeks, the train ride. The last two days they took us from these open trains to the regular cattle, closed trains. We ate the snow, we just—everybody had a blanket—it was January, so we just, we ate the snow, we ate only the snow. So the last two days when we already were in the closed-in cattle trains, suddenly I had this terrible diarrhea. But I mean terrible, terrible. And this friend, we stood together, she was a big help to me. Because from nature, she was stronger, and she didn't go through the thing with diarrhea. So when we got off the train, I felt I am dying, I said leave me here, I cannot make it, I felt I am dying, I was lying on the ground, and I almost saw my mother approaching. I felt I am dying, I'm telling you.

This was Fela's entry into Ravensbrück. Rather than leaving her, several friends picked her up and carried her to the nearby barracks. She recalled the conditions there:

> When we arrived in the barracks, they put us in the room where there were a lot of showers. And in the wall there were faucets. Everybody ran for this water to drink, and the same thing, me. And again diarrhea, and the toilets were overflooded, and there was a big line, you know, to go to the toilets. So while we were walking to the toilets, we passed by, like a barrack, and I saw there a woman in a white outfit, like a nurse. So I figure what do I have to lose, so I went in and I told her I have this problem. And in Germany they have a pill [that] looks like a

Replica of three-tiered bunk beds used in the camp. Photo from an exhibit at the Ravensbrück memorial, 1984–1994. Collection of MGR/SBG.

black coal, a round pill, and she gave me a couple pills, and this helped me. Okay. They settled us in the barracks, and there were three tiers-bunk beds, usually there were two tiers-bunk beds. Here there were three tiers, and it was only boards, there was nothing [that] makes a little softer, straw or something, nothing.

So this girl . . . her married name is Regina Weisfelner, her maiden name is Steinbok—so she was very good to me, she was like a sister, and they could not serve the soup at the same time to all the girls, the group [that] we were. It was twelve o'clock at night, they served the soup. But this is not the worst thing. The German woman who served the soup is a woman [who] was in jail, she had a green triangle. So she had a board, and if she thought that you were here before, she gave you over the head with the board. But this Regina, she didn't look, because the minute, if I would go out from this bunk bed, the Polish girls, [who] came from the uprising from Warsaw, they stole the boards. So you could not leave the bunk. So she brought me the soup, and then she went for herself for the soup. But somehow the soup was a little nourishing, because I was so weak.

They counted us twice a day, in the morning and in the evening. And they didn't count us in five minutes—it took hours. So I was sitting in the mud, that's how weak I was. So what do I know from Ravensbrück? The only thing [that] I know from Ravensbrück, the soup was a little thick, it was not so watery, and they didn't catch us to go to work, we could just sit around.

And I don't know, we didn't have a calendar, but it's approximately we were there like three weeks, or maybe a couple days more, and one day they said, they put us in a column of five, they gave us again a piece of bread, maybe half a bread, I don't remember, and a piece, it was some bologna, salami, I don't know. I think it was liverwurst—aha, it was liverwurst. They gave a nice piece of liverwurst, and we went in a regular normal train. And we arrived in Neustadt-Glewe.

Fela's story continues in the next chapter, which describes Ravensbrück's satellite work camps.

MANYA FRIEDMAN'S ARRIVAL FROM GLEIWITZ

Manya Friedman of Bethesda, Maryland, also came to Ravensbrück from Gleiwitz. She sent me her brief recollection of her arrival, which echoes some of Fela's descriptions:[2]

The trip in the open freight cars from Gleiwitz to Ravensbrück, through Czechoslovakia, (the railroad lines were bombed) took almost as long as our stay in Ravensbrück. In January 1945 when the Soviet army was advancing west, the Germans decided to transfer us to central Germany. As we were leaving our camp, a transport from Auschwitz was waiting at the gate to get in.

When we finally arrived in Ravensbrück it was the middle of the night, and, because of the blackout, we could not be allocated to the barracks. Instead, we were directed to the bathhouse to spend the night. Knowing already what bathhouses and showers represent, we were expecting the worst. I so vividly recall that incident. My best friend and I were sitting on the floor hugging each other and saying goodbyes. I was so anticipating the end that I thought I can smell gas. To this day I am puzzled by this phenomenon, how one's mind can play tricks. You can imagine our relief when at dawn the first rays of light crept through the shades.

After Gleiwitz, a work camp, Ravensbrück was hell. First of all, it was like the Tower of Babel. So many people from different locations, speaking different languages, and among them many Gypsies. After the first night on a bunk bed with several other women, my friend and I lost everything we had.

I do not remember much more, except . . . the pushcarts laden with emaciated, naked corpses, their limbs often hanging over the side of the cart. Once in a while some would fall off . . . being picked up and thrown back on the heap. Standing for hours in the bitter cold at roll call, aim-less registrations, and of course standing in endless lines. Our group was soon sent to Rechlin. I do not recall exactly how long we stayed in Ravensbrück. In those days dates and time had very little meaning.

GLORIA HOLLANDER LYON'S LONG JOURNEY TO RAVENSBRÜCK

Another survivor, Gloria Hollander Lyon, arrived at Ravensbrück at an unusually late date by way of a convoluted route, and her departure soon afterward miraculously brought her from near death to rescue. Of all of the Jewish survivors who spent any time at the camp, I know of none who arrived after her—more or less on 17 April 1945. I met Gloria at the 1995 ceremonies marking the camp's fiftieth anniversary of liberation and imme-diately noticed her youthful vivaciousness and ability to articulate.

Gloria was born on 20 January 1930 in Nagy Bereg, the daughter of David Holländer, a businessman and farm manager, and Helén Gelb Holländer, a housewife who ran a small store. At the time, this small town in the Carpatho-Ukraine was part of Czechoslovakia.[3] Gloria had a sister and four older brothers. Her mother survived Auschwitz-Birkenau but died in 1948 from illness related to the hardships she had suffered. Her father, who was in Auschwitz and several other camps, died of a heart attack in 1977.

The region where Gloria grew up was annexed to Hungary in the Munich Agreement of 1938 and was one of the first Hungarian deporta-tion zones in the spring of 1944. Gloria and her family were rounded up immediately after Passover on 15 April 1944 and sent with other area Jews to Beregszasz, the provincial capital. She was fourteen at the time. The Jews were first kept in the synagogue, then in a sealed brick factory. After four weeks, they were deported to Auschwitz in cattle cars, "packed in like sardines" for four days.

Gloria worked alongside her mother and sister for seven and a half months sorting clothing in *Kanada,* the deposit for items taken from Jew-ish prisoners. She was then selected for the gas chamber by Dr. Josef

Mengele, the camp's notorious chief doctor. However, the Hungarian guard from the *Kanada* deposit was in charge of the truck to the gas chamber, and he gave her and some other women tacit permission to jump off. Naked in the freezing weather of late December, Gloria hid in a culvert. The following night she climbed out and followed a light to an unknown barrack, and the next day was transferred with about six to eight hundred women to Bergen-Belsen.

"I must have arrived in Bergen-Belsen on 1 January 1945," Gloria said. "There we were housed in tent barracks that didn't even have bunk beds, and the rain just kept washing the soil under the tent in there. I'll never forget, this was the most horrible place because of all this mud that we had to be sitting in, and it was very cold." Besides her other problems, Gloria was now alone, without the comfort or support system of her mother and sister. She was in Bergen-Belsen for a few weeks, and then in five additional camps, including Ravensbrück. From Bergen-Belsen she was sent to the city of Braunschweig, where she had to help clear the major streets from the debris of bombardments.

A few weeks later she was shipped from Braunschweig to Hanover, where she worked in a gas mask factory. Soon afterward, she was sent from there to Hamburg to again clear the major streets of debris, then shipped out again. The approximate date was toward the end of March 1945. Her next destination was Beendorf, a small town that later became part of the German Democratic Republic. She worked twelve hundred feet underground in a salt mine. "Hitler, fearing Allied air attacks, moved his most important armaments industry underground to protect it from Allied bombardments, and moved us into the factory," she said. "And for this job I was 'hand-picked.' We all had to hold up our hands." She was among the women with small hands who were chosen to work on precision instruments for V-1 and V-2 rockets.

It is unclear exactly how long Gloria was at Beendorf, but she evidently was shipped from there to Ravensbrück in the second half of April 1945, arriving about a week before the Swedish Red Cross rescue effort that included Jewish women began on 24 April. She recalled the terrible trip to the camp and her short stay there:

> And from there I was sent to Ravensbrück, without any provisions on the road, and it was never just going directly from camp to camp. These short distances, a trip of about fifty miles would take anywhere from two to four days sealed in a boxcar, and it took a tremendous toll on the human body, especially in our fragile condition and weak condition. So each time we would arrive in a camp, there were all these dead people, especially toward the end.
>
> By the time I reached Ravensbrück, I was in pretty bad shape. I remember on the way there was a lady in the cattle car who was the

oldest—I thought she was my mother, you know? And she had all these—I don't know, looked like boils all over her body, and they were large ones, and I couldn't even imagine what they were. But she was in a lot of pain, so I said to her, "Maybe you two could switch seats so you'll be in the middle, and I'll hold my hands in the middle to keep people from brushing against you." And that's what I did most of the way. She told me about her daughter and she doesn't know if she's alive or not, and she had these wonderful shoes from home yet, because she was not selected to die, as I was. I lost my shoes from home in that selection from Auschwitz. After that, it was a matter of trying to take off a pair of wooden shoes from a dead person so that I have something under my feet. But she still had these wonderful shoes.

Anyway, so toward the end she said to me I can have her shoes when she dies. I said, "You won't die. You have a daughter. You just hold on to yourself, because she's fighting to find you and you are fighting to find her, and you will see each other yet." I tried to keep her spirits up. Gosh, you know, when I think of her, I always become over-whelmed, because I just wanted her to stay alive so much. But she died right there, right there as I had my hands up, and then I had some room to sit down. I even sat on her, this little lady. You know, one would think that one becomes hard, but it really sensitized me, that human beings are so fragile, and yet they are so strong at the same time. She couldn't just hold on. She died on the way.

GLORIA'S SHORT STAY IN RAVENSBRÜCK

Gloria, who was only fifteen when she arrived, believes she was in Ravensbrück for about a week, and she was in "the worst shape" by then. "By this time we were very, very weak and dazed. We were just not ourselves anymore," she said. "I can't remember exactly how long, maybe a little longer, and then they just ordered us into cattle cars." Despite her short time at the camp, she has vivid memories. "This lake was so beautiful, and the surrounding trees were reflected in this beautiful lake," she said. "One couldn't even imagine what was behind it. And almost at the rim of the lake—I can't tell which is north and south, so I cannot describe it—was the gas chamber and next to it the crematorium. And then the other side, continuing from there was this tall wall, a brick wall. Wow! It was like two stories high, maybe three. And nobody could climb up that wall, unless you could throw something over it. No escape. And on top they had several rows of barbed wire, I remember."

One of Gloria's memories of her time in the camp is so chilling that she seems to have repressed it for years:

But I do remember something in Ravensbrück that was extraordinary, and for a long time I remembered that something happened to these people, and it took me a long time. I actually dreamt it, and through the dream I remembered what happened, not so long ago, just a few short years ago.

We stood for head count for hours and hours and hours, and it was terrible. They asked us what our blood type was, and they asked for certain blood types, people to raise their hands. I had no idea what my blood type was, and I was surprised when a number of people raised their hands. Not that many, but a few people raised their hands. Two people were asked to step forward, and a nurse came and drew blood from them in a—like a jar. I can't say vial, because it was much bigger, from both of them. And then we were all excused, and we had to go wherever we had to go.

In the morning, when it was again time to stand in line, those two people were tied to two stakes, and they were dead. We figured that they probably drew all their blood out and let these people die. But this was very hard on me. And at the end I just couldn't believe that they'd do that, but it was an experimental camp and there were many people who were experimented on. Thank God, I was not subjected to any of these cruel experiments.

Although Gloria was not forced to submit to "medical" experiments, she arrived at Ravensbrück with a medical problem, which she described. "I have a lot of marks on my body that are beginning to show up now as I get older," she said. "I don't know if you can see it now, but here. I have all kinds of marks all over my right leg. But these are malnutrition problems that I had, deep wounds all over . . . I already had it in Beendorf. By the time I was in Ravensbrück, they were huge. Actually I could see the bone, the shin of my right foot. But it would start as a little pimple, and they would multiply, because one, larger and deeper, became infected, refused to heal, because my body actually was consuming itself. And so it took months, even later when I was free, before they would even begin to heal."

In reflecting about her time at Ravensbrück and other camps, Gloria offered an important insight into an often overlooked difference between Jewish and non-Jewish prisoners. While non-Jews were frequently able to keep in contact with their families and even receive food parcels, this was not possible for the Jewish women. She explained:

You know that the Jewish people were taken with their entire families and wiped out totally. Most of them were wiped out totally. Those of us who are alive were one or two, maybe a mother, very rarely, or a sister. Of course, we didn't know about the menfolk. Now, the non-Jews were usually only that person who was involved in the act, political prisoners. . . . So she was able to correspond with the others. The Jewish people didn't have any "back home." If somebody was hidden, you wouldn't dare write a letter there. You couldn't anyway, because you were Jewish. And so neither of you knew of the other at any time. Imagine getting a letter from home. It would be enough to keep you wanting to live, no matter how starved you are, and to get a little package. They were censored. Letters were censored, and the packages were small, but, gee, I know that in Auschwitz we had people who shared their packages with us, even if it was just a quarter of a little cookie. You know, just the very idea that someone wants to share—or they got salami. That's the only salami I had.

Gloria arrived at Ravensbrück soon before the Swedish Red Cross intervened, the death marches began, and the Soviet Army ultimately arrived on 3 May 1945. She later discovered that she arrived in Sweden with the first group of Jewish women from the camp, so she must have left on around April 24 or a little earlier.

GLORIA'S DEPARTURE FROM RAVENSBRÜCK

Gloria did not actually leave on the Red Cross transport, but they seem to have caught up with her group and rescued them along the way. She remembers her departure from the camp, but was unconscious for part of her voyage to freedom:

One day we were just ordered into cattle cars, and the train just kept moving and stopping quite aimlessly. It could be that the railroad was bombed and they couldn't go any farther, but we just didn't make much headway. And there we were, locked up in these cattle cars completely without food or drink. Finally we arrived at a place, and we were ordered to get off, and we went by a huge farm. There were no homes at all. There were these farm buildings. I would suppose they would store hay in them, but they were huge farm buildings. In fact, they were brick red, painted brick red in color. I'll never forget. We were ordered into this one, we thought for the night, and opened the huge front doors which had latches like this which opened and closed. And as we went in, to our right there was this big pile of striped clothes, not grays. Like, you know, in Auschwitz—like some people had—these striped clothes actually were just leftovers from the Russian prisoners whom they murdered in the Auschwitz gas chambers. But how do they get here? I'm not sure whether they were all striped, but mostly striped clothes, and why were they there, and they were all damp. You know, almost wet, but not really wet. So we began to wonder what happened to the people to whom these belonged.

So we went in, and there was nothing there. We just sat down on the floor, on the ground, and they closed the latch on us. So at first we thought nothing of it. But in the back of minds you wonder, "I hope we're safe." You just didn't feel safe anywhere, anything they did with us. And then we saw two pipes. The upper window, way up high, you couldn't possibly reach it by stretching out or by standing on another person easily, and this white steam was coming in. And we heard a motor, and this white steam was coming in. We thought it was steam. Anyway, we didn't smell anything. I couldn't smell anyway. In Auschwitz I lost my sense of smell. But the girls were saying, "It doesn't smell like gas," or something like that.

However, Gloria remembers that the women were concerned, and one of them took off her wooden clog and broke some of the windows to let some fresh air in. "Then she took her other clog off and broke some more," Gloria said. "And suddenly we heard the Germans come, and I thought they were going to shoot us all, but they didn't. They just stopped putting the steam in or whatever that was, and we stayed there that night quite anxious. Are they going to shoot us now, murder us all?" While the hot steam was coming in, it was so warm that some of the women took off their coats, Gloria said. "So then this girl finally decided to let some air in, but then the Germans outside were afraid that we climbed up on top of each other and were trying to shoot—I don't know why they would even have thought of that, because we were completely unarmed. But anyway, we thought they must be getting after us some— they'll get us one way or another, but what is it? We could never outguess them," she said

"Well, when morning came, it was kind of a march," she continued. "At this point we marched, and I don't know whether you would call it a death march, but the shape we were in—I think you can call it a death march. But I've heard of people marching much farther. And people did drop here and there. We were just too weak to take very much anymore," she added. "So we were wondering what's waiting for us after this experience in the barn, and we really weren't sure what we experienced."

So we walked all the way to the train and were ordered into cattle cars, and that train just kept moving and stopping. Finally we arrived at our destination out in an open field. There was nothing there except gentle, rolling hills. And before we even were let out, we heard the Nazis outside discuss our fate. We were all going to be shot. Oh, I remember all these reactions that set in. I personally felt numb. I couldn't believe that it would end like this after all I've endured. And some people fell into deep apathy, and others began to scream or to become delirious. But then the doors opened, and, "*Raus,* out, out, everybody."

We were ordered to push out the dead and the sick. This couldn't have been far from Ravensbrück, just not far, but I don't know how far and where exactly it was. And we should push out the dead and the sick, and about half or more of the people were dead from exhaustion, malnutrition, diseases and hunger, whatever. So we decided in our cattle car that if we're going to be shot anyway, we're going to let the sick

146

stay, come what may. So they'll shoot us here instead of somewhere else. So we pushed out the dead, and then those of us who still could walk were ordered to stand in line or walk in a certain direction in an orderly fashion. . . . I saw that two women were doling out something from burlap sacks, and [it] must have been the food of the guards, because they doled out a handful of just sugar, crystallized sugar, and a handful of raw macaroni to people.

I didn't have a dish to put it in, so I held up my gray dress to receive my ration. And I kept looking, and I was completely unaware that there were holes in my dress, and the macaroni and sugar just spilled on the tall, mushy, wet grass. So as if in slow motion, I remember just going down to pick up some of the macaroni, because the sugar was a total loss, and just as this was happening I was hit, and I was hit again, and then I remember I just blacked out, and I collapsed and lost consciousness. I really would have died there had not some of my fellow prisoners still been capable of human feelings and compassion.

Gloria learned later that some of the women carried her onto the train, where she remained unconscious for more than three days. During this time the Nazis evidently fled, and the Swedish Red Cross rescue team gathered up Gloria and the women who were with her. When she regained consciousness, her friends told her that they were with the Swedish Red Cross, and that they had stopped at several other camps to pick up other prisoners to bring them to Sweden.

"When I came to, I was on an entirely different train," she recalled. "I was on a real passenger train, and I was crossing the Danish countryside. . . . And I thought I was hallucinating at this time, because nothing that I heard made sense. I said, 'Weren't they just about to shoot us? Wasn't I just beaten up?' and I was feeling myself and feeling sore. And then they said that, 'We are free.' And you know how much I would have loved to believe this, but there were so many rumors throughout my incarceration period that never materialized that it just didn't seem possible," she said.

Fortunately for Gloria, she was not hallucinating, and she had indeed been rescued. She later learned that at the last moment the Swedish rescue team had caught up with the train she was on and liberated the group. "The train pulled to a stop in Copenhagen, and friendly faces by the thousands greeted us behind barricades," she said. "But they broke through the barricades, and they had brown bags and little Swedish flags in their hands. They broke through the barricades and came up to the train and handed us these brown bags. I remember the chocolate and boiled, peeled, and neatly cut-up potatoes still warm, something in the bag, and I just looked at it. I wasn't hungry. I couldn't eat, but I watched everybody eat, and they were eating ferociously, you know, and they got so sick, so sick, and some of them died right there after freedom, after they reached freedom on Danish soil already. People were really dying like flies all the way through to Sweden."

GLORIA'S RECOVERY IN SWEDEN

Like other Ravensbrück survivors who were rescued directly from the camp or one of its satellites, Gloria was taken by ferryboat from Copenhagen to Malmö, Sweden. Arriving on 3 May 1945, she was brought to a public shower. "Somebody tried to tell us, 'water, shower,'" she recalled. "And they had to turn it on before we believed that it was going to be a shower. But what I remember most is the full-length mirrors there. I'll never forget when I looked at myself for the first time. I got scared. I did this to hide myself. You know, I was skin and bones sticking out all over and these big hollow eyes, and I said to myself, 'This is not the Hunzi [Gloria's name then] that I saw last.' It was so incredible."

Her rescue in Sweden is unusual because she was only fifteen, and two Swedish families wanted to adopt her. However, she turned both of them down. Although she moved in with one of the families in August, she did not want to be adopted and was longing for news of her own family. She had no idea if anyone had survived. "I started writing right away home, Hungarian and Czech, the Czech address and Hungarian address, the same place, but different names," she said. She heard nothing in reply while she was in quarantine and in the recuperation center. She suffered from nightmares, and had been ordered by the doctors not to work and to continue resting. Suddenly, she said, something stirred in her memory:

> But one night—one night—I still hadn't heard from my mother. I was beginning to feel that I'm the sole survivor of my family, and that was my biggest threat, and at the age of fifteen I had to start making arrangements for my life, what do I want to do. I decided that if nobody in my family will be alive, then I'm going to Israel, I'm going to help build a Jewish homeland, because after all I went through, I think that can be the only home that I would accept.
>
> But I kept trying. I used to know my aunts' and my uncles' addresses, because I mailed Mother's letters at the post office, and I would write under her letters very often, but I forgot. I remembered the names and I remembered the cities, but it wasn't like today, call 411, or information or operator, and certainly not the telephone books. So you couldn't find out. But one night—I was already with the Swedish family—and Gullan, my Swedish sister, and I shared one room. I woke up, and I said, "Gullan! Gullan, I just dreamt that my uncle's address was 5236 Del Mar, Saint Louis, Missouri, M-O, St. Louis, Missouri." I didn't know actually what it was. And so she ran for paper and pencil. She says,

"Write it down, because by morning you'll forget." And how wise she was to do that, because I probably would have forgotten. And in the morning she pressed me to write that letter right away. I wrote it, and my uncle got my letter in St. Louis, Missouri, and I missed his address by two numbers within the same block. So maybe by the time I wrote it down, I didn't remember. And he notified my aunt in Kansas City and my first cousins in New Jersey and Arizona.

Soon Gloria had a family in the United States, but she still didn't know anything about her nuclear family in Europe. She eventually received a letter from her mother and recalled her emotions:

I couldn't believe it. I had a good cry before I could even read it. I'll never forget giving that letter such a kiss, as if it could just kiss back. And my mother wrote, then, that she and Annushka [Anna, Gloria's sister] were liberated soon after we were separated and that she never expected me to be alive, that the radio announced periodically long lists of survivors here and there, and that people would be glued to the radios, and that people came to tell her that I am alive and I'm in Sweden. And she refused to believe it, and she told them nobody ever came back from the gas chambers, that perhaps it's somebody else by that name. And then other people came, too. And so she was beginning to feel maybe there's something to that, but she didn't dare to believe it, she wrote.

Gloria's mother then sent her brother Michael to Budapest to check the Red Cross lists and verify her survival. He had been the first member of the family to be liberated and to come home after the death marches. Michael returned from Budapest with a copy of a comprehensive Red Cross list of survivors that included Gloria's name. "Mother still couldn't believe it," Gloria said, "until she had my own letters, six of them at the same time. You know, in the aftermath of the war, there was so much chaos, the postal service was totally irregular," she said. She also explained how she had to make a difficult choice about her future:

And so then came the question of what to do with my life. I had to make a quick decision, because the Swedish Red Cross was anxious to unite families, but most of us had nobody. And if they knew that my mother was alive, then they would send me home. To warn me about this, my uncle wrote from St. Louis, "Do not tell the Swedish Red Cross if you hear anything from your parents, because we already started making our papers for you to come to the United States." I wanted to go home and be with my mother. This separation was so hard on me, that I just was dying to be with my mother. But she wrote to me that, "As much as we would have you come home, we think you will have a better life in America." And so I obeyed her advice, with pain in my heart, knowing that I would never, ever see her again. And my mother died three years later from hardship suffered in the camp.

GLORIA'S LIFE IN THE UNITED STATES

Meanwhile, after two years in Sweden, Gloria immigrated to the United States and settled in Kansas City, where part of her family lived. She worked during the day and went to night school. She met her husband, Karl Lyon, a German Jew who had fled Germany in 1937, and they were married in 1949. They settled in San Francisco, where Karl was studying law, and they had two sons, David and Jonathan. Gloria worked there for twenty years as a banking research analyst. She then began a successful "bed and breakfast" business in San Francisco. Encouraged by discussions with guests in her home and others, she began to speak publicly about her experiences.

Although Gloria never had the opportunity to see her mother again, she was eventually reunited with the other surviving members of her family. She received permission to visit them in the Ukraine, then part of the Soviet Union, and afterward managed to bring out her father, and her sister and two brothers, along with their families. The Holocaust not only murdered millions of Jews but it also broke up families, and some survivors have never been reunited with other surviving members of their families. Gloria's struggle to bring her family to the United States is a continuation of the story of her experiences during the Holocaust.

Gloria has made an effort to trace the odyssey of her time in seven camps, by visiting the sites, talking with other survivors, and studying the Red Cross Arolsen records in Germany. "I've learned, from other survivors, that Ravensbrück was much worse than it appeared to me," she said. "It's not that I was evaluating Ravensbrück, because they were all terribly horrible, just horrible, but since they were there longer, they were exposed to much more than I was during the short time, and that people were continuously beaten up unnecessarily, illogically, mistreated, and experimented on in great numbers."

Like the Jewish survivors from Auschwitz who came to Ravensbrück during its last months, Fela Kolat, Manya Friedman, and Gloria Lyon stressed the importance of the nurturing support they received from family and close friends. They were all in Ravensbrück for a relatively short time, but all have vivid memories of the horrors they witnessed.

11

The Satellite Work Camps

MANY Jewish women who entered Ravensbrück were sent off to do slave labor in the main camp's satellite work camps, especially Malchow and Neustadt-Glewe. While individual survivors have shared with me their recollections of some of Ravensbrück's satellites or subcamps, much documentation has been lost, and it may never be possible to compile accurate details and statistics that provide an overall view.

Ravensbrück's first subcamps were created in 1941–1942. After 1943, many satellites affiliated with the main camp were constructed alongside already existing factories involved in war production.[1] Some were not actually camps but locations in cities, where slave labor was needed in factories or other activities. Ravensbrück also supplied workers to other camps that were not directly under its command, which causes confusion about statistics regarding the main camp's prisoner population.

In addition, some women were sent to camps that were at first satellites of Ravensbrück, but after the fall of 1944 came under the jurisdiction of Buchenwald, Sachsenhausen, Flossenbürg, or Mauthausen. Incomplete documentation proves a minimum of 31,000 female inmates moved during 1944–1945 to the satellite camps belonging to Buchenwald or Flossenbürg concentration camps. More than 4,300 female inmates were sent from Ravensbrück to satellite camps subordinated to Neuengamme concentration camp in June–September 1944.[2]

Malchow, a satellite of Ravensbrück that had an underground armament factory, will be discussed in the next chapter, because it was on the route of the death march out of Ravensbrück. Most of the Jewish survivors of subcamps who shared their stories with me were in either

Memorial marker at Neustadt-Glewe, one of the subcamps of Ravensbrück, located in the Neustadt-Glewe airfield, Mecklenburg. Photo by Karl Heinz Schütt.

Malchow or Neustadt-Glewe. In addition to eyewitness recollections of Neustadt-Glewe, there is information from research done on the camp by a current inhabitant of that town, Karl Heinz Schütt. Distressed by the tragic events that had taken place where he was living, he wrote a small book and two supplements about the subcamp, and compiled a partial list of inmates.[3]

The Satellite Work Camps

FELA KOLAT IN NEUSTADT-GLEWE

Fela Kolat of Sosnowiec, who described coming from Gleiwitz to Ravensbrück in the previous chapter, spoke in detail about her days in Neustadt-Glewe. Her last memory of Ravensbrück was receiving "a nice piece of liverwurst" for the trip to the satellite camp. Throughout the ordeal she was with her friend, Regina Weisfelner.[4] Fela recalled:

> In Neustadt-Glewe it was again a standing, we could not go into the barracks. Stand, counted, stand. So this Regina Weisfelner, we needed a drink, we needed a drink, I don't know, somehow, like I said, she was stronger. We all had on a piece of rope here, we had a cup, so she somehow had a cup of water, and she figured she was going to share the water with me, and while she poured the water in my cup, this German came over and put my head in her head, like this, and a tooth right away was shaky.
>
> And again, we could not go in the barracks, I think, until almost the evening. When we got in, they checked us, so like I said, I had a couple of pair of panties—I don't know if I had two or three, T-shirts. And this German woman started to slap my face so hard, because I had more than one pair of the panties. And when we went into the barracks, there were no bunk beds, just the floor. So Regina and I, and there were the Zion sisters . . . and there was Sala Teichner (she is in Canada), and Etka Fridberg—we were at the wall. Somebody else was sitting in between the legs. There was no room to lie down. It was so crowded. And there the soup was just plain water. And the piece of bread was like you take a slice of white bread toast . . .
>
> So it was much worse—the food in Neustadt-Glewe—than it was in Ravensbrück. And the walls were covered with lice, like bedbugs. This Regina Weisfelner, I put my head in her lap, and she picked the lice, and that's how we spent the days. We had no water, we had no shower, we had—the conditions were the worst of the worst of the worst.

There were no work assignments, but Fela heard about a volunteer job and thought it might be a way to obtain extra food:

> In one corner was this friend from Paris, a girl, I don't know when she arrived because she had still a little nice color on her cheeks and she still had some energy, and one day she said, "You know, when we walked in the trenches." That means they were volunteers, and this, one of the Germans gave her a couple cigarettes, and the woman who gave out the soup, if you gave her the cigarettes, she gave you from the bottom, the thick stuff, otherwise she took the ladle and she gave you the watery stuff. So Regina said to me, maybe it's an idea to go volunteer to work in the trenches.
>
> So one day we did. So we walked to the woods and to dig the trenches, but I had no muscles, I was very weak, and it was already

started, the trench, so this German said, "Why don't you work?" So I said, "I don't know how. I never had a shovel in my hand." So he went in and he tried to show me, and meanwhile there was a German woman who was in charge of us, too. And she said to this German that she was going to report him—that he is doing my work, I couldn't do it. The day was over, it was in the woods, it was fresh air. I could hardly walk and I could hardly hold the shovel walking home. Up to me walked a woman who used to be a nurse in the Jewish Hospital in Sosnowiec, and she took the shovel and carried [it] for me. And the next day, because I was not used to work, every muscle in my system was hurting. When you don't, when you sit every day, sit, sit, sit, and suddenly you want to walk, it's unbelievable how bad it is.

In addition to the kindness of the German male guard and the nurse from Sosnowiec, Fela remembered the comfort of sharing the scarce food at the camp. "There were three sisters—they are from Lodz," she said. "The youngest one, I don't know how—she went to the garbage, she found things. Nobody else could find things. I don't know how she did [it]—she brought in some things. We were starving. So there was this girl, Lola Lipschitz, from my city, it was Passover. I'm never going to forget this. It was Passover. Suddenly she had a cup of potatoes in the skin—boiled potatoes. So she took a slice, and shared a slice. She gave all us a slice of the potato—this was our Passover meal."

Several incidents from the days immediately before liberation also remained vivid in Fela's memory:

So that's how it was in Neustadt-Glewe, and one day I still had a watch that I carried in my shoe. Stupid me, it was almost ten days before the liberation, or maybe a week before the liberation, I figured they don't look anymore, they don't check anymore, so I took out the watch and I put it between the lining of the coat. One day [a Nazi overseer] walked over and touched it, and she found it. Did she slap me! Oh! Did she slap me so hard! She found the watch. And that's—every day was the same.

Before May second, that means maybe it was May first, or the last of April . . . it was a couple of days before the liberation. Suddenly, the German woman who gave us the soup gave us—everyone—like a teaspoon, maybe it was a tablespoon, of this powdered milk. They came already, some packages from the Red Cross, but [the Nazis] stole it because the whole amount that they gave was maybe a tablespoon of powdered milk. So I remember taking a little water and making a paste, but we were already so weak, like I said, the way they gave us the food, it was not to live, and not to die. Like I said, the soup. She gave from the top the watery stuff, and the rest she did for a cigarette, or for something.

So a couple of days before May second we noticed that the Germans put on the civil[ian] clothes, on the morning of May second, even May first, they didn't give out the soup. They didn't give the piece of bread. Nobody showed up. We didn't see a German face, May first, May second. I said to Regina, "Look at this, this girl is carrying maybe seven breads." I walked out and I just took from her a bread, so Regina saw I have this bread. Somebody told her there are potatoes. Nobody from the Germans are there, so she brought a couple of potatoes, we made a fire, and we baked a couple of potatoes on the fire.

The Soviet Army soon arrived and Regina, Fela's friend, was able to speak with them in Russian. "So the Russians came," Fela said. "So this Regina was born in Lvov, Lemberg, and she didn't come to Sosnowiec as a baby, she was already ten years old or something. So she knew to talk in Russian. So because she talked Russian, she talked to the first guy, and this guy right away said he was going to kill a pig. He did, he killed a pig. But naturally I said I'm not going to eat the pig, I like my baked potato. And whoever ate from the pig got very sick."

The Soviet soldiers told the former inmates to move into the barracks that their Nazi guards had occupied, in order to improve their living conditions. Fela suspects that the soldiers wanted to take advantage of the young women in the barrack. "Two Russians guys come in with a flashlight, shined us in the face," she recalled. "So this Regina said, 'we are sick girls,' and this guy, maybe he was intelligent, I don't know, he left . . . the next day we had to take . . . a piece of furniture from metal. So where the door is, we put this outside so they would not see the door. So we were afraid."

Some of the former inmates took over the homes of local Germans who had fled the Soviet soldiers. Fela and Regina decided to find fresh clothes in one of the empty houses and get rid of their lice-infested clothing. "So we started out to go to the German houses," Fela said. "But because there were four thousand women, we could find nothing from women's clothes. Because the women from Poland, from the uprising, they emptied already the women's clothes. So when we walked in this house, I found a men's jacket, a sport jacket, the sleeves were to here, a men's shirt, so we took these two pieces." Someone then helped her make a skirt out of the drapes. To replace her worn out shoes, she took some ice skates and removed the blades. The most valuable item they found was a container of "black pills" in the medicine cabinet. "The girls who had diarrhea from the pig, it saved their lives," Fela said.

Fela and the group of young women from her barrack moved into the headquarters of the Russian commandant, where they felt safer. However, during the two weeks they were there, they were required to scrub the living quarters and to peel the potatoes. At the end of that time, the commandant told them it was time to go home, and after many hours of travel she finally arrived in Sosnowiec.

LEA GELBGRAS FERSTENBERG IN NEUSTADT-GLEWE

Lea Gelbgras Ferstenberg of Warsaw, whom we met in chapter 9, arrived in Ravensbrück with the evacuees from Auschwitz. When we interrupted Lea's story in that chapter, she was doing nothing but waiting, and then she was shipped to Neustadt-Glewe. Like Fela, Lea spoke of the hunger she felt at the satellite camp and about her liberation.[5] "When we were liberated in Neustadt-Glewe, the second they opened the gate for us to go out, I remember being just out of my mind," Lea said. "I was screaming and crying. . . . I realized that I'm alone. So the next day, the Russians forced us to go out from the camp because it was really—sickness was coming. It was dirty." The Russian soldiers evacuated the prisoners and burned the camp down to prevent disease, Lea said. She and a group of young women were brought to the town of Pritzwalk, where, like Fela and her friend, they began looking for some clothing and a safe place to sleep.

"We were trying to organize some clothes, some clothes to be dressed, to have something," Lea said. "So I remember like today, we went out in Pritzwalk, on the street." However, at first she had a problem taking clothing from the German civilians in the town. "A man was standing in the window and he looked like my father," she said. "I was talking about revenge. We went in and went out. I couldn't even take from him his shoes that were in the house. In the house were shoes. I went in and went out. I couldn't. I couldn't." Finally she was able to take something to wear from another house. "There were some empty houses," she said. "People were afraid of us and they were hiding in basements. So you went and you found some clothes. I even found a *renard*, a fox [fur piece]."

Like Fela's friend Regina, one of Lea's friends knew Russian and spoke to a soldier. He gave them two horses and a wagon, and the six women in Lea's group, along with two male survivors, traveled toward Warsaw. When their belongings were stolen from the wagon, they complained to a Russian soldier who brought Lea a winter coat. They finally reached the Polish border and managed to get a train to Warsaw. "Warsaw was destroyed," she said.

RESEARCH ON NEUSTADT-GLEWE

Thanks to Neustadt-Glewe resident Karl Heinz Schütt's diligent research, we have some general information to substantiate Fela's and Lea's individual recollections.[6] The camp was founded to supply workers for Dornier-Werke, an airplane factory that had been relocated to the airbase at Neustadt-Glewe after the original one in Wismar had been destroyed in 1943. When the camp was initiated, ten barracks that had been part of the airport were fenced in with electrified barbed wire. A second opaque barrier was added, along with guard towers armed with machine guns. The camp was opened with three hundred female inmates in the fall of 1944, and by the end of December there were an estimated nine hundred prisoners, with some women even sleeping in hallways. Beginning in January 1945, larger transports arrived and the overcrowding led to catastrophic hygienic conditions. Additional barracks, unheated and unfurnished, were requisitioned from the airbase.

The conditions in the camp caused an increase in deaths from hunger and disease after 1944, but there are no concrete figures or even estimates of the total number of deaths at this point. Since there are no complete lists of names or designated camp numbers, many of the women remain anonymous. Most prisoners died after severe malnutrition made them more susceptible to typhus, tuberculosis, or dysentery. Various gravesites were later discovered in the woods, as well as in the town cemetery. Inmates apparently transported the dead on a handcart through town to the cemetery, where local visitors were told to leave while the burials took place.

Overall, Schütt believes that we have to assume that the number of women who died in the camp far exceeded five hundred, with deaths sharply increasing after mid-March 1945 (a time period for which there is no documentation of deaths). In the beginning of March, the corpse detail buried eighty women in one week. Estimates suggest at least forty to seventy deaths a week in the infirmary, not counting those women who were transported back to Ravensbrück to be murdered in the gas chamber. Survivor Rena Kornreich Gelissen, who worked in the corpse detail in Neustadt-Glewe, recalled: "There is a huge mountain of corpses, two meters tall." She added: "the camp stinks of decomposing bodies."[7]

By the time that Fela and Lea were sent to Neustadt-Glewe, prisoners were no longer assigned to slave labor. However, for most of the camp's existence, the female inmates started working in two twelve-hour shifts immediately after arrival, assembling wings, motors, and fuselages at the airport. Others were detailed to hard physical tasks, such as moving planes onto runways, cutting trees in the surrounding woods, and providing labor in a nearby concrete factory, always under guard. Transports arrived until the end of April 1945. While the exact total number of inmates cannot be determined, it is assumed to have been more than five thousand. More than sixty percent of the women were Jews from Hungary, Poland, Czechoslovakia, the Soviet Union, Yugoslavia, Holland, France, Belgium, Greece, and Germany, as well as Roma and Sinti women from some of these countries. Some inmates were political prisoners, for example those arrested during the Warsaw uprising.[8]

On the morning of 2 May 1945, the guards fled the camp, along with inmates who had worked for them. French male prisoners-of-war then came from their nearby camp, disabled the electrified fence, and opened the gate. Women in barracks outside the fence liberated themselves by breaking through the doors and undoing the barbed wire outside their windows. Many of the women then left the camp, and some returned with a U. S. Army patrol that they came across in the vicinity. However, because the area was not part of their zone, the American soldiers soon went away. In the late afternoon of 2 May, Red Army tanks liberated the town and camp of Neustadt-Glewe.

Some of the women returned immediately to their home countries, and, as Fela and Lea described, some remained in the town or nearby in abandoned houses to recover strength for their travels. Bus transports were organized for the weak and sick. About three hundred severely ill women were tended in a makeshift hospital in a local school. Some of the sick women who could be transported were flown home out of Ludwigslust or Schwerin-Goeries. The camp and airbase were briefly used by the Red Army and later dismantled.

Before liberation, Ravensbrück had supplied guards, work details, and infirmary personnel to its Neustadt-Glewe subcamp, and reports were constantly sent to the main camp. Because the statistics for Neustadt-Glewe and other satellites were generally included with those for the main camp, there is very little documentation for these subcamps. Furthermore, almost all information on Neustadt-Glewe was destroyed when the fleeing Nazis tried to suppress evidence. Because of this lack of documentation, the testimony provided by Fela Kolat, Lea Ferstenberg, and other survivors interviewed for this book, as well as Schütt's research, is all the more valuable. Other Ravensbrück survivors who told me that they were in Neustadt-Glewe include Hilda Kreuzer of The Bronx, New York; Esther Peterseil of Lawrence, New York; Agnes Werber of Royal Palm Beach, Florida; Esther Goldman of Norfolk, Virginia; Clara Rosenbaum of Montreal, Canada; and Martha Rothman of San Diego, California.

ESTER WEISZ GRUN IN MEUSELWITZ

While Neustadt-Glewe and Malchow are the two satellite camp destinations most often mentioned by the Jewish survivors that I have encountered, they were not the only subcamps to which Jewish Ravensbrück prisoners were shipped. For example, Ester (Eliz) Weisz Grun was sent to Meuselwitz. Ester was introduced in chapter 7, which described her harsh outdoor work at Ravensbrück. Deported from Satoraljaujhely, Hungary, to Auschwitz in the spring of 1944, she arrived in Ravensbrück that December. Ester spoke of her experiences in Meuselwitz, an almost unknown satellite camp near Leipzig where she was sent at the end of

January 1945.[9] She remembered being selected to leave the main camp, along with fifteen other young women:

> Sixteen of us. We were all young. So all of a sudden we were going on feet, walking to a train station, which took about two hours. It is bitter cold weather, four o'clock in the morning. Shoes. I have a pair of shoes . . . that has no shoelace or socks, and my feet [were] frozen, terribly frozen, which I suffered for the rest of my life having a frozen pair of feet, and after all, no underwear. Just one layer of dress. So we [were] walking and walking. We got to a train station, and then finally one girl, Anikó—the SS were near her. Now, you know, sixteen people are taking up room, and she had the courage to ask him, "Where are we going?" He said that he is taking us to an *Arbeitzlager* [work camp], to an ammunition factory and a town called Meuselwitz. He also said, "Do not worry. You are going to go to work every day, one week, nights, one week during the daytime, and you will be okay," and that was the whole conversation. . . . Then we were in the train. The train went like seven hours. This was a regular train.

Ester had vivid memories of her group's introduction to the new camp:

> We arrived [at] the station in Meuselwitz, that's the name of the town. Then we have to get on our feet again for about two hours, walking to the concentration camp in Meuselwitz, and the SS took us to the *Revier*, which is like a little hospital. There was a nurse who was welcoming us, checking our hands, hair. By then my hair is growing. I really had . . . long hair almost like now. Then she is looking and checking [for lice], taking out like section by section [of hair] with a pencil, and I am shivering, is she going to find something. But there was one girl in Ravensbrück that we were religiously checking each other's hair daily to make sure, because I can't begin to tell you how awful the flies, disease, the filth, the dirt, the bacteria that were just covering us. We made sure with this girl, checking our hair, and luckily this nurse could not find anything. She said that my head is clean. She's not going to touch my hair, and I, of course, said, "Thank you."
>
> Well, after they finished checking our complete body from head to toe, we were taken into a shower room, and I can't begin to tell you how frightened we were. What is this shower going to be? The same SS woman and the same SS man are looking over us, and, of course, we had to take our clothes off, and we were frightened, we were panicking. We were embarrassed, also. Nobody ever saw me naked. But anyway, and they gave us a little bit of soap, and they let us shower. And we put on our clothes.
>
> We did take the shower, yes. It was a real shower with water. Finally after all those months, we have a shower that we can take. From there we were taken and given a room for ourselves in Meuselwitz. The sixteen young girls had their own room. So that was such a relief. We felt

like we are in paradise. . . . It was just that we were together, sixteen of us. It became like a little family, like sisters. Then we got to know each other more and more, you know, like we woke up together, we went to sleep together. We were there until 1945, April.

Ester added that she was glad that she was "at least under the roof." She said the women "received a tiny bit of bread a day, and also a little bit of lukewarm water at night before we would retire. We also had a room where we had heat given to us, because there was a fireplace in the center of the room. They gave us a blanket. We slept in our clothes. They gave us a little wood, firewood, and we were able to make a little fire." Ester remembers that Meuselwitz was a very large concentration camp, where five thousand Polish non-Jews were working when she arrived.[10]

Except for a Jewish woman she knew who was posing as a non-Jew, she believes her group of sixteen were the only Jews at the camp. Her slave labor assignment was in "an ammunition factory where we are producing war weapons, bullets," she said. "I was put on a very special machine that I was producing hundreds of bullets daily," she explained. "We had one week [of] daytime work for about twelve hours, and one week, at night we worked. The SS would come, taking us into the factory . . . producing bullets, thousands of bullets. We had like a holder where we had to place [them] when we were ready with the bullets, to drill it through and put it right in to insert it. Then two people had to hold it on each side to carry it where they were collecting."

The concentration camp, including the ammunition factory, was bombed several times, and Ester had to do construction work to repair the damage. After the destruction became too severe, the commander announced that the camp would be evacuated. The women were "herded right like animals into these open wagons," Ester recalled, "and we were just going with the train, where we don't know, just going. We were trying to avoid where the war was really going on, so first their aim is to leave the area, the concentration camp. Then they bombed the train. There were a lot of incidents," she said. "Terrible. Some people were badly hurt. The wagon is open, and they were bombing from the air, and they had to be taken to the hospital, and because of the tracks bombed, we could not go anymore. Everybody had to get out of the wagon. The SS crew was marching with us. We were marching for three solid nights and days in the bitter cold weather, because April in Germany, it's still snowy, cold conditions."

The evacuees from Meuselwitz continued marching through mountainous terrain until they finally reached farmland. They were allowed to rest for only two hours each night, and they walked from farm to farm. Meanwhile, the SS shot anyone who could not go on. Ester said she was in "terrible condition" during the forced march:

My shoe broke—the wooden shoe. I can barely walk because my feet are off balance. The mud, the ice, the water, everything goes into my left foot, left shoe. Well, I am swollen, my knees, my ankles, my elbows, my wrists are frozen. It's a huge farm. We are there. They had not given us food. This is the third week already, night and day in the freezing cold. One day the Red Cross showed up on the highway giving us a raw potato. One day we receive a boiled potato, [from the] Red Cross also.

Well, anyway, this is a farmland. I am exhausted, I'm crying, I'm helpless like everybody else, five thousand people, and this SS commander and their crew are cruel, like marching through a mountain hill, and in April the buds, the beautiful tender little green buds already breaking through the trees, the little branches. So . . . I pinched off a bud. The SS woman had spotted me. She saw that I pinched it off. I never forget, she comes over to me, hit my hand so badly that I still feel it, telling me, "Don't you dare, or you'll be dead if you do it again."

ESTER GRUN'S ESCAPE

Ester and the women with her continued into the forest, reaching another farm along the way. She suddenly decided to take action that would result in either escape or death. She described the situation:

Then everybody settles down on the ground. It's snowing, bitter cold, and I'm standing. I said, "I can't lie down on the snow." I'm shivering. There is a huge straw stack, a straw stack. . . . I am standing there, and I'm praying, again, talking to God to help me and saying my own prayer . . . and God is telling me that I should try to squeeze myself into this straw stack, and hopefully the SS is not going to watch me or see me, because he's going to shoot me to death. Nobody saw me. I managed to squeeze myself into it. I remained there all through those two hours. Four o'clock, we know when it was four o'clock, we heard, I heard. The SS announced it, the commander, "*Achtung! Achtung!*" [Attention! Attention!] We have to get up, get ready, and continue marching.

I did not come out from the straw stack. I remain there, and I said to God, "I cannot get out of here because the SS is searching now. He's going to see me coming out, and he's going to shoot me right there. I have to take a chance to stay there." And you know what? Suddenly I feel something. This is the SS, who is pushing his bayonet through, into the stack, and I feel that point of it right in the middle of my stomach, but luckily, he did not push it farther and he left. . . . Well, I hear everybody's marching away. I waited there for at least two hours, [it] must have been like six o'clock, seven o'clock. It's daylight. I could see the light coming through the straw. I managed to come out, but I threw myself on the ground because I couldn't stand up; I was frozen. So I lie down on the ground and just pick my head up and looked around if there is anyone, God forbid, because if there is anyone from the SS group, they [are] going to shoot me.

Ester saw a barn and crawled to it on her stomach. There she asked in Hungarian whether anyone else was hiding, and two of her comrades from Ravensbrück and Meuselwitz, Eva and Shari, answered her. "I can't begin to tell you, when we met each other, we just fell on the floor, all three of us crying," she recalled. "We were happy to be together and found each other, but thinking, what's going to be from here on. . . . Oh, you have no idea the feeling that we were like clinging to each other and crying and just were happy, and now, but what should we do?"

The three young women waited a few hours, and then headed down the road until they saw another farm. They tried two more farms and a home that had a sign saying that it belonged to the mayor of the next town, but no one would take them in. "We looked horrifying, filthy, dirty, raggedy," Ester said. The mayor yelled at them, and they ran away in fright. At the next farm they approached, the woman who answered the door told them there was no room but they could stay for the night in the washroom. "We were just so grateful to her being after all these weeks in the filth, in the mud, in the bitter cold, that we were going to have a night in the washroom. She asked her housekeeper to warm up the washroom. She gave us a huge tub of hot water to wash down," Ester said. Their hostess also sent them hot soup and was "very gracious and very nice," Ester added.

In the morning their rescuer sent a Hungarian woman to talk to them. They were terrified when she knocked, but she said she had been sent to help them. She told them she had gone to the City Hall earlier and had a drummer announce that three "young girls" were looking for any kind of work. Three farmers came forward and offered to have the friends work separately on their individual farms. Every Sunday afternoon they were allowed to meet each other. "Of course, we were thrilled and we were grateful," Ester said.

"We worked very, very hard," she continued. "I did all kinds of dirty, filthy work for the farmer, because there was no other way. I had to clean the stable from the animals. I had to drag it out with the wagon. I had to feed the animals. I had to keep them clean. I had to feed the chickens," she said. "The war was going on. They were bombing constantly." When there was a bombing raid, the farmer and his family disappeared. "I was the only one [who] remained on the farm, because I had to take care of everything, the animals," she said. "And I didn't see them. When the bombing would quiet down, they would come back. But again, shortly after, they would disappear again, and I wouldn't see them for days."

Ester was living in the kitchen, and the farmer's wife fed her one meal a day, unless the family had gone to their shelter. At such times, Ester stayed behind but had no access to food. She soon learned to steal eggs from the hens, swallow them raw, and bury the shells. She survived this way until she heard on a loudspeaker that Hitler was dead. "All of a sudden Shari and Eva appeared," she said. "They came over to me, and we are hugging each other, we are crying, we are happy, we are tearing, and you just don't know what to say or how to express our feelings." The man she was working for told all three friends they could stay on his farm, but they replied, "Thank you very much. We want to go home to our own families."

From there Ester and her friends began walking down the highway hoping to find transportation home:

> We walked up to a certain point, but then we found the Red Cross, who saw our condition, and we were just three *nebbish* [harmless] young girls, and they wanted to help us. So they sent a truck with a German, but that German was already a human, at least, and they had like benches in the truck and the three of us sat on the bench, and he took us to a school where they were trying to get people who needed help and collected all these people in this big school. We stayed there for a few days, just lying on the floor, and they sent in a little food through Red Cross. Then again they picked us up, and they were trying to go as far as they were able to, because everything was destroyed, the road, the tracks.
>
> The Nazis were still, some of them, shooting from the forest, and, you know, the Red Cross authorities, they have to be very careful to protect us. So when they find that it's okay to continue, then they would send another truck, and we would just slowly manage to get all the way to Vienna. In Vienna, the Red Cross was already waiting with a train. By then hundreds of us who survived were able to be put into the train, and they gave us a hot meal and some bread and they gave us like a washcloth. Then from there on, we were heading back to Hungary.

DORIS FUKS GREENBERG IN NEUBRANDENBURG

Neubrandenburg is another subcamp of Ravensbrück that is not widely known.[11] We met one survivor of Neubrandenburg, Doris Fuks Greenberg, in chapter 6. She arrived in Ravensbrück with the false papers of a non-Jew after the 1944 Warsaw uprising and was soon sent on to do slave labor at this satellite camp. Arrested as a non-Jewish political prisoner, she retained this designation at the subcamp.

Like Neustadt-Glewe, Neubrandenburg was near an airfield and a factory that made airplane parts.[12] "There were buildings right in the forest. They were just sticking out a little bit, but covered by the tree-tops," Doris remembered. "They had factories of parts for airplanes, and that's where they put us to work. Also, at the beginning they put us to work on a railroad. You know those narrow railroads. Not the regular railroad. We laid those rails." Doris worked in the factory until 8 March 1945, when she was shipped on to work on a farm.

Micheline Maurel, a non-Jewish political prisoner from France who arrived about a year before Doris, wrote that the camp was "a no man's land, a forsaken and forlorn outpost where no one would ever be able to find us." She described an enclosure with electrified barbed wire, a parade ground, and a kitchen that looked like a "black and windowless fortress." As for the "sanitary installations," they were "[t]wo buildings a few hundred feet away, one of which contained pipes and faucets, the other housing a single concrete bench, the top of which was pierced by twelve holes, six on a side. Between Block Three [where the French prisoners were housed] and the watchtowers, on a piece of ground that was still grassy, was another building, the delousing bathhouse, one part of which served as a jail."[13] Beyond the watchtowers, hills and a pine forest concealed the airfield. The factory where the women worked was between the camp and the town of Neubrandenburg. Throughout her book Maurel described the harsh conditions that included beatings, lice, disease, and severe hunger. She also listed the women's rations:

> For breakfast, at four in the morning, an unsweetened infusion that was called coffee. Nothing else.
> For lunch, a soup made of cabbage or turnips. Nothing else. No meat and no fat; just water and grit.
> For dinner, a slice of bread (in early months, about nine ounces; in the second year, half this amount). With the bread, merely the liquid part of the cabbage or turnip soup.
> On Sundays, in place of the soup, we had a ladleful of coffee, a microscopic pat of margarine and a slice of *cervelas*, or dry sausage. That was all. We were toiling twelve to fourteen hours a day, not counting the roll calls, the *Strafstehen* [punishments] and the extra details.[14]

On 28 April the Nazi overseers fled, and the women were able to walk out of the camp. The Soviet Army arrived in the area two days later.

BRACHA BLATTBERG SCHIFF IN RECHLIN

Bracha Blattberg Schiff included information about Rechlin, another sub-camp of Ravensbrück, in an unpublished testimony that she wrote for her children and grandchildren. She shared with me the pages on Ravensbrück and Rechlin.[15] Bracha arrived at Ravensbrück on the January 1945 death march from Auschwitz. "I didn't expect luxury there," she wrote, "but reality was even worse than I imagined." After about a week at Ravensbrück, she noticed that a group was being organized to be sent to a work camp and she joined them. "I knew from past experience that it might be a cover-up for a deportation camp, but I was so hungry that I didn't have anything to lose," she recalled:

> We boarded large trucks that left the camp's gate and continued on the roads westward. We traveled until we reached a village or small town named Rechlin. Next to the town was a small camp. It was a new experience for me.
>
> Here too, the day started with an *Appell* but without all the ceremony as in Auschwitz. Straight afterward we left for work. Close to the camp was a military airport. Our job was to dig ditches on the sides of the roads. We took out the dirt and prepared hiding places for civilians. The military men had more sophisticated bunkers. The air raids and bombing continued almost every night and also during the day. It was probably British planes. The bombings didn't scare me, maybe they gave me some hope. Our guards here were older military men. During an air raid they were the first to jump into the ditches. Our other job was to help clear the surface of debris after the air raids.

Bracha once again took a chance when she heard inmates were being transferred to another camp. "After some time in the camp I felt that the 'joy of revenge' of the air raids must have had a good influence on my emotional state," she recalled. "But the small food portions and the difficult physical work outside caused me to lose more weight. It was dangerous when you are already malnourished. Bathing was difficult and also limited. When they looked for candidates to be transferred to another camp, I was one of the first volunteers."

Bracha was deeply shocked when she realized that the transport was taking her back to Ravensbrück. However, after receiving a shower, clean clothes, and a Red Cross food package, she found herself on a bus on the way to freedom in Sweden.

Neustadt-Glewe, Meuselwitz, Neubrandenburg, and Rechlin are but four subcamps that were part of a vast empire of slave labor camps that used Ravensbrück prisoners in a brutal regime for the Nazi war effort.[16] The size of these installations varied from less than one hundred inmates to more than twenty thousand, and conditions depended on the overseers, increasing crowding, and the progress of the war. Even the best conditions included twelve-hour shifts and punishment, and the worst included death by starvation, illness, or more deliberate means. This chapter offers only a glimpse of the hundreds of subcamps of Ravensbrück and other major concentration camps, and this is an area of Holocaust history that still needs substantial investigation.

12

Malchow and the Death Marches

A LONG with Neustadt-Glewe, Malchow was the next destination for many of the Jewish women who arrived in Ravensbrück from Auschwitz in late January or early February 1945. Since the main camp was severely overcrowded by then, some women were soon sent on to subcamps such as Malchow, which was about forty-five miles northwest of Ravensbrück. Here, Malchow is treated separately from the other subcamps because it played the dual role of slave labor camp and one of the stops along the route of the death march from the main camp at the end of April 1945. Earlier prisoners in Malchow worked in a nearby underground munitions factory, which was camouflaged by a forest that had been planted above it. Malchow was also the site of a camp for male prisoners-of-war.[1]

All of the Malchow internees who spoke with me arrived so late that their slave labor was no longer required in the munitions factory. The women were sent there from Ravensbrück in February or March to die from disease or starvation. Those who arrived on the final death march from Ravensbrück came later and stayed briefly, leaving the main camp on 27–28 April. The women on the death march numbered somewhere between twelve thousand and twenty thousand, probably closer to the higher number.[2]

I. JUDITH BERGER BECKER AND RACHEL ROZENBAUM HOCHERMAN REMEMBER MALCHOW

I. Judith Berger Becker, whose vivid description of her time in Ravensbrück has already been recounted, was among those women sent to

The Mother Group. Sculpture at Ravensbrück memorial site, by Fritz Cremer. Photo by Diwischek, Lychen. Collection of MGR/SBG.

Malchow from the main camp in February.[3] "There was no work. We were just there to die," she said of her six weeks in Malchow. "I was looking for worms, or anything on the ground, to eat, and there weren't any worms!"

The women were given nothing but water, and during that time a typhus epidemic broke out, according to Judith. She believes that the prisoners were housed in a stable. "Because our barracks, I think most of the barracks, had two wings, and in the center was a water trough," she said. "And the water trough was definitely at the height of horses. And the two wings had nothing but a strip of wood that would probably be like a stall or an area for hay. Because it had a walk that would accommodate maybe two horses, and the rest of it was long, like the size of a bed, kind of a division on the floor, and there was no straw, there was nothing there. And we slept there."

Many of the women were ill, especially with typhus, Judith Becker recalled. "The sickness was just awful," she said. "After a while the girls were very much afraid because the dying were polluting the area, with emissions from the body. So they wanted to take them out before they were dead, while they could still be *schlepped* [dragged or carried], rather than carry dead weight, because nobody had strength." However,

Judith's mother, who was also lying on the floor and ill with typhus, prohibited this for religious reasons. "She lifted her head, and she said nobody is going to take a person out to bring on their death, and she explained to them the Jewish law," Judith said. She was referring to the prohibition against acting in a way that would hasten a person's death.

"And there was a big uprising," Judith continued. "And they said, 'Who are you, you cannot tell us this is going to preserve life.' But she says, 'No, it's not going to preserve life. It's going to kill your inner life. And your life is in the hands of God, and your inner life, you have to cultivate, and you cannot take these women out until they are dead.' Because of that, she asked everyone, 'If you feel you are dying, move out from the area where you are sleeping, and lie down on the walk, so it will be easier to carry [you] out,' because we just couldn't do it. So there were some scenes that were not to be believed."

Rachel Rozenbaum Hocherman, whose story is told in chapter 13 on rescue to Sweden, was also sent from Ravensbrück to Malchow in February 1945.[4] Like Judith Becker, she recalls that people died of starvation there. "Women were living on potato peels and water, and there was very little food," she said. However, she managed to find something extra to eat. "One day I went near the kitchen where a woman from my former gardening group was working, and I asked her for some soup that the *Volksdeutsch* [ethnic German] workers received," she told me. "This helped me and slowly I began to be able to eat and I recovered." When the prisoners-of-war incarcerated in another area of Malchow discovered Rachel and other nearby slave laborers, they shared their Red Cross food packages, she said. Rachel volunteered to be a gardener and began working in the hothouse. Two French male prisoners-of-war who worked there gave her bread and soup, much better food than the other prisoners received.

ROSE FROCHEWAJG MELLENDER MARCHES FROM MALCHOW

Rose Frochewajg Mellender, introduced in chapter 9, was also a prisoner in Malchow, arriving by way of Auschwitz and Ravensbrück.[5] She was not in Ravensbrück very long when she heard an announcement that, "The transport that just came is going farther. You're going to a very nice camp," she recalled. "So we thought, 'Ah-oh. God knows where we're going.' They marched us from Ravensbrück to places where we didn't even know what it is, what place it is, what day it is, snowing, and lucky it was snowing. Because of the snow, we survived. They took us to a place, Malchow. It was called Malchow. Clean, nice. We thought we came to heaven," she said. Rose continued:

We didn't do anything, but they at least gave us some food once a day. In the morning we got tea and a piece of bread. Then they gave you like two or three potatoes. So you cut the potatoes like it would be, you know, God knows what. Put it on the bread with a little salt and that's how you ate.

We were treated okay there, not beaten or anything. We were able to wash, not to bathe. There were no bathing facilities. It was a training camp . . . or something like this. They were going farther, so they gave us their clothes. We prayed to God, "Please let us stay here." We stayed three weeks.

Out. Underway. Why? Did we find out? Because the front was coming closer and closer, from one side the Americans, and from the other side the Russians. So they said, "This will be the end of you. We [are] looking for a place where we could destroy you completely. Nobody will find you ever." So we made already up that this is it, this is our destiny, and we wouldn't live.

We were walking ten miles in snow, sleeping outside in snow. We came to two big places where we saw men . . . in airplane hangers, and dead people piled up one on top of the other, burned to death. We said: "This is probably our destiny. That's where they bring us."

The Nazis didn't seem capable of finding a suitable place to deposit the women, and they kept marching them from one place to the other. They were in an area not far from Leipzig, Rose said. "We slept outside and on top of each other to keep warm. We got up in the morning all swollen like that, and the hands swollen from the cold. In the morning when the sun shines, we said, 'Oh, it's warm, let's take [our clothes] off,' and we used to wash ourselves with snow." The group continued on their forced march:

Then we came to a big place where they were shooting horses because the horses couldn't go any farther. They said you could cut the meat off the horses and eat. And people did. The liver they took, not cooked, they ate like that. I said, "I'd rather die than do that. I don't want it." And I ate snow and I had a few potatoes left.

As we were marching, a big woman, a Jewish woman, or maybe she wasn't Jewish, because I don't think that a Jewish [woman] would do this, she saw I had a few potatoes in a sack, because I ate a piece and I shared with my cousin. So we shared the potatoes for twice, three times. She saw that I had the five potatoes. She was a big husky woman, and she wanted to grab the sack up with the potatoes. She figured the little girl, she's weak anyway, she's going to die anyway. She wanted to grab my potatoes, and I started to put on a resistance. I said, "This is mine. Why are you taking them?" "No," she said, "you stole it from me." I said, "How did I steal? I wasn't even near you."

Everybody said [to the other woman], "What the hell are you talking about? You're stealing hers." The German saw what's going on, he came and said, "What's going on here?" You know, in German. She says, "She took my potatoes." When she said that, he took the gun and he wanted to shoot me. And they said, "No, no, it's the other way around! She wants to steal hers!" So he didn't know what to do, so he hit her with the carbine, hit me, and that's how—and my aunt protected me. She said to the woman, "If you come near her or to me, I'm going to kill you." So she never doubted that.

After Rose and her group continued on the forced march for days, she realized that the situation might be changing for the better:

We came to Leipzig, and all of a sudden they said to us, "There is a big place with the vegetables. Go take it. Take whatever you want." So we knew already something is cooking, you know. We look and they disappeared. The Germans disappeared. That was already March. By [the] end of March [more likely April], they disappeared. Nobody was around, because if we would know that's the end, we would tear them apart as much as we had no strength. But, you know—that we could have done. They disappeared and I grabbed a big—what is it called in English? It's like a yellow vegetable and you cook it and it has a smell to it. . . . A big smelly—like it looks like a big radish. A turnip. A big turnip [or related root vegetable]. I was set, you know, I held that. I didn't want—because I didn't know whenever I will eat that. At least [it] is a little sweet. You could eat, you know. I was liberated with that.

When Rose and her friends were freed near Leipzig, they pled with the local population for food and asked, "Throw us some bread." Instead, she said, the people threw hot water at them from the windows. Rose and the others continued to seek food and shelter:

We were told, "On one side are the Americans, on the other are the Russians. You're better off to go to the Americans, because the Russians rape the women." Who had strength to go across the Elbe by the water? We didn't have strength. But we stayed where we are. We started grouping, you know, and walking and begging the Germans—they should give us [something] to eat. Some gave us and some said, "Get the hell out. We're going to kill you." I said, "No, you're not, we're going to kill you now if you don't give us what we want."

So they gave us some food. They didn't let us in the houses. We stayed in the big school. They cooked some soup, the Red Cross. Whoever got, got. If you weren't very pushy, like I, I didn't get it. So good that I had that turnip. I kept cutting and eating.

Then at night some [survivor] men also, that were there already, came and they said, "Here is a camp for displaced people. We have food. We have everything. You could come." There were like two hundred, three hundred women—we went there. They gave us to eat and we got very sick, because we weren't used to eating. This was in Leipzig.

The warning that the Russian soldiers would try to rape Rose and her friends was then proven true. "They were right," she said. "The Russians did come and seek out some girls, you know, and we pretended that we are so very sick they shouldn't touch us. They were animals, because they didn't see a woman for such a—what did they care if she is a concentration camp, if she's sick, has lice or not? They didn't care. They had the lice, too, you know. And they raped some girls. So we had to hide under beds and things. It was a struggle all along, all along."

Finally Rose and a friend met a Polish officer who helped them return to Poland. "Then in that camp we met some people from Poland, a very intelligent officer," she said. He was going back to Poland and offered to take Rose and her friend. "If we want to go, he's going to take us. So we trusted him. He took us on the station wagon and he brought us to a town, let us go. There we went to the Red Cross and they sent us into a Jewish organization. That's how we survived. From there we went to Poland," she said

ERNA ELLERT ON THE DEATH MARCH TO THE ELBE

Erna Ellert was also sent to Malchow from Ravensbrück, shortly after her arrival there from Auschwitz. She was on the death march from Malchow and arrived at the Elbe River near Schwerin at about the same time as the Allied and Soviet forces. Erna was actually born in the city of Auschwitz, or Oswiecim, Poland; her father was from Breslau and her mother from Vienna, so she spoke fluent German. A trained nurse, she was in various camps beginning in November 1940, later ending up back in Auschwitz as a prisoner. Erna told me an amazing story as we rode on a bus from Berlin to Ravensbrück in April 1995.[6] She was already in the gas chamber at Auschwitz-Birkenau with the door closed, when some SS guards opened the door to add a mother and newborn infant to those destined for annihilation. Erna was naked except for a silver fox fur that she had draped around her. All of a sudden she heard one of the SS men ask, "Who is the girl from the jungle?" She ran to him and said, "Please save us," adding that she was a nurse and had been born in Auschwitz.

Inexplicably, he released Erna, two other nurses, and a doctor from the gas chamber and sent them to Block Eleven, which housed non-Jewish Polish political prisoners. She was sent to neighboring Block Ten to assist during experimental surgery on young women, and later to work in the *Union,* the munitions factory in Birkenau. She was there on 18 January 1945 when the workers were lined up and sent out of the camp on the death march and the open train ride to Ravensbrück.

Erna believes she arrived in Ravensbrück during the first few days of February and soon afterward was sent on to Malchow. "And then we went to Malchow, and it was better," she said. "We had a place in the barracks and more food. We ate whatever they gave us. Water was very rare—it was frozen. We still had the ice and the snow. To clean ourselves was impossible. So you took one part of your blouse and made it a little bit wet and you washed yourself." She does not know the exact date, but at some time in mid-April the women in Malchow were sent out of the camp, finally arriving at the Elbe River. Erna was almost killed there, as she recalled:

> There was a very large bridge, and I went with a girl who [now] lives in Israel in Holon, and with a Christian girl. And she said to me, "We are going up on the bridge. We have to pass the bridge to the other side." So I said, "Adella, I want to know something. When they sent us on the bridge and they closed the bridge with the SS and don't let us pass off the bridge [on the other side], something is going on. I don't want to go. Wait. We don't have to be the first ones." And she said, "You are right, we won't go."
>
> And at this time they were building a house there on the water, and the Russian workers built something there, a very big pipe system, and I saw that something would happen. So I took a big strong iron and I put it in my arm, where I had my number. And I made a hole to take away my number. I said that if something happens and we have to run, they shouldn't see my number. It was not where most people's was. So the three of us went into the pipes, and I don't know what time it was, but it was already late. And we went far into the pipes. At night, when it was dark, they blew up the bridge, and a full bridge of girls fell into the water. And the next day, it was very quiet. No one was there and we went out and started to walk. And all of a sudden some workers came who were working for the Germans. But the Germans had run away.
>
> The Russians were going to come, and on the other side, where they stopped the people, the Americans were there already. So we started to go and then a Russian man came and said, "I work here where they have a liquor factory, and come with me." We were very afraid that if the civil Germans will know we are Jewish, they will kill us. So he took us to the place where he was working, took us to the cellar, and brought us a very large plate with potatoes. We were crazy. We were crying, we were eating the hot potatoes. The Christian girl didn't know we were Jewish. There were three girls, two Jews and one who was Christian.

The three young women started walking. "It was very dangerous to go, very dangerous," Erna said. "The Russians were taking the girls for pleasure and so we were sleeping in sauerkraut barrels and one day we went already closer to go home. We asked the way to the border with Poland, and at night we saw the main place where the officers were. So we went up to a house and we wanted to lie down to sleep. Then all of a sudden we heard boom, boom, boom and a soldier came. And he was drunk and he came to me and lay down in the bed. And I was crying but it didn't help. But he was drunk and he slept. But I couldn't get up, and what happened? Straight from where the bed stood on the other wall was an old, old cupboard with the door with a mirror. When I heard he was sleeping I jumped out from the bed—I was very skinny. But he got up and took his revolver, but he didn't know it, but he shot into the mirror."

Erna was saved by a Jewish soldier from Warsaw who had run away from Poland and joined the Russian army. He heard the noise and rushed upstairs, called some other soldiers, and they took away the man who was trying to shoot her. He told her that he knew she was Jewish and said, "Don't worry, tomorrow morning I don't have a car, but I have a motorcycle with a sidecar." He took Erna and her friends to the Polish border about one hundred miles away, and they were safe. She eventually settled in Ramat Hasharon, Israel.

JUDITH ROSNER GERTLER ON THE RAVENSBRÜCK DEATH MARCH

Judith Rosner Gertler, whose story as a child in Ravensbrück was told in chapter 5, has gripping memories of the death march out of that camp.[7] Unlike Judith Becker, Rachel Hocherman, Rose Mellender, and Erna Ellert—all sent from Ravensbrück to Malchow in February 1945—Judith Gertler arrived there on the death march from Ravensbrück at the end of April. Her aunt, who was her surrogate mother in Ravensbrück, had contracted typhus and was in the *Revier* at the end of March. Judith managed to avoid going on a transport without her; soon after her aunt was released from the *Revier*, the Nazis prepared to evacuate the camp. Judith remembers everyone lining up near the gate:

> Of course, we were anxious to leave, and they emptied out. Everybody was leaving, and as soon as we left the camp, they started to bomb with firebombs on the road. The Russian army was very close. We heard already the shooting and the cannons. But we couldn't make a decision to stay behind, because we were afraid of the fire. And sure enough, when they started these fire bombings, we went into a forest. We were in a forest.
>
> And the fires were coming from all sides. It was a terrible scene. Wherever you ran, you could see the trees are falling, like in a movie, and getting on fire. The firebombs, they were not heavy. They were espe-

cially for a forest. And this night didn't end. It was just unending, until finally we found a little lake, and we sat by the lake and we figured, whatever happens, we'll go into the lake.

We stayed there for a few hours, and by then the whole camp dispersed. We didn't see the Germans, and everybody was trying to find a place. We knew that something was coming to an end. But when you saw this big fire, everything was more dangerous even than in the camp. And the next morning, all you saw was smoke from all sides.

There was a group together, somehow together. And we found another little girl who we knew from Budapest, and she lost her family. They added her to my aunt and us. Everybody was trying to go on the main road, because the German population was evacuating, also, and they all wanted to run to the American or English, towards the west. They didn't want to be occupied by the Russians. I guess the Russians frightened them. So we wanted to go with them, but it was impossible during the day to go, because they came down with the planes and they were shooting on the population. The Russians and the Allies, whoever it was. This was the last ditch that they did. It was about two weeks before the war had ended, and they just wanted to kill everybody, of course.

Although it seemed to Judith that the entire camp was liquidated, some three thousand women who were too ill to walk were left behind. The Nazis intended to use explosives to murder them in the camp, but some of the prisoners from the adjacent men's camp were able to prevent this. Dr. Antonina Nikiforova and other Soviet prisoners-of-war who were medical practitioners remained behind to care for these women.

Because Judith Gertler's aunt walked slowly and had Judith and another child with her, their small group had a problem finding others willing to walk with them. "They wanted to go very fast and they said, 'You wouldn't be able to go fast. You will stay always behind,'" she recalled. "We walked pretty fast, but my aunt had problems with her feet, because by then we had no food, and everything was like—she had wooden shoes that rubbed her. And I developed mumps. I blew up terribly. I knew what it was, but what could I do? There was nothing I could do. And we were trying to always join another group of women, because we were afraid to stay alone."

Judith and the others continued walking along the main roads of Germany, hoping to be liberated by the Americans, the British, or even the Russians. "This was like the front," she said. "Everything was pushing together. And you couldn't stay behind, because every time you turned around, there was always fire and the smoke from the burning, and I guess the Germans wanted to burn everything behind them. Even the private homes they wanted to burn. They didn't want the Russians to come in and find everything there."

Judith Gertler continued until she reached Malchow, but the camp had already been evacuated. One German had remained behind to accompany them on a bicycle as their death march resumed. "He was still in charge," she said. "He was maneuvering with his gun, and he was telling us to march. And at night, even he disappeared. I guess they all had their plans already how to get rid of the uniform and what to do. We were completely alone, and we decided we had to find someplace for the night."

Judith and the women in her group stayed overnight in a big barn, and the next morning they discovered that refugees from other camps and some prisoners-of-war had also slept there. Some American tanks and jeeps passed by but did not stop, and about two days later, the Russians arrived. Judith and her aunt moved into a small house in the village, along with some other young women who spoke Hungarian. "That was already under the Russian occupation, but the war hadn't ended yet," she said. "It was maybe another week before the war had ended, and it was very frightening. . . . The other women who were in this house, they were much older than I and they realized the Russian army is quite dangerous for young women, so we barricaded the house."

Judith and her aunt then stayed on an abandoned German farm until midsummer. The Russian soldiers were not interested in helping the women return to their homes, and instead told them they were needed to take care of the farm animals. The soldiers promised to find a way to get them home afterward if they would stay for a while and work on the farm. However, Judith and the others stayed for weeks and the Russians still did not help them leave. Finally, in the middle of the summer, the Russians transported them by horse and buggy to a refugee camp, where they slept "under the stars." Afterward, Judith Gertler and her aunt had a difficult time returning home, because her hometown of Munkács (later Mukachevo) had changed hands from Czechoslovakia to Hungary and then the Ukraine. They traveled across Germany, Poland, and White Russia (Byelorussia) by truck and were sent to a DP camp in Russia. Finally, a Jewish commandant helped them, and they were sent home to Mukachevo by train.

NEW RESEARCH ON THE DEATH MARCH

These personal recollections of Malchow and the death march from that subcamp and Ravensbrück are individual pieces that help comprise the larger picture of the death march. Each of the survivors knows only what happened to her, and there is no comprehensive record of the satellite camps. A new book in German addresses the death march, but it may never be possible to accurately document the satellite camps or the death marches.[8] None of the recollections of the women who shared their experiences in Malchow and the death march exactly matches this new study that tries to geographically analyze the route from Ravensbrück either to or through Malchow.

The death march can be divided into four geographic stages heading northwest, according to this latest research on the final phase of Ravensbrück's history. The women were marched from Ravensbrück to Mirow, from Mirow to Röbel, Röbel to Malchow, and then Malchow to Schwerin.[9] One plan was for the women to walk to Retzow, a satellite camp near Rechlin. In the Rechlin-Retzow area, the SS gave men from the village uniforms and posted them as guards. However, many of the village men disappeared.[10]

At the Rechlin-Retzow location, there were not only women marching from Ravensbrück but also inmates marching from Sachsenhausen, fleeing civilians, and the *Wehrmacht*. In the vicinity of Mirow-Röbel there were many Hungarian Jews, as well as women from Slovakia, Yugoslavia, and Poland. During this stretch of the death march, a Hungarian Jewish mother and daughter, Isabella and Judith Fischer, fled to Lärz, and Ilona Gottschalk and Anni Sindermann, to Röbel.[11]

The satellite camp of Malchow was the supposed destination for the women on the third stretch from Röbel. At Malchow the women from Ravensbrück were joined by others from Neubrandenburg, which was evacuated on 28 April. A smaller group that reached Malchow continued in the direction of Goldberg (Plau) and Lübz, but the majority of the women who arrived were driven into Malchow as their final destination. The SS drove them into the camp, shoved them in barracks, locked the doors, and fled. Malchow was liberated by the Red Army on 2 May 1945. There is a cemetery there, with fifteen hundred Jewish and other women and men from Ravensbrück and Sachsenhausen, but there are no names of the dead.[12]

The last stretch of the death march was for a small group that went from Malchow to Schwerin. The women were no longer well guarded, and the march disintegrated as people slowly left and the SS took flight. Men and women of different nationalities formed small groups to defend themselves from the SS, and they ran in the direction of Schwerin. For those from Sachsenhausen and the small group from Ravensbrück who survived the march, it ended at Raben Steinfeld, near Schwerin. They were freed there by the Allies. On 2 May 1945 Schwerin was under the jurisdiction of the United States, and later the British, and from 1 July 1945 the Soviet Union.[13]

The evacuation of Ravensbrück and the four stretches of the death march can be considered the last organized criminal acts of the Nazi regime. The twelve thousand to twenty thousand women were sent on the death march without appropriate clothing or shoes and insufficient food.

Already in fragile health, they were forced to sleep outdoors in the still wintry April nights. As they marched along in an ever-narrowing corridor between the Eastern and Western fronts, those who were too ill or too tired to continue were shot. Some of the women tried to flee along the way. However, in addition to being ill and weak, many of the prisoners were foreigners who could not speak German and had no idea where they were going. Furthermore, it is important to have a sense of the general chaos of the situation, with the women on the death march intermingling with other fleeing individuals and groups, as well as the heavy congestion on the roads. Since there are no records, very few of the deaths can be confirmed, and the number is difficult to determine.[14]

At the April 1995 ceremonies marking the fiftieth anniversary of Ravensbrück's liberation, there was a special commemorative photographic exhibit. The English text about the camp's last days said:

> On 27–28 April [1945], more or less twenty thousand women were marched toward Neustrelitz and Malchow. The SS abandoned the [Ravensbrück] camp on 29 April, turning off the electricity and water, and abandoning three thousand sick women, along with their inmate doctors and nurses. At noon on 30 April 1945, the Forty-ninth Army of the Second Belorussian Front, headed by Major Bulanow, liberated those left in the camp. They set up a hospital for those who had been left behind and some of the women who returned to the camp from the death march. The liberated prisoners returned home between May and July 1945. The last were the Austrians, who left on 16 July.[15]

After more than six years, the slave labor, starvation, suffering, torture, "medical" experiments, disease, and murder at Ravensbrück women's concentration camp finally came to an end.

A survivor and a driver of a Red Cross white bus that liberated women from Ravensbrück to Sweden in the spring of 1945. They stand in front of an authentic bus at the ceremonies marking the fiftieth anniversary of the camp's liberation in April 1995. Photo by Rochelle G. Saidel.

Polish Jewish survivor Mina Lewkowicz Goldstein, *center,* with her father, Moshe Leib Lewkowicz, and her mother, Zlata Keinigszstain Lewkowicz, in the Lodz ghetto wearing yellow stars, 1940. Goldstein collection, United States Holocaust Memorial Museum, Washington, D.C.

This photo of Hungarian Jewish survivor Ester Weisz Grun was taken in 1939 and sent to her aunt in the United States. Courtesy of Ester Weisz Grun.

Jewish survivor Hannah Cukier Horon in her hometown of Sosnowiec, Poland, in 1941. She now lives in New York. Photo courtesy of Hannah Cukier Horon.

Jewish survivor Lidia Rosenfeld Vago, Budapest, 11 March 1944. She now lives in Israel.
Photo courtesy of Lidia Rosenfeld Vago.

Dutch Jewish child survivor Sali Solomon Daugherty recovering in Sweden, after she was rescued by the Red Cross. From the exhibit *Women of Ravensbrück: Portraits of Courage,* Florida Holocaust Museum, St. Petersburg, Florida.

Right, Margaret (Margo) Wohl Guiness, recovering in Malmö, Sweden, with two other survivors, six months after liberation. Photo courtesy of Margaret Wohl Guiness.

Jewish survivor Gloria Hollander Lyon (then Hajnal Holländer), age fifteen, 2 June 1945 in Landskrona, Sweden. Photo courtesy of Gloria Hollander Lyon.

Belgian Jewish survivor Rebecca (Becky) Teitelbaum with her son, Abe, born in Brussels in 1947. © Vancouver Holocaust Education Centre 2002, reproduced with permission of the Vancouver Holocaust Education Centre, Canada.

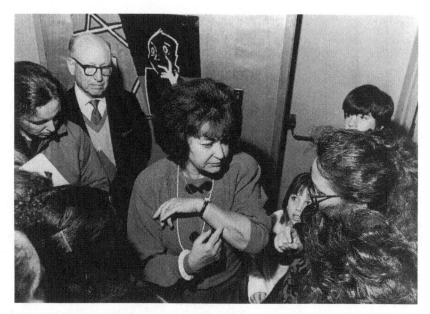

Gloria Hollander Lyon surrounded by students inspecting her tattooed concentration camp number, Oakland California, 1987. Photo courtesy of Gloria Hollander Lyon.

Jewish and non-Jewish survivors from Europe, the United States, Israel, and elsewhere, gathered at the 1995 Ravensbrück memorial ceremonies marking the fiftieth anniversary of liberation. Photo by Rochelle G. Saidel.

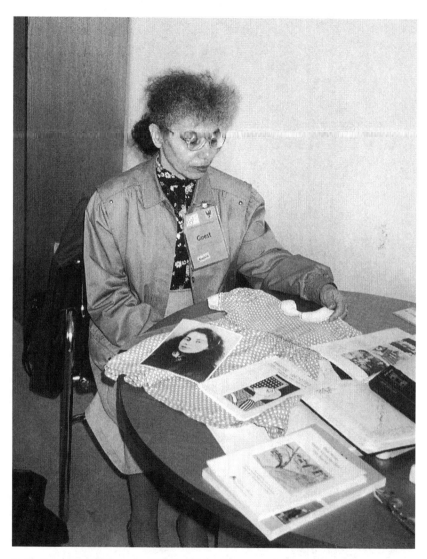

Stella Kugelman Nikiforova, a Jewish child survivor now living in St. Petersburg, Russia, shows the dress she wore in Ravensbrück. She presented the dress to the camp memorial museum in April 1995. Photo by Rochelle G. Saidel.

Jewish survivor Rachel Rozenbaum Hocherman, Berlin, 1995. She was born in Kurow, Poland, and lived in Israel until her death in 2000. Photo by Rochelle G. Saidel.

Jewish survivor Erna Ellert, Berlin, 1995, at the fiftieth anniversary of Ravensbrück's liberation. She was born in Oswiecim (Auschwitz) and now lives in Israel. Photo by Rochelle G. Saidel.

Joanna Krause, a Jewish survivor from Dresden, Germany, 1995, at the fiftieth anniversary of Ravensbrück's liberation. She was arrested and sterilized for marrying a non-Jew. Photo by Rochelle G. Saidel.

Two Dutch Jewish sisters: *left,* Chaja Moskovits Dana; *right,* Nomi Moskovits Friedmann, front row; at the 1995 ceremonies marking fifty years since the liberation of the camp. Child prisoners in Ravensbrück, they now live in Netanya, Israel. Photo by Rochelle G. Saidel.

Rear center, Dr. Sigrid Jacobeit, director of the Ravensbrück memorial, dances the hora with Israeli and other survivors. Ravensbrück, fiftieth anniversary of liberation, 1995. Photo by Rochelle G. Saidel.

Standing at left rear, Ravensbrück memorial director Dr. Sigrid Jacobeit meets with Israeli survivors in Berlin, April 1995, to discuss plans for future memorialization. Photo by Rochelle G. Saidel.

A recent photo of Jewish survivor I. Judith Berger Becker, who survived Ravensbrück and other camps with her mother, Pepi, and her sister, Marlit. She now lives in Jerusalem. Photo courtesy of I. Judith Berger Becker.

Left to right: Jewish survivors Edith Eisler Denes, Lilly Eisler, and Viola Eisler Baras in Florida, 1987. The two sisters and their mother survived together from their arrest until their liberation. Photo courtesy of Viola Eisler Baras.

A recent photo of Margaret (Margo) Wohl Guiness, now living in California with her husband, Herbert Allen Guiness. Photo courtesy of Margaret Wohl Guiness.

A recent photo of Jewish child survivor Judith Rosner Gertler, who was deported to Ravensbrück from Mukachevo, Hungary. She now lives in New York. Photo courtesy of Judith Rosner Gertler.

A recent photo of Jewish survivor Lidia Rosenfeld Vago, posing with a photo taken of her in 1943. She now lives in Israel. Photo courtesy of Lidia Rosenfeld Vago.

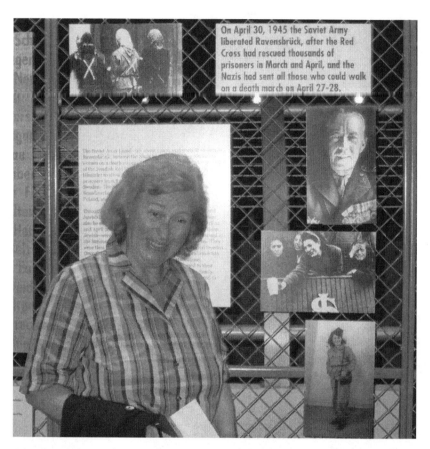

On April 30, 1945 the Soviet Army liberated Ravensbrück, after the Red Cross had rescued thousands of prisoners in March and April, and the Nazis had sent all those who could walk on a death march on April 27-28.

Sali Solomon Daugherty at the *Women of Ravensbrück: Portraits of Courage* exhibit, Florida Holocaust Museum, April 2001. Sali stands in front of a panel displaying a photo of her recuperating in Sweden and the photo given her by Count Folke Bernadotte. Photo by Rochelle G. Saidel.

13

Rescue to Sweden

A BOUT one thousand Jewish women from Ravensbrück or some
of its satellites were rescued during the camp's last days and
brought to Sweden by the Swedish and Danish affiliates of the
International Committee for the Red Cross. Sali Solomon Daugherty,
Gloria Hollander Lyon, and Rebecca Buckman Teitelbaum already
shared their stories about Sweden in previous chapters, and four more
women liberated by the Red Cross tell about their experiences here. In
addition to their personal recollections, I also bring to light the background behind this extraordinary rescue effort, as well as the existence of
early interviews with Polish Jewish and non-Jewish survivors in Sweden.

Mina Lewkowicz Goldstein, Hannah Cukier Horon, Rachel Rozen-
baum Hocherman, and Rosa Korman Fajerstajn were among those Jewish-
Polish women from Ravensbrück and the Malchow subcamp who were
brought to Sweden as the result of an agreement worked out by Count
Folke Bernadotte, vice president of the Swedish Red Cross, *Reichsführer*
Heinrich Himmler, and the representative of the Swedish section of the
World Jewish Congress. The women's stories give the statistics of the Red
Cross white bus rescue effort an individual and personal perspective.

MINA LEWKOWICZ GOLDSTEIN AND HANNAH CUKIER HORON

The details of Mina Lewkowicz Goldstein's arrest and her slave labor in
the clothing factory in Ravensbrück's *Industriehof* (industry courtyard)
were detailed in chapter 7. Born in Lodz and now living in Los Angeles,
California, she was known as Inka in Sweden.[1] She remembers that during the last two weeks that she was at Ravensbrück, the Russians were

Prisoners liberated by the Red Cross on their way to Sweden. From the exhibit, *Ich grüsse Euch als freier Mensch* (I greet you as a free person), MGR/SBG, 1995. Courtesy of MGR/ SBG (no known provenance).

coming very close. At exactly midnight one night there were sirens, and then the factory lights were shut off as the Russians bombarded the camp's surroundings. The slave laborers had to wait and could not return to work until three or four o'clock in the morning. Mina said that during her last days in the camp the Jews at the *Industriehof*, where she worked, received packages from the American Red Cross. At first there was one package to be shared by ten people, and she and nine others once took their package outside to divide its contents. Two SS men with a dog deliberately walked on the blanket and everything went into the sand, she said. She also remembered that the Jewish women were afraid the Russian and Polish women would kill them for their food, so they kept it between their legs when they slept.

Mina was liberated from Ravensbrück by the Swedish Red Cross on either 25, 26, or 28 April 1945, arriving in Sweden by way of Denmark, she said.[2] Once in Sweden, she was first placed in quarantine for two weeks. Her roommate was Hannah Horon, whose story is also told here. Mina was the second person in her group to hear news about a living relative, her father. He had been liberated by the Americans in Hamburg and returned to Lodz. After she left Sweden, she went to Lodz to be with him, and then her brother returned from Russia. She later traveled from

Poland to Germany, where, in 1949, she married a survivor who had been born in Lodz. She had not known him before the Holocaust, and he had gone to Cracow before the ghetto was closed. She jokes that at first she didn't want to get married after the war and "go to another jail." The couple first went to Israel, and in 1960 they received permission to enter the United States. Mina's husband died in 1984. She is proud that she was able to receive her high school diploma at the age of forty-nine.

While Mina came to Ravensbrück in 1944, the other three women whose stories are recounted here were shipped there from Auschwitz after its evacuation in January 1945. Hannah Cukier Horon's journey to Sweden began in Sosnowiec, Poland, in Eastern Upper Silesia, where she was born on 7 December 1924, three years before her only brother.[3] Her father was a tailor, and her mother maintained their comfortable home and helped her father when she had time. Hannah attended public school until a year before World War II began, and then, at age fifteen, studied in the local business school for a year. She belonged to *Hashomer Hatzair*, a left-wing Zionist youth organization.

Because of her father's influence in the community, Hannah worked as a volunteer in the Jewish communal office. She later continued in the *Judenrat* office, supervised by the Germans, and received food for her work.[4] She and her family were soon sent to a ghetto in a farm village outside of the city, after being forced to leave all of their valuables with the Nazis. There was one small building for four or six families, and Hannah's family lived together in one tiny room.

Hannah remained with her parents in the ghetto and was able to use her connections in the office to bring them vegetables from outside. Then, at the end of August 1943, she recalls hearing talk about the Nazis "liquidating everything, everyone."[5] Her mother wanted to save her by sending her over the Czech border to a region the Germans had not yet reached, but this never materialized. After she left to meet her contact in Sosnowiec, the Nazis arrested her parents and said they would release them only if she came back. Hannah returned to the ghetto, but her parents were not released and subsequently were sent on a transport to Auschwitz. A few months later, in August 1943, she, too, was on a train to Auschwitz. She learned from acquaintances there that her parents had been sent directly to the gas chamber.

Hannah worked in the munitions factory at Auschwitz-Birkenau, and her job was carrying baskets containing metal pieces from the machines to barrels of hot soapy water, where she washed away the oil. Once the basket was so heavy that she fell and suffered from a rupture in the groin. She also had another serious medical problem in Auschwitz, an infected nipple. As she was afraid to show it to a nurse or a doctor, she continued going to work. Luckily, the abscess broke on a Sunday, when she was not working, and some of her friends helped her to deal with it. Both of Hannah's medical problems affected her in later life. Throughout her ordeal Hannah was concerned that she no longer got her menstrual period, because she thought she would not be able to have children. However, she said that "in a way it was good because the hygiene was very . . . you couldn't shower every day, we didn't have soap, we didn't have towels, so it was much healthier."

Hannah was shipped by freight train to Ravensbrück in January 1945 and remained there until her rescue to Sweden. "The war was on when we left Ravensbrück," Hannah correctly recalls. "The Red Cross sent buses, and the Germans gave us packages with food that came from America. First we didn't know where we going. We didn't believe that we were going to freedom, so we didn't care anymore. We were traveling with the Swedish Red Cross during the day, and during the night we were in the woods. And the Swedish soldiers were giving us chocolate, and we were afraid to take it, because we thought maybe it was poison. And they were talking in Swedish to us, but we didn't understand. And they were smiling, 'take it, good, good,' but we were afraid. So we traveled for a few days, three or four days."

The buses traveled from Germany to Copenhagen, where Hannah remembers receiving food. "And there we got for the first time, milk, white bread, and whatever food they gave us. So a lot of girls were so hungry for the food they overate at night, and in the morning they were lying dead." After staying overnight, the group went by boat to Malmö, Sweden. There they received clothing, food, and medical attention, and were then transported to different towns.

Like Mina, Hannah was first placed in quarantine in Sweden. "You know, when we came to Sweden on the first quarantine, we saw the wires [of the fences]," she said, "and we didn't want to go in. We refused, because we thought we are coming to freedom! And here we see wires again. The Jewish representative explained to us we would go to a different place, but it was the first quarantine. The doctor and nurses were taking our temperature every day, and every week or every day, whatever, systematically, a piece of bread more, a little more soup, not in one shot, big quantities. And from Sweden, I only have good, good memories."

"The Swedish people were very good," she said. "I came to a town, where the first thing, we went to a school, and we were in an auditorium, and we were lying on those straw sacks with paper sheets, and the doctor examined us. And on the steps to the stage there were clothes, different styles, different sizes, toothbrushes, and underwear. They grabbed us to give us a good rubdown, you know, a shower and a good rubdown, because they were afraid that we might have brought a disease with us. And we could pick up our clothes, and if it wasn't enough that night, they called up a factory and in the morning they brought more clothes. None of us who went to Sweden had one bad word about the Swedish." Hannah was given an office job; she was pleased that her employers were kind, helpful, and allowed her to take off the days of Rosh Hashanah.

Hannah met her future husband, Herszlik Horonczyk (later Henry Horon), when she went to visit a friend's husband in a men's convalescent home. "This was the first time we were with boys that were our kind," she said, "because I had dated Swedish boys. But who can understand us better than the one who went through the same thing?" Her future husband's brother came to visit and offered to pay for an engagement party, held in the local hotel in August 1946. In May 1947 Hannah and Henry were married in Sweden, and despite her earlier fear of infertility, their oldest daughter was born a year afterward. After the Joint Distribution Committee located her uncle in The Bronx, Hannah and her family immigrated to the United States, and she then had a second daughter.

RACHEL ROZENBAUM HOCHERMAN

Rachel Rozenbaum Hocherman also began her journey to Ravensbrück, and then Sweden, in Poland.[6] She was born in the small town of Kurow (near Lublin) on 14 October 1927, the daughter of Golda Korenblitt Rozenbaum and Mendel Rozenbaum. Her father had a small dairy factory, where he made butter and cheese, and her mother administered a delicatessen and cheese store associated with the factory. Rachel was a proud Jew and an active Zionist.

One year before the war began, Rachel went to live with her two aunts in Warsaw in order to attend secondary school. She was in Warsaw in September 1939 when the war began and returned to Kurow when the bombing stopped four weeks later. Rachel's father was then imprisoned, but she and her mother were able to get him released. Rachel returned to Warsaw in January 1940, and by the end of that year or the beginning of 1941, she was required to wear an armband with a Star of David.[7] While she was in Warsaw, in the spring of 1942, her family was taken from Kurow and probably gassed at Chelmno. When she returned to Kurow from Warsaw soon afterward, no one from her family was left (except for a brother hiding on a farm). Polish friends gave her an unsophisticated document with a false identity. Rachel looked for her brother, and then returned to Warsaw, to her aunts. The aunts lived in the area that became the ghetto, and Rachel, then fifteen, did not want to stay there.

She again returned to Kurow, where the villagers now refused to help her, but she found Jews who had fled from Czechoslovakia. She met Mikolasz Weisz, a twenty-seven-year-old Czech Jew from Bratislava who had contact with the Polish underground. She helped him with the Polish language, and he gave her an authentic-looking identity card from someone two years older who had died. She thus became Anna Yanina Dolczewska. She obtained train tickets for Mikolasz and his family, and carried false identity cards for him. Rachel assisted Weisz in his flight from Poland by going on the train with him and staying in the dining car to serve as his cover. Afterward, he sent her some money and tried to help her. Remaining near Kurow, she could no longer contact her aunts because the Warsaw ghetto had been sealed.

Rachel also aided two other Jews from Slovakia, by taking them on the train. Ukrainian guards caught them and took them to the police. She, with her Polish identity, was free, but she bravely went to the police to try to save these people. Although she had Polish papers, there was a death penalty for helping Jews. She was placed in a prison near the Carpathian Mountains, probably in late November 1942, and remained in jail for two months, supposedly awaiting trial. She was then placed in another cell with people who had been picked up from the street for forced labor, and was sent with them directly to Auschwitz. As a "non-Jew," Rachel did not have to face a selection but nevertheless received a tattooed number, 35673. She wore the red triangle of the political prisoners. Her transport arrived in Auschwitz around 20 January 1943. Of this transport of non-Jewish Poles, only twenty percent survived the two-day train ride, she said.

When she arrived in Auschwitz, Rachel's good leather boots were confiscated and replaced by wooden shoes. Another Jew posing as a Pole, whom she remembered only as Luba, was working at the clothing distribution depot, *Kanada*. She recognized Rachel as a fellow Jew passing as a Pole, retrieved her boots, and gave her warm clothing, a needle, and thread. Rachel said that Luba saved her life. Rachel worked in Birkenau for five months. Then she was moved to Rajsko, a work camp near Birkenau, and became an *Aufseherin,* a work supervisor. However, she wanted a simple job like the other women. She obtained permission to relinquish her supervisory job and did vegetable farming instead.

At the beginning of 1945, Rachel was given the new job of cleaning the SS headquarters, and there she received extra food that helped her to survive the imminent evacuation and forced march. She said she was told the women left the camp on 18 January 1945, but she was not sure of the exact date. They walked and walked, throwing away everything in order to walk without any extra weight. She saw many women who had been shot because they were unable to walk and were lying dead on the road. She felt she was walking toward freedom, but in fact she was walking toward Ravensbrück. She believed that her good boots saved her life. She took them off once during the march and her feet were so swollen that it took some time before she could get them on again. After that, she never took them off during the forced march.

She thought about running away, but there was no place to run. She was not even sure whether she was in Poland or Germany. The women walked for two days or more until they reached the German border, guarded by Nazis with dogs. When they reached Germany, they were put into a closed train and continued to travel. She didn't know how long the trip took, but they finally reached Ravensbrück at night. They were put into a large barrack and had to place their belongings on the floor. A friend offered her food, but she was too sick to eat anything. Like others who arrived at that time from Auschwitz, she recalled that the camp was "a horror." "There was no place to sleep—nothing. Thousands arrived and there was no preparation for us. We were sleeping in corridors, on the floor," she said. After one month of this "horror," Rachel was sent to Malchow, which Count Bernadotte of the Swedish Red Cross included in his white bus operation.

After the Red Cross took the women to Sweden by way of Denmark, Rachel was placed in a rest camp called Doverstorp, near Lund. Afterward, she went to Stockholm, stayed with a family, and enrolled at the *gymnasium* (secondary school). Still afraid to declare herself Jewish, she continued using her false Polish identity. She later declared herself Jewish to the authorities and took back her real name, Rachel Rozenbaum. She stayed in Sweden until she decided to go to Rio de Janeiro, Brazil, to find her father's brother in July or August 1946. She worked in a clothing store there, joined a Zionist organization, and served as a private secretary for the WIZO (Women's International Zionist Organization) president. While visiting a friend in São Paulo in 1947, she met her future husband, Moyses Hocherman, and they were married on 16 November of that year. She gave birth to four daughters in Brazil: Esther, Ida, Sonia, and Ruth.

Rachel had always dreamed of going to Israel but opted instead to find her only living family in Brazil. She made friends there, married, and was well integrated into the São Paulo Jewish community. However, in 1969, after twenty-three years in Brazil, Rachel, a life-long Zionist, moved to Israel with her husband and family. Rachel's husband died of a stroke in January 1995, after forty-seven years of marriage; Rachel died of cancer in Israel in June 2000.

Rachel was not the only Jewish Ravensbrück prisoner who entered Sweden posing as a Polish non-Jew. For example, Chaya (Helen) Kaplan Luksenberg of Philadelphia, a survivor from Radom, Poland, remembered one survivor who revealed her Jewish identity on her first Friday night in Sweden. Chaya and her roommate decided to kindle *Shabbat* (Sabbath) candles and to say a blessing of thanksgiving. "At that moment there was a knock on the door," she recalled. "Standing there was a Polish girl that I had known in the camp by the name of Maria. I asked her what she wanted. She immediately started to sob and told me her name was Miriam and that her father had been a rabbi in Lodz, Poland. When she left home she promised her mother that if she survived she would light *Shabbat* candles every Friday night."[8]

ROSA KORMAN FAJERSTAJN

While Rachel Hocherman and Miriam from Lodz were temporarily afraid to reveal their Jewish identity even in Sweden, Rosa Korman Fajerstajn admitted soon after her arrest that she was Jewish and had false papers. Rosa was born on 15 March 1919 in Opole, Poland (near Lublin), the daughter of Hinda and Moshe Aron Korman.[9] Her father, an observant Jew, was an accountant. Rosa attended the Beis Yacov religious school for girls, and wanted to continue her education in secondary school in Lublin. However, when she was fifteen, the family's financial circumstances forced her to begin working in a store, while also giving Polish lessons.

At the beginning of World War II, Rosa tried to cross the border to Russia but then returned to Opole. She spent time in Warsaw and the Opole ghetto, as a courier for a group of left-wing partisans. Like all the Jews in Opole, she was forced to wear a white armband marked "Zion," beginning in late 1940 or early 1941. "The ghetto in Opole was worse than Auschwitz," she said. Her parents were taken away to the Sobibor death camp in April 1942, and then she was alone. On 29 April 1943, like Rachel Hocherman, she was arrested with her false identity papers. Unlike Rachel, she was afraid she would be discovered and admitted that she was a Jew before being taken to Auschwitz. In Auschwitz she wore both a yellow Star of David and a red and white circle that identified her as a political prisoner.

When Auschwitz was liquidated in January 1945, Rosa was sent to Ravensbrück, arriving after the death march that most of her comrades did not survive. Like the other women who came at that time, Rosa recalled that conditions in Ravensbrück were extremely overcrowded and harsh. She was forced to live in a muddy tent with hundreds of other women. From there, she too was sent to the Malchow satellite slave labor camp, then rescued and brought to Sweden by the Red Cross.

While recovering in Sweden, Rosa contacted close friends from Poland, Dora Zamberg Goldman and Wolf Goldman, who had immigrated to Brazil in 1937. They sent for her, and at the age of twenty-seven on 2 October 1946, she arrived in Brazil. The couple took care of her and treated her as though she were their daughter, she said. Jacob Fajerstajn, a man from her hometown of Opole, was living with the Wolf family. Three months after meeting each other, on 5 January 1947, Rosa

and Jacob married. Rosa adjusted well to life in São Paulo, where everyone was kind to her. She was unhappy, though, that she and Jacob had
no children, especially after her first child was stillborn. After a miscar-
riage in 1950, she gave birth to her son in 1952. She miscarried again
later, before giving birth to her daughter. "I was pregnant six times to
have two children," she said.

Rosa had worked outside her home before World War II and continued to do so, helping in her husband's store until it closed in 1971. Afterward, she found private customers. "I got out of Hitler's war, and here,
in a free country, where people can do what they best understand, am I
going to get lost?" she asked.

COUNT BERNADOTTE AND HEINRICH HIMMLER

Compared with most Jewish women who passed through Ravensbrück,
Mina Goldstein, Hannah Horon, Rachel Hocherman, and Rosa Fajerstajn
were among the luckier ones. The good fortune that ended their terrible
experiences included a seemingly unbelievable but documented meeting
between Himmler and Norbert Mazur, representative of the Swedish Section of the World Jewish Congress, at the SS–Gut Hartzwalde, an estate
outside Berlin, on 21 April 1945. The initiation of efforts by the Red Cross
to bring concentration camp inmates to safety in Sweden had begun two
months earlier, when Red Cross officials held a meeting with the head of
Reich Security and Himmler's right-hand man, Walter Schellenberg.

By late 1944, some of Hitler's closest aides, including Himmler, had
begun to recognize that Germany was losing the war. At the request of
Swedish foreign minister Christian Günther, Schellenberg and Felix Kersten arranged for a meeting between Bernadotte and Himmler. Kersten,
a Latvian-born Finn who was Himmler's masseur, had offered to serve
as a go-between to help the Swedish rescue effort.

Bernadotte arrived in Berlin secretly on 16 February, and at the meeting, held in a hospital about seventy miles to the north, Himmler agreed
to Bernadotte's request to allow Swedish Red Cross workers to rescue
thirteen thousand Scandinavians.[10] The goals of the Red Cross were to
enter Ravensbrück and nearby Sachsenhausen concentration camp with
food packages, and ultimately take over the camps to avoid their evacuation before the Red Army arrived.[11] Bernadotte returned to Stockholm
on 23 February and reportedly assured the head of the World Jewish
Congress in Sweden, Hillel Storch, that "some positive results [for Jews]
should be achievable."[12] At the same time, Storch was also using Kersten
as an intermediary to persuade Himmler to release Jews to Sweden.[13]

Bernadotte returned to Germany on 5 March with twelve white buses
and twelve trucks filled with medical and other supplies. At that time he

brought 4,400 Danes and Norwegians from concentration camps to the Neuengamme camp on the Elbe River, near the Baltic port of Lübeck, where they were under Red Cross care. A week later, on 12 March, Himmler drafted a document by hand, which he titled "A Contract for Humanity," signed by Kersten and Himmler. It promised that concentration camps would not be blown up; a white flag would be raised over the camps when the Allies approached; Jews would be treated like other prisoners and not executed; and Sweden could send packages to Jewish prisoners.[14]

After the rescue of Norwegian and Danish prisoners had been carried out, the next step was to make a proposal to the Nazis regarding more Scandinavians. Bernadotte met with officials of the Foreign Office in Stockholm on 26 March, and the resulting policy allowed him to "request that a number of Jews be sent to Sweden."[15] By a mandate of the Swedish government, Count Bernadotte offered to use the Red Cross white buses to rescue and transport non-Scandinavian prisoners; there were also weighty discussions with Himmler about liberating citizens of West European nations. At about the same time, Himmler tried through Schellenberg to get a sense of the possibility of contact with U.S. general Dwight D. Eisenhower regarding a separate ceasefire.

All of these earlier negotiations led to a meeting on 20–21 April between Himmler and Mazur, and then to another on 21 April between Himmler and Bernadotte. Himmler reportedly told Mazur that he could take out one thousand Jewish women, but then told Bernadotte that he could take all of the surviving Jewish women from Ravensbrück.[16] Within the next week, it was possible to liberate about seventy-five hundred women from the camp. On the night of 22 April, two hundred sick French women were taken out, and at four o'clock in the morning on 23 April, the Swedish Red Cross took away eight hundred women from the Benelux countries. Himmler reportedly repeated to Bernadotte at their last meeting on 23 April that he could take anyone he wished. On the evening of 24 April, one thousand more women were taken out of the camp by truck, under Swedish Red Cross coordination. Then, on the afternoon of 25 April, twenty buses from the Danish Red Cross evacuated more prisoners, including many Polish Jewish women, pregnant women, and thirty children. The Swiss delegate to the International Committee of the Red Cross, Paul de Blonay, also worked out an agreement to use German trains to transport prisoners to Padborg. On 26 April a train was sent with sixty cargo cars from Ravensbrück in the direction of the Danish border, with four thousand women aboard. The end of the liberation action was the transport by the Red Cross of twenty-six sick women on 28 April.[17]

At a press conference held on 30 April 1945, Bernadotte revealed the previously secret rescue action. He announced that by the end of April,

fifteen thousand women, including eight thousand Danes and Norwegians and seven thousand women of other nationalities, had been
liberated from various concentration camps and brought to Sweden
on what were known as the "white buses" and by other means.[18] The
Ravensbrück survivors included Mina Goldstein, Hannah Horon, Rachel
Hocherman, Helen (Chaya) Luksenberg, and Rosa Fajerstajn, as well as
Marya Friedman, Gloria Hollander Lyon, Sali Solomon Daugherty, Basia
Rubinstein, and Rebecca Teitelbaum (who recuperated in a Copenhagen
hospital). They were among about one thousand Jewish women, mostly
Polish, who were rescued from Ravensbrück and its satellite work camp
of Malchow. Margo Guiness, who was sent from Ravensbrück to Bergen-
Belsen, was brought to Sweden from that camp.

THE LUND INTERVIEW PROJECT

Of the women who recounted their experiences in Sweden to me, Basia
Rubinstein's story has an added dimension. She was among twenty-one
Jewish women from Poland who were interviewed in 1945–1946 about
their time in Ravensbrück. I found her name in a special archive in Lund
University, Sweden, in 1998, three years after meeting and interviewing her.

This archive is from an early interview project coordinated by Dr.
Zygmunt Lakocinski (1905–1987), an art historian and professor of
Polish at Lund University. Along with Professor Sture Bolin, a history
professor, Dr. Lakocinski formed a committee to document the experiences of the survivors. The project was called *Polski Instytut Zródlowy*.
With financial support from the Swedish Institute for International Affairs and the Government Labor Committee, Bolin planned the interviews
and Lakocinski supervised the Polish-speaking interviewers, eventually
assuming the responsibility of preserving the results of the study.[19]

The interviewers visited all of the Swedish displaced persons camps
where the survivors had been brought and tried to persuade people to
talk about their experiences. Not all of these survivors were from
Ravensbrück, nor were they all women or Jewish. The project managed
to accumulate some five hundred interviews in Polish in 1945–1946.
Most of the interviewees were Catholic, and my research at the archive
found that a maximum of only twenty-one of the interviewees identified
themselves as Jewish Polish women rescued from Ravensbrück.[20] They
generally did not speak in detail about Ravensbrück, but even the little
available information from their testimonies demonstrates the variety of
routes they were forced to follow as they made their way from their birth-
places, usually via other camps, sometimes then to Malchow or elsewhere, and finally to Sweden.[21]

14

Reconstructing Lives in the Aftermath

T HE LIVING nightmare that Ravensbrück inflicted on its female victims did not completely end with rescue by the Red Cross or the
liberation of the camp by the Soviet Army on 30 April 1945. The
women's days in the camp have continued to affect them throughout their
lives. Ravensbrück has left its victims with physical and emotional scars,
which in some cases have prompted them to actively try to ensure that
no future generation suffers a similar fate. Some of the women who managed to survive Ravensbrück against all odds talked about their lives
afterward, beginning with their experiences in displaced persons (DP)
camps and continuing until the present. Their lives were interrupted and
changed in irreparable ways, but they seem to have remarkable capacities
that enabled them to build new lives.

OLGA WEISS ASTOR

Olga Weiss Astor, one of the Jewish survivors who arrived at Ravensbrück in 1944, was introduced in chapter 6, and her slave labor sorting clothing was described in chapter 7. When I met her in her home near
Chicago in 1997, she was still suffering from physical problems connected with Ravensbrück.[1] She recalled what happened to her when she
was liberated, after she had been shot and wounded in Allach:

> But, you know, now I say to myself, I was in Ravensbrück, Burgau,
> Turkheim, Dachau. I mean, Dachau [I] just went through because they

She Who Carries by artist Will Lammert is clearly reflected in the Schwedtsee, which contains the ashes of an unknown number of the victims of Ravensbrück. Photo by Heinz Heuschkel, Berlin. Collection of MGR/SBG.

couldn't terminate us, and I got to Allach. In Allach, I was wounded. Then they took me from one hospital to the other. I was in Schwabinger Hospital in Munich, which the nuns had, and for the first time it was a bed with pillows and white sheets. I mean, you never saw anything more beautiful. They didn't have X-ray machines. They were not ready for this type of stuff. I mean, I was on a machine of sorts, and they bored through underneath my knee, and they put it in traction. And I was lying there, and I was happy as a lark. I couldn't think of tomorrow if you would have killed me.

An American officer got a special doctor from Italy to see me, and he said, "She will never walk again." And I thought, I don't give a hoot if I can walk or not walk. I can be in this bed as long as I live. Who know? I mean this is—it was a luxury. And then they transferred me to all sorts of other places until finally I got to Allach, and the ambulance took me to the hospital in Allach. This was in 1945 in May, June, July, August, maybe.

From Allah, Olga was taken to a hospital in Feldafing, the location of a large DP facility. "And when we arrive in Feldafing, two men came to pick me up from the ambulance," she said. "One guy, he picked me up, and I looked at him, and I was screaming bloody murder because he had a *Wehrmacht* uniform on. I said, 'You——,' I mean I started cursing in German. I know how to curse in many languages. I am very talented. And he showed me his number from Auschwitz. So that satisfied me, and I tell you, I had to hug him, you know, because he carried me in his hand, and I almost fainted, he had such a good smell. And he became my husband."

Olga's future husband, a survivor wearing the discarded *Wehrmacht* uniform, was then named Heinz Osterlitz, from Breslau. He changed his name to Henry Astor when the couple immigrated to the United States. The man who helped Henry take Olga from the ambulance was Sigmund Shuftan, who later married Olga's Ravensbrück friend and hospital roommate, Esther Tuvel. When I met Olga in 1997, she and Esther Tuvel Shuftan were still close friends, living as neighbors in Glenville, Illinois. Olga introduced me to Esther, who told me that a book of her sister's memoirs was about to be published posthumously.[2]

Olga's injury was serious, and she was put in a body cast in Feldafing. She was appalled by the bad conditions in the hospital, which was in the area under the jurisdiction of the United States. When General Dwight D. Eisenhower paid a visit, she managed to complain to him about the hospital's problems. As a result, he arranged for a better facility, and she and others were moved to a luxury hotel in Feldafing.

After they left the DP camp but while still in Germany, Olga married Henry and Esther married Sigmund. The two couples were married on the same day, and the two brides took turns wearing the same dress and shoes. Olga said of the shared outfit and the two weddings: "I have a nine-and-a-half foot, she has a seven—don't ask. Yes, we were married in Germany, and we had even a Jewish ceremony. The rabbi didn't have ten people together, of course. Where would he get ten Jews? So he sent down the *shamus* [caretaker] to the street. 'Bring somebody up. We have to have ten guys.' God knows what Nazi was standing there and saying, 'Yes,' whatever they had to say."

When I met Olga thirteen years after Henry's death, the lifelong love affair between them was still reflected in Olga's comments about him and their marriage. She even said that it was worth going through the travails of concentration camps in order to meet him. "I'll tell you why it was worth it," she explained. "He knew, because he took me to the operating table—he was a nurse. That's the kind of man he was. After the liberation, Henry wanted to learn nursing and take care of the people. Anyway, he knew that I will have a lifetime problem, and he loved me. He did not know if I am fat or skinny, tall or short, because I was in a body cast. [It was not until] four weeks before we got married that he saw me without a body cast. And then, as it should happen, I had to walk on crutches. He used to play football, and he had a knee injury or something, and they had to put his knee in a cast. So he was hopping around and I was hopping around. And I tell you, he was my best friend, he was my lover, my husband, the best father you can have."

Olga and Henry arrived in the United States on 20 December 1946, when she was twenty-two and he was twenty-five. When the immigration officer in New York could not spell their name, Osterlitz, they remembered hearing of the Astor Hotel and so changed their name to Astor. They at first stayed with an aunt and uncle; then they were able to help Olga's sister immigrate. Finally they managed to get their own apartment. "You had to have an apartment, and you had to have a job," Olga recalled. "It wasn't enough to sign. You had to have a job. You had to have an apartment, because you had to give an actual affidavit that they will not be a burden to the state. And you know, when you are here in this country for a year and you have a baby and you live in a tenement and your husband earns five dollars a day, and he worked in a dime store, and we had to get the money, every day the five dollars, and he got it in pennies, nickels, and dimes—in those days a dime store was a dime store—because otherwise we didn't have any money to go [the] next day to buy something to eat."

Olga managed to work to supplement the couple's income, even after she gave birth to her daughter. "At the beginning I worked," she said. "There was a dressmaker across the street from where we lived, and she was German-Jewish, she and her husband. They came up in 1938, so they had no . . . but she needed somebody to help her. She worked at home, and she hired me for twenty-five cents an hour. I told her I have a baby, and she says, 'Well, you just bring her, too, and put her in a laundry basket.' And Henry every morning brought Charlotte over in the laundry basket, put it there in the room, and I could breast-feed her there and so on. And that's how it was." Olga's greatest sadness is that her beloved Henry died only three months before their only grandchild was born, and that grandfather and granddaughter never had a chance to know each other.

TOVA FLATTO GILADI

Another survivor, Tova Flatto Giladi, was one of the children who recounted (in chapter 5) her experiences at Ravensbrück and before her arrival.[3] Today she lives in Kew Gardens in Queens, New York, with her husband, Ben, and their daughter, Iris. Like Olga Astor's, her account of recovery begins in a hospital for displaced persons. Tova and her mother were sent from Ravensbrück to Bergen-Belsen in February 1945, and Tova was critically ill with typhus when the British army arrived there on 15 April. She was sick for months and had to learn how to walk again.

"Can you imagine, in such a short time in the concentration camps, my weight was like a baby, like this, and I had, probably, tuberculosis, I don't know," she said. "I was very sick, and they took me. I was in and out of hospitals. I was in a hospital, and a German doctor—because this was in Germany—so there were German nurses and German doctors. One doctor treated me, and I said to my mom, 'I don't want this man to touch me. I think he's an SS.' My mother said, 'This is your imagination. They wouldn't allow him here to take care of people.' I said, 'Mom, I can't stand him.' In fact, he went to a bathroom to shave, and a woman walked in by mistake, and she saw, because they were all tattooed, the 'SS,' and he was an SS."

After this encounter with a doctor who was said to be from the SS, Tova was treated by an unusually caring physician. He saved her life, she said:

> But then, I have to tell you something very beautiful about a British doctor, British man, that liberated us. I was in and out of hospitals because I could not digest food at all. For instance, if I ate a potato, it came out the same color, the same way. It didn't look any different than on the plate. And this was going on, because those were the symptoms of the illnesses, that you got terrible diarrhea, fever, so this is the way people died.
>
> So he wrote home to his wife, and he was a doctor. In those days, they gave penicillin, antibiotics only to soldiers, because this was something very new. So he wrote home, and she sent him—he explained the symptoms of my illness—and she sent him the medication, and he was

treating me. You can say like you treat a baby. I couldn't walk. I couldn't eat. Till today, this is so many years later, I have problems with my stomach. I have a very nervous stomach. . . . Something has probably affected my insides from the experience.

After liberation, mothers with children, including Tova and her mother, were moved from the barracks to the former SS housing, so they could be more comfortable. However, Tova first saw the horrors of the camp. "There were piles of dead people higher than people," she said. "I can tell you, when you see the movies, this is the way Bergen-Belsen looked, and I was there. When Anne Frank died, this was in the time when I was in Bergen-Belsen."

Tova's father survived Buchenwald and a slave labor camp, and managed to return to the family's hometown of Piotrkow, in Poland. He found his wife's name on a survivor list compiled by UNRRA, the United Nations Relief and Rehabilitation Administration. Tova's name was not on the list, and she believes the authorities did not expect her to live. She was so weak that when schools were created in the DP camp, she had to be specially driven to school.

One day she came home from seeing a movie with a group of children from her school, and a celebration was in progress. She complained to her mother, "We don't know where Daddy is, and you are making here such a—celebration." Her mother had even baked a little cake. "There wasn't so much food after the war, either," Tova said. "It took some time. And my father was sitting in a corner, because he found where my mother is and he came to see. And he didn't believe that I'm alive, because he came and I wasn't there. He was sitting in a corner, and I was, in a way, angry. What's the big party here? We don't know where Daddy is. And I come in, and I saw my father. We embraced, and none of us could say a word for, it seemed like forever."

Tova and her parents were able to immigrate to Israel. "And then we were very fortunate," she recalled. "I had a grandmother that left Poland before the war, and she settled in Israel. And when she found out that my parents, my father, her son, is alive, she sent us papers. In 1947 we went to Israel, and I went to school." Tova also met her husband in Israel. "My husband comes from the same hometown as I do, from Piotrkow," she said. Ben Giladi is six years older and she did not know him before, but she had been with his sisters in Bergen-Belsen. "Six years now is nothing, but six years—I started going to kindergarten, so he already almost was on the way [to] finishing school," she said.

Tova was in the army in Israel, an experience that generally helps immigrants adjust to their new homeland. However, Tova had problems that stemmed from her earlier days in Nazi Germany. "I was in the army," she said. "I went for all kinds of courses. But I was very unhappy in the army, because it reminded me of the camps, of the roughness of the sergeants, and it brought back to me certain things from my childhood, which I didn't like." She found out later that her unhappy letters to her parents had been intercepted and censored. "I was writing home letters that my parents didn't receive, because I was writing how I feel about the army, and you're not supposed to write such a thing," she said. "So one day my father came with goodies and begged them to let him in to see his daughter. They didn't let anybody, but they felt for him. They let him in."

At around the same time, Tova met her future husband. "Ben was also new in the country, and we were dating a very short time, maybe three months, and he asked me if I wanted to go through life with him," she said. "Maybe if I wouldn't be in the army at that time, we would have been dating for a longer period of time. But you could leave the army if you got married. Then you had only to make a month a year for the reserve. We got married, and exactly we got married three days before Passover, and three days before Passover to the year our little girl was born."

Tova married Ben on 19 April 1951, and their daughter Iris was born on 6 April 1952. The combination of responsibility for a family and the threat of war convinced Ben that they should leave Israel for the United States, and they immigrated in 1959. Tova explained that their decision was related to the Sinai Campaign:

> As long as my husband was single, he didn't mind. But when he was married and had a little girl and he was going to the army, and he never knew if he's going to come back. His sister in America promised his mother. . . . She promised that she's going to take care of him, because he was the baby, the youngest. He was the youngest child. So she promised to take care. So when she heard about the Sinai action and how many soldiers were killed, so she sent out papers. . . . She wanted to feel that she fulfilled her mother's promise, and she sent papers. I didn't even dream about America. I didn't want to go anywhere, and so forth. When he got his affidavit from the American consulate, a cousin came from America. [Ben] said, "You see how I feel? I didn't even open it."
> At that time I knew English, because I finished high school in Israel. But he didn't speak English at the time. So [the cousin] said, "If you are not going to go now, you're losing your chance." So my father said to him, "You know what? Go. We'll help you." Because times in Israel were very difficult. He said: "I'll help you. Go, and you will not feel guilty that you missed an opportunity."

Tova spoke of her own arrival in America with her small daughter, and of the problems she had to overcome:

> Then I came with Iris, and she started school, and I didn't want her to go through what I went through, because I started to learn in Polish, then I started to learn Yiddish, and then Hebrew, and then English. I

would have probably gone farther than that if I would not have those interruptions in my life. So I was afraid to do it to her.

When I came to America, I [had] finished high school in Israel, which is on a much higher level than the one in the United States. So I wanted to put my child in a Hebrew school, because she didn't speak English. She spoke Hebrew. The teachers in public school wanted to be helpful. They spoke Yiddish, but she did not speak Yiddish. She spoke Hebrew. So I said if I could get a job as a kindergarten teacher in a Hebrew school, I'd put her in a private school, because I couldn't afford to put her in a private school.

So I enrolled her in a school, and I told them how much my husband earns. He was going to school, to the university, and he was working in a liquor store, carrying bottles at the time. I showed them and I said, "I don't want any [special] charge here. I wasn't raised that way. If you give me a job, I'll pay you as much as others do, and I'll be happy with the rest that will be left."

Tova was accepted as a teacher for a year, but she did not have a license and was required to work alongside another teacher. She earned very little after paying her daughter's tuition and also had problems with the woman who taught with her. "And I gave my heart to them," she said. "I was too sincere, and I took it too seriously. And I came home with very little money, because I had to pay. They charged quite a lot for a private school." When she realized her daughter could speak English, Tova enrolled her in public school and sought other employment.

At first, Tova didn't know that her daughter could actually speak English, because she had never heard her do so, and the school taught in both English and Hebrew. "She didn't speak a word [of English]," Tova said. "And kids were hitting her because they thought she's such a proud little girl. One day she started to talk, and when she started to talk, she talks without a trace of an accent. She has a beautiful command of the English language. So when she started to talk English freely, I said I was already in the Diaspora. I know the feeling. I want her to mingle with all kinds of people, and I don't want her to be raised in a prejudiced situation, and so forth. So she went to a public school, and I went to work."

At first Tova worked for years as a bookkeeper and cashier in a restaurant. After the owner retired, she took some courses and worked in an office for twenty-five years as a bookkeeper. Tova's forced labor for the Nazis continued to trigger her fear in the workplace in later years. She had made ammunition boxes for the *Wehrmacht,* and was often beaten from behind when she seemed not to be working enough. Many years later, working in a New York office, she said: "My boss could never approach me from the back, because if he said [anything] from my back, I was jumping. This is so many years. Because you never know from which side you're going to be hit. This was the utmost fear."

She also continues to have a fear of riding in subways, and says this was why she retired at age sixty-three. "The thing that pushed me to stop is not the work," she said. "I always like to be very busy. But the subways. I used to faint at times. There was no air-conditioning, and the people were pushing and shoving you, and the stench, the dirt. I said, 'I went through so much in my life. Why do I have to?' You cannot be very rich from working, so why should I kill myself? It doesn't pay."

Speaking a few years after her retirement, Tova said she regretted the decision. "Because I thought I'm going to go back to school, but when you are sixty-five, your memory, your head holds so much, your memory is bad. And I had a very good memory." She had worked most of her life and found it boring to stay at home, often doing puzzles. "It was a very difficult way to change," she said. "First of all, I had a certain lifestyle, and I felt that if you're working, even though sometimes your job is tedious and you feel it's not interesting, you learn every day something when you're out in the world. When you are away from it all, you feel like you are on an island somehow. I am not too happy about it, but it's already done." She was considering taking noncredit college courses in English literature, but thought it might be too difficult for her to make the commitment. "And then to be with younger people, I don't know how I'm going to feel about it," she said.

Meanwhile, Tova is concerned about her daughter Iris, who has suffered the tragedies of a young marriage and early widowhood. "Sometimes I felt very guilty, because I told her about my experiences and it was spoken at home," she said. "My mother talked about it. My father talked about it. I talked. You have to know, I'm talking to you now, this is a matter of fifty years or more. So I am afraid. We raised a child. She is so good—not because she's my daughter—and she paid a bitter price for being so good. And I'm afraid that maybe we should not have told her so much, because she wanted to correct the world. She wanted to do things, and she hurt herself terribly with it. My daughter had a nervous breakdown."

Tova regrets not only her daughter's suffering but also that of her parents. "I was an only child left to my parents," she said, "and I would never give them any shame, because they lost two beautiful sons. I carried such a responsibility that I have to be a good girl and not to bring any shame or anything to my parents. And the biggest experience that I went through, and it was a sickening one, when I had to go to America, I had to go after my husband, and I was an only child and left them behind. This was a tragic time for me. And I lost my father. He wasn't even seventy. Then my mother lived with us, and she was very sick. She had a terrible illness, a blood disease, and we suffered for many, many years."

However, her greatest sadness is that she had only one child and that child is not unscathed. "What hurts me the most is that, once I said to my friends, 'Maybe we should not have had children, because we are so damaged,'" she recalled. But she later told her mother, "If you are not going to have children it's like Hitler would win. We want to have children." She arrived in the United States with her daughter and was afraid to have more children because her parents were in Israel and she needed to work. "What aches me the most [is] that I have an only child, and she is weaker and she suffers more than I do, that I have a better life," she said. "She is with us now, and she's treated very well, but she went through, in comparison to me, her going through affected me maybe more than my own life."

ROSE FROCHEWAJG MELLENDER

Rose Frochewajg Mellender, who lives in the Bronx, New York, also shared her thoughts on the aftermath of the Holocaust. We met her earlier and left her as a Polish officer was helping her return to her hometown of Bedzin, Poland.[4] "Boy, was I disappointed when I was liberated," she recalled. "I had no food. I had nobody to talk to. I mean to talk to, to turn to. It was the same hatred that I went in, the same hatred when I came out. The Russians hated the Jews and the Ukrainians hated the Jews and the Poles hated the Jews. Everybody. So I said, 'Is that what we dreamt of? That I would come out and I'd be carried on your hands, on people's hands?' It's the same thing over and over. The world didn't learn anything. Nothing whatsoever."

Once Rose arrived in Poland, her situation began to improve somewhat, but she still faced anti-Semitism. At first she didn't find any relatives in her hometown, but there were people that had been with her in Auschwitz. They had been liberated in January, after she was sent to Ravensbrück. They had organized a Jewish committee to find surviving relatives. She stayed with these acquaintances for a few weeks, and then a man who had worked for her family took her in. There were six other young women living there with her. "You made like communes, you know, and you lived to survive," Rose said. "I came to Poland, and, mind you, we stayed in line for bread, and the Poles chased us out. They said, with a curse word, 'So many are still left, and you are staying here. You want to eat our bread?' And chased us out and didn't let us get bread. The next day [my cousin] came, he took me away. I said, 'I don't ever, ever want to go back and look at them.'"

Rose's cousin Abraham had discovered she was alive and had come to find her. He worked for the U.S. Army and was able to take her to the American zone of Germany. She lived there in a large home with twelve young women and seven young men. "And that's how my life started getting a little better," she said. At that time Rose also discovered that her brother David had survived. She stayed in the Feldafing DP camp near Munich, where she met her husband, Isaac Mellender, among a group of her friends.

The couple registered to immigrate to Israel, Australia, or the United States. "My husband opened a business in Germany, worked very hard," she said. "I got married. As you saw there [in a photograph], that was the Jewish wedding. I had the baby, my first son. But we wanted to get out [in] the worst way. I had a nanny and I had a maid, but I said, 'I don't want their nannies and I don't want their maid. I want to get out. So whatever will come first, there we will go.' So the United States came first. They came, the CIA came to interview us. So we were the first to be put on the list, and we came here in 1950 and had a very good life."

In addition to their son Leon, born in Germany in 1946, Rose and Isaac had a son Andrew, born in the United States. Unlike Tova Giladi, who worries that she spoke too much with her daughter about her experiences during the Holocaust, Rose insists that it was imperative to talk to her children:

> We talked constantly. We told them what happened, because of hatred, because we were Jewish and things like that. We took them to Israel. We traveled a lot and showed them . . . what we went through. How kids died and only because of hatred, nothing else. So, I put it out in the open. I talked about it. I went to lecture. You understand? I have friends still today that never spoke to the children about it. They covered it up. They are not all right here. They're afraid of every little thing. You see, we talked about it. My children knew. One of the lectures, my oldest son came, got up and said, "I am the son of a survivor. If you think they're crazy or whatever, I had the best life ever. My parents were the most normal parents, the best parents that could be." Stood up and spoke in front of everybody. So, my children weren't deprived of anything, maybe because we were so young.

Considering the physical abuse that Rose suffered during the Holocaust, she was remarkably healthy for many years afterward. A doctor was shocked when she told him she had been in camps. "Yes," she told him. "And I ate snow and slept outside on the snow. I was swollen for almost five weeks." He assured her that she was fine. However, she suffered from terrible nightmares. "Oh, my God," she told the doctor, "the dreams. Every night I wake up, which is true, in a cold sweat, and I start screaming because I think they [are] coming," she said. "I was fine. I was never sick. Not even a cold. Let me tell you that. Only those dreams."

Rose's husband was ten years older than she, and his health became more problematic. "My husband got cancer," she said. "He was such a fighter. They told him he's going to live three weeks to three months, because it was caught in the fourth stage already, lymphoma. We came in, my children and I, to the room, and we probably looked very forlorn, very upset. He says, 'What's the matter? They told you I have cancer? Cancer is not going to get me.' And in fact, it did not, for ten more years."

"Do you know, he lived ten years with it, and lived a life, not being sick, but worked," Rose said. "The last minute, when he went into the hospital, because he had chemotherapy for ten years. He's written up in the medical books, because nobody gets it for ten years. He lived with it until the cancer didn't kill him, but the chemotherapy killed him, ate up everything inside. He had leukemia then." Rose's husband died in 1988, and meanwhile she had suffered a heart attack. "I couldn't take it," she said. "Everything that was good just turned upside-down. I ask why? I suffered. I gave so much. Why more? Why more? Why am I being punished?"

Rose believes she recovered because her husband kept saying, "You have to live. I'm going to die because I'm doomed. I have cancer. This is it. But you have to live. You're young. Fight it." As for her future, Rose said: "I survived and now it's—I don't know. They say the heart is okay. I'm doing well with it. But evidently it's too much. I can't take it that much. It's stress. Stress is killing me. They think maybe I need tranquilizers or whatever, because my stomach isn't good. They say, 'Oh, it shows like it's from stress.' So I just pray to God."

Rose always wanted to be a teacher, and makes a point of lecturing to school groups about her experience. When her children were small, she volunteered at their school, and went for special training to work with students who had reading problems. She also worked with disabled people and as a supervisor for the Housing Department. She is especially gratified by her lectures at universities:

> When I go to the colleges and I talk about it and they show movies and they show the piles of people, I start by telling them, "You see, on one of those piles, I left my sister." And from there, I go on telling them. I just stress, the thing that I stress most is hatred. If you hate, then that's the end of everything. If I could reach even one person tonight that when you go home and you could tell your friend or your mother or whomever, your brother or sister, that hatred is the most heinous thing that could ever be, because you're a Jew or you're a Gentile or you're Spanish or you're black, you hate them without any reason, without any cause, this is the end of humanity.
>
> They only give me fifteen minutes they could ask questions, but I stay on like an hour. They have so many questions to ask. They are so interested. They cry with me and they take my telephone [number]. They write me letters that I reached them—that I reached them and they believe. Because they try to tell you that it never happened. I say, you see, it never happened. Where are my parents? What is with all those things? Eisenhower was there and he saw, and what did he write? Ask your

parents. That it's the end of humanity. That this is it, because of hatred. I say, "Please go home and just stop hating because one is black or white or green." That's what I leave them with.

ESTER WEISZ GRUN

Like Rose Mellender, Ester Weisz Grun of White Plains, New York, is dedicated to teaching future generations about hate and prejudice as a warning for the future. We were already introduced to her and learned about her experience as a slave laborer.[5] As soon as possible after her liberation, she went back to her home in Hungary to see if any family members were alive. She learned that her younger brother had survived Theresienstadt and also returned. "He came home like a toothpick," she said. "He was fifteen when he came home, sick, suffering from typhus, and it attacked his heart and he came down with heart trouble. I came down with heart trouble and lung trouble, and we both had to be hospitalized." A few months later, her older brother, who had been sent to a labor camp with her father in 1940, came home after four years in a Russian prison.

Ester continued to seek news of her father, and in 1948, a month before she came to the United States, she received a postcard in Hungary that said, "My dear child, here I am, and I am hoping to see you soon." However, like Gloria Hollander Lyon, whose story is told in chapter 10, she had already been invited to the United States by a relative, one of her father's two sisters. "I waited for three years, from 1945 until 1948, and my father still didn't come home," she said. "Then my aunt says to me, 'You must come. Otherwise, you're going to lose all your papers.'" Her father returned to Hungary after eight years of imprisonment in Russia. By then her brothers had left Hungary to avoid being conscripted for labor, and her aunt also helped them to enter the United States via a German DP camp, France, and Cuba.

Ester married Soltan Grun on 21 September 1948; she gave birth to two daughters, Olga in 1949 and Linda in 1953. She speaks about her past in public, Jewish, and Catholic schools and colleges, as well as churches. "I am teaching [about] the Holocaust for the rest of my life," she said. "I am going, and I am invited from school to school on the higher level, high schools, colleges. They are inviting me back to talk about my experiences. The only thing I am asking the future generation [is] to remember, never forget, because I am speaking for the six million who cannot be here with us and tell their story. So I am asking the future generation to make sure that they will remember, and we should never, never forget."

Meanwhile, Ester herself can never forget, and a physically and emotionally painful experience in 1994 brought her back to her days in

Ravensbrück. While taking a walk in her suburban neighborhood and only a block from her home, she was suddenly attacked by a German Shepherd dog. "When I saw the dog biting into my arm, it was the most horrifying, terrifying episode," she said. "It traumatizes me for the rest of my life." Explaining how these dogs were used to mistreat people at Ravensbrück, she said: "Every SS [guard] had a German Shepherd, and that was their protection. This is why we were so intimidated. There's no way that anyone, anybody, would even try to revolt."

OTHER RAVENSBRÜCK SURVIVORS TODAY

Every survivor's life story after liberation is a testimony to the fact that Ravensbrück in many ways always stayed with her, and Olga Astor, Tova Giladi, Rose Mellender, and Ester Grun offered examples that illustrate this. I would like to briefly mention some other women I met who have the strength to use their devastating experiences as a way of teaching others. We have seen how Gloria Hollander Lyon traced her forced itinerary throughout Europe during the Holocaust, and now lectures and writes about her past. Likewise, Margaret (Margo) Guiness speaks about her experiences, composes poetry, and has written a moving memoir. When I met her in Long Beach, California in 1998, she was walking with crutches but still actively telling her story. She shared with me the unpublished manuscript of her memoir, and in 2001 she had it published.[6]

Dr. Lore Shelley, a survivor of Auschwitz and Ravensbrück who lives in San Francisco, has made an important scholarly contribution by compiling and documenting the stories of Auschwitz survivors, some of whom were also in Ravensbrück.[7] I met Lore at the Ravensbrück commemoration at the camp memorial in 1995. Another survivor, Alice Birnhak of Brooklyn, wrote a memoir that included her time at Ravensbrück and Malchow, and she often lectures about her experience. I met her on 14 October 1997 at the 92nd Street Y in New York, where she was speaking in connection with the publication of her book.[8] A native of Kielce, Poland, she was sent from Auschwitz to Ravensbrück in November 1944 and soon sent on to Malchow. Telling me of the few weeks she had stayed in Ravensbrück, she said: "After all these years, I still remember the impression that camp made on me. I shiver whenever I think about it."

Lidia Rosenfeld Vago, of Petach Tikva, Israel, has done an extraordinary amount of work to coordinate the survivors of her group from the *Union* factory in Auschwitz-Birkenau. As most of them were sent to Ravensbrück with her in January 1945, she also helped to locate them in connection with the 1995 commemoration at the camp memorial. She was involved in a forceful but unsuccessful court case in Germany about payment for slave labor, and has written a memoir, part of which is published in an anthology, and part of which is quoted in chapter 9.[9] She is an articulate writer and speaker on her experiences during the Holocaust.

Perhaps the best way to conclude this sampling of how Ravensbrück affected women later in their lives is with questions that remain unanswered. Sali Solomon Daugherty of Jaffa, Israel, who shared her story as a child in the camp in chapter 5, told me when we met in Jerusalem in 2000:[10]

> After the war—this I would not like to speak about. Because if I ever speak about it, or write about it—I have had a very difficult life for forty years after the war. And I only realize that today. If I would speak, I would also speak on a psychological level—what did it do to me finally? How did I behave? How have I lived until fifty years after the Shoah? What has become of me? What have I personally suffered because of the camps? And this is another story and this is something I could speak about, I could lecture about, and that I even might myself write about. Because that is very very important—and only the end would be what I realize. . . . I came to the answer truly only a month ago. I finally had the answer of what it did to me and what the final result was of the camp. And I think that what I didn't realize that happened in the camps, I realize today because of what happened to me thereafter. But that's another story. So let's say I did not come on this earth to pluck roses. So that's about it.

I can think of no words more eloquent than Sali's to demonstrate that the effects of being in Ravensbrück or any concentration camp can never be erased. When I interviewed her in Jerusalem, her final statement was: "I realize today that I am very successful in a way that I consider the success of the *neshama,* of the soul. I consider myself successful that I have survived the years of survival."

15

Gender and Women's Bodies

W E have heard about Ravensbrück from its first days until its last, and about how it continues to affect some of its victims. Throughout this book, Jewish survivors have shared many stories and individual recollections, some of which clearly demonstrate situations unique to women. However, as most of the former prisoners of Ravensbrück are not accustomed to speaking in today's feminist terms, we sometimes have to read between the lines of their testimonies to understand how gender considerations made their experiences unique to women. While making a point about this is not something that most survivors consciously think about or explicitly express, being female was a significant factor that influenced life and death during the Holocaust in general and in concentration camps in particular.

GENDERED BEHAVIOR

Gender refers to the social, political, and economic relations between men and women, and how the societal structure imposes certain behavioral expectations and norms that are different for men and women. The victims of Ravensbrück we have met lived in a time and place in which women's and men's roles were more clearly separated than they are today, in a society that was even more defined by patriarchy. This was true even for such a prominent and unusually highly educated woman as Dr. Käthe Pick Leichter, who was gassed at Bernburg in the winter of 1942. She had received a doctorate magna cum laude, was a Socialist party leader and early feminist in Vienna, and had held high level government

Drawing of a pregnant prisoner comforted by a camp sister, by artist Helen Ernst, a survivor of Ravensbrück, 1946. Collection of Museen der Landeshauptstadt Schwerin, Stadtgeschichtsmuseum, Schwerin.

positions. Nevertheless, she waited too long to escape the Nazis because she was taking care of her children and her household.

None of the women who were "special prisoners" or hostages were held on their own merit. Instead, they were held as negotiating pawns because of their relationship to important men. For example, Gemma LaGuardia Gluck would have been treated like any other Hungarian Jewish woman, but she had special privileges as the sister of the powerful mayor of New York, Fiorello LaGuardia. Likewise, relatives of Charles de Gaulle and Winston Churchill were treated as special prisoners. Even Olga Benário Prestes, who was not in this special category, was arrested because of the man in her life. She was deported from Brazil to Nazi Germany because of her husband's prominence as the leader of the Brazilian Communist party.

The women who were deported to Ravensbrück from Germany and Central Europe generally came from more progressive social situations than those from Poland and other countries in Eastern Europe, but all of the women, to some extent, were victims of gender inequalities before the Holocaust began. Their previous socialization in a gendered patriarchal world affected their lives once they were in Ravensbrück. In some ways their status as women offered them advantages, and in others, disadvantages. Obviously, gender cannot be considered in a vacuum, and other factors such as social class, nationality, political affiliation, religious beliefs, age, health, and even luck influenced how women experienced the Holocaust.

Some of the prisoners who came to the camp from Poland had already been disadvantaged as women in various ghettos. With almost no exceptions, male Nazis and *Judenrat* members controlled communal affairs and people's lives in the ghettos.[1] Rachel Hocherman's and Rosa Fajerstajn's stories demonstrate how single young women without male protectors were especially vulnerable in ghettos in Poland. However, women had in their favor the fact that circumcision could not give them away, and they were able to pass as Polish Christians more easily than a man.

Hannah Horon's low-level work for the *Judenrat* gave her a little protection in the ghetto, such as inside information and extra food, but she obtained her job only because of her father's influence in the community. Male protection was important for women at that time, because their own social status and economic condition depended on it. On the other hand, many women in ghettos rose to the occasion and performed courageous acts that were not part of their socialization. For example, like many other women in similar circumstances, Rachel Hocherman and her mother had the courage to obtain her father's release from jail during the early days of the occupation.[2] Rachel's and Rosa Fajerstajn's underground activities in the ghettos also demonstrate the bravery of young women in such extraordinary circumstances. However, they were not given leadership roles in the organized structure of the Nazi-imposed Jewish councils, and the general mode was for women to be subordinate to men.[3]

Not only were women socialized to need male protection, but they were also usually conditioned to be followers rather than leaders. This seems to have been the case for some of the survivors of Ravensbrück who shared their stories here. Both Mina Goldstein and Rachel Hocherman were offered supervisory positions in concentration camps, but they preferred to blend in with the others and not assume responsibilities of authority that made them stand out.

Modesty is another attribute that society has imposed on women. At the time of the Holocaust, women, especially Orthodox Jewish women, were trained from childhood to be modest. This aspect of gendered behavior made life in Ravensbrück and other concentration camps particularly traumatic for women. The women were required to parade naked in front of each other, as well as before male and female Nazi personnel. Women who had never seen their own mothers without clothing were suddenly faced with the shocking sight of their mothers' naked bodies. The overcrowding and resulting close contact between the women in the barracks, and especially in the latrines, made it impossible for women to retain their inbred sense of modesty, and this caused severe mental, as well as physical, torment.

Lidia Vago put into words what most survivors still cannot even talk about, regarding how her sense of modesty affected her bodily functions:[4]

> What I want to tell you is a horrible thing from a sanitary point of view and I know you are interested in this problem of women in the camps. So we had that bowl. And at night I don't know how that bowl was kept by me and my sister, and we were not allowed to go out to the latrine. And all of us had dysentery. And I had it after a long period of constipation. I remember two weeks, but if it is impossible from a physiological point of view, it may have been ten days. Because of inhibitions starting from the train [to Auschwitz], I simply could not use that bucket in the middle of the car in front of all of those people. There was a sheet around it, but I had inhibitions and I could not use it. And the same happened later in Auschwitz in the first days. And that's why I was constipated. And so in the end, after about ten days or two weeks, when everyone had dysentery and at night we were not allowed to go out, you can imagine what a horrible situation was there in the block. And we did it in the bowl. And then my sister took it to the sewage ditch and washed my pants, because I was in horrible condition. I thought I would die there. And she washed my pants and she washed the bowl from which we went on receiving our soup. So it's unbelievable.

"CAMP SISTERS" AND "WOMEN'S WORK"

While gender considerations such as submissiveness and modesty resulted in undue mental and physical stress for women, some aspects of their socialization as women helped them to survive. Lidia Vago's description of how her sister assisted with her hygiene is an example of the phenomenon of "camp sisters." This term, which refers to blood sisters, other female relatives, or unrelated women who bonded to help each other survive in concentration camps, has been explored in many women's memoirs and analyses of them.[5] Most accounts conclude that women were more prone to bond emotionally and form surrogate families than were men. While this seems likely from survivor testimonies, it probably cannot be scientifically proven. However, most of the women whose testimonies were recounted here spoke of bonding with other women.

Some of them entered the camps with their mothers, sisters, or aunts, while others arrived with good friends or soon found a new friend. There are many examples of camp sisters throughout the book, and I will briefly review a few. Mina Goldstein had her own mother with her for most of her time in concentration camps and refused to abandon her when she had the opportunity to leave Ravensbrück for Oranienburg. Hannah Horon said that her camp friends helped treat her abscessed breast, and Rachel Hocherman recounted how Luba befriended her and saved her life by giving her back her boots. Fela Kolat spoke repeatedly of her closeness with Regina Weisfelner, and how Regina helped her and gave her strength.

As an outgrowth of this bonding and forming surrogate families, some of the women cooperated in communal childcare when there were children in the camp. When a child's biological mother went out on a work detail, another woman would watch the child. Likewise, when a mother was murdered or died of disease, another woman always stepped in to take care of the orphaned child. Basia Rubinstein even helped to sneak her friend's small son into Ravensbrück. In order to protect both four-year-old Michael Kaplan and his hysterical mother, Basia hid the child under her skirt.

In accordance with the societal norms of the times, the Nazis generally considered children the responsibility of their mothers, not their fathers. For this reason, mothers were sent to the gas chambers with their children at Auschwitz-Birkenau, while fathers' lives were spared—at least while they were considered productive slave laborers. This is a gendered aspect of the Holocaust that is generally overlooked and requires more research.

Giving gifts and writing recipe books, two splendid gendered activities through which women tried to remember home, were discussed in the context of how they raised the women's spirits. There are outstanding drawings, poems, embroideries, recipe books, and other gifts now in museums that were originally handmade and given to friends in Ravensbrück. While there may be some exceptions, these exchanges of gifts and recipes seem to be phenomena unique to women. It is striking that such items are a highlight of the museum exhibit at the Ravensbrück memorial, while the comprehensive memorial museum at the nearby men's camp at Sachsenhausen shows no sign that gift giving took place there.

It was almost impossible to write recipes, and even more so to then manage to hide a small recipe book and, in some cases, keep it until liberation. If a woman was found in possession of paper and a writing instrument, she was subject to severe punishment. Even when the women could not write down their recipes, they talked about food and recipes from home. Some of the recipes that survived in books can actually be used to cook the dishes named, and others are only sketchy recollections of a remembered dish. In either case, sharing recipes helped the women retain a sense of "before" and a hope of "afterward." Like the giving of gifts, it may have also helped them keep their sense of themselves as women.

Giving gifts and sharing and writing down recipes were practices related to general nurturing and homemaking skills, part of the gendered roles that women were taught as they grew up female. These roles in the social structure served them well in the abnormal conditions of camp life. For example, women knew how to make the scarce rations last longer and how to combine, trade, or share their own portions to improve the food situation. They were also accustomed to washing and sewing clothes, and they tried to do their best to keep themselves and their clothing as neat and clean as possible under the circumstances. Since they were used to tending to the hygienic needs of children and other members of the family, they adapted to such tasks as picking each other's lice and helping those who were ill. All of these nurturing and homemaking activities, which could well be described as survival skills, are related to or parallel to activities that society allotted to women living at home before the Holocaust.

WOMEN'S BODIES

In addition to the social relations of gender, physiological considerations made the experiences of women unlike those of men. For decades feminist social scientists have pointed out that biology is important for humans mainly in the context of how the norms of culture and society interpret it, and feminist biologist Anne Fausto-Sterling explores this issue from a physiological point of view.[6] She points out that "since the 1950s, psychologists, sexologists, and other researchers have battled over theories about the origins of sexual difference, especially gender identity, gender roles, and sexual orientation. Much is at stake in these debates.

Our conceptions of the nature of gender difference shape, even as they reflect, the ways we structure our social system and polity; they also shape and reflect our understanding of our physical bodies."[7]

I agree that gender considerations influence how we think about biological differences between the sexes, but these very differences gave women in Ravensbrück unique women's experiences. There is an interconnection between gender and the physical body, with each contingent on the other. Menstruating and the inability to do so, becoming pregnant, and giving birth indeed have cultural aspects and are interpreted in different ways in different societies, but they are specifically women's biological functions. All of these female physiological conditions made women especially vulnerable in concentration camps. Many female survivors, including most women interviewed for this book, stressed that their ability to bear children after the physical tortures that their bodies endured was one of their greatest achievements. As one example, Hannah Horon, sure she would not be able to get pregnant after the absence of her menstrual period, was happily surprised when she conceived after recuperating in Sweden. While one can argue the case that the desire to become pregnant is a gender issue instilled by society, pregnancy is also a physiological function unique to women.

Menstruation was an overwhelming problem in Ravensbrück and other camps. First of all, it is not true that no women menstruated. There were exceptions, as prisoners continued to have their periods. They were not provided with sanitary napkins or any other means of absorbing the flow, and the blood ran down their legs as they stood at *Appell* or their work assignments. Even though most women's periods stopped in the camps, they still had to suffer through at least one last period. Again, Lidia Vago eloquently and frankly spoke of an issue to which most survivors only delicately alluded, if they mentioned it at all. Speaking of her experience at Auschwitz, before she was sent on the death march to Ravensbrück, she told me:

> We got something to drink that was not coffee but was called coffee. There was bromide in it, and supposedly it was not just for tranquilizing us but it had another aim. I don't know if it is true or not—but it was to stop our menstruation. But that was anyway stopped by the very poor diet we had to live on, or to vegetate on. Because the *blockovas* and the *stubovas*, or the personnel, also Jewish women, were better fed. They got more food—I don't know how. And they remained women. But we did not. And of course in those conditions nobody thought what will happen after the war, if we stay alive maybe we will be unable to bear children. That was not our first concern. It was the very last priority.
>
> For us it was very good that we didn't have our periods. Because of the horrible sanitary conditions. Because all of us had it for the last time, and you can imagine what filth there was because of it. And there

was no paper whatsoever for the toilets, latrines. Because paper was dangerous. It could be a means of communication, and any sabotage or underground activity could be organized by means of paper and pencil. Nobody had it, and it was punishable by death.[8]

Some women were pregnant when they arrived at Ravensbrück, and they, as well as their fetuses, were at great risk. At Ravensbrück it might have been appropriate to coin a word "childdeath" to go hand in hand with the occasion of childbirth. There are many testimonies about forced abortions (often including sterilizations), secret stillbirths, and even the killing of newborns by prisoners in order to save the life of the mother.

Lola Goldstein Taubman, whom I met when I was giving a lecture on Ravensbrück in Orlando in 1997, shared with me some testimony that she had sent to the Conference on Jewish Material Claims against Germany. She testified to the Claims Conference, "While in Ravensbrück, a woman in the bunk next to me gave birth to a dead baby. We didn't have any scissors, so they tore the umbilical cord and threw the baby away." Lola was born in Svalava (Szolyva) and came to Ravensbrück after Auschwitz was evacuated in January 1945.[9]

One of the Nazis' solutions for unwanted pregnancies and births was forced sterilization. There is an order on record from SS *Obersturmbann-füher* (Major) Brandt to Dr. Carl Clauberg requesting the sterilization of one thousand Jewish women in Ravensbrück.[10] As mentioned in the case of Wanda in chapter 2, Sinti and Roma women and girls over the age of twelve also underwent forced sterilization in the camp, with Professor Clauberg sterilizing some 120 to 240 Gypsy women and young girls during the first week of January 1945. Complete figures are not available for the Jewish and Gypsy women and adolescents who were forcibly sterilized in Ravensbrück.

Joanna Lindner Krause told me that she was sterilized even before arriving in Ravensbrück. She spoke with me at the fiftieth anniversary of the camp's liberation.[11] Born in Dresden in 1907, she married a non-Jewish artist in Germany on 21 October 1935. She was arrested four days later for violating the Nazi racial purity laws. Joanna was then in and out of jail for eight years and was pregnant when she was arrested in Dresden in 1943. She was placed in forced labor in a laundry, but her colleagues knew she was pregnant and protected her from heavy work. When an SS man approached her and asked why she wasn't working as hard as the others, she told him that she was pregnant. As a result, she was subjected to a forced abortion and sterilization in Dresden during her seventh month of pregnancy. She arrived in Ravensbrück in January 1944, coming from a work camp.

If we include women's breast-feeding experience, there are two poignant stories of women forced to abandon their infants before entering Ravensbrück. German Jewish political prisoner Olga Benário Prestes was allowed to give birth in the *Barnimstrasse* prison in Berlin and to keep her baby until she was weaned. Destined for adoption by an "Aryan" family, the child was rescued by her grandmother. Olga was later gassed at Bernburg. Dutch political prisoner Aat Breur, who was arrested in November 1942, was sure that she would be in prison for only a few days. She brought along her five-month-old daughter Dunya, in order to breast-feed her. Aat was shipped to Ravensbrück without her daughter, and both mother and child survived.

In addition to what we can term physiological considerations related to the reproductive system, women were at another physical disadvantage. Ravensbrück was designed to be a slave labor camp, and the Nazis were not concerned that women have less muscular strength than men.[12] They were forced to do hard labor such as paving roads, loading bricks, digging ditches, and felling trees, and many of them simply would not have had the stamina even under normal conditions. Starvation, sleep deprivation, illness, and beatings did not improve their chances of successfully completing their physically demanding tasks. If women, on the other hand, were given relatively lighter work than men, it was because their physiognomy lent itself to doing the job better. For example, women were not chosen to assemble V-1 and V-2 electronic rocket parts for Siemens in order to spare them more difficult physical labor. As Gloria Hollander Lyon explained about her work in a subcamp, women were employed at such tasks because their smaller hands were more efficient at this kind of job.

RAPE AND FORCED PROSTITUTION

In cases of rape and forced prostitution, societal gender considerations and those related to female physiology are integrally intertwined. Both rape and forced prostitution were inflicted on women in Ravensbrück not only because of their female anatomy but also because of the patriarchal male-controlled structure of society that has encouraged these two heinous activities among some men for much of history. "Woman's biological sexual self is never just that because of the gendered (socialized, culturalized, economized, politicized) relations of patriarchy, which continuously seek to hierarchically differentiate woman from man," in the words of feminist political scientist Zillah Eisenstein.[13]

No woman I interviewed told me that she was raped, although several said they knew about the rape of other women. While I cannot provide personal testimony from survivors for specific cases of rape at Ravensbrück, it is more than likely that there was rape and fear of rape. Rape is not only physical abuse but also a demonstration of "superiority" over a powerless victim, and a concentration camp for women was an ideal setting for such exploitation. Accounts of torture of women by male aggressors throughout history generally include rape. For example, before she was shipped from Brazil to Nazi Germany and ultimately to Ravensbrück, Elisabeth Saborowski Ewert was raped in front of her husband.

Although the Nazi racial laws that prohibited sex between an "Aryan" and a Jew should have protected Jewish women from being raped, this was not always the case. A Nazi male could merely deny that he had raped a Jewish prisoner, and her testimony would not have been considered. Ruth Elias testified that sexual violence against women, including Jewish women, was common in concentration camps, and she wrote of her experience in Auschwitz: "Drunken SS men sometimes made unexpected appearances in our block; the door would suddenly be flung open, and they would roar in on their motorcycles. Then the orchestra was ordered to play, and the SS men would sing along while they continued to drink, their mood getting ever more boisterous. Young Jewish women would be pulled from their bunks, taken away somewhere, and raped. Raping Jewish women wasn't considered *Rassenschande* (race defilement), therefore it was allowed." Explaining that she was spared because she lived on the third tier of the bunks, she concluded: "Any woman who refused to go with the SS men was savagely beaten, so no one offered any resistance. I cannot describe the pitiable state of these poor women when they came back to the barracks."[14]

A number of Jewish women who survived death marches from Ravensbrück or its satellites and then found themselves in territory controlled by the Soviet Army told me that rape by the Russian soldiers was common. However, no one said that she herself had been raped.

The issue of prostitution and prostitutes in Ravensbrück is twofold. First of all, women arrested as prostitutes in Germany were incarcerated in the camp as "asocials." Both Nanda Herbermann and Margaret Buber-Neumann were assigned as block elders for barracks with prostitutes, and in their memoirs they gave testimony about these women's behavior in the camp. Buber-Neumann wrote how difficult it was to discipline them but described them with sympathy as victims of society.[15] They were indeed victims of a gendered patriarchal society. While the women arrested as prostitutes were considered "asocial," the men who frequented them had no such stigma attached to them.

This observation brings us to the second part of the issue of prostitutes and prostitution in Ravensbrück. While some women were arrested for the "illegal" practice of prostitution and placed in the camp as "asocials," women from Ravensbrück and other camps were used "legally" to serve as prostitutes in bordellos in men's camps. This shocking reality should put to rest any questions about whether gender considerations in a patriarchal society caused men and women to have different experiences in concentration camps. Some women prisoners were sent to men's camps to serve as prostitutes, and some male prisoners were entitled to the services of prostitutes. According to Hans Marsalek, this was the case in the bordello in the Mauthausen concentration camp. This "privilege" applied only to German and Austrian prisoners, mainly criminals, and some non-German prisoner bureaucrats in 1942–1943. Beginning in 1944, with the exception of Russian and Jewish prisoners, foreigners could also visit the bordello, which was "staffed" by female concentration camp prisoners drafted for this "work detail."[16]

Although none of the women I spoke with had personal knowledge about inmates forced into prostitution in some of the men's camps, there are first-hand testimonies and documentation.[17] One is by Anja Lundholm, who was deported to Ravensbrück in 1944 as a political prisoner and a "half-Jew."[18] Another is that of Margarethe W., a German woman who was arrested as an "asocial" because she had an affair with a "half-Jew." She was brought to Ravensbrück on 15 December 1939 and provided details about being sent to "work" in the Buchenwald bordello in 1943. One of sixteen Ravensbrück prisoners transported to Buchenwald to serve as prostitutes, she tried to commit suicide.[19]

There were bordellos for the SS or privileged prisoners in camps such as Mauthausen, Buchenwald, Sachsenhausen, Neuengamme, Dachau, Flossenbürg, and Mittelbau-Dora, and most of the women forced into prostitution in these camps came from Ravensbrück.[20] This victimization of women as women, for the pleasure of men (some of whom were themselves prisoners of the Nazis), shows that in addition to any other reason for their arrest by the Nazis, women were considered inferior to men.

LESBIANS

The legal treatment of lesbians as opposed to male homosexuals is further demonstration of gender differentiation. While male homosexuals were prosecuted by the Nazis under article 175StGB, based on the original anti-homosexual law of 1871, paragraph 175n, lesbians did not even have the distinction of being considered in a special category as homosexual. Instead they were considered "asocial," a title that proves that socialized gender issues played a role in the culture and society of Nazi Germany.[21] Male homosexuals had their distinct pink triangles to mark them as homosexual in concentration camps, but lesbians at Ravensbrück wore the black triangles that designated them as "asocial" or not fitting into society.

Although the Jewish women who spoke to me of lesbians at the camp painted them as aggressors, there were, no doubt, positive lesbian relationships that helped women bond and survive. As mentioned in chapter 2 regarding a groundbreaking conference on women and the Holocaust in 1983, some of the Jewish survivors have their own biases against lesbians, which may have colored their recollections. Writing of this stigmatization of lesbians and prostitutes, Hester Baer and Elizabeth Baer noted, "It is very difficult to get a clear and honest picture of relationships between women in Ravensbrück, particularly because there are no extant accounts of the camp written by prostitutes or lesbians, and other women's accounts may be untrustworthy because informed by such prejudices."[22]

The context of life in a concentration camp disrupted women's concepts of themselves, as well as the interconnections between minds and physical body functions in the social settings of their former lives. Changes in their bodies made them feel in some ways that they had ceased to be women, even as they struggled to keep a semblance of their normal lives and social conditions as women.

Epilogue

Ravensbrück Still on My Mind

T HE FATES of the women who suffered at Ravensbrück, especially the forgotten Jewish victims, have haunted me for twenty-three years. When I first visited the camp memorial site in the German Democratic Republic (GDR) in October 1980, the absence of Jewish victims in the memorialization exhibits and monuments shocked me. As a result, I have spent more than two decades seeking out their stories.

Since the day of my first visit to Ravensbrück, I have met and developed friendships with some of the Jewish women who had the good fortune to survive—against all odds—this camp's brutality. Their moving and extraordinary stories have been recounted here. In addition to these survivors, I talked with non-Jewish survivors and with relatives of Jewish victims who perished in the camp, as well as studying records and testimonies in the United States, Israel, Europe, and Brazil. Meanwhile, my emotional and intellectual connections with the women who suffered at the camp continued to grow.

My 1980 trip to the GDR and visit to Ravensbrück took place because of three colleagues who also became close friends. The GDR invited writers from three Jewish publications to demonstrate the absence of anti-Semitism to the Jewish community of the United States (and overt manifestations were indeed suppressed). Charles R. Allen, Jr., a gifted journalist who was one of the first to expose Nazi war criminals in the United States, made the connection with the GDR and suggested that I represent the Jewish Telegraphic Agency (JTA) news service. Murray Zuckoff, then editor of JTA, gave me the opportunity to do so as a freelance reporter.

Women of Ravensbrück: Portraits of Courage. One of seven photo transfer and mixed media panels created by Florida artist Julia Terwilliger in 1996 to remember and honor the women of Ravensbrück, Florida Holocaust Museum, St. Petersburg, Florida. Photo by Rochelle G. Saidel.

Aviva Cantor, a founding mother of *Lilith,* the Jewish feminist magazine, insisted that I must visit Ravensbrück while I was in the GDR. Quite frankly, I had not even heard of the camp in 1980, but I trusted Aviva's instincts on issues related to Jewish women's history and followed her firm recommendation.

Ravensbrück was not on the itinerary that our Communist hosts had prepared for us, and they tried hard to convince me that I really did not need to see it. Embarrassed by my threat to get there on my own and my suggestion that they seemed to be hiding something, they finally agreed to a short visit. As I mentioned in the introduction, the most information I could obtain about Jewish victims from the Communist survivor who served as my guide in 1980 was that German Communist heroine Olga Benário Prestes was coincidentally Jewish and that there had been a Jewish barrack. However, the memorial site had no evidence that any woman had ever been imprisoned there as a Jew.

Once I learned that there had been a Jewish barrack, I realized the exhibits at the memorial were negating the history of the Jewish victims.

Although I then had no idea of its considerable size, I was quite adamant in 1980 about the necessity of mentioning a Jewish presence as part of the camp's exhibits. GDR officials brushed aside my complaints, explaining that in compliance with the Communist practice of the times, the women were remembered according to nationality, and not religion. For example, the Polish Jewish victims of the camp, along with their Catholic Polish camp sisters, were supposedly "remembered" by means of a memorial room that featured a large crucifix. Both the explanation and the resulting reality enraged me. Aron Hirt-Manheimer, the editor of *Reform Judaism* who accompanied me to Ravensbrück, later told me that I "went crazy" there that day. And much later, in 2001, I learned that my angry reaction in 1980 about the camp memorial's failure to honor the Jewish victims had been noted in a GDR file at a high governmental level.[1]

Evidently, I had convinced Werner Händler, our official GDR government host in 1980, that I was going to follow through on the issue of memorializing the camp's Jewish victims. After my initial shock at their absence in the camp's memorial presentations on my October 1980 visit, I began writing him to urge GDR officials to create a memorial to the Jewish victims. He was at the time a Communist official who had been assigned through the *Liga für Völkerfreundschaft* (League for friendship among people) to accompany me and the other two American Jewish journalists. A Sachsenhausen survivor who later became General Secretary of the International Sachsenhausen Committee, Händler, then a nonpracticing Jew, evidently took my suggestion seriously. After his visit to the United States in 1985, he wrote a letter on 25 July to Hermann Axen, Member of the GDR Politburo, which stated, in part:

> I also had several conversations with Jewish press and organizations [in the United States]. Therefore, I could verify that in the last decade a wide tide of identification with Judaism developed mainly in the United States as a reaction to the Nazi extermination policy and under the influence of the State of Israel. People who are not religious feel themselves today as Jews and want to express it. It has to do with a strong emotionally characteristic process not yet consolidated that should be taken into account especially in our collaboration with the USA and the Americans. Also, in the visits to the memorials to the former concentration camps, whether there is an appropriate level of commemoration of the Jewish victims is frequently taken into account. The accusations made by the American journalist Rochelle Saidel after the visit in Ravensbrück in the fall of 1980 should be remembered in this connection. As, in spite of numerous attempts, no changes could be achieved in Ravensbrück, the Friendship Committee GDR-USA had since then taken the visitors from the USA only to Buchenwald and Sachsenhausen, where there are no problems, bypassing Ravensbrück.[2]

In this letter, Händler indicated that he had already tried to initiate some changes at Ravensbrück, and warned that the failure to do so would cause problems in relationships then being sought with the United States by the GDR. After his letter, the situation very slowly began to change, and by 1988, when the camp's site was still part of the GDR, a Jewish memorial was finally installed at Ravensbrück. The inscription is in honor and memory "of the countless Jewish and other victims of fascist racial-madness." The old "party line" of politicizing memorialization to glorify Communism and keeping exhibits *Judenrein* (free of Jews) thus had changed somewhat even before the end of the GDR. This is an important historical fact that needs to be emphasized, because it is often assumed that there was no change in this regard until after unification. After the Jewish memorial was created, one of the prison block cell exhibits was dedicated to Jewish victims, as I heard in correspondence from Händler and later from researchers at the memorial.

It was only when I returned to the camp memorial site in March 1994 and Germany was in the process of reunification that I learned that indeed there had been quite a "secret" in Ravensbrück in 1980. My offhand and ingenuous comment that my hosts were hiding something had been right on target, because in 1980 some twenty thousand Soviet soldiers were stationed at the camp as part of the Cold War missile program. In 1994 the site was in a state of transition from its GDR days to a new Western approach. Even though the Berlin Wall had fallen in November 1989, the last Soviet soldiers, stationed on Ravensbrück's grounds since the end of World War II, did not leave until the summer of 1993. I cannot forget the incongruous symbol of westernization that I spotted right outside the entrance to the Ravensbrück memorial site in 1994, a sign in English advertising, "Sylvia's Fitness Center."

My most haunting memory of that long and dreary 1994 winter day spent at Ravensbrück is that of the presence of many Siberian cats, abandoned by the Soviet soldiers and their families when they returned home. The cats wandered the newly accessible huge area of the camp, lonely, hungry, chilled, crying for help, and possibly destined for extermination. They seemed to be apparitions of the women who had a similar fate fifty years earlier, and their plight heightened the feeling of horror that the wasteland of razed barracks instilled in me.

After the troops finally withdrew, the grounds they had occupied and the entire former concentration camp came under the jurisdiction of the *Stiftung Brandenburgische Gedenkstätten* (the State of Brandenburg Memorials Foundation). The nearby town of Fürstenberg was suffering from the economic shock of losing the Soviet troops and their families, a long-term presence that had quadrupled the local population. One possible resolution that would have raised urgently needed revenue for the area, building a shopping center on land that had been part of the original camp, was halted after an international outcry. On the same day I visited Ravensbrück in March 1994, the Fürstenberg town officials were meeting to discuss this very proposal.

When I visited that year, the exhibits in the cells of the prison block, created by national survivor committees of individual countries, were in the process of renovation. The new Jewish memorial room was then among the exhibits in the cells. I was told that the Ravensbrück memorial staff had created it (unlike the others). As the museum in the prison cells was being redone for the forthcoming 1995 fiftieth anniversary ceremonies, it was closed to the public. However, I was allowed into the building, accompanied by staff member Christa Schulz. I could not see the Jewish exhibit, because that cell was locked and its contents were being dismantled. She said it was being moved to a larger cell space as there had been criticism that it was too small.

In 1994 I could see for the first time the vast former barracks area, occupied by the Soviet troops and hidden from view in 1980. The Soviet Army had razed all original Ravensbrück barracks. The crematorium, shooting corridor, and sculptures were as I remembered them, and I was also able to walk around the unmarked adjacent area that had been the site of the Siemens factory and barracks. I was fortunate to see the memorial in its transitional state in 1994, while it was still a muddy and untidy wasteland. Even then, with few exceptions, there was little encouragement for my interest in the Jewish victims of the camp. By then, I had met and interviewed a few more Jewish survivors, verified that the literature in English on the camp in general was almost nonexistent, and begun to gather whatever books I could find in French and German. However, even the foreign-language books were not about or by Jewish victims, although some of them included important information on them.

By the time I returned for the ceremonies marking the fiftieth anniversary of liberation in April 1995, the site had been "gentrified." The camp memorial's texts and exhibits had also been changed to reflect the camp's figurative relocation to the West. The Communist interpretation of what had happened during the Third Reich had been revised to conform to the new post-Soviet political reality, and a new presentation about the Jewish victims of the camp was then prominent among the exhibits in the prison cells of the punishment bunker.

After the discouragement and dearth of information on Jewish victims, I was astounded in April 1995 by the large number of Jewish women who attended the anniversary ceremonies, mostly from Israel but also from the United States, Europe, and elsewhere. While I was concerned about the survivors who were facing their unthinkable memories at the reunion, some of the women from Israel, in turn, were playing their roles of "Jewish mother" and worrying that I didn't have enough to eat.

I was deeply moved by two Jewish sisters now living in Israel, who had been deported from Amsterdam to Ravensbrück with their mother and brother in 1943. Many of the survivors had asked why I was at the fiftieth anniversary, why I was so interested in the camp, and if I, myself, was a survivor. I had given the same answer many times, "As a Jewish child born in 1942, there was no way I could be a survivor." I was born in the United States, but if, instead, I had been born in Europe and brought to this camp, I was sure that I could not have lived. Then I met the sisters, and one of them, Chaja Moskovits Dana, had been born in 1942. I was absolutely awestruck to meet her. She had entered the camp when she was sixteen months old, and by some miracle had survived both Ravensbrück and Bergen-Belsen.

I had another powerful emotional experience that day, also connected with the year 1942. The circumstances of my own life have given me a coincidental personal connection with Olga Benário Prestes and Dr. Käthe Pick Leichter, two early Jewish political prisoners who were taken from Ravensbrück and gassed in the winter of 1942. I am acquainted with their children, and I sometimes feel as though I actually knew these brave, intelligent, and idealistic women who were murdered by the Nazis, even though their deaths occurred the year I was born. Because my husband is Brazilian and I sometimes live in São Paulo, I am more familiar with Olga's history than most Americans. I have also had the opportunity to meet and correspond with her daughter in Rio de Janeiro, historian Dr. Anita Leocádia Prestes. And through my work in the New York State Senate for nine years, I befriended Käthe's son, former New York State Senator Franz Leichter. Olga Benário Prestes and Dr. Käthe Pick Leichter are inspirational heroines to me, and I was moved to tears by their enlarged photos side-by-side in the 1995 exhibit on Jewish prisoners.

Among the some thirteen hundred Jewish and non-Jewish survivors who attended the 1995 ceremony, there were about two hundred Jewish women. In striking contrast to the many years when Jewish victims were left out of the camp's story, the camp memorial's officials arranged a special meeting with the delegation of Israeli survivors to ask them how they would like to see the memorial evolve. I attended this meeting and saw how their input was specifically solicited. The attendees were told that their suggestions would be taken into consideration. Two years later the German-Israeli Foundation began to fund a sociological study of the camp's Jewish victims.[3]

This 1995 event was a turning point for my work, because I began to interview some of the Jewish survivors in attendance and gathered names for further contacts and interviews. Soon afterward, my long-term idea of including their presence and their stories in the history of the camp began to take shape. The United States Holocaust Memorial Museum helped by sending out cover letters, along with my letters, to the some three hundred Ravensbrück survivors in their registry. After receiving about sixty responses, which sometimes provided the names of other survivors, I sent out questionnaires and interviewed as many women as possible. The interview process is psychologically painful not only to the interviewee but also to a sensitive interviewer. One survivor sounded so deeply depressed and unreasonably demanding on the telephone that I was afraid to go visit her. I was sorry to lose her story but felt the need to protect myself. In general, however, speaking with the survivors was not only upsetting but also an intimate and gratifying experience. Some of them had personal questions about me and my life, and I thought it was only fair to answer them.

The recollections of the women in this book help to fill in some of the gaps from the specific point of view of Jewish Ravensbrück survivors, and of Jewish female Holocaust victims in general. Admittedly, these testimonies are at best a blend of memory and history. First of all, individual women's experiences cannot give us a comprehensive overview of the camp. Like the political prisoners who kept secret notes, they can only know what they saw, in a specific location and at a specific time. Furthermore, with all due respect to their taking the time and the emotional effort to share their stories, with the exception of Basia Rubinstein's 1945 testimony in the Lund University archive, they were talking about events that happened to them more than fifty years ago. Does time play tricks on memory? Even if this is sometimes the case, collectively, their stories are extremely vital to our understanding of life in Ravensbrück. Because of their generosity in sharing their painful experiences, we are richer in our knowledge about the camp in general, the unique ways that women suffered, and the experiences of Jewish women there in particular.

Sometimes a woman told a story that no one else mentioned. For example, Judith Becker described in chapter 9 that she saw a barrack filled with young women who had no tongues. In the same chapter, Lidia Vago reported that she was scientifically measured with an apparatus upon her arrival at the camp. Gloria Lyon told us in chapter 10 that she had seen women whose blood had been removed to the point that they were left to die. And only Olga Astor, in chapter 6, reported that Jewish prisoners were forced out into the cold naked for *Appell* on Christmas day 1944. All of these women used phrases indicating they would never forget what they saw.

We can either dismiss any or all of these stories as improbable or consider them precious information that only one survivor remembered. Unless and until proven otherwise, I tend to subscribe to the latter possibility. Even if we had no other reason to take their word for it, I don't believe anyone could have a vivid enough imagination to invent such stories. When the testimonies of the women in this book are put together, along with writings from non-Jewish survivors, reports on those who did not survive, historically accepted facts, war criminal trial transcripts, and Nazi documents, they serve to corroborate each other in a way that gives us an overview of the experiences of the Jewish victims of the camp.[4]

While I was interviewing survivors and working on this book, I was invited in 2000–2001 to serve as curator for an exhibit on Ravensbrück for the Florida Holocaust Museum in St. Petersburg. This exhibit, *Women of Ravensbrück—Portraits of Courage: Art by Julia Terwilliger*, enabled me to present in historic context the loving creations of a talented artist and friend whose premature and sudden death interrupted her own tribute to the Ravensbrück victims. Through my lectures related to this exhibit and on other occasions, I had the opportunity to meet more Ravensbrück survivors and their families. It was a special treat in February 2003 to see Rebecca Teitelbaum's tiny Ravensbrück recipe book at the Vancouver Holocaust Education Centre and then taste *gateau a l'orange* (orange cake), her nephew Alex Buckman's favorite recipe from the book.

Meanwhile, I had returned to Ravensbrück in June 2001, along with my friend and colleague Dr. Sonja Hedgepeth, to verify some details of my research. The landscape of the site had been expanded and changed, and the empty area that had held the Soviet troops was coated with black slag, with markers indicating the sites of barracks and other buildings. One of the former SS houses at the entrance to the camp was being readied as a conference center, especially for educational programs for youth groups. Including Jewish victims in memorialization at the camp was accepted without question. In fact, the report on the memorial's fifty-fifth anniversary ceremonies held 13–16 April 2000 begins by mentioning that, "commemorations started with the arrival of the first three guests from Israel."[5]

In the more than twenty-three years that I have been familiar with the camp, the absence of a Jewish presence has come full circle, and today the professional staff of the camp memorial and other researchers are seriously involved with including the history of Jewish victims. It is not difficult to comprehend the reason that Jewish victims were previously left out, or why they are now included. The way we memorialize any event is colored by who is doing the remembering and for what purposes.

When I first visited Ravensbrück in 1980, I had no idea that so many years later I would still be immersed in it. The victims' stories have become a part of me, and sometimes hearing and writing about them makes me so sad that I need an uplifting break. On one such occasion, I went to a *Storahtelling* production in a New York synagogue, created and enacted by Amichai Lau-Lavie. An Israeli living in New York, Amichai has developed a way of making the Torah (The Five Books of Moses) come alive as an interactive experience. He has his own Holocaust background, because his father, then age nineteen, and his uncle, then age eight, were liberated from Buchenwald on 11 April 1945. Soon afterward, they learned that their mother, Chaya Frankel-Teomim Lau, had not survived. "In addition to being a devoted and loving wife, mother, and housewife, she was also active in community affairs. She devoted a great deal of time to looking after the needy and counseling and comforting the many who turned to her for help," one of her sons wrote.[6]

Perhaps Ravensbrück and the fate of its Jewish victims will always torment me. I could not get away from the camp at *Storahtelling*, even while I was trying to imagine myself as wandering with the Israelites in the desert. Amichai, portraying Moses, invited those who appreciate and find holiness in nature to come up for an *aliyah* to the Torah. As I went up to say the blessings, I began thinking about nature, and especially the beautiful lake in the Adirondack Mountains that has always been part of my life. But then I remembered the Schwedtsee, the lake next to Ravensbrück, as well as an unpublished short story that Amichai wrote in 1995 and shared with me. It was about his grandmother, Chaya Lau. He wrote:

> My grandmother is now a lake. "The ashes," mother says, "were spread in the lake that was next to the camp, divided by a brick wall." Now there is no wall, just a blue lake in green German scenery. My grandmother is now a lake. Before that she was a corpse, open eyed and open mouthed in a mass of crowded corpses. Before that she was an identifiable corpse next to a woman skeleton who saw and recognized and maybe gently closed the dead eyes, and then removed her to the mass of other bodies. In barracks for 250 they crowded one thousand.[7]

Chaya Lau, like so many uncounted other Jewish victims to whom this book pays tribute, died of starvation and typhus a few days before liberation in Ravensbrück.

Appendix

The Jewish Ravensbrück Survivors

A special thank you to all of the Ravensbrück survivors and their families who granted interviews or provided written information for this book. The following Jewish survivors who cooperated in the study are mentioned in the book, ranging from quoting an extensive testimony to listing a name in a footnote.

Olga Weiss Astor, Glenwood, Illinois
Viola Eisler Baras, Tamarac, Florida
Alice Berger, Pembroke Pines, Florida
I. Judith Berger Becker, Jerusalem, Israel
Alice Strum Birnhak, Brooklyn, New York
Lotte Brainin, Vienna, Austria
Chaya Moskovits Dana, Netanya, Israel
Sali Solomon Daugherty, Jaffa, Israel
Edith Eisler Denes, Tamarac, Florida
Renee Duering, Daly City, California
Lilly Eisler, Tamarac, Florida
Erna Ellert, Ramat Hasharon, Israel
Rosa Korman Fajerstajn, São Paulo, Brazil
Ilona Klein Feldman, Chicago, Illinois
Lea Gelbgras Ferstenberg, New Rochelle, New York
Manya Friedman, Bethesda, Maryland
Nomi Moskovits Friedmann, Netanya, Israel
Shimon Gerecht, Holon, Israel

Judith Rosner Gertler, Brooklyn, New York
Tova (Guta) Flatto Giladi, Kew Gardens, New York
Esther Wondolowicz Goldman, Norfolk, Virginia
Mina Lewkowicz Goldstein, Los Angeles, California
Doris Fuks Greenberg, Stamford, Connecticut
Jacqueline Schweitzer Gropman, Canton, Michigan (z"l)*
Ester (Eliz) Weisz Grun, White Plains, New York
Margaret (Margo) Wohl Guiness, Laguna Niguel, California
Rachel Rozenbaum Hocherman, Ramat Gan, Israel (z"l)*
Hannah Cukier Horon, Jackson Heights, New York
Blanka Adler Kahan, Bayside, New York
Stella Ginsburg Kipman, Ville Mount-Royal, Quebec, Canada
Fela Szyjka Kolat, Worcester, Massachusetts and Monsey, New York
Susan Jakubovic Kornhauser, Downsview, Ontario, Canada
Johanna Lindner Krause, Dresden, Germany
Hilda Zajac Kreuzer, Bronx, New York
Helen (Chaya) Kaplan Luksenberg, Philadelphia, Pennsylvania
Gloria Hollander Lyon, San Francisco, California
Rose Frochewajg Mellender, Bronx, New York
Olga Friedman Mittelman, Toronto, Ontario, Canada
Lonia Kirshenbaum Mosak, Skokie, Illinois
Irmgard Muller, Chapel Hill, North Carolina
Stella Kugelman Nikiforova, Saint Petersburg, Russia
Elisabeth Koevesi Pavel, Brooklyn, New York
Esther Himmelfarb Peterseil, Lawrence, New York
Clara Szabo Rosenbaum, Montreal, Quebec, Canada
Martha Hoffman Rothman, San Diego, California
Basia Zajaczkowska Rubinstein, Lincolnwood, Illinois
Bracha Blattberg Schiff, North Miami Beach, Florida
Dr. Lore Shelley, San Francisco, California
Esther Tuvel Shuftan, Glenwood, Illinois
Katerine Stone, Silver Spring, Maryland
Lola Goldstein Taubman, Longwood, Florida
Elizabeth Kroó Teitelbaum, Brooklyn, New York
Rebecca (Becky) Buckman Teitelbaum, Ottawa, Canada (z"l)*
Lidia Rosenfeld Vago, Petach Tikva, Israel
Edith Gabor Vidos, Briarwood, New York
Regina Steinbok Weisfelner, Bronx, New York
Agnes Bloch Werber, Royal Palm Beach, Florida
Ida Yardeni-Tavor, Atlanta, Georgia

Appendix

Thank you also to other survivors who provided information that contributed to this study, but whose names do not appear:

Sala Szmulewicz Achtman, Brooklyn, New York
Edith Ales, West Orange, New Jersey
Henrietta Szpigelman Altman, Melbourne, Victoria, Australia
Vera Beckhard, New York, New York
Batsheva Dagan, Holon, Israel
Ilona Wiesner Demeter, Rego Park, New York
Guta Fischel, Sarasota, Florida
Rosl Mauskopf Forsberg, Solvesborg, Sweden
Lily Gliksman Zaks Friedler, Coconut Creek, Florida
Marysia Wegier Gordon, Riverdale, New York
Hanna Kallus Greenfeld, Dix Hills, New York
Eugenia Wein Nelken Gwozdz, Corpus Christi, Texas
Anne Hadley, Boca Raton, Florida
Stephanie Heilbrunn Heller, Melbourne, Victoria, Australia
Bernice Horon, Lewistown, Pennsylvania
Rose Szpiler Katz, Brighton, Massachusetts
Helena Kaufman, Hallandale, Florida
Esther Herskovits Klein, Far Rockaway, New York
Agnes Kroo, Geneva, Switzerland
Nelly Kurianski, Sarasota, Florida
Dora Bursztain Langsam, Philadelphia, Pennsylvania
Ilana Lehner, Jerusalem, Israel
Ruth Krautwirth Meyerowitz, West Orange, New Jersey
Regina Feingold Oksman, West Roxbury, Massachusetts
Gerda Perley, Montreal, Quebec, Canada
Germaine Pitchon, Clearwater, Florida
Edith Klein Platschek, Budapest, Hungary
Ana Riesenberg-Czajkowski Praszkier, Melbourne, Victoria, Australia
Tova (Tola) Rosmant, Tel Aviv, Israel
Feiga Rosz, South Euclid, Ohio
Lilly Rosenberg Schwartz, Haifa, Israel
Margot Fuchs Stern, Seal Beach, California
Guta Weintraub, Rockville, Maryland

*known to have died during the time of the study (*z"l* is a Hebrew acronym for "of blessed memory")

Notes

INTRODUCTION

1. Most memoirs in English by non-Jewish survivors were originally in another language. From German, for example, Margarete Buber-Neumann, *Under Two Dictators*, trans. Edward Fitzgerald. (London: Gollencz, 1949); Nanda Herbermann, *The Blessed Abyss: Inmate #6582 in Ravensbrück Concentration Camp for Women*, trans. Hester Baer, ed. Hester Baer and Elizabeth Baer (Detroit: Wayne State University Press, 2000). From French, for example, Charlotte Delbo, *Auschwitz and After* (New Haven: Yale University Press, 1995); Denise Dunfurnier, *Ravensbrück: The Women's Camp of Death* (London: Allen and Unwin, 1948); Michelene Maurel, *An Ordinary Camp* (New York: Simon and Schuster, 1958; also published as *Ravensbruck*, London: Blond, 1958); and Germaine Tillion, *Ravensbrück: An Eyewitness Account of a Women's Concentration Camp* (New Yosrk: Doubleday, 1975). From Polish, for example, Wanda Póltawska, *And I Am Afraid of My Dreams,* trans. Mary Craig (New York: Hippocrene Books, 1987); Wanda Symonowicz, ed., Beyond *Human Endurance: The Ravensbrück Women Tell Their Stories.* (Warsaw: Interpress Publishers, 1970). From Dutch, Corrie Ten Boom, *The Hiding Place.* (New York: Bantam, 1971).

2. Every museum, especially when the subject is as politically and emotionally charged as the Holocaust, has its own agenda, or framework, within which to tell its story. The case in East Germany is particularly obvious, because the framework changed after the fall of the Berlin Wall. For information on the history of memorialization at the Ravensbrück memorial, see Insa Eschebach, Sigrid Jacobeit, and Susanne Lanwerd, eds., *Die Sprache des Gedenkens: Zur Geschichte der Gedenkstätte Ravensbrück 1945–1995* (The language of memorialization: toward a history of the Ravensbrück memorial 1945–1995) (Berlin: Edition Hentrich, 1999). For general information on the politics of memorialization of Holocaust museums and memorials, see Claudia Koonz, "Germany's Buchenwald: Whose Shrine? Whose Memory?" in *The Art of Memory: Holocaust*

Memorials in History, ed. James Young (Munich and New York: Prestel-Verlag and The Jewish Museum, 1994); Rochelle G. Saidel, *Never Too Late to Remember: The Politics behind New York City's Holocaust Museum* (New York: Holmes & Meier, 1996); James Young, *The Texture of Memory: Holocaust Memorials and Meaning* (New Haven: Yale University Press, 1993); James Young, ed., *The Art of Memory: Holocaust Memorials in History* (Munich and New York: Prestel-Verlag and The Jewish Museum, 1994). See also Ruth Linden, *Making Stories, Making Selves: Feminist Reflections on the Holocaust* (Columbus: Ohio State University Press, 1993).

3. Insa Eschebach, "Engendered Oblivion: Commemorating Jewish Inmates at the Ravensbrück Memorial 1945–1995," unpublished paper presented at *Gender, Place and Memory in the Modern Jewish Experience,* an international conference held 2–4 January 2001, Bar-Ilan University, Israel. The book she referred to is *Ravensbrück,* published by Komitee der Antifaschistischen Widerstandskämpfer in der Deutschen Demokratischen Republik (Committee of antifascist resistance fighters in the GDR) (Berlin, 1960), 7 (German version), 45 (English version).

4. *Ravensbrück,* Komitee der Antifaschistischen Widerstandskämpfer, 11, 49, cited by Eschebach, "Engendered Oblivion."

5. Ibid., 129, 143.

6. "Die Geschichte lehrt: Alles für den Frieden" (The history teaches: everything for peace), Komitee der Antifaschistischen Widerstandskämpfer der Deutschen Demokratischen Republik, 30 April 1985, 40; "Jahrestag der Befreiung des Faschistischen Konzentrationslagers Ravensbrück" (Anniversary of the liberation of the Fascist concentration camps, Ravensbrück), (Berlin, 1985), 7–19, cited by Eschebach, "Engendered Oblivion."

7. See Herta Soswinski, "Why We Have to Tell about It," in *Auschwitz: The Nazi Civilization,* ed. Lore Shelley (Lanham, Md.: University Press of America, 1992), 125–44. The camp was not free of Jews for very long, because, for example, Sali Solomon Daugherty arrived with her mother and aunt toward the end of November or early December 1942.

8. For example, memoirs by Halina Nelken, *And Yet, I Am Here!* (Amherst: University of Massachusetts Press, 1999) and Rena Kornreich Gelissin, *Rena's Promise* (Boston: Beacon Press, 1995) include their experiences at Ravensbrück, as does the posthumously published memoir by Sara Tuvel Bernstein, *The Seamstress* (New York: Putnam, 1997). Alice Birnhak briefly mentions her time in Ravensbrück in her memoir, *Next Year, God Willing* (New York: Shengold Publishers, 1994). Margaret Guiness, who shared her unpublished manuscript with me, later self-published her remarkable story that includes Ravensbrück, *When the Sky Rained Umbrellas* (Laguna Niguel: Royal Literary Publications, 2001). While these five memoirs could be considered those of "typical" Jewish victims, there is also a memoir by an "atypical" victim. See Gemma LaGuardia Gluck, *My Story,* ed. S. L. Shneiderman (New York: David McKay, 1961).

9. Although no exact records are available, an estimated 20 percent of the total population was Jewish. The estimated statistic used at the Ravensbrück memorial site in 1995 was that 10 percent of the population was Jewish, but I believe this figure was too low. By 2000 this estimate was changed to about 15 percent,

but the actual number was probably even higher. In a 1995 interview at her home outside of Paris, the president of the French Amicale de Ravensbrück, survivor Dr. Marie-Jo Chombart de Lauwe, said that many women passed through the camp on the way to Auschwitz or other camps and were never included in the count of those interned. Many of these women who were taken to other camps were Jews. There will never be specific numbers for any of the groups of women at the camp because the Nazis burned many records in the crematorium before fleeing.

10. I am indebted to excellent research assistants, Dr. Evie Joslow and Susan Sapiro, who sensitively and ably conducted some of the interviews in the United States for me.

11. See Karl W. Deutsch, *The Nerves of Government* (London: Free Press of Glencoe, Collier-Macmillan, 1963); and Peter L. Berger and Thomas Luckmann, *The Social Construction of Reality* (Garden City: Anchor Books, Doubleday, 1966).

12. Shulamit Reinharz, *Feminist Methods in Social Research* (New York: Oxford University Press, 1992), 127.

13. Gluck, *My Story*. The estate of Mr. Shneiderman has granted the author permission to augment and republish the book.

1. A SPECIAL HELL FOR WOMEN

1. For more information, see Monika Herzog and Bernhard Strebel, "Das Frauenkonzentrationslager Ravensbrück" (Ravensbrück women's concentration camp) in *Frauen in Konzentrationslagern: Bergen-Belsen Ravensbrück* (Women in concentration camps: Bergen-Belsen, Ravensbrück), ed. Claus Füllberg-Stolberg, Martina Jung, Renate Riebe, and Martina Scheitenberger (Bremen: Edition Temmen, 1994), 14.

2. May 1939 is generally accepted as the month of the first transport. According to Erika Buchmann, *Die Frauen von Ravensbrück* (The women of Ravensbrück) (Berlin, GDR, 1959), 28, the first women's transport arrived at the Fürstenberg train station on 23 March 1939.

3. See Soswinski, "Why We Have to Tell about It," 125–44. An Austrian Jewish political prisoner who survived, Soswinski arrived on 14 January 1942 and was sent to Auschwitz in October 1942.

4. Gluck, *My Story*, 71.

5. Hubert Fischer, "Ärztliche Versorgung, Sanitäre Verhältnisse und Humanversuche im Frauenkonzentrationslager Ravensbrück," (Medical care, sanitary conditions, and human experimentation in the Ravensbrück women's concentration camp) in *Gesnerus*, Switzerland, 1988, 45 (1), 51, 53.

6. See Herzog and Strebel, "Das Frauenkonzentrationslager Ravensbrück," 15.

7. Ibid.

8. Buber-Neumann, *Under Two Dictators*, 186–87.

9. Ibid., 187–88.

10. Ibid., 211.

11. See Herzog and Strebel, "Das Frauenkonzentrationslager Ravensbrück,"

15, which cites the official *Stärkemeldungen* (prisoner counts) of 24 May 1940 (3,199 women) and 9 August 1941 (5,235 women). Copies at Ravensbrück Memorial archive. In 1941 a camp for male inmates was constructed next to the women's camp and subordinated to it, and the total number of male inmates registered there from that date until April 1945 exceeded twenty thousand.

12. Fischer, "Ärztliche Versorgung, Sanitäre Verhältnisse und Humanversuche im Frauenkonzentrationslager Ravensbrück," 50.

13. See Herbermann, *The Blessed Abyss,* 110–11. The memoir was originally published in German in 1946.

14. The 14f13 project was part of the euthanasia program known as T4 (as its address was Tiergartenstrasse 4, Berlin). The program was designed for adults who were mentally or physically "unacceptable" by Nazi racial standards and were murdered at one of four euthanasia centers, including Bernburg. See chapter 3 for more details about Jewish women from Ravensbrück who were murdered at Bernburg.

15. See Herzog and Strebel, "Das Frauenkonzentrationslager Ravensbrück," 15, which cites the official prisoner count for April 1942 as 6,389 women, and also cites a report of *Wirtschafts-Verwaltungshauptamt* (WVHA–Economic Administrative Authority: the bureau responsible for the economic exploitation of deportees) dated 30 April 1942, which numbers prisoners at 7,500. Copies at Ravensbrück Memorial archive. After Reinhard Heydrich, head of the Reich's Central Security Office and the Deputy Reich's Protector of Bohemia and Moravia, died of wounds he received in the Czech village of Lidice in May 1942, all the village women were sent to Ravensbrück.

16. Fragments of arrival lists and inmate numbers from 1 January to 31 December 1943, with 15918–25891, Ravensbrück Memorial archive.

17. Germaine Tillion, in *Ravensbrück,* 244, cites a figure of about 43,700. A considerably lower maximum number of 32,050, which still reflects untenable overcrowding, has been used in memorial exhibits at the camp. According to Bernhard Strebel, an SS list of the *Wirtschafts-Verwaltungshauptamt* (WVHA) listed a total of 46,070 women in Ravensbrück and its satellites on 15 January 1945. "Ravensbrück-das zentrale Frauenkonzentrationslager" ("Ravensbrück, the central women's concentration camp"), in *Die nationalsozialistischen Konzentrationslager. Entwicklung und Struktur* (The national socialistic concentration camps—development and structure), ed. Ulrich Herbert, Karin Orth, and Christoph Dieckmann. (Göttingen: Wallstein Verlag, 1998), 240.

18. Fischer, "Ärztliche Versorgung, Sanitäre Verhältnisse und Humanversuche im Frauenkonzentrationslager Ravensbrück," 58.

19. See Strebel, "Ravensbrück-das zentrale Frauenkonzentrationslager" 225–27.

20. Charlotte Müller, *Die Klempnerkolonne in Ravensbrück: Erinnerungen des Häftlings Nr. 10787* (The plumber column of Ravensbrück: recollections of prisoner No. 10787) (Berlin: Dietz Verlag, 1981), 184.

21. I. Judith Berger Becker, interview with Rochelle G. Saidel, Jerusalem, 17 February 1997, archive of the author.

22. See Herzog and Strebel, "Das Frauenkonzentrationslager Ravensbrück," 21–22; and Fischer, "Ärztliche Versorgung, Sanitäre Verhältnisse und Humanversuche im Frauenkonzentrationslager Ravensbrück," 61.

23. Strebel, "Ravensbrück—das zentrale Frauenkonzentrationslager," 235. Fischer uses the figure of 5,693 women "said to have been gassed" at the camp, 62.

24. Gluck, *My Story,* 70–71.

25. Martin Guse, "'Wir hatten gar nicht angefangen zu leben': Eine Ausstellung zu den Jugend-KZ Moringen und Uckermark 1940–1945" ("We didn't even begin to live": an exhibition of the youth camps Moringen and Uckermark, 1940–1945) (Moringen: 1992), cited in Herzog and Strebel, "Das Frauenkonzentrationslager Ravensbrück," 20.

26. Dagmar Hajkova, *Ravensbrück* (Prague: 1960), 163, quoted in Herzog and Strebel, "Das Frauenkonzentrationslager Ravensbrück," 20.

27. Lotte Brainin, letter to Rochelle G. Saidel from Vienna, 16 January 1996, archive of the author.

28. Wanda Kiedrzynska, *Ravensbrück: Kobiecy obóz koncentracyjny* (Ravensbrück: women's concentration camp) (Warsaw: 1961), 134–46, cited in Herzog and Strebel, "Das Frauenkonzentrationslager Ravensbrück," 20.

29. The first public event on the question is recorded in Esther Katz and Joan Ringelheim, eds., *Proceedings of the Conference of Women Surviving the Holocaust* (New York: The Institute for Research in History, 1983). More recent analytical studies include Dalia Ofer and Lenore J. Weitzman, eds., *Women in the Holocaust* (New Haven: Yale University Press, 1998); Nechama Tec, *Resilience and Courage: Women, Men, and the Holocaust* (New Haven: Yale University Press, 2003); and Elizabeth Baer and Myrna Goldenberg, eds., *Experience and Expression: Women, the Nazis, and the Holocaust* (Detroit: Wayne State University Press, 2003).

30. Strebel, "Ravensbrück-das zentrale Frauenkonzentrationslager," 229.

31. Ibid., 219. Strebel cites Kiedrzynska, *Ravensbrück: Kobiecy obóz koncentracyjny,* as a source for the figure of 132,000.

32. Kiedrzynska, *Ravensbrück,* cited in Strebel, "Ravensbrück-das zentrale Frauenkonzentrationslager," 243.

33. For example, researcher Insa Eschebach stated: "According to rough estimates, there were about twenty thousand Jewish prisoners at Ravensbrück and its satellite camps, figures which require further investigation, as do the numbers and fate of the Jewish prisoners." "Engendered Oblivion."

34. Lea Ferstenberg, interview with Evie Joselow for Rochelle G. Saidel, New Rochelle, New York, 12 February 1998, archive of the author.

35. Fela Kolat, interview with Rochelle G. Saidel, Worcester, Massachusetts, 24 June 1996, archive of the author.

2. TRIANGLES OF MANY COLORS

1. See reference list. The following accounts by political prisoners are translations in English: Buber-Neumann, *Under Two Dictators*; Herbermann, *The Blessed Abyss*; Genevieve de Gaulle Anthonioz, *The Dawn of Hope: A Memoir of Ravensbrück* (New York: Arcade Publishing, 1999); Delbo, *Auschwitz and After*; Dunfurnier, *Ravensbrück*; Maurel, *An Ordinary Camp*; Tillion, *Ravensbrück*; Wanda Póltawska, "Ravensbrueck between Life and Death" (Poland:

No. 6/106,1963), 17–19; and *And I Am Afraid of My Dreams*; Symonowicz, *Beyond Human Endurance*; Ten Boom, *The Hiding Place*.

2. Information about Elisabeth Saborowski Ewert is from Fernando Morais, *Olga: Revolutionary and Martyr* (New York: Grove Weidenfeld, 1990); Ruth Werner, *Olga Benário: A História de uma Mulher Corajosa* (Olga Benário: A history of a courageous woman) (São Paulo: Editora Alfa-Omega, 1987); Katja Haferkorn, "Kämpfer für das deutsche und das brasilianische Volk: Arthur Ewert" (Fighter for the German and Brazilian people: Arthur Ewert), in *Beiträge zur Geschichte der deutschen Arbeiterbewegung* (Contribution on the history of the German workers movement) (Berlin: Sonderdruck, 1968); and Maria Kuhn-Wiedmaier, "Sabo Ewert," Archive of Ravensbrück Memorial, RAI-7-2-26.

3. A letter written by her, now in the Ravensbrück Memorial archive, places her arrival at about 2 June 1939. RAII/6–1-44.

4. The information about Sabo at Ravensbrück is based on Kuhn-Wiedmaier, "Sabo Ewert." The exact date of her death is undocumented.

5. Charlotte Uhrig had been arrested because, like her husband, she had been an active resistance fighter. When she spoke to me at the camp memorial in 1980, she stressed the heroism of the Communist prisoners and minimized the presence of others.

6. Buber-Neumann, *Under Two Dictators* was translated into English from German but is long out of print. Herbermann's *Blessed Abyss* is a recent addition to accounts in translation. Morais's *Olga*, is an English translation from Portuguese about Olga Benário Prestes but is fictionalized. Among memoirs by German Communist prisoners that have not been translated is that of Müller, *Die Klempnerkolonne in Ravensbrück*.

7. Herbermann's memoir, *Der gesegnete Abgrund. Schutzhäftling Nr. 6582 im Frauenkonzentrationlager Ravensbrück* was published in Germany in 1946. The English translation edited by Hester Baer and Elizabeth Baer, *The Blessed Abyss*, was published in 2000. In a paper, "Complicating the Holocaust: Who Is a Victim? What Is a Holocaust Memoir?" presented at the Remembering for the Future 2000 Conference, Oxford University, 18 July 2000, Elizabeth Baer wrote that, "Herbermann's occasional anti-Semitic remarks [in her memoir] identify her as a product of her country and her religion."

8. Hester Baer and Elizabeth Baer, introduction to Herbermann, *The Blessed Abyss*, 45–46.

9. The memoir is Sister Theodolinde/Katharina Katzenmaier, *Vom KZ ins Kloster* (From concentration camp to convent) (St. Ottilien: 1996). Information on Sister Theodolinde was provided by Britta Pawelke of Mahn- und Gedankstätte Ravensbrück, the camp memorial. Sister Theodolinde's story was part of an exhibit at the camp, "Christliche Frauen im Widerstehen gegen den Nationalsozialismus: Häftlinge im Frauenkonzentrationslager Ravensbrück von 1939–1945" (Christian women in resistance against national socialism: prisoners in Ravensbrück from 1939–1945), 18 October 1998–20 October 1999, Mahn- und Gedenkstätte Ravensbrück/Stiftung Brandenburgische Gedenkstätten (Ravensbrück Memorial/Brandenburg Memorials Foundation).

10. Strebel, "Ravensbrück-das zentrale Frauenkonzentrationslager."

11. Póltawska, *And I Am Afraid of My Dreams*.

12. Póltawska names medical doctors Oberheuser, Rosenthal, Karl Gebhardt, Fischer, and Schidlausky as involved in the experiments, *And I Am Afraid of My Dreams*, 74, 80, 84.

13. Books by French Ravensbrück survivors that have been translated into English include: Delbo, *Auschwitz and After*; Dunfurnier, *Ravensbrück*; de Gaulle Anthonioz, *The Dawn of Hope*; Maurel, *An Ordinary Camp*; and Tillion, *Ravensbrück*.

14. Marie-Jo Chombart de Lauwe, interview with Rochelle G. Saidel, Paris, 1 February 1995. The title of the book on which she collaborated is *Les Françaises à Ravensbrück* (The French women at Ravensbrück) (Paris: Éditions Gallimard, 1965). She became head of the French Amicale of survivors. She later wrote her own memoir, *Toute une vie de résistance* (An entire life of resistance) (Paris: Éditions Grapheln FNDIRP, 1998).

15. The English version is Tillion, *Ravensbrück*. Earlier versions, in French, include a shorter account titled "Ravensbrück" in a collection, *La Baconnière*, ed. Albert Béguin, 1946; and "Réflexions sur l'étude de la déportation" (Reflections on the study of the deportation), in *Revue d'histoire de la Deuxième Guerre Mondial* (Review of the history of World War II), nos. 15–16 (July–September 1954), 3–38. The English version is a translation of *Ravensbrück* (Paris: Éditions du Seuil, 1973).

16. See Carol Rittner, Stephen D. Smith, and Irena Steinfeldt, eds., *The Holocaust and the Christian World* (Nottingham: Beth Shalom Holocaust Memorial Centre, 2000), 167. They give her last name as Skobtsova. Monika Herzog, archivist at Mahn- und Gedenkstätte Ravensbrück, uses the name Skobzoff.

17. See Sigrid Jacobeit, *Ravensbrückerinnen* (Women from Ravensbrück), (Oranienburg: Stiftung Brandenburgische Gedenkstätten, 1995). According to Monika Herzog, archivist at the camp memorial, the names of the two nuns were on the so-called Mittwerda list of 6 April 1945, which had 469 prisoners' names. This list was prepared after the women were gassed. "Mittwerda" was a coded term for the gas chamber, although the women were informed they were being sent to a camp in Silesia, where they would receive good treatment. The specific date of the death of the two women cannot be established and is assumed to have been 30 or 31 March 1945. (Communication from Monika Herzog to the author, 3 April 2001.)

18. For a complete account, see Ten Boom, *The Hiding Place*. There is a summary biography in Rittner, Smith, and Steinfeldt, *The Holocaust and the Christian World,* 169.

19. Stennie Pratomo-Gret, e-mail correspondence with the author. Stennie and her husband, Djajeng Pratomo, were extremely helpful when I was preparing an exhibit and catalogue on the camp for the Florida Holocaust Museum in 2001. See also, "Short History of Dutch Women in Ravensbrück, 1940–1945," in Carol Adams, ed., *Women of Ravensbrück: Portraits of Courage,* booklet for exhibit by Julia Terwilliger, University of Central Florida, 1997, 9–11, archive of the author.

20. See Eva Fogelman, *Conscience & Courage: Rescuers of Jews during the Holocaust* (New York: Anchor Books, 1994), 213–17, 244–47.

21. Information on the Soviet Army women in Ravensbrück is from Vera Unverzagt, "'Das soll sich nicht wiederholen'—Weibliche Kriegsgefangene der

Roten Armee im KZ Ravensbrück" (This should not repeat itself—female prisoners-of-war of the Red Army in Ravensbrück concentration camp) in *Frauen in Konzentrationslagern,* ed. Füllberg-Stolberg et al., 307–12. Antonina Alexandrowna Nikiforova's book, *This Should Not Repeat Itself,* came out in the Soviet Union in Russian in 1958 and has not been translated into English.

22. Testimony of Johann[es] Schwarzhuber, charged jointly with committing a war crime at Ravensbrück between 1939 and 1945 as a member of the staff—ill treatment and killing of Allied Nationals interned therein. He was also *Lagerführer* (camp leader) from 12 January to 29 April 1945. Accused under charge of ninety-eight Pioneer Corps, Ravensbrück Trial, Hamburg, 5 December 1946, WO 235/317, Public Record Office, London (now called the National Archives of England, Wales, and the United Kingdom). Schwarzhuber testified that there were twelve British and fourteen American women in the camp (page four of document), but this has never been confirmed. For more information on Violette Szabo, see R. J. Minney, *Carve Her Name With Pride* (London: George Newnes, 1956); and Susan Ottaway, *Violette Szabo: 'The Life that I Have . . .'* (Annapolis: Naval Institute Press, 2002).

23. "Jehovah's Witnesses," booklet, Washington: United States Holocaust Memorial Museum. See also Christine King, *The Nazi State and the New Religions: Five Case Studies in Non-Conformity* (New York: Edwin Mellen, 1982).

24. Gluck, *My Story,* 55–56.

25. Magdelena Kusserow Reuter, conversation with Rochelle G. Saidel, São Paulo, 27 May 1999. I met Magdalena when we spoke about Ravensbrück on the same platform in Brazil in May 1999. She had come for events in Rio de Janeiro and São Paulo in connection with the release of the Portuguese version of the video *Jehovah's Witnesses Stand Firm against Nazi Assault.*

26. Quoted from the *Watchtower* magazine, Brooklyn, N.Y., 1 November 1979.

27. Buber-Neumann. *Under Two Dictators,* 222–38.

28. Martina Scheitenberger and Martina Jung, "Fürsorge–Arbeitshaus–KZ, Betty Voss" (Care–workhouse–concentration camp, Betty Voss), in *Frauen in Konzentrationslagern,* ed. Füllberg-Stolberg, et al. 300.

29. See Katz and Ringelheim, *Proceedings of the Conference of Women Surviving the Holocaust,* for more details about the conference in general.

30. Desig # 491.73 (Homosexuals–Prisoners/mug shots–concentration camps), W/S #71929, CD #0026. "Mug shot of Henny Sara Schermann who was condemned to death for 'unnatural fornication.'" United States Holocaust Memorial Museum Photo Archives, (accessed 24 April 2002). Original document in Staatsarchiv Nürnberg (photo NO-3060) uses Jenny as her first name, and correspondence from that archive insists that is the correct name. Claudia Schoppmann, *Days of Masquerade: Life Stories of Lesbians during the Third Reich* (New York: Columbia University Press, 1996), 22–23, also writes that Schermann's first name was Henny, and provides information about her and Mary Pünjer.

31. Scheitenberger and Jung, "Fürsorge—Arbeitshaus—KZ, Betty Voss," 305.

32. Hannah Horon interviewed by Susan Sapiro for Rochelle G. Saidel, New York, 8 December 1997, archive of the author.

33. Mina Goldstein, telephone interview with Rochelle G. Saidel from Los Angeles, 20 October 1997, archive of the author.

34. The survivor does not wish to be identified. She provided this information at a session on women and the Holocaust, Annual Scholars' Conference on the Holocaust, Philadelphia, 6 March 2001.

35. Elizabeth Kroó Teitelbaum, interview with Rochelle G. Saidel. Brooklyn, 20 October 1997, archive of the author.

36. See Michael Berenbaum, "A Mosaic of Victims: What about Non-Jewish Victims of the Nazis?" in Rittner, Smith, and Steinfeldt, *The Holocaust and the Christian World*, 68–72. For a detailed account about Sinti and Roma women, see Sybil Milton, "Hidden Lives: Sinti and Roma Women," in *Experience and Expression: Women, the Nazis, and the Holocaust* (Detroit: Wayne State University Press, 2003), 53–75.

37. See Heike Krokowski and Bianca Voigt, "Das Schicksal von Wanda P.—Zur Verfolgung der Sinti und Roma" (The destiny of Wanda P.—the persecution of the Sinti and Roma), in *Frauen in Konzentrationslagern*, ed. Füllberg-Stolberg, et al., 259–68.

3. OLGA BENÁRIO PRESTES AND KÄTHE PICK LEICHTER

1. Information on Olga Benário Prestes is based on visits to the Ravensbrück memorial; correspondence with memorial (Mahn- und Gedenkstätte Ravensbrück) archivist Monika Herzog; Morais, *Olga*; Werner, *Olga Benário*; Rita de Cássia Buzzar, "Olga," in *Não Olhe nos Olhos do Inimigo* (Don't look in the eyes of the enemy) (São Paulo: Paz e Terra, 1995), 17–31; and Anita Leocádia Prestes, "Olga Benário Prestes, minha mãe" (Olga Benário Prestes, my mother), in *Não Olhe nos Olhos do Inimigo*, 13–16.

2. Jutta von Freyberg and Ursula Krause-Schmitt, *Moringen-Lichtenburg-Ravensbrück: Frauen im Konzentrationslager 1933–1945* (Moringen-Lichtenburg-Ravensbrück: women in concentration camps) (Frankfurt: VAS–Verlag für Akademische Schriften, 1997), 133.

3. Ibid.

4. Ibid.

5. Ibid.

6. Anita Leocádia Prestes dates her mother's death as April 1942, but most other sources say February or March.

7. One (fictionalized) book originally published in Portuguese in Brazil has been translated into English and republished in the United States. See Morais, *Olga*.

8. Morais, *Olga*, 241–42.

9. The information on Käthe Leichter is based on an interview with her son, Henry O. Leichter (New York, 7 August 1998); Henry O. Leichter, "Childhood Memories" (unpublished English manuscript, 1995); and Herbert Steiner, *Käthe Leichter: Leben und Werk* (Life and work) (Vienna: Europa Verlag-AG, 1973).

10. Leichter, "Childhood Memories," 38.

11. Ibid.

12. Ibid., 59.

13. Steiner. *Käthe Leichter*, 8–9.

14. SA is the abbreviation used for *Sturmabteilungen,* the stormtroopers or Brownshirts, founded in 1921 as the Nazi Party's private army. They were later eclipsed by the SS (*Schutzstaffel*).

15. Leichter, "Childhood Memories," 122–23.

16. Ibid., 136.

17. Steiner, interview with Rosa Jochmann, April 1970, *Käthe Leichter,* 262.

18. Ibid.

19. Erika Buchmann, "Der 'Judenblock'" (the Jewish Block), in von Freyberg and Krause-Schmitt, *Moringen-Lichtenburg-Ravensbrück,*132.

20. Steiner, *Käthe Leichter,* 262.

21. Ibid, 263.

22. Herta Soswinski, "Why We Have to Tell about It," 129–30.

23. See Strebel, "Ravensbrück-das zentrale Frauenkonzentrationslager," 235.

24. See Herzog and Strebel, "Das Frauenkonzentrationslager Ravensbrück," 20–21.

25. Soswinski, "Why We Have to Tell about It," 125–44.

4. RESISTANCE THAT LIFTED THE SPIRIT

1. The Ravensbrück memorial has many such items on display. The Florida Holocaust Museum, St. Petersburg, was given four items as part of the exhibit of art by Julia Terwilliger, *Women of Ravensbrück: Portraits of Courage,* which opened in the museum in 2001. These items were given to artist Terwilliger by Dutch survivor Anna Maria Berentsen-Droog. Elizabeth Kroó Teitelbaum, a survivor of Ravensbrück and other camps, gave to The Museum of Jewish Heritage in New York City an embroidered handkerchief made for her by a friend at a labor camp. *Der Wind weht weinend über die Ebene: Ravensbrücker Gedichte* (The wind blows crying over the plain: Ravensbrück poems), ed. Christa Schulz (Fürstenberg: Ravensbrück Memorial, Mahn- und Gedenkstätte Ravensbrück, 1991) is a collection of the women's poetry from the camp, as is Constanze Jaiser's *Poetische Zeugnisse. Gedichte aus dem Frauen-Konzentrationslager Ravensbrück 1939–1945, (Ergebnisse der Frauenforschung, 55)* (Poetic testimonies. Poems of the women of Ravensbrück concentration camp, 1939–1945, Results of Research on Women, 55), (Stuttgart/Weimar: J.B. Metzler: 2000). Examples of women's memoirs that relate such occurrences are too numerous to list.

2. See, for example, Cara De Silva, ed., *In Memory's Kitchen: A Legacy from the Women of Terezin* (Northvale: Jason Aronson, 1996); Myrna Goldenberg, "Food Talk: Gendered Responses to Hunger in the Concentration Camps," in *Experience and Expression,* Baer and Goldenberg, eds., 161–79; Maurel, *An Ordinary Camp,* 95–96; Dagmar Schroeder-Hildebrand, *"Ich sterbe vor Hunger!" Kochrezepte aus dem Konzentrationslager Ravensbrück* (I'm dying of hunger! Cooking recipes from Ravensbrück concentration camp) (Bremen: Donat, 1999); Bernstein, *The Seamstress,* 229, 237–38.

3. Alex Buckman, telephone conversation with Rochelle G. Saidel, 8 August 1998. As young children, Alex and his first cousin Anny were hidden together

during the Holocaust. When Alex's parents did not return, his aunt and uncle, Becky and Herman Teitelbaum, became his legal guardians.

4. "Rebecca's Legacy: A Ravensbruck Cookbook," in *Zachor*, the newsletter of the Vancouver Holocaust Education Centre, No. 1, January 1998, 4.

5. The following information is from an unpublished talk by Alex Buckman, 15 February 1998, when his aunt's recipe book was displayed in connection with a reception for *In Memory's Kitchen*, sponsored by the Vancouver Holocaust Education Centre; and Buckman, correspondence with the author, 26 September 2002. The author is grateful to Mr. Buckman for his help. The recipe book was again displayed at the Vancouver Centre from February through May 2003, in an exhibit, *Ravensbrück: The Forgotten Women of the Holocaust*.

6. The exhibit was in place in 1999–2003, and the closing date is unknown. The coordinator of the exhibit told me in a telephone conversation that Francesca was no longer living, and that her sister or daughter had donated the notebook to the museum. She also said that this relative did not want to be interviewed, and that she would not put me in touch with her.

7. Schroeder-Hildebrand, *"Ich sterbe vor Hunger!"*

8. Anna Maria Berentsen-Droog arrived in the camp on 9 September 1944 and was liberated by the Red Cross on 24 April 1945. In addition to her recipe book, she gave Julia Terwilliger a book cover embroidered with "J A" and "in stille uren." This literally means "in silent hours" and implies, "when you have time on your hands." It was made by Brigitte Albrecht, a Dutch prisoner who arrived in the camp on 20 September 1941 and was liberated by the Swedish Red Cross on 24 April 1945. She also gave Terwilliger a small purse, a gift from Brigitte Albrecht to a friend, and an Easter card in colored pencil. They are included in the exhibit *Women of Ravensbrück: Portraits of Courage* and are part of the Florida Holocaust Museum's permanent collection. Al Terwilliger, Julia Terwilliger's husband, donated the artifacts to the museum.

9. Information about Renee Duering, Daly City, California, is from correspondence and telephone conversations with the author. Ella Shiber's drawings are in *The Union Kommando in Auschwitz: The Auschwitz Munition Factory Through the Eyes of Its Former Slave Laborers*, ed. Lore Shelley (Lanham, Md.: University Press of America, 1996), 106–26.

10. The drawings of Aat Breur are in Dunya Breur, *Een verborgen herinnering* (A hidden memory) (Nijmegen: Sun Publisher, 1995). Additional biographical information is from "Frauenkonzentrationslager Ravensbrück—Kalender 2000" (Ravensbrück women's concentration camp calendar for 2000), (Berlin: Senatsverwaltung für Arbeit, Berufliche Bildung und Frauen, 1999).

11. Violette Rougier-Lecoq, *Témoignages: 36 Dessins à la Plume: Violette Lecoq* (Thirty-six pen drawings) (Paris: Les Deux Sirènes, 1948). Additional information about Violette Lecoq is from *Informationen*, Frankfurt, No. 35, October 1992, 16.

12. Monika Herzog, *Drawings of Ravensbrück: "Hope, which lives in us eternally,"* (Fürstenberg: Mahn- und Gedenkstätte Ravensbrück, 1993). Reproductions of the drawings of Aat Breur, Violette Lecoq, and others are dispersed throughout Jack Morrison's *Ravensbrück: Everyday Life in a Women's Concentration Camp, 1939–45.* (Princeton: Markus Wiener Publishers, 2000), and are also part of the exhibit and catalogue, *Women of Ravensbrück: Portraits of*

Courage—Art by Julia Terwilliger, Rochelle G. Saidel, guest curator, Florida Holocaust Museum, St. Petersburg, 2001.

13. For examples, see Breur, *Een verborgen herinnering,* especially 163–66. The exhibit, *The Last Expression: Art and Auschwitz,* organized by the Mary and Leigh Block Museum of Art, Northwestern University, and shown at the Brooklyn Museum, March–June 2003, provides evidence that men as well as women created greeting cards.

14. Gluck, *My Story,* 46–47.

15. Kristin Congdon, "Giving as Resistance," in *Women of Ravensbrück: Portraits of Courage—Julia A. Terwilliger,* exhibit booklet, ed. Carole Elizabeth Adams (Orlando: University of Central Florida, 1997), 8.

16. Ibid., 41–42.

17. See selected references at the end of this book. The best-known book in English (translated from French) about the women of the French resistance in the camp is Tillion's *Ravensbrück.* Póltawska, *And I Am Afraid of My Dreams,* describes resistance by Polish prisoners.

18. Henry O. Leichter, interview with Rochelle G. Saidel, New York, 7 August 1998; Christa Schulz, ed., *Der Wind weht weinend über die Ebene* (Fürstenberg: Ravensbrück Memorial, 1991).

19. The original German is in Schulz, *Der Wind weht weinend über die Ebene,* 62–63. The poem was translated and given to the author by Henry O. Leichter. The information on the memorization of the poem by the young Communist prisoner is from Rosa Jochmann in Steiner, *Käthe Leichter,* 262.

20. Rosa Jochmann quoted in Steiner, *Käthe Leichter,* 262.

21. Werner, *Olga Benário,* 261.

22. Gluck, *My Story,* 36–37.

23. Ibid., 51–52.

24. Ibid., 42–43.

5. JOYLESS CHILDHOODS

1. Sali Solomon Daugherty, interview with Rochelle G. Saidel, Jerusalem, 28 December 2000, archive of the author. The photograph is part of an exhibit about the camp, *Women of Ravensbrück: Portraits of Courage,* Florida Holocaust Museum, St. Petersburg, February–September 2001. Sali had given the photograph to Julia Terwilliger, the artist whose works are featured in the exhibit. See the photograph on page 218.

2. Sali also remembers another mother with a child named Micha Carmen, and she believes they immigrated to Australia. Both female and male children were sometimes in the camp with their mothers, even though it was a camp only for women. There was a separate auxiliary camp for men nearby.

3. This photo is also part of the exhibit, *Women of Ravensbrück: Portraits of Courage.* (See the photograph on page 000, and see chapter 13 for more details of rescue to Sweden.

4. Stella Kugelman Nikiforova. Interview with Rochelle G. Saidel, São Paulo, Brazil, 2 November 1994, archive of the author. (In Russian, with Dr. Alla Millstein Gonçalves as interpreter.)

5. Evidently Stella's mother was not identified as a Jew by the Nazis when she was arrested, or she and Stella would have been forced to wear a yellow triangle along with the red one.

6. Some of these toys can be seen in the exhibits at the Ravensbrück memorial, Mahn- und Gedenkstätte Ravensbrück.

7. Gluck, *My Story*, 38–39.

8. See Naphtali Lau Lavie, *Balaam's Prophecy: Eyewitness to History: 1939–1989* (New York: Cornwall Books, 1999), 25, 77.

9. Tova Giladi, interview with Evie Joselow for Rochelle G. Saidel, New York, 27 January 1998, archive of the author. Tova's husband, Ben Giladi, also from Piotrkow, publishes a newsletter for survivors.

10. I met Judith Gutter when she attended a lecture I gave at the Rosenthal Institute for Holocaust Studies at the Graduate School and University Center, City University of New York, in the fall of 1997. Information is from her interview with Susan Sapiro for Rochelle G. Saidel, New York, 10 April 1998, archive of the author.

11. Gluck, *My Story*, 52.

12. See Herzog and Strebel, "Das Frauenkonzentrationslager Ravensbrück," 19. They quote Wanda Kiedrzynska's statistics regarding children as well as teenagers in Ravensbrück. According to her, incomplete ledgers suggest 882 children were deported to Ravensbrück. Also, between September 1944 and April 1945, 560 births were registered. Most of the newborns lived only briefly and then were murdered by the Nazi doctors and nurses. See also Britta Pawelke, "Als Häftling geboren—Kinder in Ravensbrück"(Born to prisoners—children in Ravensbrück) in *Frauen in Konzentrationslagern*, 157–65. Pawelke states that the figure in the incomplete ledgers is 881 children, of whom 263 were Jewish.

6. A YEAR OF COMINGS AND GOINGS, 1944

1. Margaret (Margo) Guiness, interview with Rochelle Saidel, Long Beach, California, 13 March 1998, archive of the author.

2. Because of this experience, Margaret Guiness titled her memoir *When the Sky Rained Umbrellas*. She published the manuscript of her memoir as a ninety-nine-page book of the same name in 2001. Her manuscript (undated) is in the archive of the author.

3. Margaret (Margo) Guiness dedicated her memoir to the memory of her sister Bozena. For details about the rescue of Jewish women from Ravensbrück to Sweden, see chapter 13. The Red Cross evacuated women from both Ravensbrück and Bergen-Belsen.

4. Olga Astor, interview with Rochelle G. Saidel, Glenville, Illinois, 28 September 1997, archive of the author.

5. Esther Tuvel Shuftan became Olga's neighbor in Illinois when they immigrated after World War II. Sara wrote a book, published posthumously, which supplements Olga's testimony. See Bernstein, *The Seamstress*, esp. 184–250. I met Esther in Olga's home in Glenville, Illinois, in 1997.

6. For another account of traveling in a sealed cattle car from Ravensbrück to Burgau, see Eva Langley-Dános, *Prison on Wheels: From Ravensbrück to Burgau* (Einsiedeln: Daimon Verlag, 2000).

7. Elisabeth Pavel, interview with Evie Joselow for Rochelle G. Saidel, Brooklyn, New York, 29 November 1997, archive of the author.

8. More likely, it was an *X* painted on the back, which was used to easily identify a fleeing woman if she tried to escape.

9. Ilona Feldman, excerpt of unpublished manuscript and questionnaire sent to Rochelle G. Saidel on 13 March 1996, archive of the author.

10. Doris Greenberg, interview with Evie Joselow for Rochelle G. Saidel, New Rochelle, New York, 12 February 1998, archive of the author.

11. The women were given numbers that were sewn on their clothes. They were not tattooed at Ravensbrück.

12. See chapter 11 for Doris Greenberg's experiences in the Neubrandenburg subcamp.

13. Susan Kornhauser, interview with Robin Ostow for Rochelle G. Saidel, Toronto, 1 June 1998, archive of the author.

14. By the time that Susan Kornhauser and her mother arrived in the camp at the end of December 1944, a gas chamber was in operation.

15. For Alice Birnhak's experiences during the Holocaust, and a few details about Ravensbrück, see her book, *Next Year, God Willing*. I met and interviewed her in New York on 14 October 1997. While she is extremely articulate and lectures widely on her experiences, she had little to recount about her limited time at Ravensbrück.

7. WOMEN AT WORK

1. According to Christopher Simpson, *The Splendid Blond Beast: Money, Law, and Genocide in the Twentieth Century* (New York: Grove Press, 1993), 306–7, 310, the following German companies used slave laborers from Ravensbrück (often in satellite camps): AEG electronics; Ardelt Werke (munitions); Chemische Fabrik Malchow, Erprobungstelle d RLM, Dornier-Flugzeugwerke (aircraft); Flugplatz Rechlin (airport); Gerätewerke Pommern (missile assembly); Havelschmelzwerk GmbH, Heinkel-Werke AG (aircraft); Hugo Schneider AG (HASAG) (munitions); IG Farben (film factory); Ikaria-Werke, GmbH, Kabel-und Metallwerke Neumeyer AG, Luftfahrtgerätewerk, Markgraf und Heger, Mechanische Werkstätten GmbH (munitions); Metallwerke Holleischen GmbH (munitions); Munitionsfabrik Finower Industrie (munitions); Munitionsfabrik Silberwerke Treuenbrietzen Zweigwerk Röderhof (munitions); Polte-Gruneberger-Metall-Konzern (munitions); Polte-Werke (flak munitions); Siemens Bauabteilung (construction); Siemens und Halske (electronics); Silva-Metallwerke GmbH (munitions); Sprengstoff Chemie-Werke (munitions); Veltener-Maschinenbau GmbH (aircraft components). For more information on the Nazis' organized slave labor empire, of which Ravensbrück was an integral part, see, e.g., Benjamin Ferencz, *Less Than Slaves* (Cambridge: Harvard University Press, 1979); Joseph Borkin, *The Crime and Punishment of I. G. Farben* (New York: Free Press, 1978); Christopher Browning, *Nazi Policy, Jewish Workers, German Killers* (New York: Cambridge University Press, 2000); Wolfgang Sofsky, *The Order of Terror* (Princeton University Press, 1999); Peter Hayes, *Industry and Ideology: I. G. Farben in the Nazi Era* (New York: Cambridge University Press, 2000).

2. Margaret (Margo) Guiness, interview with Rochelle G. Saidel, Long Beach California, 13 March 1998, archive of the author.

3. The above testimony by Basia Rubinstein is based on her conversation with the author at the Ravensbrück memorial in April 1995, archive of the author. She also gave more than two hours of testimony to the Yad Vashem Archive in 1991 (or possibly 1981), but the tape is inaudible and even the date of the interview is questionable.

4. The following information is from Basia Rubinstein, interview by Luba Melchior for the Polish Research Institute, Lund University, Sweden, 12 December 1945, in *Polski Instytut Zródlowy Archive,* interview number fifty, Lund University Library. Translated for the author by Moshe Borger, Jerusalem, September 2000, archive of the author. See chapter 13 for more information on the archive at Lund University.

5. The measure "dkg," also called "dag," is a dekagram, or ten grams. The women received three hundred grams of bread, a portion that was cut to 180 grams, according to Basia Rubinstein.

6. Mina Goldstein, telephone interview with Rochelle G. Saidel, 20 October 1997, archive of the author.

7. Biebow established a central inventory station at Pabianice, eight miles southeast of Lodz, which sorted all of the belongings from the Warthegau ghettos and the Chelmno extermination camp. Some of these goods, especially furs, were sent to Ravensbrück for repair and distribution to the *Waffen-SS.* See Hilberg, *The Destruction of the European Jews* (New York: Holmes & Meier, 1985), 948, 952.

8. Michal Unger at Yad Vashem lecture, "Hans Biebow: From Merchant to Perpetrator," Second International Conference on Education and the Holocaust, The Memory of the Holocaust in the Twenty-first Century, 12 October 1999.

9. The Lodz Ghetto was wiped out by the end of August 1944 when 73,563 people were deported, according to the files of the Statistical Office of Lodz. "By the end of August the ghetto was empty except for a small cleanup Kommando. The victims were shipped not to Germany, to work in plants, but to the killing center in Auschwitz, to be gassed to death." See Hilberg, *The Destruction of the European Jews,* 517–18, 1209. If Mina was in Lodz with a group that was sent to Germany in October 1944, this must have been a special case that Biebow arranged for his own benefit.

10. Herzog and Strebel, "Das Frauenkonzentrationslager Ravensbrück," 19–20.

11. Olga Astor, interview with Rochelle G. Saidel, Glenville, Illinois, 28 September 1997, archive of the author.

12. Ester Grun, interview with Evie Joselow for Rochelle G. Saidel, White Plains, New York, 15 December 1997, archive of the author.

8. GEMMA LAGUARDIA GLUCK

1. There were other American women at the camp. According to Póltawska, *And I Am Afraid of My Dreams* (136), Aka Kolodziejczak, a Polish woman who was an American citizen, was released from the camp in December 1943. She

gives no further details. Margaret Rossiter, *Women in the Resistance* (New York: Praeger, 1986) 204–10 mentions a native-born American at Ravensbrück named Virginia D'Albert Lake. She had married a French aristocrat and joined the resistance with him. She was sent to Torgau subcamp, and in February 1945 her mother convinced Secretary of State Cordell Hull to have her transferred to a Red Cross camp at Lake Constance.

2. Gluck, *My Story*. The book has been out of print for many years, and the author has been given permission by the Shneiderman estate to have it republished with a new introduction and epilogue.

3. Saidel, *Never Too Late to Remember*.

4. Shneiderman's books in English include: *Between Fear and Hope* (New York: Arco Publishers, 1947); *The Warsaw Heresy* (New York: Horizon, 1959); *The River Remembers* (New York: Horizon, 1970). He was also the editor of *Warsaw Ghetto: A Diary by Mary Berg*, (New York: L. B. Fischer Publisher, 1945).

5. Nazi "racial theory" considered as Jewish any person who had one Jewish grandparent. Jewish religious law considers as Jewish any person who is born of a Jewish mother. According to her memoir, Gemma LaGuardia Gluck went to church in Budapest but reminded her husband to go to the synagogue on the High Holy Days. Her Catholic father had insisted that she say the Hebrew prayer, "Shema Yisrael," every evening at bedtime, because of his pride in her mother's "Jewish heritage." Gemma's maternal grandmother, Fiorina, was a Luzzato, a member of a very prominent Italian Jewish family. See Gluck, *My Story*, 13.

6. Gemma's younger brother, Richard, was born in 1885 and died of a heart attack at age forty-two.

7. Gluck, *My Story*, 13.

8. The second daughter was named for Gemma's mother, who died in Budapest in 1915. Irene evidently moved to the United States before World War II.

9. Background information on Hungary based on Leni Yehil, *The Holocaust: The Fate of European Jewry* (New York: Oxford University Press, 1990), 501–20. See also Hilberg, *The Destruction of the European Jews*, 796–860; Randolph Braham, *The Politics of Genocide: The Holocaust in Hungary* (Detroit: Wayne State University Press, 2000), as well as other volumes by Braham on Hungary.

10. In *My Story*, Gluck wrote that she was arrested by SS officers. In a questionnaire that she answered in Berlin on 7 May 1946, she wrote she had been arrested in Budapest by the Gestapo. *Fragebogen* (Questionnaire) Gemma Glück, RA-Nr. I/3-3-10 (Archive of Mahn- und Gedenkstätte Ravensbrück).

11. Gluck, *My Story*, 23.

12. S. L. Shneiderman, preface to Gluck, *My Story*.

13. Israel Police Document, letter to von Thadden, TR3 1020, (Jerusalem: Archive of Yad Vashem). There were other political hostages in the camp, including the niece of Charles de Gaulle. See de Gaulle Anthonioz, *The Dawn of Hope*.

14. The dates of her arrest and arrivals are in *Fragebogen* Gemma Glück, RA-Nr. I/3-3-10, (Archive of Mahn- und Gedenkstätte Ravensbrück). For more details of her arrest, see Gluck, *My Story*, 17–26.

15. Gluck, *My Story*, 27.

16. Ibid., 31.
17. Ibid., 32–35.
18. Ibid., 51.
19. Ibid., 60–61.
20. Ibid., 71.
21. Ibid., 74.
22. Ibid., 79.
23. Ibid., 83.
24. Gemma LaGuardia Gluck, letter to Mayor Fiorello LaGuardia from Berlin, 15 July 1945 (New York: LaGuardia and Wagner Archives, LaGuardia Community College, City University of New York).
25. Harvey Gibson, letter to Mayor Fiorello LaGuardia, 12 September 1945; Mayor Fiorello LaGuardia, letter to Harvey Gibson, 31 October 1945 (New York: LaGuardia and Wagner Archives, LaGuardia Community College, City University of New York).
26. Mayor Fiorello LaGuardia, letter to Gemma LaGuardia Gluck, 31 October 1945 (New York: LaGuardia and Wagner Archives, LaGuardia Community College, City University of New York).
27. Mayor Fiorello LaGuardia, letter to General Dwight D. Eisenhower, 7 January 1946 (New York: LaGuardia and Wagner Archives, LaGuardia Community College, City University of New York).
28. Gemma LaGuardia Gluck, letter to Fiorello LaGuardia, 2 April 1947 (New York: LaGuardia and Wagner Archives, LaGuardia Community College, City University of New York).
29. On 21 May 1947 the Moore-McCormack Lines sent a bill to Fiorello LaGuardia for passage from Copenhagen to the United States. The cost for Gemma, ticket no. 11817, and Yolanda, ticket no. 11818, was $310 each, and for Richard, ticket no. 11818, $155. (New York: LaGuardia and Wagner Archives, LaGuardia Community College, City University of New York.)
30. Gluck, *My Story,* 100.

9. JEWISH EVACUEES ARRIVE FROM AUSCHWITZ

1. Lidia Vago, interview with Rochelle G. Saidel, traveling from Berlin to Ravensbrück, 22 April 1995, archive of the author.
2. Mina Goldstein, Los Angeles, telephone interview with Rochelle G. Saidel, 20 October 1997, archive of the author.
3. During the last months of World War II, the International Red Cross made several inspection trips to the camp and also sent food packages. For details of the rescue effort that followed, see chapter 13. There are various documents in the archive of the International Red Cross, Geneva (with copies in the archive of the author), that mention the inspections and the food packages, and several interviewees in this book refer to the packages.
4. Rose Mellender, interview with Susan Sapiro for Rochelle G. Saidel, New York, 1 February 1998, archive of the author.
5. I. Judith Becker, interview with Rochelle G. Saidel, Jerusalem, 17 February 1997, archive of the author.

6. I have never heard from any other survivor or read in historical sources that there was such an orchestra at Ravensbrück. Either there is confusion with the women's orchestra at Auschwitz, or this was a unique event.

7. I inquired of the staff of the archive of the Ravensbrück Memorial in June 2001 whether there had been other reports of such a group of women without tongues, and they said this was the first they had heard of it.

8. Gloria Deutsch, "A hundred years of faith," *Jerusalem Post* special supplement, 18 December 1998, 6–7.

9. Hannah Horon, interview with Susan Sapiro for Rochelle G. Saidel, New York, 8 December 1997, archive of the author. See chapter 13 about rescue in Sweden.

10. Lea Ferstenberg, interview with Evie Joselow for Rochelle G. Saidel, New Rochelle, New York, 12 February 1998, archive of the author.

11. Lidia Vago, interview with Rochelle G. Saidel, 22 April 1995. For more information on her experiences during the Holocaust, especially in Auschwitz, see "One Year in the Black Hole of Our Planet Earth: A Personal Narrative," in *Women in the Holocaust,* ed. Ofer and Weitzman, 273–84.

12. The following information is from Lidia Vago's unpublished manuscript, 54–64.

13. K.L. stands for *Konzentrationslager,* which is German for concentration camp. It is usually abbreviated KZ.

14. Viola Baras, Edith Denes, and Lilly Eisler, interview with Rochelle G. Saidel, Tamarac, Florida, 14 February 2001, archive of the author.

15. Lotte Brainin, letter to Rochelle G. Saidel, Vienna, received 16 January 1996, archive of the author.

16. Larry Gropman, letter to Rochelle G. Saidel, 5 March 1996, archive of the author.

17. See Shelley, ed., *The Union Kommando in Auschwitz,* for accounts of Auschwitz survivors from the *Werkunion* who arrived in Ravensbrück. She recounts the stories of other Auschwitz survivors who arrived in Ravensbrück in January/February 1945 in *Auschwitz: The Nazi Civilization* and *Secretaries of Death* (New York: Shengold, 1986).

18. There were others that I did not have the opportunity to intensively interview, but who nevertheless shared parts of their stories with me in brief letters or telephone conversations. They include: Esther Peterseil of Lawrence, New York; Stella Kipman of Ville Mount-Royal, Quebec, Canada; Lonia Mosak of Skokie, Illinois; Alice Berger of Pembroke Pines, Florida; Katerine Stone of Silver Spring, Maryland; Esther Goldman of Norfolk, Virginia; Irmgard Muller of Chapel Hill, North Carolina; and Ida Yardeni-Tavor of Atlanta, Georgia.

10. LATE ARRIVALS FROM OTHER CAMPS

1. Fela Kolat, interview with Rochelle G. Saidel, Worcester, Massachusetts, 24 June 1996, archive of the author.

2. Manya Friedman, letter to Rochelle G. Saidel, 23 January 1996. See also *Echoes of Memory* (Washington, D.C.: U.S. Holocaust Memorial Museum, 2003), 19–29.

3. Gloria Hollander Lyon, interview with Evie Joselow for Rochelle G. Saidel, San Francisco, 14 May 1998, archive of the author. See also Claus Füllberg-Stolberg, "Die Odyssee einer ungarischen Jüdin" (The odessy of a Hungarian Jewish woman), in *Frauen in Konzentrationslagern,* ed. Füllberg-Stolberg, et al., 279–90. Gloria also made a film of her story, *When I Was 14: A Survivor Remembers* (1995), distributed by University of California, Extension Center for Media and Independent Learning, Berkeley.

11. THE SATELLITE WORK CAMPS

1. There is no final number for the camps affiliated with Ravensbrück, and the figure has varied with time. Bernhard Strebel, Ravensbrück das zentrale Frauenkonzentrationslager," 233–34, says that much research is needed on the subject of these satellites. He lists the names of only twelve satellite camps, locations, and numbers of inmates working (if available), as well as beginning and end dates. Jack Morrison, in *Ravensbrück* (206–22), says there were more than seventy subcamps, but he does not distinguish which camps later became subordinated to other camps.

2. Strebel, "Ravensbrück-das zentrale Frauenkonzentrationslager," 233–34.

3. See Karl Heinz Schütt, *Ein vergessenes Lager? Über das Aussenlager Neustadt-Glewe des Frauen-KZ Ravensbrück* (A forgotten camp? On the Neustadt-Glewe subcamp of Ravensbrück women's concentration camp) (Berlin: GNN-Verlag Sachsen, 1997), and two supplements. I was able to put some survivors I knew in contact with him, so that their names could be included in his work.

4. Fela Kolat, interview with Rochelle G. Saidel, Worcester, Massachusetts, 24 June 1996, archive of the author.

5. Lea Ferstenberg, interview with Evie Joselow for Rochelle G. Saidel, New Rochelle, New York, 12 February 1998, archive of the author.

6. The following information on the camp is from Schütt, *Ein vergessenes Lager?*

7. Schütt, *Ein vergessenes Lager?* 23.

8. Wanda Póltawska, a Polish political prisoner, recounts her starvation and illness at Neustadt-Glewe in *And I Am Afraid of My Dreams,* 155–57. Aurelia Pollak, a Jewish prisoner who was sent to Ravensbrück from Auschwitz in January 1945 and then to Neustadt-Glewe, recalls her days in the camp in *Three Years of Deportation* (Ra'anana: DocoStory, 1999), 117–25.

9. Ester Grun, interview with Evie Joselow for Rochelle G. Saidel, White Plains, New York, 15 December 1997, archive of the author.

10. Morrison, *Ravensbrück,* 208, says there was a maximum of 150 people working at the munitions factory in Meuselwitz in 1944. His note says his information is "put together from several sources, chiefly the testimony of Fritz Suhren at Nuremberg on 17 June 1946." (note 2 to chapter 16, 331.)

11. Micheline Maurel wrote a book about her time in the camp from the fall of 1943 until its liberation. See Maurel, *An Ordinary Camp.* There is a study of the camp in German by Heinz Barche, *Mahnung und Verpflichtung: Leben, Ausbeutung und antifaschistischer Widerstandskampf weiblicher Häftlinge in den Konzentrationslagern Neubrandenburgs, 1943–1945, Kommentare,*

Dokumente, Berichte (Memory and commitment: life, exploitation, and anti-fascist resistance struggle of female prisoners in Neubrandenburg concentration camps, 1943–1945, commentary, document, report). This undated study was prepared for the *Kommission zur Erforschung der Geschichte der örtlichen Arbeiterbewegung bei der Bezirksleitung Neubrandenburg der SED, Komitee der antifaschistischen Widerstandskämpfer der DDR, Bezirkskomitee Neubrandenburg* (Committee of the anti-Fascist resistance struggle of the German Democratic Republic, Neubrandenburg district committee). It is in the archive-library of Mahn- und Gedenkstätte Ravensbrück, the Ravensbrück memorial, which made a copy available for the archive of the author.

12. The company was the Neubrandenburg Engineering Workshops, *Mechanischen Wertstätten Neubrandenburg Gmbh*, or *MWN*. See Morrison, *Ravensbrück*, 211–12. Morrison cites Maurel that there were two thousand women in the camp in late 1943, but she wrote there were twenty-two thousand women. See Morrison, 212n. 9, and Maurel, *An Ordinary Camp*, 18, 24, regarding this discrepancy.

13. Maurel, *An Ordinary Camp*, 9.

14. Ibid., 93.

15. Bracha Blattberg Schiff, letter to the author dated 8 December 1995, North Miami Beach, Florida, and unpublished manuscript, 13–19, archive of the author.

16. See Morrison, *Ravensbrück*, "Chapter 16—The Subcamps," 206–22 for a partial list of the camps and more details.

12. MALCHOW AND THE DEATH MARCHES

1. There are two publications in German about the camp at Malchow: *Das Munitions- und Sprengstoffwerk in Malchow (Meckl.) 1938–1945, Heft 2 zur Geschichte der Stadt Malchow (Meckl.)* (The munitions and explosives factory in Malchow, 1938–1945, booklet 2 on the history of the city of Malchow) (Malchow: City of Malchow, text by Alfred Nill et al., 1995); and *Treu—aber wem? Bestraft—doch wofür? Malchower Jungendliche erleben den Zusammenbruch 1945, Teil 2, Heft 5 zur Geschichte der Stadt Malchow (Meckl.)* (Faithful—but to whom? Punished—but for what? Malchow young people experience the 1945 breakdown, part 2, booklet 5 on the history of the city of Malchow) (Malchow: City of Malchow, no author listed, 1997). The publications are in the archive-library of Mahn- und Gedenkstätte Ravensbrück, which gave copies to the author's archive.

2. Three sources give different figures for the total of women on this death march from Ravensbrück, and one even gives an earlier date. According to Martin Gilbert, *Atlas of the Holocaust* (New York: William Morrow, 1993), 227, seventeen thousand women left Ravensbrück on 15 April. According to an exhibit prepared by Mahn- und Gedenkstätte Ravensbrück for the April 1995 ceremonies marking the fiftieth anniversary of liberation, about twenty thousand women were marched toward Neu Strelitz and Malchow on 27–28 April 1945. According to Delia Müller and Madlen Lepschies, *Tage der Angst und der Hoffnung: Erinnerungen an die Todesmärsche aus dem Frauen-Konzentrationslager*

Ravensbrück Ende April 1945 (Days of terror and hope: memories of the death march from women's concentration camp Ravensbrück at the end of April 1945) (Stiftung Brandenburgische Gedenkstätten/Mahn- und Gedenkstätte Ravensbrück, undated, probably 1999–2000), twelve thousand women started on the march on 27 April.

3. I. Judith Becker, interview with Rochelle G. Saidel, Jerusalem, 17 February 1997, archive of the author.

4. Rachel Hocherman, interview with Rochelle G. Saidel, Berlin, 25 April 1995, archive of the author.

5. Rose Mellender, interview with Susan Sapiro for Rochelle G. Saidel, New York, 1 February 1998, archive of the author.

6. Erna Ellert, interview with Rochelle G. Saidel, Germany, 22 April 1995, archive of the author.

7. Judith Gertler, interview with Susan Sapiro for Rochelle G. Saidel, New York, 10 April 1998, archive of the author.

8. Müller and Lepschies, *Tage der Angst und der Hoffnung.*

9. Ibid., 43–47.

10. Ibid., 84.

11. Ibid., 94.

12. Ibid., 107.

13. Ibid.,122.

14. Ibid., 123–24.

15. A book in German edited by Sigrid Jacobeit, *"Ich grüsse Euch als freier Mensch"* ("I greet you as a free person") (Oranienburg: Stiftung Brandenburgische Gedenkstätten, 1995) is a more extensive treatment of the 1995 exhibit on the camp's liberation. Captain Boris Makarow was the officer in charge, according to Morrison, *Ravensbrück,* 305.

13. RESCUE TO SWEDEN

1. Mina Goldstein, interview with Rochelle G. Saidel, 20 October 1997, archive of the author.

2. It was most likely on the afternoon of 25 April, when twenty buses from the Danish Red Cross evacuated prisoners, including many Jewish Polish women. See Simone Erpel, "Rettungsaktion in letzter Minute" (Rescue at the last minute) in *Ich grüsse Euch als freier Mensch,* ed. Jacobeit, 53–54.

3. Hannah Horon, interview with Susan Sapiro for Rochelle G. Saidel, New York, 8 December 1997, archive of the author.

4. Sosnowiec had a population of 130,000, including 20,805 Jews, at the time of the 1931 census. See Gilbert, *Atlas of the Holocaust,* 32. The Sosnowiec *Judenrat* was established immediately after the German conquest on 6 September 1939. See Yehil, *The Holocaust,* 156, 207–9.

5. The Sosnowiec ghetto was liquidated in August 1943. See Yehil, *The Holocaust,* 448.

6. Rachel Hocherman, interviewed by Rochelle G. Saidel, Berlin, 25 April 1995, archive of the author.

7. The Warsaw Ghetto was created over a period of six weeks in October–November 1940. As early as November 1939, *Generalgouveneur* Hans Frank ordered Jews over the age of twelve to wear white armbands bearing a blue Star of David. See Hilberg, *The Destruction of the European Jews,* 2:216, 221, 226.

8. Helen (Chaya) Luksenberg, unpublished and undated testimony sent to the author on 12 December 1995, archive of the author.

9. Rosa Fajerstajn, interviewed by Anita Pinkuss and Anabela Sereno of the *Divisão de História Oral do Arquivo Histórico Judaico Brasileiro* (Oral history division of the Jewish-Brazilian history archive), São Paulo, 12 June 1995, archive of the *Divisão de História Oral do Arquivo Histórico Judaico Brasileiro,* which gave a copy to the author.

10. Kati Marton, *A Death in Jerusalem* (New York: Pantheon Books, 1994), 75–76.

11. Erpel, "Rettungsaktion in letzter Minute," 24.

12. Marton, *A Death in Jerusalem,* 78.

13. Folke Bernadotte, *The Curtain Falls* (New York: Knopf, 1945), 69.

14. Netherlands Institute for War Documentation, Kersten File, quoted in Marton, *A Death in Jerusalem,* 78.

15. Memorandum of 27 March 1945, Red Cross Archives, Stockholm, Bernadotte File, quoted in Marton, *A Death in Jerusalem,* 78.

16. Marton, *A Death in Jerusalem,* 80. Erpel, "Rettungsaktion in letzter Minute," 55, cites Norbert Mazur, *En Jude talar med Himmler* (A Jew meets with Himmler) (Stockholm, 1945, 24–26) that one thousand Jewish women were taken by the Red Cross. Mazur wrote that at his meeting with Himmler, the *Reichsfürer* said, "I agree that one thousand Jewish women will be liberated from Ravensbrück concentration camp if you can have them taken by the Red Cross."

17. Erpel, "Rettungsaktion in letzter Minute," 53–54. According to Marton, *A Death in Jerusalem,* 20, Bernadotte's negotiations resulted in a total of 21,000 citizens of more than twenty countries being rescued, including 6,500 Jews. However, not all of these were from Ravensbrück, and her statement is confusing. According to Herzog and Strebel, "Das Frauenkonzentrationslager Ravensbrück" (22–24), on 22 April several hundred women were evacuated by the Swedish Red Cross to Denmark and Sweden. More liberation transports followed, and the last one, with 3,960 women, predominantly Polish, left Ravensbrück on 26 April and headed toward Denmark and then Sweden. The total number of women liberated in this way was about 7,500. These women were mostly from Scandinavia, the Netherlands, France, and Poland.

18. See Erpel, "Rettungsaktion in letzter Minute," 22. The total number of women liberated from Ravensbrück and its satellites is still not totally verifiable, and data vary between 7,500 and 14,000, according to information published by the Ravensbrück memorial. It has been most often stated that about 7,500 women were brought to Sweden via Denmark (and three hundred to Switzerland), yet this number seems not to include the eight thousand Danes and Norwegians that were repatriated. Background for archival material at Lund University in Sweden cited a higher number, although there is no verification provided, and the figure seems much too high. According to Birgitta Lindholm, the director of the manuscript division of the Lund University Library, more than 21,000 people,

including 5,000 to 6,000 Jews, were brought to southern Sweden by the Red Cross white buses (Interview with Rochelle G. Saidel, Lund, Sweden, 28 June 1999). The Lund figures correspond with those of Steven Kobelik and may be based on his earlier work. According to Kobelik, "by the end, Bernadotte's mission had rescued nearly 21,000 inmates, citizens of more than twenty different countries. An estimate of the number of Jews saved was about 6,500." Kobelik, *The Stones Cry Out: Swedish Response to the Persecution of the Jews 1933–1945* (New York: Holocaust Library, 1988), chapter 4, cited in Marton, *A Death in Jerusalem*, 80.

19. Pia-Kristina Garde has completed a book in Swedish based on another early study of survivors rescued in Sweden, which resulted in a 1945 book by Einar Tegen and Gunhild Tegen, *De dödsdömda vittna* (The dead who were doomed to die witness), published in Stockholm by Wahlström & Widstrand. According to Garde, Dory Engströmer and a group of interviewers gave questionnaires to survivors in 1945, and most of the material in the 1945 book is based on these questionnaires. However, many of the originals are missing. They were often translated in two steps, from the original language to German, and from German to Swedish. The questionnaires, some of which were preserved in all three languages, are in the Einar and Gunhild Tegen Collection in the Uppsala University Library. This collection contains questionnaires from a survey of some 600 survivors who had been in Ravensbrück, Auschwitz, Stutthof, Neuengamme, Bergen-Belsen, and other camps. The questions in this Stockholm-based investigation were similar to those in Lund, and some survivors even participated in both studies. The idea in 1945 was to carry out and publish a scientific investigation, but the Tegens instead produced a less scientific book based on 192 questionnaires and interviews. Garde discovered the Tegen book in 1980, and immediately began searching for these 192 survivors. She is seeking a publisher in Sweden for "The Love of My Parents," her Swedish manuscript about the original 1945 study, her search, and her interviews with the survivors. Information on this study is from Uppsala University professor Stéphane Bruchfeld, 1 October 2002 conversation with the author, and e-mail from Pia-Kristina Garde to the author, 22 October and 30 October 2002.

20. Interviewers of the twenty-one Jewish women were Sabina Szmulowicz and Luba Melchior.

21. The Lund University website now has information on the interviews. See www.lub.lu.se/handskrift/projekt-ravensbruck. The Lund Jewish community in 2000 was trying to undertake a project to verify which of the women were still living, and to seek them out. The author has been in touch with the head of the community, but no further information has been received. By coincidence, at the 1995 fiftieth anniversary of the liberation of Ravensbrück, the author briefly interviewed one of the women in the archive, Basia Zajackowska-Rubinstein. She was then living in the Chicago area. Efforts to reestablish contact after discovery of the archive have not been successful. See chapter 7 for more information on Basia.

The twenty-one women in the Lund University archive are the following: Basia Zajackowska-Rubinstein, from Kielce, arrived in Ravensbrück from Pionki, and was a slave laborer for Siemens. Gustawa Kaplan, born on 3 March 1905, in Cracow, went from Pionki to Auschwitz in April 1944, to Ravensbrück in September 1944, then to Malchow. Erna Solewicz, born in Cracow on 1 September 1920, was in the *Jugendlager* part of the camp. Lida Holcer, born on 26 January 1916 in Tarnow, in Ravensbrück from March 1945 for a short time, and then sent to the Beendorf ammunition factory. Rachela Gottfried, born in Cracow on 27 October 1914, in Plaszow and the Tarnow ghetto in 1942–1943, then in Pionki, in Auschwitz from 1 August to 15 November 1944, in Ravensbrück from November until December 1944, then until 26 April 1945 in Malchow. Cecylia Skorecka, born on 14 June 1907 in Cracow, arrived in Ravensbrück in November 1944, sent on 23 or 24 November to Malchow, and liberated there on 26 April 1945. Genia Rotman, born in Lodz on 10 April 1918, sent to Radom on 8 November 1943, then to Auschwitz, then to Ravensbrück and stayed there from 3 November 1944 until 22 November 1944, then to Malchow until she was liberated on 24 April 1945. Rozalia Goldband, born in Cracow on 15 April 1908, sent to Auschwitz on 25 July 1944, arrived in Ravensbrück in October 1944, on 11 November 1944 sent to Malchow and liberated on 26 April 1945. Maria Miodownik, born in Chmielniku on 16 May 1920, brought to Ravensbrück from Auschwitz on 1 November 1944, then sent to Malchow on 22 November, liberated from there on 26 April. Estera Melchior, born on 22 February 1926 in Warsaw, in Auschwitz (no. A-24 766) from 27 July 1944 until 1 November 1944, then in Ravensbrück for three weeks, until 22 November 1944, then taken to Malchow, where she was liberated on 26 April 1945. Lajka Mandelker, born on 5 March 1920 in Cracow, taken to Auschwitz in June 1943 and stayed there until October, from October 1943 until 24 April 1945, in Ravensbrück and worked for Siemens. Masza Pszczol, born on 18 August 1916 in Lodz, in Auschwitz from 20 August 1944 until 1 September 1944, and then sent to Neukolln from September 1944 until April 1945, in Ravensbrück from April 1945 until her liberation to Sweden on 24 April 1945. Helena Bard-Nomberg, born on 2 March 1908, sent to Auschwitz in June 1943 and remained there until 18 January 1945, when she was sent to Ravensbrück. Estera Krajanek, born on 10 September 1917 in Warsaw, and was in Auschwitz, and then in Ravensbrück from November 1944 until 28 April 1945. Tola Sommer, born on 27 June 1918 in Radom, in Auschwitz from August 1944 until 1 November 1944 (with the number A-24888), in Ravensbrück from 2 November 1944 until 21 November 1944, and then in Malchow until liberated on 24 April 1945. Felicja Hauptman, born on 16 January 1916 in Cracow, in Auschwitz until 18 January 1945, and then in Ravensbrück, sent to Malchow on about 15 February 1945, and liberated on 26 April 1945. Helena Szykman, born on 5 April 1915 in Bedzin, in Auschwitz from some time in 1943 until 1 November 1944 (with the number 51810), in Ravensbrück from 1 November 1944 until 22 November, and then in Malchow until liberated on 24 April 1945.

The stories of the last four of the twenty-one names are not as clear as the others. Estera Bergman, born in Deblin on 8 February 1900, was in Czestochowa, then Ravensbrück (no. 96253), Beendorf, and Hamburg, and it is not clear from where she was rescued. Estera Borenstein, born on 11 October 1926 and was sent from the Lodz ghetto to Auschwitz, arriving on 27 August 1944, in Ravensbrück for only two weeks, from 30 August 1944 until 15 September 1944, then sent to Mauthausen from 20 September 1944 until 27 February 1945, and then to Bergen-Belsen from 3 April 1945 until 6 June 1945. She seems to have been liberated from Bergen-Belsen (not Ravensbrück) and brought to Sweden from there, but the June date is irregular. None of the handwritten information for Genendla Szuldman was possible to decipher, and the interview for Hela Kurek was missing.

14. RECONSTRUCTING LIVES IN THE AFTERMATH

1. Olga Astor, interview with Rochelle G. Saidel, 28 September 1997, Glenville, Illinois, archive of the author.

2. See Bernstein, *The Seamstress*.

3. Tova Giladi, interview with Evie Joselow for Rochelle G. Saidel, New York, 27 January 1998, archive of the author.

4. Rose Mellender interview with Susan Sapiro for Rochelle G. Saidel, New York, 1 February 1998, archive of the author. Her story from before her arrival in Auschwitz until her departure from Ravensbrück is told in chapter 9, and her time in Malchow and at liberation in Leipzig, in chapter 12.

5. Ester Grun, interview with Evie Joselow for Rochelle G. Saidel, White Plains, New York, 15 December 1997, archive of the author. Her background is in chapter 6, her slave labor experience in Ravensbrück is in chapter 7, and her time in Meuselwitz, in chapter 11.

6. Guiness, *When the Sky Rained Umbrellas*.

7. See Shelley, *Auschwitz, Secretaries of Death*, and *The Union Kommando in Auschwitz*.

8. See Birnhak, *Next Year, God Willing*.

9. See Lidia Vago, "One Year in the Black Hole of Our Planet Earth," 273–84.

10. Sali Solomon Daugherty, interview with Rochelle G. Saidel, Jerusalem, 28 December 2000, archive of the author.

15. GENDER AND WOMEN'S BODIES

1. Regarding special problems of single women, see, for example, Dalia Ofer, "The Status and Plight of Women in the Lodz Ghetto," in *Women in the Holocaust*, ed. Ofer and Weitzman, 123–42. A number of testimonies by interviewees for this book spoke of the difficulties of surviving without male protection in the ghetto.

2. For other stories of Jewish women who had to assume new roles and save their husbands, see Marion Kaplan, *Between Dignity and Despair: Jewish Life in Nazi Germany* (New York: Oxford University Press, 1998), 50–73.

3. Gisi Fleischmann of Bratislava, a woman who had a leadership role in the Slovak Central Refugee Committee, is a notable exception. See Yehuda Bauer, *Rethinking the Holocaust* (New Haven: Yale University Press, 2001), 167–85. The underground resistance movements included such women leaders as Zivia Lubetkin, Vitka Kempner, Chaika Grossman, and Vladka Meed, but they were not part of the communal structure in charge of the ghettos.

4. Lidia Vago, interview with Rochelle G. Saidel, Berlin, 22 April 1995, archive of the author.

5. See, for example, Myrna Goldenberg, "Memoirs of Auschwitz: The Burden of Gender," in *Women in the Holocaust*, ed. Ofer and Weitzman, 327–39; Brana Gurewitsch, *Mothers, Sisters, Resisters: Oral Histories of Women Who Survived the Holocaust* (Tuscaloosa: University of Alabama Press, 1998), 95–218; Nechema Tec, *Resilience and Courage: Women, Men, and the Holocaust* (New Haven: Yale University Press, 2003); Judith Baumel, *Double Jeopardy: Gender and the Holocaust* (London: Vallentine Mitchell, 1998), 67–99; Baer and Goldenberg, *Experience and Expression*; Sybil Milton, "Women and the Holocaust: The Case of German and German-Jewish Women," in *Different Voices: Women and the Holocaust*, ed. Carol Rittner and John Roth (New York: Paragon, 1993), 229–30. A number of testimonies by interviewees for this book also spoke of bonding with real or adopted sisters in the camp.

6. See, for example, Michelle Rosaldo and Louise Lamphere, "Introduction," in *Woman, Culture, and Society*, ed. Michelle Rosaldo and Louise Lamphere (Stanford: Stanford University Press, 1974); Anne Fausto-Sterling, *Myths of Gender: Biological Theories about Men and Women*, rev. ed. (New York: Basic Books, 1992); and Fausto-Sterling, *Sexing the Body: Gender Politics and the Construction of Sexuality*, (New York: Basic Books, 2000). *Sexing the Body* has an extensive bibliography that deals with this issue.

7. Fausto-Sterling, *Sexing the Body*, 44.

8. Lidia Vago, interview, 22 April 1995. The question of whether bromide was in fact given to women to stop menstruation or whether malnutrition produced this result has not yet been satisfactorily resolved.

9. Lola Goldstein Taubman, undated testimony prepared for the Conference on Material Claims, archive of the author.

10. See Janet Anschütz, Kerstin Meier, and Sanja Obajdin, ". . . *dieses leere Gefühl, und die Blicke der anderen*. . ." (. . . these feelings of emptiness and the glances of the others), in *Frauen in Konzentrationslagern*, ed. Füllberg-Stolberg, et al., 128–29.

11. Joanna Lindner Krause, interview with Rochelle G. Saidel, Ravensbrück, 23 April 1995, translated by Carolyn Gammon, archive of the author.

12. According to feminist biologist Anne Fausto-Sterling, "Height and shape differences are not absolute, but it may be that strength differences are. . . . Much of the muscle size differences between males and females result from disparities in fiber growth rather than fiber number. Both hormones and physical activity play a role." See Fausto-Sterling, *Myths of Gender*, 216.

13. Zillah Eisenstein, *Feminism and Sexual Equality* (New York: Monthly Review Press, 1984), 150.

14. Ruth Elias, *Triumph of Hope: From Theresienstadt and Auschwitz to Israel* (New York: John Wiley, 1998), 120. There are no statistics and no ways of proving how much rape or forced prostitution of Jewish women took place.

15. See Herbermann, *The Blessed Abyss,* 124–39 and passim; and Margarete Buber-Neumann, *Prisonnière de Staline et d'Hitler. 2: Déportée à Ravensbrück* (Prisoner of Stalin and Hitler, part 2: deportee in Ravensbrück) (Paris: Seuil, 1988), 19–27 and passim.

16. Quoted in Christa Schulz, "Weibliche Häftlinge aus Ravensbrück in Bordellen der Männerkonzentrationslager" (Female prisoners of Ravensbrück in bordellos in men's concentration camps), in *Frauen in Konzentrationslagern,* 145. On the same page there is a reproduction of a blank pass that was issued to prisoners in Dachau giving them permission to go to the camp brothel. See also Herbermann, The Blessed Abyss, 131–32.

17. See Christa Schulz, "Weibliche Häftlinge aus Ravensbrück in Bordellen der Männerkonzentrationslager," 135–46.

18. Anja Lundholm, *Das Höllentor. Bericht einer überlebenden* (The gates of hell. Account by survivors) (Reinbek bei Hamburg: 1988), 125 ff., quoted in Schulz, "Weibliche Häftlinge aus Ravensbrück," 141.

19. The interview with Margarethe W., quoted in Schulz, "Weibliche Häftlinge aus Ravensbrück," 142, was taken from Reinhild Kassig and Christa Paul, "Bordelle in deutschen Konzentrationslagern" (Bordellos in German concentration camps) in *Krampfader—Kasseler Grauenmagazin,* 1990, Heft 1, 26–31.

20. See Strebel, "Ravensbrück-das zentrale Frauenkonzentrationslager," 229.

21. Martina Scheitenberger and Martina Jung, "Fürsorge—Arbeitshaus—KZ, Betty Voss," 305.

22. Herbermann, *The Blessed Abyss,* 136n. 2.

EPILOGUE

1. Insa Eschebach, a researcher from Humboldt University, came across the letter about me as part of her studies on how Ravensbrück's memorialization has changed over time. She told me about it when I met her at a conference at Bar Ilan University in Israel in January 2001. Letter dated 25 July 1985 from Werner Händler to Hermann Axen, Member of the Politburo, Archive of *Stiftung Brandenburgische Gedenkstätten/Mahn- un Gedenkstätte Ravensbrück* (MGR–Brandenburg Memorials Foundation/Ravensbrück Memorial), RAI/3–5 VI 1007, copy in archive of author.

2. Letter from Werner Händler to Hermann Axen, 25 July 1985. See also Insa Eschebach, "Jahrestage. Zu den Formen und Funktionen von Gedenkveranstaltungen in Ravensbrück, 1946–1995" (Anniversary: The form and function of memorial events in Ravensbrück, 1946–1995), in *Die Sprache des Gedenkens,* Eschebach, Jacobeit, and Lanwerd, eds., 92.

3. This research had two phases. The first is "Victims and Survivors: Jewish women prisoners in the Ravensbrück concentration camp during and after World War II. Historical, sociological, and political research," German Israeli Foundation Research Project 1997–1999. The second is "Victims, Victimizers and survivors: a multidisciplinary research on Jewish women in the concentration camp of Ravensbrück and their environment," German Israeli Foundation Research Project 2001–2003.

4. See Pascale Rachel Bos, "Women and the Holocaust: Analyzing Gender Reference," in *Experience and Expression: Women, the Nazis, and the Holocaust,* ed. Baer and Goldenberg, 23–50, for more insights into survivor testimony and gender.

5. "Ravensbrück Memorial Center, 13–16 April 2000," in *55th Anniversary of the Liberation of Prisoners from the Sachsenhausen and Ravensbrück*

Concentration Camps, and the Brandenburg Penitentiary, 14 to 16 April 2000, 27 April 2000 (Stiftung Brandenburgische Gedenkstätten, 2000), 35.

6. Naphtali Lavie, *Balaam's Prophecy,* 25. Amichai Lau-Lavie's father is Ambassador Naphtali Lau Lavie, a former Consul General of Israel in New York, and his uncle is Rabbi Israel Lau, former chief Ashkenazi rabbi of Israel. They were rounded up by the Nazis in their hometown of Piotrkow, Poland. Their mother Chaya, known as Helena in Polish, was born 1 January 1900. See *Balaam's Prophecy* for more details.

7. Amichai Lau-Lavie, "Bitter Herbs, Passover Eve 1995," unpublished short story, archive of the author.

Selected Reference List

RAVENSBRÜCK

Adams, Carol, ed. *Women of Ravensbrück: Portraits of Courage*. Booklet for exhibit by Julia Terwilliger. Orlando: University of Central Florida, 1997

Amicale de Ravensbrück et de ses Commandos. *L'Ordre Nazi: Les Enfants Aussi* (Also the children). Paris: L'Amicale de Ravensbrück, 1979.

————. *Revivre et Construire Demain* (To live again and build tomorrow). Paris: Amicale de Ravensbrück, 1994.

Anthonioz, Genevieve De Gaulle. *The Dawn of Hope: A Memoir of Ravensbrück*. New York: Arcade, 1999.

Apel, Linde. *Jüdische Frauen im Konzentrationslager Ravensbrück 1939–1945* (Berlin: Metropol Verlag, 2003).

Barche, Heinz. *Mahnung und Verpflichtung: Leben, Ausbeutung und antifaschistischer Widerstandskampf weiblicher Häftlinge in den Konzentrationslagern Neubrandenburgs, 1943–1945, Kommentare, Dokumente, Berichte* (Memory and commitment: life, exploitation, and anti-fascist resistance struggle of female prisoners in Neubrandenburg concentration camps, 1943–1945, commentary, document, report). Committee of the anti-Fascist Resistance Struggle of the German Democratic Republic, Neubrandenburg District Committee, undated.

Bejarano, Esther. *"Man nannte mich Krümel": Eine jüdische Jugend in den Zeiten der Verfolgung* ("People called me crumb": A Jewish youth in the time of persecution). Hamburg: Curio-Verlag, 1991.

Benedict, Susan. "The Nadir of Nursing: The Nurse-perpetrators of Ravensbrück Concentration Camp." *Nursing History Review* 11(2003): 129–46.

Bernadac, Christian. *Camp for Women: Ravensbrück*. Geneva: Ferni Publishing House, 1978.

Bernadotte, Folke. *The Curtain Falls*. New York: Knopf, 1945.

Bernstein, Sara Tuvel. *The Seamstress*. New York: Putnam, 1997.

Birnhak, Alice. *Next Year, God Willing*. New York: Shengold Publishers, 1994.

Reference List

Breur, Dunya. *Een verborgen herinnering* (A hidden memory). Nijmegen: Sun Publisher, 1995.

Buber-Neumann, Margarete. *Déportée à Ravensbrück* (Deported to Ravensbrück). Paris: Éditions du Seuil, 1985.

———. *Under Two Dictators*. Translated by Edward Fitzgerald. London: Gollencz, 1949.

Buchmann, Erika. *Die Frauen von Ravensbrück* (The women of Ravensbrück). Berlin: GDR, 1959.

Chombart de Lauwe, Marie-Jo. *Toute une vie de résistance* (An entire life of resistance). Paris: Éditions Graphein FNDIRP, 1998.

Chombart de Lauwe, Marie-Jo, et al. *Les Françaises à Ravensbrück* (The French women at Ravensbrück). Paris: Éditions Gallimard, 1965.

Christliche Frauen im Widerstehen gegen den Nationalsozialismus: Häftlinge im Frauenkonzentrationslager Ravensbrück von 1939–1945 (Christian women in resistance against national socialism: Prisoners in Ravensbrück concentration camp from 1939–1945). (Exhibition Catalog, October 1998–October 1999). *Stiftung Brandenburgische Gedenkstätten/Mahn- und Gedenkstätte Ravensbrück* (Brandenburg Memorials Foundation/Ravensbrück Memorial).

Das Munitions- und Sprengstoffwerk in Malchow (Meckl.) 1938–1945, Heft 2 zur Geschichte der Stadt Malchow (Meckl.) (The munitions and explosives factory in Malchow, 1938–1945, booklet 2 on the history of the city of Malchow). Malchow: City of Malchow, text by Alfred Nill et al., 1995.

Delbo, Charlotte. *Auschwitz and After*. New Haven: Yale University Press, 1995.

Dunfurnier, Denise. *Ravensbrück: The Women's Camp of Death*. London: Allen and Unwin, 1948.

Elling, Hanna, and Ursula Krause-Schmitt. "Die Ravensbrück-Prozesse vor dem britischen Militärgericht" (The Ravensbrück trial before the British military tribunal). *Informationen 35*. Frankfurt am Main (October 1992): 13–37.

———. "Die Ravensbrück-Prozesse vor dem französischen Militärgerichten in Rastatt und Reutlingen" (The Ravensbrück trial before the French military tribunal in Rastatt and Reutlingen) *Informationen 37/38*. Frankfurt am Main (November 1993): 22–36.

Eschebach, Insa. "Engendered Oblivion: Commemorating Jewish Inmates at the Ravensbrück Memorial 1945–1995," unpublished paper presented at *Gender, Place, and Memory in the Modern Jewish Experience*, international conference, 2–4 January 2001, Bar-Ilan University, Israel.

———. "Interpreting Female Perpetrators: Ravensbrück Guards in the Courts of East Germany, 1946–1955." In *Lessons and Legacies: The Holocaust and Justice*, vol. 5. Edited by Ronald Smelser. Evanston: Northwestern University Press, 2002.

Eschebach, Insa, Sigrid Jacobeit, and Susanne Lanwerd, eds. *Die Sprache des Gedenkens: Zur Geschichte der Gedenkstätte Ravensbrück 1945–1995* (The language of memorialization: toward a history of the Ravensbrück memorial 1945–1995). Berlin: Edition Hentrich, 1999.

Feig, Konnilyn. *Hitler's Death Camps: The Sanity of Madness*. New York: Holmes & Meier, 1979.

Reference List

55th Anniversary of the Liberation of Prisoners from the Sachsenhausen and Ravensbrück Concentration Camps, and the Brandenburg Penitentiary, 14 to 16 April 2000, 27 April 2000. Stiftung Brandenburgische Gedenkstätten, 2000.

Fischer, Hubert. "Ärztliche Versorgung, Sanitäre Verhältnisse und Humanversuche im Frauenkonzentrationslager Ravensbrück" (Medical care, sanitary conditions, and human experimentation in the Ravensbrück women's concentration camp). *Gesnerus 45* (1988)1: 49–66.

Füllberg-Stolberg, Claus, Martina Jung, Renate Rieb, and Martina Scheitenberger, eds. *Frauen in Konzentrationslagern Bergen-Belsen Ravensbrück* (Women in concentration camps Bergen-Belsen, Ravensbrück). Bremen: Temmen, 1994.

Gelissen, Rena Kornreich. *Rena's Promise: A Story of Sisters in Auschwitz.* Boston: Beacon Press, 1995.

Gluck, Gemma LaGuardia, *My Story.* Edited by S. L. Shneiderman. New York: David McKay, 1961.

Grohs-Martin, Silvia. *Silvie.* New York: Welcome Rain Publishers, 2000.

Helen Ernst: 1904–1948, Berlin–Amsterdam–Ravensbrück, Stationen einer antifaschistischen Künstlerin (Stations of an Antifascist Artist). Exhibition catalogue, Das Verborgene Museum. Berlin: Traum & Raum, 1994.

Herbermann, Nanda. *The Blessed Abyss: Inmate #6582 in Ravensbrück Concentration Camp for Women.* Edited by Hester Baer and Elizabeth Baer. Detroit: Wayne State University Press, 2000. (Originally published in Germany as *Der gesegnete Abgrund. Schutzhäftling Nr. 6582 im Frauenkonzentrationslager Ravensbrück,* 1946.)

Herzog, Monika. *Ravensbrücker Zeichnungen. Drawings of Ravensbrück: "Hope, which lives in us eternally."* Stiftung Brandenburgische Gedenkstätten/Mahn- und Gedenkstätte Ravensbrück, 1993.

Hübner, Hans. "Martha, die Kartenlegerin von Ravensbrück" (Martha, the fortune-teller from Ravensbrück). *Informationen 40.* Frankfurt am Main (Dec. 1994): 10–17.

Jacobeit, Sigrid. *Ravensbrückerinnen* (Women from Ravensbrück). Oranienburg: Stiftung Brandenburgische Gedenkstätten, 1995.

———, ed. *"Ich grüsse Euch als freier Mensch"* (I greet you as a free person), Oranienburg: Stiftung Brandenburgische Gedenkstätten, 1995.

Jacobeit, Sigrid, and Grit Philipp, eds. *Forschungsschwerpunkt. Ravensbrück. Beiträge zur Geschichte des Frauen-Konzentrationslagers* (Focused research. Ravensbrück. Contribution on the history of women's concentration camps). Stiftung Brandenburgische Gedenkstätten, No. 9. Berlin: Edition Hentrich, 1997.

Jacobeit, Sigrid, and Lieselotte Thoms-Heinrich. *Kreuzweg Ravensbrück: Lebensbilder antifaschistischer Widerstandskämpferinnen* (The way of the cross, Ravensbrück: Life portraits of antifascist resistance fighters). Leipzig: Verlag für die Frau, 1987.

Jahresbericht der Stiftung Brandenburgische Gedenkstätten, 1999 (Annual report of the Brandenburg memorials foundation, 1999). Stiftung Brandenburgische Gedenkstätten, 1999.

Reference List

Jaiser, Constanze. *Poetische Zeugnisse: Gedichte aus dem Frauen-Konzentrations-lager Ravensbrück 1939–1945 (Ergebnisse der Frauenforschung, 55)* (Poetic testimonies: poems of the Ravensbrück women's concentration camp, 1939–1945, results of research on women, 55). Stuttgart : J. B. Metzler, 2000.

Katzenmaier, Katharina [Sister Theodolinde]. *Vom KZ ins Kloster* (From concentration camp to convent). St. Ottilien: EOS–Verlag, 1996.

King, Christine. *The Nazi State and the New Religions: Five Case Studies in Non-Conformity.* New York: Edwin Mellen, 1982.

Klier, Freya. *Die Kaninchen von Ravensbrück: Medizinische Versuche an Frauen in der NS-Zeit* (The rabbits of Ravensbrück: medical experiments and women in the time of national socialism). Munich: Knaur, 1994.

Knapp, Gabriele, *Frauenstimmen: Musikerinnen erinnern an Ravensbrück* (Women's voices: musicians remembering Ravensbrück). Berlin: Metropol Verlag, 2003.

Krause-Schmitt, Ursula. "Zwangsarbeit bei Siemens—die Lager" (Forced labor in the Siemens camp) and "Der Weg zum Krematorium führte am Siemenslager vorbei" (The way to the crematorium passed along the Siemens camp). *Informationen* 37/38. Frankfurt am Main (November 1993): 38–46.

Krause-Schmitt, Ursula, and Christine Krause, eds. *Mit den Augen der Überlebenden. Ein Rundgang durch die Mahn- und Gedenkstätte Ravensbrück* (With the eyes of survivors. A tour of the Ravensbrück memorial). Essen: Lagergemeinschaft Ravensbrück/Freundeskreis, 1999.

Lacouture, Jean. *Le témoignage est un combat: Une biographie de Germaine Tillion* (Testimony is a struggle: A biography of Germaine Tillion). Paris: Seuil, 2000.

Langley-Dános, Eva. *Prison on Wheels: From Ravensbrück to Burgau.* Einsiedeln: Daimon Verlag, 2000.

Lavie, Naphtali Lau. *Balaam's Prophecy: Eyewitness to History: 1939–1989.* New York: Cornwall Books, 1999, 25, 77.

Limbächer, Katja, Maike Merten, and Bettina Pfefferle, eds. *Das Mädchenkonzentrationslager Uckermark* (Uckermark young women's concentration camp). Münster: UNRAST, 2000.

Marton, Kati. *A Death in Jerusalem.* New York: Pantheon Books, 1994.

Maurel, Michelene. *An Ordinary Camp.* New York: Simon and Schuster, 1958.

Maurice, Violette. *N. N.* Paris: Encre Marine, 1991 (first issued, 1946).

Milton, Sybil. "Women and the Holocaust: The Case of German and German-Jewish Women." In *Different Voices.* Edited by Carol Rittner and John K. Roth. New York: Paragon House, 1993.

Morais, Fernando. *Olga: Revolutionary and Martyr.* New York: Grove Weidenfeld, 1990.

Morrison, Jack. *Ravensbrück: Everyday Life in a Women's Concentration Camp, 1939–45.* Princeton: Markus Wiener Publishers, 2000.

Müller, Charlotte. *Die Klempnerkolonne in Ravensbrück: Erinnerungen des Häftlings Nr. 10787* (The plumber column of Ravensbrück: Recollections of prisoner No. 10787). Berlin: Dietz Verlag, 1981.

Müller, Delia and Madlen Lepschies. *Tage der Angst und der Hoffnung: Erinnerungen an die Todesmärsche aus dem Frauen-Konzentrationslager Ravens-*

brück Ende April 1945 (Days of terror and hope: memories of the death march from Ravensbrück women's concentration camp at the end of April 1945). Stiftung Brandenburgische Gedenkstätten/Mahn- und Gedenkstätte Ravensbrück, undated, ca. 2000.

Nelken, Halina. *And Yet, I Am Here!* Amherst: University of Massachusetts Press, 1999.

Noyce, Wilfrid. *They Survived: A Study of the Will to Live.* London: Heinemann, 1962.

Ottaway, Susan. *Violette Szabo: "The Life That I Have. . . ."* Annapolis: Naval Institute Press, 2002.

Owings, Alison. *Frauen. German Women Recall.* "Solidarity and Survival," chapter on Charlotte Müller, and "A Job in its Own Category," chapter on Anna Fest. New Brunswick: Rutgers University Press, 1994, 155–71, 313–41.

Philipp, Grit. *Kalendarium der Ereignisse im Frauen-Konzentrationslager Ravensbrück, 1939–1945* (Calendar of Events in Ravensbrück women's concentration camp, 1939–1945). Berlin: Metropol, 1999.

Pollak, Aurelia. *Three Years of Deportation.* Ra'anana: DocoStory, 1999.

Póltawska, Wanda. *And I Am Afraid of My Dreams.* 1964. New York: Hippocrene Books, 1987.

———. "Ravensbrueck between Life and Death." Poland, No. 6/106 (1963): 17–19.

Raban, Havka Folman. *They Are Still With Me.* Lohamei Haghetaot: Ghetto Fighter's Museum, 2001, 180–88.

Ravensbrück. Berlin: Komitee der Antifaschistischen Widerstandskämpfer in der Deutschen Demokratischen Republik (Committee of antifascist resistance fighters in the GDR), 1960.

Ravensbrück National Memorial. "Der Zellenbau Ravensbrück: The cellblock at Ravensbrück women's concentration camp." Brochure, 1987.

Ravensbrück National Memorial. "National Memorial of Ravensbrück— Museum." Brochure, undated.

Rittner, Carol, Stephen Smith, and Irena Steinfeldt, eds. *The Holocaust and the Christian World.* Nottingham: Beth Shalom Holocaust Memorial Centre, 2000.

Rossiter, Margaret. *Women in the Resistance.* New York: Praeger, 1986.

Rougier-Lecoq, Violette. *Témoignages: 36 Dessins á la Plume: Violette Lecoq* (Thirty-six pen drawings). Paris: Les Deux Sirènes, 1948.

Saidel, Rochelle G. "Fifty Years after the Horror: Women Survivors Recall Indignities Unique to Them." *Jewish Telegraphic Agency Daily News Bulletin.* New York: 4 May 1995.

———. "Integrating Ravensbrück Women's Concentration Camp into Holocaust Memorialization in the United States." In *Women in the Holocaust: Responses, Insights and Perspectives. Selected Papers from the Annual Scholars' Conference on the Holocaust and the Churches, 1990–2000.* Edited by Marcia Littell. Philadelphia: Merion Westfield Press International, 2001, 63–74.

———. "Ravensbrück." In *Herança Judaica.* São Paulo: B'nai B'rith, October 1995.

————. "Ravensbrück, Memory, Memorialization." Paper presented at the Second Bi-Annual Holocaust Studies Conference, Middle Tennessee State University, Murfreesboro, April 1998.

————. "Ravensbrück Women's Concentration Camp: Before and after Liberation." In *Remembrance, Repentance Reconciliation: The 25th Anniversary Volume of the Annual Scholars Conference on the Holocaust and the Churches.* Edited by Douglas F. Tobler. Lanham, Md.: University Press of America, 1998, 165–75.

————. "Ravensbrück Women's' Concentration Camp: The Brazil Connection." Paper presented at *GenDerations*—Seventh International Interdisciplinary Congress on Women, University of Tromso, Norway, June 1999.

————. "Recovering the Memoirs of Jewish Women Victims of the Holocaust: The Cases of Ravensbrück Concentration Camp and Immigrants to Brazil." Paper presented at the Twenty-seventh Annual Scholars' Conference on the Holocaust and the Churches, University of South Florida, Tampa, March 1997.

————. "Ravensbrück Concentration Camp and Rescue in Sweden." In *Remembering for the Future: The Holocaust in an Age of Genocide,* vol. 1. Edited by John K. Roth and Elisabeth Maxwell. London: Palgrave, 2001.

————, curator. *Women of Ravensbrück, Portraits of Courage: Art by Julia Terwilliger.* Exhibit catalog. St. Petersburg: Florida Holocaust Museum, 2001.

Salvesen, Sylvia. *Forgive—But Do Not Forget.* London: Hutchinson, 1958.

Schikorra, Christa. *Kontinuitäten der Ausgrenzung: "Asoziale" Häftlinge im Frauen- Konzentratonslager Ravensbrück* (Continuation of exclusion: "Asocial" prisoners in Ravensbrück women's concentration camp). Berlin: Meropol, 2001.

————. "Prostitution of Female Concentration Camp Prisoners as Slave Labor: On the Situation of 'Asocial' Prisoners in Ravensbrück Women's Concentration Camp." In *Dachau and the Nazi Terror 1933–1945, Studies and Reports,* vol. 2. Edited by Wolfgang Benz and Barbara Distel. Dachau: Verlag Dachauer Hefte, 2002.

Schoppmann, Claudia. *Days of Masquerade: Life Stories of Lesbians during the Third Reich.* New York: Columbia University Press, 1996.

Schroeder-Hildebrand, Dagmar. *"Ich sterbe vor Hunger!" Kochrezepte aus dem Konzentrationslager Ravensbrück* ("I'm dying of hunger!" Cooking recipes from Ravensbrück concentration camp). Bremen: Donat, 1999.

Schulz, Christa, ed. *Der Wind weht weinend über die Ebene: Ravensbrücker Gedichte* (The wind blows crying over the plain: Ravensbrück poems). Stiftung Brandenburgische Gedenkstätten/Mahn- und Gedenkstätte Ravensbrück: Editions Tirésias Michel Reynaud, 1991, 1995.

Schütt, Karl Heinz. *Ein vergessenes Lager? über das Aussenlager Neustadt-Glewe des Frauen- KZ Ravensbrück* (A forgotten camp? On the Neustadt-Glewe subcamp of Ravensbrück women's concentration camp). Berlin: GNN-Verlag Sachsen, 1997.

Schwarz, Helga, and Gerda Szepansky, eds. *Frauen-KZ Ravensbrück . . . und dennoch blühten Blumen: Dokumente, Berichte, Gedichte und Zeichnungen vom Lageralltag* (Ravensbrück women's concentration camp . . . and still flowers bloomed—documents, reports, poems and drawings from camp life). Potsdam: Brandenburgische Landeszentrale für Politische Bildung, 2000.

Shelley, Lore, ed. *Auschwitz: The Nazi Civilization*. Lanham: University Press of America, 1992.

———. *The Union Kommando in Auschwitz*. Lanham, Md.: University Press of America, 1996.

Shneiderman, S. L. "LaGuardia's Sister: Eichmann's Hostage." Midstream 7 1 (1961): 3–19.

Simpson, Christopher. *The Splendid Blond Beast: Money, Law, and Genocide in the Twentieth Century*. New York: Grove Press, 1993.

Sommer-Letkowitz, Elizabeth. *Are You In This Hell Too?* London: The Menard Press, 1995.

Soswinski, Herta. "Why We Have to Tell about It." In *Auschwitz: The Nazi Civilization*. Edited by Lore Shelley. Lanham, Md.: University Press of America, 1992.

Stadt Fürstenberg/Havel Land Brandenburg—Bundesrepublik Deutschland. Dokumentation Internationaler Landschaftsplanerischer Ideenwettbewerb. "Ehemaliges Frauen- Konzentrationslager Ravensbrück" (City of Fürstenberg/Havel, state of Brandenburg, Federal Republic of Germany. Documentation of international landscape planning idea competition. "Former Ravensbrück women's concentration camp"). 2000.

Strebel, Bernard. "Ravensbrück-das zentrale Frauenkonzentrationslager" (Ravensbrück, the central women's concentration camp). In *Die nationalsozialistischen Konzentrationslager. Entwicklung und Struktur* (The national socialistic concentration camps—development and structure). Edited by Ulrich Herbert, Karin Orth, and Christoph Dieckmann. Göttingen: Wallstein Verlag, 1998, 215–59.

Steiner, Herbert. *Käthe Leichter: Leben und Werk* (Käthe Leichter: life and work). Vienna: Europa Verlag-AG, 1973.

Symonowicz, Wanda, ed. *Beyond Human Endurance: The Ravensbrück Women Tell Their Stories*. Warsaw: Interpress Publishers, 1970.

Ten Boom, Corrie. *The Hiding Place*. 1971. New York: Bantam, 1983.

Tillion, Germaine. *Ravensbrück*. New York: Doubleday, 1975.

Toulouse-Lautrec, Béatrix de. *J'ai eu vingt ans à Ravensbrück: La Victoire en Pleurant* (I was twenty years old in Ravensbrück: the victory of mourning). Paris: Librairie Académique Perrin, 1991.

Treu-aber wem? Bestraft- doch wofür? Malchower Jungendliche erleben den Zusammenbruch 1945, Teil 2, Heft 5 zur Geschichte der Stadt Malchow (Meckl.) (Faithful—but to whom? Punished—but for what? Malchow young people experience the 1945 breakdown, part 2, booklet 5 on the history of the city of Malchow). Malchow: City of Malchow, 1997.

von Freyberg, Jutta, and Ursula Krause-Schmitt. *Moringen-Lichtenburg-Ravensbrück: Frauen im Konzentrationslager 1933–1945: Lesebuch zur Ausstellung*. (Moringen-Lichtenburg-Ravensbrück: Women in concentration camps). Frankfurt: VAS–Verlag für Akademische Schriften, 1997.

Walz, Loretta. *Erinnern an Ravensbrück* (Remembering Ravensbrück). Stiftung Brandenburgische Gedenkstätten, 1998.

Werner, Ruth. *Olga Benário: A História de uma Mulher Corajosa* (Olga Benário: A history of a courageous woman). São Paulo: Editora Alfa-Omega, 1987.

WOMEN, THE HOLOCAUST, MEMORY, AND METHODOLOGY

Baer, Elizabeth, and Myrna Goldenberg, eds. *Experience and Expression: Women, the Nazis, and the Holocaust.* Detroit: Wayne State University Press, 2003.
Baumel, Judith Tydor. *Gender and the Holocaust: Double Jeopardy.* London: Valletine Mitchell, 1998.
Berger, Peter, and Thomas Luckmann. *The Social Construction of Reality.* Garden City, N.J.: Anchor Books, Doubleday, 1966.
Brodzki, Bella, and Celeste Schenk, eds. *Life/Lines: Theorizing Women's Autobiography.* Ithaca: Cornell University Press, 1988.
Cantor, Aviva. *Jewish Women/Jewish Men.* San Francisco: HarperSanFrancisco, 1995.
Chicago, Judy. *Holocaust Project: From Darkness into Light.* New York: Penguin, 1993.
Delbo, Charlotte. *Convoy to Auschwitz: Women of the French Resistance.* Boston: Northeastern University Press, 1997.
———. *None of Us Will Return.* New Haven: Yale University Press, 1992.
De Silva, Cara, ed. *In Memory's Kitchen: A Legacy from the Women of Terezin.* Northvale: Jason Aronson, 1996.
Eisenstein, Zillah. *Feminism and Sexual Equality.* New York: Monthly Review Press, 1984.
Eliach, Yaffa, and Brana Gurewitsch. *Holocaust Oral History Manual.* New York: Center for Holocaust Studies, 1991.
Elias, Ruth. *Triumph of Hope: From Theresienstadt and Auschwitz to Israel.* New York: John Wiley, 1998
Fausto-Sterling, Anne. *Myths of Gender: Biological Theories about Men and Women.* Rev. ed. New York: Basic Books, 1992.
———. *Sexing the Body: Gender Politics and the Construction of Sexuality.* New York: Basic Books, 2000.
Fuchs, Esther. *Women and the Holocaust.* Blue Ridge Summit: University Press of America, 1999.
Garber, Zev, ed. *Methodology in the Academic Teaching of the Holocaust.* Lanham, Md.: University Press of America, 1988.
Goldenberg, Myrna. "Different Horrors, Same Hell: Women Remembering the Holocaust." In *Thinking the Unthinkable: Meanings of the Holocaust.* Edited by Roger Gottleib. New York: Paulist Press, 1990.
———. "Food Talk: Gendered Responses to Hunger in the Concentration Camps." In *Experience and Expression: Women, the Nazis, and the Holocaust.* Edited by Elizabeth Baer and Myrna Goldenberg. Detroit: Wayne State University Press, 2003.
Gurewitsch, Brana, ed. *Mothers, Sisters, Resisters: Oral Histories of Women Who Survived the Holocaust.* Birmingham: University of Alabama Press, 1998.

Horowitz, Sara. "Voices from the Killing Ground." In *Holocaust Remembrance: The Shapes of Memory*. Edited by Geoffrey Hartman. Cambridge: Blackwell, 1993.

Katz, Esther, and Joan Ringelheim, eds. *Proceedings of the Conference of Women Surviving the Holocaust*. New York: The Institute for Research in History, 1983.

Koonz, Claudia. "Germany's Buchenwald: Whose Shrine? Whose Memory?" In *The Art of Memory: Holocaust Memorials in History*. Edited by James Young. Munich and New York: Prestel-Verlag and The Jewish Museum, 1994.

Kremer, Lillian. *Women's Holocaust Writing: Memory and Imagination*. Lincoln: University of Nebraska Press, 1999.

Lentin, Ronit. *Israel and the Daughters of the Shoah: Reoccupying the Territories of Silence*. New York: Berghahn Books, 2000.

Lerner, Gerda. *Why History Matters* (Part 1). New York: Oxford University Press, 1997.

Linden, R. Ruth. *Making Stories, Making Selves: Feminist Reflections on the Holocaust*. Columbus: Ohio State University Press, 1993.

Lixl-Purcell, Andreas. "Memoirs as History." In *Leo Baeck Yearbook 39*. London: Martin Secker & Warburg for Leo Baeck Institute, 1994.

Ofer, Dalia, and Lenore J. Weitzman, eds. *Women in the Holocaust*. New Haven: Yale University Press, 1998.

Quack, Sybille, ed. *Between Sorrow and Strength: Women Refugees of the Nazi Period*. New York: Cambridge University Press, 1995.

The Personal Narratives Group, eds. *Interpreting Women's Lives: Feminist Theory and Personal Narratives*. Bloomington: University of Indiana, 1989.

Rapaport, Lynn. "The Double Disadvantage—Being a Jewish Woman in Germany Today." In *Zur Geschichte der jüdischen Frau in Deutschland* (On the history of Jewish women in Germany). Edited by Julius Carlebach. Berlin: Metropol, 1993.

Reinharz, Shulamit. *Feminist Methods in Social Research*. New York: Oxford University Press, 1992.

Ringelheim, Joan. "Thoughts about Women and the Holocaust." In *Thinking the Unthinkable: Meanings of the Holocaust*. Edited by Roger S. Gottleib. New York: Paulist Press, 1990.

———. "The Unethical and the Unspeakable: Women and the Holocaust." In *Simon Wiesenthal Center Annual*. Chappaqua: Rossel Books, 1984.

Rittner, Carol, and John K. Roth, eds. *Different Voices*. New York: Paragon House, 1993.

Ritvo, Roger, and Diane Plotkin. *Sisters in Sorrow: Voices of Care in the Holocaust*. College Station: Texas A & M University Press, 1998.

Rosaldo, Michelle, and Louise Lamphere, eds. *Woman, Culture, and Society*. Stanford, Calif.: Stanford University Press, 1974.

Saidel, Rochelle G. "A Luta das Mulheres contra o Nazismo" (The struggle of women against nazism). In *Shalom Documento*. São Paulo:1993.

———. "Jewish Women Who Immigrated to São Paulo because of Nazism in Europe, 1933–1949." Paper presented at the NGO Forum on Women Beijing '95, Beijing, People's Republic of China, September 1995.

Schwertfeger, Ruth. *Women of Theresienstadt: Voices from a Concentration Camp*. New York: Oxford University Press, 1989.

Shelley, Lore. *Secretaries of Death*. New York: Shengold Publishers, 1986.

Tec, Nechama. "Reflections on Resistance and Gender." In *Remembering for the Future: The Holocaust in an Age of Genocide*, vol. 1. 552–69. Edited by John Roth and Elisabeth Maxwell. London, Palgrave, 2001.

———. *Resilience and Courage: Women, Men, and the Holocaust*. New Haven: Yale University Press, 2003.

Index

Abortions, 22, 211, 212

Agassi, Judith Buber, 15

Air raids/bombings, Allied, 179; effects on prisoners, 130, 160, 173–74; on prisoners and German civilians, 162, 174; prisoners' reactions to, 85, 129, 165; prisoners repairing damage from, 142, 160, 165; on Red Cross convoys, 67–68; targets of, 82, 116

Allach subcamp, 86–87, 189–91

Allen, Charles R., Jr., 217

Allies, 33, 117, 176. *See also* Air raids/bombings, Allied; Britain; Soviet Union; United States

An meine Brüder (To my brothers) (Leichter), 61

Anti-Semitism, 68, 112, 124, 198

Appell. See Roll call *(Appell)*

Art, resistance through, 57–59

"Asocials," 21, 213–15; categories within, 37–40

Astor, Olga Weiss, 82–87, 103, 113, 189–93, 223, 243n.5

Auschwitz-Birkenau, 52, 134, 183, 202; compared to Ravensbrück, 25, 105, 129–30; death march to Ravensbrück from, 121–23, 125, 128–30, 171–72; evacuation of, 121–36, 183, 185; gas chamber of, 51, 171, 208; Hungarian Jews sent to, 104, 112, 141; Jews sent from Ravensbrück to, 8, 18; Jews sent to Ravensbrück from, 10, 52, 104; transports to, 51, 98, 245n.9; transports to Ravensbrück from, 18–19, 21, 30–31, 39, 80, 88, 94

Austria, 39, 45, 47

Axen, Hermann, 219–20

Babies: born in camps, 19, 211–12, 243n.12; murders of, 22, 31; as survivors, 116–18, 222

Baer, Hester and Elizabeth, 215, 236n.7

Baras, Viola Eisler, 134–35

Bard-Nomberg, Helena, 254n.21

Barracks, 15, 77, 133, 139; bunks in, 139; children left in, 66, 75–77; for industrial court, 102, 122; Jewish, 52, 115, 218; at Malchow, 166, 172; medical, 92–93; at Meuselwitz, 159–60; mixed populations in, 88, 124; at Neustadt-Glewe, 153, 156–57; overcrowding in, 18, 19, 105, 126–27; prisoners in charge of, 28, 44, 48, 76, 93, 102; quarantine block, 70, 114; at Ravensbrück memorial site, 221, 224; at Siemens factory, 95, 97–98, 221; special, 114, 128; for women from Auschwitz, 125–26, 128–29

Beatings. *See* Punishment/torture

Becker, I. Judith Berger, 19, 125–28, 134, 166–68, 223

Beendorf, 142, 144

Index

Berentsen-Droog, Anna Maria, 57, 240n.1, 241n.8
Bergen-Belsen, 75, 79, 82, 89, 96, 142, 188
Bergen-Belsen Displaced Persons camp, 92, 194
Berger, Peter, 9
Berger (Schreier), Pepi, 125–26, 128
Bergman, Estera, 254n.21
Berlin: bombing of, 84; Gemma Gluck and family in, 117–18
Bernadotte, Folke, 178, 186–88, 252nn.17–18
Bernburg euthanasia center, 18, 20, 37, 234n.14; gassings at, 45, 50–51
Bernstein, Sara Tuvel, 84
Bezdin, 198
Biebow, Hans, 101, 245n.7, 245n.9
Birnhak, Alice Strum, 94, 202, 244n.11
Bloch, Denise (Denielle Williams), 34–35
Blockälteste, 28, 44, 48–50, 102, 213
Blonay, Paul de, 187
Bolin, Sture, 188
Borenstein, Estera, 254n.21
Brainin, Lotte, 21, 135
Brazil, 28, 43–44, 69, 72, 184–85, 206, 213
Breuer, Herta, 49, 61
Breur, Aat, 57–59, 212
Breur, Dunya, 58, 212
Britain, 117; liberation of camps by, 89, 176; nationals at Ravensbrück, 26, 34–35; spies for, 31, 34–35
Buber, Martin, 15
Buber-Neumann, Margarete, 15–17, 36–37, 213
Buchenwald, 151, 214
Buchmann, Erika, 49
Buckman, Alex, 54–56, 224, 240n.3, 241n.5
Budapest, 79, 83, 87, 94, 111–12, 133, 149
"Bunker" (punishment building), 13–15, 221
Burgau, 83, 87

"Camp sisters," 160, 205, 208–9
Cantor, Aviva, 218
Carmen, Micha, 242n.2
Catholics, resistance by, 29, 32. *See also* Christians

Celebrations, 86; for children, 68–70
Cemeteries, 157, 176
Chelmno, 182, 245n.7
Childcare, 66, 68, 208
Children, 64–68, 78, 97, 243n.12; camp experience *vs.* adults, 64, 66; in camps with mothers, 74–75, 208–9, 242n.2; labor by, 72–73, 75; as survivors, 64, 68–71, 187; of survivors, 197–99, 210; women's care of, 40, 60, 70–71
Chombart de Lauwe, Marie-Jo, 31, 232n.9, 237n.14
Christians, 97; Jews aided by, 32–33; Jews posing as, 89, 183–85. *See also* Catholics
Clauberg, Carl, 40, 211
Clothing, 16–17, 100, 209; bartering food for, 85, 93, 98; confiscated, 103, 134, 141, 245n.7; for death marches, 129, 176; identification on, 26, 103, 133, 244n.11; lack of warmth from, 21, 88, 98, 103, 106, 159; for liberated prisoners, 155–56, 181–82; misfitting, 80, 84, 90–91; sent back after gassings, 50–51, 134; thefts of, 18, 124
Communists, 28, 221, 236n.6; dominance in survivor committees, 7; glorified at memorial sites, 4–7, 220, 231n.2; Olga Benário Prestes as, 42–44; POWs in Ravensbrück as, 33–34; resistance by, 4–6, 44, 236n.5; use of memorial sites, 219
Concentration camp inmates, 100; abandoned, 174, 177; anti-Semitism of, 68, 124; as *Blockälteste*, 28, 44, 48–50, 76, 102, 213; condition at liberation, 67–68; escaped, 52, 98, 142, 161–62; as *kapos*, 39, 40, 84, 125–26; in positions of authority, 29, 40, 93, 101–2, 115, 207; relations among, 38, 99, 169–70, 179; used to inflict punishment, 15, 76, 140
Concentration camp inmates, liberated, 117, 163, 170, 175; condition of, 24, 77, 193; Germans and, 155–56, 172; interviews with, 97–98, 188; in Sweden, 148–50, 188. *See also* Red Cross, evacuation of inmates to Sweden; Survivors
Conference of Women Surviving the Holocaust, 37
Coping mechanisms, 84, 129, 136; disasso-

Index

France, 136; memoirs of survivors from, 237n.13, 237n.14; political prisoners from, 28, 31–32; POWs from, 157–58
Friedman, Manya, 140–41, 188
Friedmann, Nomi Moskovits, 66, 68–70
Furs, confiscated, 100, 245n.7
Fürstenberg, 12–13, 16, 220–21

Garde, Pia-Kristina, 253n.19
Gas chambers, 21–22, 50, 58, 171, 237n.17; at Auschwitz, 130–31; at Bernburg, 50–51; fear of, 76, 84, 92, 140–41, 145–46, 159; number murdered in, 235n.23; at Ravensbrück, 20–21, 157, 244n.11; selection for, 21, 30–32, 50–51, 58, 116, 141–42
Gebhardt, Karl, 82, 237n.12
Gelissen, Rena Kornreich, 157
Gender, 53, 108, 215; coping mechanisms of, 208–9; effects on camp experience, 22–23, 204, 213–14; experiences of Holocaust, 22–23; inequalities before Holocaust, 46, 206–7; physiological considerations in camps, 22, 209–12; and sexual abuse, 212–14
Gender roles, 204–6, 208–9, 255n.3
Gerecht, Simon, 69
German Democratic Republic (GDR), and Ravensbrück memorial site, 3–4, 7, 217, 219–21
Germans, 99, 123; helping prisoners, 135, 153–54, 162–63; and liberated prisoners, 170, 172. See also Guards; SS
Germany, 142, 163; camps in cleansed of Jews, 17–18; discrimination in, 35, 39; Fiorello LaGuardia trying to get family out of, 118–19; invasion of Hungary, 111–12; losing WWII, 186, 187; political prisoners from, 28; reunification of, 220
Gertler, Judith Rosner, 75–78, 173–75, 243n.10
Gestapo, 33, 43, 48, 80, 92, 117, 136
Ghettos: gender in, 206–7, 255n.3. See also specific ghettos
Gift making, 70, 208–9; artifacts in museums, 240n.1, 241n.8; resistance through, 54, 59–60
Giladi, Tova (Guta) Flatto, 72–75, 193–99
Gleiwitz, 25, 137–41

Gluck, Gemma LaGuardia, 35, 70, 109–20, 110, 206, 246n.2; liberation of, 116–18; observations by, 13–14, 20–21, 115–18; and other prisoners, 59–60, 62–63; return to U.S., 118–20; work of, 114–15
Goldband, Rozalia, 254n.21
Goldman, Esther, 158
Goldstein, Mina Lewkowicz, 38, 101–2, 122, 178–80, 188, 208
Gottfried, Rachela, 254n.21
Greenberg, Doris Fuks, 89–92, 163–64
Gropman, Jacqueline Schweitzer, 136
Gross Rosen, 138
Grun, Ester (Eliz) Weisz, 103–8, 158–63, 201–2
Guards, 74, 202, 213; abandoning camps, 154–55, 157, 174, 175; abandoning death marches, 147, 172; on death marches, 176, 183–84; trained at Ravensbrück, 13
Guiness, Margaret (Margo) Wohl, 79–83, 96, 113, 188, 202, 243n.2
Günther, Christian, 186
Gypsies, 85; in asocials category, 37, 39–40; sterilization of, 31, 58, 211

Hajkova, Dagmar, 21
Hamburg, war crimes procedures in, 20, 23–24, 34, 58, 238n.22
Händler, Werner, 219–20
Hartheim, gas chamber at, 51, 58
Hauptman, Felicja, 254n.21
Hausner, Gideon, 113
Hedgepeth, Sonja, 224
Herbermann, Nanda, 17, 29, 213, 236n.6, 236n.7
Herzog, Monika, 237n.17
Heydrich, Reinhard, 234n.15
Himmler, Heinrich, 15; and Hungarian Jews, 112; and Ravensbrück, 20, 44, 51; and Red Cross rescue, 178, 186–87, 252n.16
Hirt-Manheimer, Aron, 219
Hitler, Adolf, 111–12, 142, 163
Hochermann, Rachel Rozenbaum, 168, 178, 182–84, 188, 206–8
Holcer, Lida, 254n.21
Holocaust, 225; effects on families, 144–45, 150, 197, 225; experiences of women vs. men in, 22–23; survivors dis-

272

Index

Index

Lau-Lavie, Amichai, 224–25, 258n.8
Lavie, Naphtali Lau, 72, 258n.6
Lecoq, Violette, 58–59
Leichter, Franz, 47–48, 222
Leichter, Henry (Heinz), 45, 47–48
Leichter, Käthe Pick, 41, 42, 45–51, 204–6, 222; and cultural activities, 60–62; writings of, 61–62
Leichter, Otto, 46–48
Leipzig, 169–70
Lesbians, 37–39, 214–15
Liberation, 194, 251n.15; of death march prisoners, 176; of Gemma LaGuardia Gluck, 116–18; of Neustadt-Glewe, 31, 130, 134, 155–56, 157–58; prisoners' condition at, 67–68; from Ravensbrück, 24, 165; rumors preceding, 86, 100, 147; of satellite camps, 24, 136, 164, 176. See also liberation anniversaries, celebration of
Liberation anniversaries, celebration of, 30, 41, 221–22; death march exhibit for, 177, 250n.2; fiftieth, 8, 68–69, 97, 141, 221–22; fifty-fifth, 224; fortieth, 7; survivors at, 68–69, 141
Lice, 17–18, 75, 124, 133, 153, 159
Lichtenburg camp, 12–13, 35, 43–44
Lilith (magazine), 218
Lindholm, Birgitta, 252n.18
Lodz, 179–80, 185
Lodz Ghetto, 101, 122, 245n.9
Lublin, 182, 185
Luckmann, Thomas, 9
Luksenberg, Chaya (Helen) Kaplan, 184–85, 188
Lund Interview Project, 188, 252nn.19, 21
Lundholm, Anja, 214
Lyon, Gloria Hollander, 141–50, 178, 188, 202, 212, 223

Majdanek, 18, 51, 129
Makarow, Boris, 251n.15
Malchow subcamp, 94, 125, 151–52, 250n.2; arrivals at, 168–69; death march away from, 171–77; evacuation of, 169, 176, 188; POW camp at, 166
Mandelker, Lajka, 254n.21
Maria, Mother (Elisabeth Skobzoff), 32
Marsalek, Hans, 214
Martyrdom and Resistance (newspaper), 4

Maurel, Micheline, 164, 250n.12
Mauthausen, 31, 40, 88, 119, 151, 214
Mazur, Norbert, 186–87, 252n.16
Medical care, 70, 100, 132, 158; for abandoned prisoners, 174, 177; for diarrhea, 138–39, 155; in quarantine barracks, 92–93; in *Reviers*, 29, 132; for survivors, 68, 191, 193–94. See also *Reviers*
Medical experiments, 19, 82, 97, 143–44, 150, 237n.12; on political prisoners, 30–31; "rabbits" for, 30; Tillion recording evidence of, 31–32
Melchior, Estera, 254n.21
Mellender, Rose Frochewajg, 123–25, 168–71, 198–201
Mengele, Josef, 141–42
Mennecke, Friedrich, 37
Menstruation, 22, 181, 210–11
Meuselwitz (subcamp), 108, 158–63, 249n.10
Miodownik, Maria, 254n.21
Mittelbau-Dora, bordello in, 214
Mittwerda (*Schonungslager Mittwerda*), 20, 237n.17
Modesty, 22, 159, 207–8
Molotov-Ribbentrop Pact, 15–16
Mory, Carmen Maria, 58
Moskovits, Frida and Ben Zion, 68–69
Muckermann, Friedrich, 29
Müller, Charlotte, 19
Munkács (Mukachevo), 75, 77, 134–35, 175
Murders: of babies, 211, 243n.12; of British spies, 34–35; of children, 97; on death marches, 160, 176–77, 183; "14f13" project, 18, 51, 234n.14; of insane women, 58; of Jehovah's Witnesses, 35; of Jews from German camps, 18; at *Jugendlager*, 21, 136; methods of, 19–22; numbers of, 23–24, 235n.23; of Polish resistance fighters, 30; at Ravensbrück, 100, 116, 157. See also Gas chamber

Nazis, 164, 170; attacks on Red Cross convoys, 55–56, 163; evidence destroyed by, 21, 158; racial purity laws of, 23, 39, 211, 213, 246n.5. See also Guards; SS
Netherlands, 32–33

Index

Index

Rubinstein, Basia Zajaczkowska, 97–100, 188, 208, 253n.21
Russians. *See* Soviet Union

SA *(Sturmabteilungen)*, 47, 240n.14
Sabo (Elisabeth Saborowski Ewert), 28–29, 44, 213
Sabotage: arrests for, 70; by prisoners, 14–15, 33–34, 53
Sachsenhausen, 12, 151, 176, 186, 214, 219
Salvini, Hermine, 23
Satellite camps, 151, 164, 249n.1; deaths in, 23–24; Jews sent to, 19, 121; Ravensbrück and, 20, 235n.33; selection for, 93, 133–34, 159, 165; slave labor at, 95, 98. *See also Jugendlager;* Malchow; Meuselwitz; Neubrandenburg; Neustadt-Glewe; Rechlin
Scandanavians, Red Cross rescue of, 186–88, 252nn.17, 18
Schellenberg, Walter, 186–87
Schermann, Jenny (Henny) Sara, 37–38
Schiff, Bracha Blattberg, 164–65
Schoorl, concentration camp at, 33
Schoppmann, Claudia, 38
Schult, SS Lance Corporal, 34–35
Schulz, Christa, 221
Schum Schum (Leichter), 61–62
Schütt, Karl Heinz, 152, 156–58
Schwarzhuber, Johannes, 20, 34–35, 238n.22
Schwedtsee, 12, 16, 143, *190,* 225
Schwerin, on death march route, 171, 176
She Who Carries, statue at Ravensbrück memorial site, 5
Shelley, Lore, 136, 202
Shneiderman, S. L., 109–11, 120
Shoes, 143, 159; children's, 76; for death march, 129, 161; lack of, 16–17; theft of, 18, 77, 124; wooden, 85, 91
Shooting corridor, Ravensbrück, 19, 221
Shuftan, Esther Tuvel, 84, 191, 243n.5
Siemens factory, 53, 55, 81, 212; Gypsies working at, 39–40; political prisoners working at, 29–30, 31, 44–45; razed, 221; slave labor in, 95–100, *96*
Sinti. *See* Gypsies
Skobzoff, Elisabeth (Mother Maria), 32
Skorecka, Cecylia, 254n.21
Slave labor, 35, 55, 75, 98, 114–15, 142,

209; in airplane factories, 91, 163–64; companies using, 244n.1; declining need for, 88, 98, 103, 166; difficulty of, 49, 103, 106; effects of, 28–29, 196; at *Jugendlager,* 133–34; in munitions, 82, 121–22, 129–31, 159–60, 166, 180, 249n.10; at Neustadt-Glewe, 153–54, 156–57; outdoors, 83, 87, 103, 106, 135, 165; payment for, 202; and pregnancy, 211–12; in textile factories, 100–103; uses of, 12–13, 16, 91, 106, 107, 111; women's capacity for, 212, 256n.13. *See also* Satellite camps; Siemens factory
Smeenk, Clarin, 59
Sobibor, 185
Social Democrats, 28, 46–47
Solewicz, Erna, 254n.21
Sommer, Tola, 254n.21
Songs. *See* Cultural activities
Sosnowiec, Poland, 137, 153–55, 180, 251n.4, 251n.5
Soswinski, Herta Mehl, 50–52
Soviet Union, 3, 28, 117, 176; fear of, 172–74; and liberated prisoners, 71, 91–92, 135, 170, 172–73, 175, 201; liberation of camps by, 31, 136, 155–56, 158; liberation of Ravensbrück, 24, 177, 251n.15; Nazi relations with, 15–16; Nazi response to approach of, 17, 21, 77, 112, 116, 140, 164; POWs from, 26, 33–34, 237n.21; rapes by troops, 170–71, 173, 213; troops at Ravensbrück memorial site, 6–7, 220–21
SS *(Schutzstaffel),* 31, 62, 108, 113, 159, 193, 202, 240n.14; abandoning camps, 160–61, 176; beatings by, 99, 104–5; destruction of evidence by, 23–24; dogs of, 37, 202; and evacuation of Meuselwitz, 160–62; and gassings, 20–21, 171; sexual use of prisoners by, 23, 213; slave labor for, 35, 100, 102; treatment of inmates by, 48–49, 84, 99, 159. *See also* Guards
Starvation, 125, 130, 157; deaths from, 102, 225; at Malchow, 166–67
Sterilization, forced, 211; of Gypsies, 31, 40, 58; of Jewish women, 211
Stolz, To, 58
Storahtelling, 224–25

277

Index

Made in the USA
Lexington, KY
20 December 2018